A HUMAN RIGHTS FRAMEWORK FOR INTELLECTUAL PROPERTY, INNOVATION AND ACCESS TO MEDICINES

G000080703

A Human Rights Framework for Intellectual Property, Innovation and Access to Medicines

JOO-YOUNG LEE
Seoul National University, South Korea

Routledge
Taylor & Francis Group

LONDON AND NEW YORK

First published 2015 by Ashgate Publishing

Published 2016 by Routledge
2 Park Square, Milton Park, Abingdon, Oxon OX14 4RN
711 Third Avenue, New York, NY 10017, USA

First issued in paperback 2017

Routledge is an imprint of the Taylor & Francis Group, an informa business

British Library Cataloguing in Publication Data
A catalogue record for this book is available from the British Library.

Library of Congress Cataloging-in-Publication Data
Lee, Joo-Young, (law teacher) author.
  A human rights framework for intellectual property, innovation and access to medicines / By Joo-Young Lee.
    pages cm
  Includes bibliographical references and index.
  ISBN 978-1-4724-1061-0 (hardback) -- ISBN 978-1-4724-1062-7 (ebook) -- ISBN 978-1-4724-1063-4 (epub) 1. Human rights. 2. Right to health. 3. Intellectual property. 4. Health services accessibility--Law and legislation. 5. Medical care--Law and legislation. I. Title.
  K3240.L43 2015
  346.04'86--dc23

                                                                        2014046282

ISBN 13: 978-1-138-09444-4 (pbk)
ISBN 13: 978-1-4724-1061-0 (hbk)

Contents

Foreword

The Ebola crisis graphically demonstrates that the contemporary intellectual property regime is deeply flawed: it is not serving its social function. As the crisis deepened in mid-2014, Dr Marie-Paul Kieny, Assistant Director-General, World Health Organization, emphasised the absence of effective medicines is 'a market failure because this is typically a disease of poor people in poor countries where there is no market'.

In this valuable book, Dr Joo-Young Lee applies the international human rights 'lens' to contemporary intellectual property. She builds on the existing literature by using both the international right to the highest attainable standard of health as well as the international right to enjoy the benefits of scientific progress and its applications. While our understanding of the former has advanced by leaps and bounds since the United Nations Committee on Economic, Social and Cultural Rights adopted General Comment 14 in 2000, our understanding of the latter has lagged behind, although it received a boost when the same Committee adopted General Comment 17 in 2006. One of the striking features of Dr Lee's analysis is that she uses both of these complex international human rights to scrutinise the contemporary intellectual property regime.

Another important feature of the analysis is that while it includes a discussion of the TRIPs 'flexibilities', it also considers health innovation and financing mechanisms that seek to develop, and provide equitable access to, much needed medicines.

Two other attributes of Dr Lee's book bear emphasis. Benefitting from the insights provided by the Maastricht Principles on Extraterritorial Obligations of States in the area of Economic, Social and Cultural Rights (2011), Dr Lee addresses the responsibilities of States *beyond their borders* in relation to access to medicines. She also grasps a second thorny issue: the human rights responsibilities of business enterprises. The main focus of the book is the human rights responsibilities of States, but it also pays attention to the human rights responsibilities of pharmaceutical companies in relation to access to medicines. Thus, Dr Lee considers the United Nations Guiding Principles on Business and Human Rights (2011), as well as the more specific and operational Human Rights Guidelines for Pharmaceutical Companies in relation to Access to Medicines, presented to the United Nations General Assembly in 2008.

To date, the United Nations Working Group on business and human rights has mainly looked at the responsibilities of extractive industries. It is time for the Working Group to also scrutinise the human rights responsibilities of pharmaceutical companies – when it takes the plunge, Dr Lee's book will be essential reading for the Group's independent experts.

In the meantime, this instructive book makes an important contribution to the deepening scholarship on the human right of access to medicines for all.

Professor Paul Hunt
United Nations Special Rapporteur on the Right to the
Highest Attainable Standard of Health (2002–2008)

Preface and Acknowledgements

I first learnt about the issue of intellectual property and access to medicines around 2002 when I was working as the editor of the *Daily Human Rights News* in South Korea. I was struck by the fact that life-saving medicines were out of reach to a large number of people and a key factor was the high prices of those medicines resulting from the intensified protection of intellectual property. Several years later, I embarked on my doctoral research into a human rights framework for the regulation of knowledge creation, intellectual property and access to medicines. The engagement in this topic was also linked with my enduring interest in the human rights impact of economic norms and institutions as well as the role of human rights in transforming socio-economic relations.

Although this problem attracted much discussion for the last decade, I found that access to medicines was often addressed merely as a humanitarian issue without having a normative ground. When the language of human rights was employed to analyse this issue, two contrasting tendencies emerged. One is to conceive the intellectual property system as a rigid one that exclusively protects private interests of intellectual property holders and is inherently indifferent to human values. The other tendency is to elevate intellectual property rights to the level of a fundamental human right and condemn any attempt to balance intellectual property rights with other competing interests as 'stealing'. Overcoming the polarised views, this book stresses the role of human rights as universal values and norms in making health innovation and intellectual property more responsive to human needs, and provides the basic content of a human rights framework for that purpose.

An earlier version of this book began its life during my time of research at the University of Essex. This book could not have been completed without the generosity of a vast number of people around me. My deep gratitude goes to all who have provided me with invaluable insights and support. I would especially thank Professor Paul Hunt, who was an inspiring supervisor and continues to be an insightful colleague. During the writing of this book, he gave me generous encouragement, which has been crucial for me to keep motivated and deepen my perspectives into this research. I am also extremely grateful to Professor Peter Stone for his support. As an expert on intellectual property law, he allowed me to develop and strengthen my arguments with reasons, keeping in mind potentially different perspectives on the topic. I would also like to thank sincerely Professor Eibe Riedel and Professor Sheldon Leader. They provided me with constructive comments, encouraging compliments, and a forum for reasoned debate.

I am indebted to an academic environment of the University of Essex where I was constantly exposed to enriching discussions about human rights through lectures, seminars and other activities. In this sense, I thank all those who committed themselves to sowing the seeds of human rights through various human rights programmes at the

University of Essex, Professor Nigel Rodley, the late Professor Kevin Boyle, Professor Francoise Hampson and Dr Clara Sandoval.

I have also been very fortunate to have an opportunity to create human rights programmes and undertake human rights research at the Seoul National University in South Korea. I warmly thank Professor Chinsung Chung, Director of the SNU Human Rights Center, and other colleagues for their generous support. My work in recent years have also benefited greatly from the experiences and insights of academics in Asia including Professor Hyo-Je Cho, Professor Vitit Muntarbhorn, Ms Wan-Hea Lee and Professor Hae Bong Shin.

I would like to thank my dear friends, Soowan Kim, Leticia Osorio, Kai Yin Low, Tuba Turan, Ryan Hill, Akihiro Ueda, Andrea Sepulveda, Diana Guarnizo, Larissa Kersten, Shengnan Qiu, Edzia Carvalho, Leonardo Valladares Pacheco De Oliveira, Al-Yamamah Alharbi, Judith Schonsteiner, Eunna Lee Gong, Sufyan El Droubi and Genevieve Sander for their companionship during my journey of writing this book, which could have been more lonely without them.

Finally, my heartfelt thanks go to all my family for their support and patience. Particularly, I cannot thank enough Chang-Jo Lee, my husband. Whenever I question myself and the meaning of doing research and writing a book, he has been there to listen to me and given me unfailing support and care.

I feel hugely indebted to those working on the ground to empower marginalised people to make their voices heard. To all those who are active in pursuing human dignity, I send my admiration and appreciation for their continued commitments to making a difference. I hope my book can contribute, even in a smallest way, to these efforts to make our societies more just and humane.

List of Abbreviations

ACHPR	African Charter on Human and Peoples' Rights
ACHR	American Convention on Human Rights
ADRD	American Declaration on the Rights and Duties of Man
Berne Convention	Berne Convention for the Protection of Literary and Artistic Works
CAMR	Canada's Access to Medicines Regime
CESCR	Committee on Economic, Social and Cultural Rights
CRC	Convention on the Rights of the Child
Doha Declaration	Doha Declaration on the TRIPS Agreement and Public Health
DRD	Declaration on the Right to Development
ECHR	European Convention on Human Rights (European Convention for the Protection of Human Rights and Fundamental Freedoms)
ECtHR	European Court of Human Rights
FTA	Free Trade Agreement
GA	UN General Assembly
GATT	General Agreement on Tariffs and Trade
Guidelines for Pharmaceutical Companies	Human Rights Guidelines for Pharmaceutical Companies in relation to Access to Medicines
ICCPR	International Covenant on Civil and Political Rights
ICESCR	International Covenant on Economic, Social and Cultural Rights
ICJ	International Court of Justice
ILC	International Law Commission
IPAB	Intellectual Property Appellate Body of India
Maastricht Principles	Maastricht Principles on Extraterritorial Obligations of States in the Area of Economic, Social and Cultural Rights
MDG	Millennium Development Goals
Paris Convention	Paris Convention for the Protection of Industrial Property
REBSP	Right to Enjoy the Benefits of Scientific Progress and its Applications
Right to Benefit from the Protection of the Moral and Material Interests of the Author	The Right to Benefit from the Protection of the Moral and Material Interests Resulting from any Scientific, Literary or Artistic Production of which He is the Author

Right to Health	Right of Everyone to the Enjoyment of the Highest Attainable Standard of Physical and Mental Health
Sub-Commission	UN Sub-Commission on the Protection and Promotion of Human Rights
TRIPS	Agreement on Trade Related Aspects of Intellectual Property Rights
UDHR	Universal Declaration of Human Rights
UNESCO	United Nations Educational, Scientific and Cultural Organization
USTR	United States Trade Representative
VCLT	Vienna Convention on the Law of Treaties
WHA	World Health Assembly
WHO	World Health Organization
WIPO	World Intellectual Property Organization
WTO	World Trade Organization

Introduction

A vast number of people remain without access to life-saving and other essential medicines.[1] The cost of medicines is one major factor that affects access to medicines.[2] Another significant problem is the lack of medicines particularly relevant to health needs of people in developing countries.[3] Both issues are associated with an intellectual property system that has been used as a dominant tool to provide incentives for innovation. Intellectual property rights in the form of patents have become critical in the pricing of medicines since the exclusive right over medicines gives the patent-holding companies the leverage to set high prices for the medicines. A patent is a right to exclude others from using, selling or importing a patented product without the consent of the patent holder. The most illustrative example regarding the effect of patents on access to medicines is seen in the context of HIV/AIDS medicines. While effective medicines for prolonging the life of people with HIV exist, many who need these medicines cannot afford the high prices the patent-holding pharmaceutical companies charge.[4] The existence of public funding and health insurance may enable people to have access to such expensive medicines. However, the high cost of the patented medicines is often unaffordable for governments in developing countries.[5] The impact of patents on access to medicines has emerged as a global concern since the adoption of the Agreement on Trade-Related Aspects of Intellectual Property Rights (hereinafter, TRIPS) because TRIPS mandates World Trade Organization (WTO) members to provide patent protection for a minimum of 20 years in all fields of technology, including medicines. Prior to the adoption of TRIPS, many countries did not grant a patent for pharmaceutical products, which allowed copies of medicines patented elsewhere to be made available at affordable prices. On the other hand, a market-based intellectual property system provides insufficient incentives for health innovation addressing diseases that afflict primarily people in developing countries due to the limited purchasing power of both government and patients.

---

1 The World Health Organization (hereinafter, WHO) estimated that approximately 1.7 billion people remained without regular access to essential medicines although its proportion decreased from half of the world population in 1975 to around one-third in 1999. WHO, *The World Medicines Situation*, Geneva (2004) 61.

2 According to the WHO, affordable prices are one of the four key components for access to essential medicines. The others are rational use, sustainable financing, and reliable health and supply systems. Ibid., 64.

3 WHO, *Public Health, Innovation and Intellectual Property Rights: Report of the Commission on Intellectual Property Rights, Innovation and Public Health* (2006).

4 MDG Gap Taskforce Report: The Global Partnership for Development at a Critical Juncture (2010) 63.

5 WHO (n 1) 70.

This book examines, from a human rights perspective, the relationship between intellectual property in pharmaceuticals and access to medicines. Although this problem has attracted much discussion in recent years, access to medicines has often been addressed merely as a humanitarian issue without having a normative ground. When the language of human rights is employed to analyse this issue, two contrasting tendencies emerge. One is to conceive the intellectual property system as a rigid one that exclusively protects private interests of intellectual property holders and is indifferent to human values. Therefore, intellectual property is considered to be inherently incompatible with human rights. The other end of the spectrum is to view intellectual property rights as fundamental so that any attempt to balance intellectual property rights with other competing interests is condemned as something akin to theft.

This book explores primarily two key questions: first, whether conflicts between patents as one type of intellectual property and human rights in the context of access to medicines are inevitable, or whether patents can be made to serve human rights in the context of access to medicines; and second, what could be a normative framework that human rights might provide for patents. As to the first question, it is important to understand the nature of potential conflicts between patents and access to medicines, and the extent to which a patent system, as a social institution, can be made responsive to human values and concerns. The second question is directed to outlining the basic content of a human rights framework, something essential if human rights are to inform the direction of policies addressing issues arising from intellectual property in pharmaceuticals.

Each chapter of this book is intended to help to answer the key questions. It is necessary to have a deepened understanding of each of the two sets of norms that govern this issue, i.e. patent law and international human rights law. The first three chapters investigate the relevant dimensions of patent law while the following two chapters analyse particular human rights bearing upon the issue of intellectual property and access to medicines. The last two chapters explore the relationship between patents and human rights, in the context of access to medicines, and outline a human rights framework for intellectual property, innovation and access to medicines.

Chapter 1 traces the history of patents to understand in what context patent systems were created and how they have evolved. The historical overview of patents enables us to understand that modern patent systems were created as legal instruments to serve social objectives. It notes variations of modern patent systems adopted by countries, responding to public needs and different levels of technological development. It sheds light on the particularities of the adoption of TRIPS as an attempt to globalise the extensive protection of patents.

Chapter 2 investigates two lines of justifications for patents; a natural rights perspective and an economic incentive perspective. This chapter critically examines what insights each of these two perspectives can provide to institutions that govern the issue of creating, and allowing access to, knowledge. It also discusses whether economic efficiency theory alone is sufficient in guiding patent law and policy in situations where the extensive protection of the exclusive rights over knowledge has an increasing impact on the life of people, for instance by restricting access to seeds or medicines. It suggests that international human rights norms should inform patent law and policy.

Chapter 3 focuses on policy space allowed within TRIPS in relation to public health. This chapter examines ways in which TRIPS can be interpreted and implemented with a view to increasing access to affordable medicines. It examines some examples of using the flexibility in TRIPS, i.e. Thailand's compulsory licensing on public health grounds, Canada's compulsory licensing for exporting medicines to Rwanda, and India's application of strict standards for patentability. The analysis of the TRIPS flexibility and the country cases can shed light on how far TRIPS can go in terms of fairly balancing competing interests in the context of access to medicines.

Chapter 4 analyses the right to access to medicines as an essential element of the right to health and the right to life enshrined in international human rights law. It also considers the right to access to medicines in the context of pandemics as an emerging customary norm. This chapter looks primarily at obligations of States under the right to access to medicines, but it also addresses the need for placing human rights responsibilities upon the patent-holding pharmaceutical companies in relation to access to medicines.

Chapter 5 provides an analysis of the normative content of the right to enjoy the benefits from scientific progress and its applications (Art. 15.1(b)) and the right to benefit from the protection of the moral and material interests of the author (Art. 15.1(c)) under the International Covenant on Economic, Social and Cultural Rights.

Chapter 6 revisits potential conflicts between TRIPS and human rights in the context of access to medicines. It clarifies differences between the right to benefit from the protection of the moral and material interests of the author on one hand, and patents on the other. Also, it pays attention to the relationship between patents and the right to property under Article 1 of the First Protocol to the European Convention on Human Rights. Drawing upon studies on normative conflicts in international law, this chapter notes the normative evolution in relation to TRIPS, which seeks to readjust the balance between competing interests so as to make it possible to read TRIPS as reconciling with values intrinsic to international human rights law. It also considers that TRIPS, however critical it may be to the issue of intellectual property and access to medicines, may not provide a comprehensive solution to the lack of needed medicines in developing countries, and highlights global debates primarily at the World Health Organization about a new model for health R&D.

Chapter 7 sets out a human rights framework for intellectual property, innovation and access to medicines, in view of which intellectual property law and policy impacting upon access to medicines is reviewed and implemented. Analysis of the boundary of permitted limitations upon particular human rights most relevant to this issue helps to develop this human rights framework. Promoting innovation for primary health needs of all including people living in poverty is an important element of the right of access to medicines, and thus this human rights framework highlights the need to seek new models for health innovation, which can address the innovation gap for poverty-related diseases. Importantly, this human rights framework applies extraterritorial obligations of States under international human rights law, recognising that the universal realisation of the right of access to medicines cannot be achieved without international cooperation.

This book undertakes research on access to medicines as one particular area of the interface between intellectual property and human rights. This book emphasises that intellectual property should be understood as a social institution that has to be made responsive to human values, and human rights can help the intellectual property system to strike an appropriate balance between competing interests. It suggests that the lack of medicines addressing health needs of developing countries forces us to look beyond the existing intellectual property system because this problem is associated with the inherent limitations of a market-based intellectual property system and thus requires a new model for a needs-driven health innovation system. The outcome of this research may have implications for other areas that are governed by both intellectual property law and human rights law.

Chapter 1
Historical Overview of Patents

Introduction

> The model of intellectual property law that took shape during the nineteenth century not only plays an important role in influencing the way we think of intellectual property law, it also restricts the questions we ask about it. One of the consequences of a narrative which teaches us that, within a historical context, intellectual property law is timeless, natural and inevitable, and that it is driven by principle, is that it leads us away from the changes that occurred over the course of the nineteenth century.[1]

As pointed out in the above excerpt, intellectual property has often been misconstrued as being 'timeless, natural and inevitable'. For instance, patents, the main subject of this book, are considered a natural right to property in ideas or the only way a society can encourage invention and innovation. Looking at the history of patents may help us not only to avoid such static approaches to patents, but also to understand current issues around patent systems. This chapter attempts to provide a brief overview of the history of patents by reference to a historical division into three periods put forward by Peter Drahos.[2] It should be noted that the early history of patents confines itself to a description of the development of patents in European countries as not all societies relied on a notion of intellectual property as a means of encouraging invention and innovation. For instance, imperial China is known as 'a society that achieved spectacular outcomes in science and innovation without relying on intellectual property rights or a customary equivalent'.[3]

The territorial period is marked by the principle of territoriality; 'the principle that intellectual property rights do not extend beyond the territory of the sovereign which has granted the rights in the first place'.[4] The section looking at this period traces back to the origin of the patent system which saw the Crowns giving monopoly privilege in most of medieval Europe. It moves on to later patent systems and considers whether or not the laws in the French Revolution engendered the notion of a natural property right in ideas by looking at the relevant discussions during the Revolution. In addition, the patent

---

1 Brad Sherman and Lionel Bently, *The Making of Modern Intellectual Property Law: The British Experience, 1760–1911*, Cambridge University Press (1999) 219.

2 Peter Drahos, 'Intellectual Property and Human Rights' (1999) 3 *Intellectual Property Quarterly* 349–71, from Westlaw. His original account of the positivist history of intellectual property had four period stages: the territorial period, the international period, the global period and post-TRIPS. For the purposes of this book, the latter two periods are dealt with together.

3 Peter Drahos, *A Philosophy of Intellectual Property*, Ashgate Publishing (1996) 15.

4 Drahos (n 2).

controversy in mid-nineteenth-century Britain, Switzerland and the Netherlands is briefly dealt with. This is followed by reflection on a variation among patent systems seen in nineteenth-century Europe and North America.

The international period is triggered by the growing demand for international regulation of intellectual property in the context of enormous technological developments and the expansion of international trade. The adoption of the Paris Convention for the Protection of Industrial Property (Paris Convention) in 1883 was a landmark event. National treatment of foreign applicants of a patent was established as an international principle. Nevertheless, increasing international cooperation in regulating patents by no means culminated with a harmonisation of national patent rules in this international era. In the US, there existed scepticism over patents in relation to free trade and anti-monopoly policy until the late twentieth century. Developing countries adopted a patent system which would serve their development goals and social policy. This section therefore looks in turn at the adoption of the Paris Convention, the discussion on patents and its relationship with anti-monopoly policy within the US, and patent systems in developing countries.

The global period sees increasing attempts to harmonise patent rules. This section discusses the context within which the Agreement on Trade-Related Aspects of Intellectual Property Rights (TRIPS) was adopted in 1994, alongside the increasing competition between world economies and the shift in ideas which places more emphasis on knowledge as property and regards the protection of patents to be favourable to free trade. This section also examines what TRIPS requires World Trade Organization (WTO) Member countries to do and what the issues have been after the adoption of TRIPS. It also considers key features of intellectual property provisions in bilateral or regional free trade agreements, so-called 'TRIPS-Plus' standards, as well as the debates over issues of intellectual property and access to medicines in a number of international and national forums.

The Territorial Period

Patent as the Prerogative-based Monopoly

Patents have their beginning in the prerogative-based monopoly system of medieval Europe.[5] Based on the prerogative power of grant, the Crown could grant individuals exclusive monopolies over particular trades. Examination of the English patent system at this time shows that patents were a device 'to encourage the transfer of valuable trades and technologies to England'.[6] Therefore, monopolies would be granted not only to those who had invented something but also to those who had brought technologies from abroad.

---

5 See Drahos (n 3) 29–33; Christopher May and Susan Sell, '3. The Emergence of Intellectual Property Rights', '4. Commerce vs. Romantic Notions of Authorship and Invention', *Intellectual Property Rights: A Critical History*, Lynne Rienner (2006).

6 Drahos (n 3) 31.

With some kind of innovation or technology, '[p]atentees were required to implement their invention without delay and ensure its continuance by communicating the necessary skills to native workmen'.[7]

However, the practice of the Crown giving monopolies was not consistent with the designed purpose. Patents were often granted to the wrong persons who were neither inventors nor specialists but were rather favourites of the Crown. Moreover, patentees were given the same power as the Crown 'to supervise, search, and seize the goods of infringers as well as the ability to levy fines and penalties for infringement'.[8] The abusive exercise of the Crown grant monopolies led to a proclamation from the Queen in 1601 which introduced judicial review so that the courts could give their view on the validity of a grant of monopolies.[9]

The response of the English common law courts to the grant of monopolies can be seen in *Darcy v. Allein*[10] which is regarded as an early landmark case on monopolies. The case established that 'monopolies are a profound interference in the liberty of subjects to trade' and 'are void at common law'.[11] The court found that monopolies which prevented others from working and trading contravened the common law, which gave freedom of trade a primary status. Another concern raised by the court was that monopolies were used for the private gain of the monopolist. Furthermore, the ability of the monopolist to decide the price would affect everyone and could therefore undermine public welfare.

In 1623 the English Parliament passed the Statute of Monopolies[12] which reflected the prevailing view of the common law court. The statute criticised that many grants, based on 'misinformation and untrue pretences of public good', had been 'unduly obtained and unlawfully put in execution', and it declared all monopolies to be contrary to the laws of the realm and therefore to be void.[13] As an exception, section 6 of the statute allowed patents to be granted only to those who made new manufactures within the territory for limited periods (14 years – the duration of two training periods for craft apprentices). Even such grants were given only with the proviso that they were not 'mischievous to the state', for instance through raising prices. Although the Statute of Monopolies was commonly accepted to lay down the legal foundations for patents,[14]

---

7 Christopher MacLeod, *Inventing the Industrial Revolution: The English Patent System, 1660–1800*, Cambridge University Press (1988) 12.

8 May and Sell (n 5) 81.

9 Ibid., 81.

10 *Darcy v. Allein* 77 Eng Rep 1260 (KB *1602*) is widely known as the Case of Monopolies.

11 Drahos (n 3) 30. Edward Darcy was granted by the queen exclusive rights to sell and import all playing cards. When Allein sought to sell cards, Darcy sued Allein accusing him of a breach of the patent. The central issue in the case was whether monopoly over a trade was proper.

12 Statute of Monopolies 1623 (c.3).

13 See the original text available at http://www.statutelaw.gov.uk/content.aspx?activeTextDoc Id=1518308, last accessed 16 March 2015.

14 Sherman and Bently rebut the commonly held account that the Statute of Monopolies had a foundational role in patent law stating that 'the foundation or basis of patent law lay in the Royal Charters and Royal Letters Patent of the Crown and not, as present-day histories often suggest,

patents remained to be seen as a creature of prerogative-based privilege until the late eighteenth century.[15]

The Emergence of Modern Patent Systems and Patent Controversy

Most European countries, with the notable exception of Switzerland, established modern patent systems in the first half of the nineteenth century.

The French Revolution and a natural right to property in ideas

The French Revolution abolished the privileges granted by the Old Regime and established a modern intellectual property system.[16] The laws during the Revolution were often stated as laying a foundation for the idea of the natural rights of inventors or authors. Section 1 of the French law of 1791 stated: 'All new discoveries are the property of the author; to assure the inventor the property and temporary enjoyment of his discovery, there shall be delivered to him a patent for five, ten or fifteen years.' Here, the right of authors or inventors was seemingly perceived to be one that was recognised rather than created by legal instrument. However, the debates during the French Revolution reveal that there existed a tension between private interests in ideas and public enlightenment.[17] One argument about ideas was that 'ideas were social rather than individual in origin'; 'the progress of enlightenment depended upon public access, rather than private claims to ideas'.[18] The contrasting argument was that the sanctity of individual creativity should be protected as a natural right. Although these debates are primarily concerned with authorship, they may also provide insights in the field of patents.

The 1791 law itself appeared not to be coherent with the natural rights argument. While it recognised an author's right as a natural property right, it limited the term of protection after which the works of authors would become part of the public domain. Classical natural rights would have no expiry dates. Furthermore, the decree adopted later in 1793 put more emphasis on the notion of the public domain. The grant of a limited property right to authors was presented as 'a mechanism for promoting and ensuring public enlightenment by encouraging and recompensing intellectual activity'.[19] Therefore, it may not be fair to say that the legacy of the French Revolution on intellectual property is confined only to the notion of a natural property right in ideas.[20] The recognition of the public domain during the French Revolution deserves adequate attention.

---

the Statute of Monopolies', Sherman and Bently (n 1) 209. However, these discussions go beyond the remit of this book.

15 May and Sell (n 5) 87; Sherman and Bently (n 1) 134.

16 This part is extensively indebted to the work of Carla Hesse, 'Enlightenment Epistemology and the Law of Authorship in Revolutionary France, 1777–1793' (1990) 30 *Representations* 109–37; Robert Post (ed.), *Law and the Order of Culture,* University of California Press (1991) 109–37.

17 Hesse (n 16); Post (n 16).

18 Ibid.

19 Ibid.

20 Drahos (n 2) 32.

Patent controversy in the nineteenth-century United Kingdom

During the period of industrial revolution between 1750 and 1850 in the United Kingdom, patents were considered to be an important element of technological change.[21] According to Harold Irvin Dutton, 'very few important inventions bypassed the system'.[22] Arguments that supported patents at this time did not much rely on the natural rights thesis which assumes that inventors have a natural right of property in ideas. Support for patents was more advanced by the argument that patents encouraged inventive activity by monopoly-reward and that this eventually benefited the public.[23] However, such arguments about the public benefit of patents were not sustained without critique. For instance, James Watt's patents on his steam engine[24] and Richard Arkwright's patents on methods of spinning cotton[25] encountered massive criticisms. Nevertheless, the opposition to a number of individual patents was not directed to the patent system per se until the 1850s.[26]

The 1852 Patent Law Amendment Act changed the content of the anti-patent debate. 'The Crown's abuse of Royal prerogative and its use of patents as a source of patronage and revenue were no longer the issues of contention.'[27] As the 1852 Patent Amendment Act established a more effective system of registration that simplified the obtaining of patent protection, patents were perceived as a creature of legal instrument rather than as a product of Royal Grant.[28] Now the patent-abolitionist argument was mainly directed to the impact of patents on free trade.[29] The abolitionists argued that patents restricted free trade in goods, including technology. R.A. Macfie, Liverpool sugar-refiner and leading abolitionist, highlighted 'their [patents'] incompatibility with Free Trade'.[30] Abolitionists also criticised patents for not being effective incentives to invention, and argued that unnecessarily expensive licence fees which were allowed by patents imposed hardships on domestic manufacturers. Nevertheless, few denied the necessity of rewarding invention. How to devise alternative forms of rewarding inventors was one of the primary concerns of the abolitionists.[31] With the emergence of protectionism, the abolitionist movement faded away in the United Kingdom and the patent controversy ended up with another

---

21 Harold Irvin Dutton, *The Patent System and Inventive Activity during the Industrial Revolution 1750–1852*, Manchester University Press (1984).

22 Ibid., 203.

23 Ibid. May and Sell (n 5).

24 Watt's patents on his steam engine were considered to stifle further advancement; many improvements in the steam engine came about after the expiration of his patent in the early nineteenth century. May and Sell (n 5) 98–9.

25 Ibid., 109–10. Richard Arkwright's patents on methods of spinning cotton also invited massive opposition of spinners who feared 'the prospect of being forced to pay Arkwright license fees to use his equipment'. This ended up in a court decision cancelling Arkwright's patent in 1785.

26 Dutton (n 21) 27.

27 Ibid., 24.

28 Sherman and Bently (n 1) 134.

29 Dutton (n 21) 24; Sherman and Bently (n 1) 130; May and Sell (n 5) 115–16.

30 Robert Andrew Macfie, *Recent Discussions on the Abolition of Patents for Invention*, 1869, 3, cited in Dutton (n 21) 24.

31 Dutton (n 21) 25.

reform, the 1883 Act, which reduced further the initial cost of a patent and thus led to greater access to the patent system.[32]

The Netherlands and Switzerland

In the late nineteenth century, patent controversies raged in other European countries too. Switzerland and the Netherlands are examples that showed 'industrialisation without national patents'.[33] Switzerland had no patent law between 1850 and 1888. The Netherlands abolished its patent system in 1869 as a result of successful lobbying by domestic enterprises. Small and medium-sized domestic enterprises saw patents as an obstacle to their growth, making them vulnerable to disruption of litigation brought by foreign patent holders. Both Switzerland and the Netherlands observed rapid technological advancement and economic growth during this period.[34] The absence of national patent law enabled domestic enterprises to introduce foreign innovations, without having to pay expensive license fees, and to produce good-quality goods for reduced costs.[35] However, both domestic and foreign pressures led to the enactment of patent legislation respectively in Switzerland in 1888 and in the Netherlands in 1912.[36] Still, the 1888 Patent Law of Switzerland excluded chemical substances and processes from patentability in effect. This exclusion lasted until 1907.

A wide variation among patent systems

Patent laws in Europe and North America in the late nineteenth century presented wide variations in many respects. Graham identified some key areas of variation among national patent systems. These included 'interpretations of novelty, the length of protection terms, the issue of whether or not patents needed to be 'worked' domestically, and exceptions to patentability', which are considered in the following.[37]

In some countries, such as France, Turkey and Italy, prior knowledge, use, or publication destroyed novelty, regardless of the origin.[38] However, in most other countries, foreign use or knowledge, if not published, could still be patented.[39] The UK was exceptional in that only public manufacture, use or sale in its territory constituted a lack of novelty. Protection terms also varied from 14 years in the UK to 17 years in the US. Local working requirements

---

32 Christine MacLeod, 'Would There Have Been No Industrial Revolution Without Patents?' Paper presented at ESRC Research Seminar Series, Intellectual Property Rights, Economic Development and Social Welfare: What Does History Tell Us? Ironbridge Gorge Museum, Coalbrookdale, UK, 26 April (2004) 4.

33 For more extensive discussions, see Eric Schiff, *Industrialisation Without National Patents: The Netherlands, 1869–1912; Switzerland, 1850–1907*, Princeton University Press (1971).

34 Graham Dutfield, *Intellectual Property Rights and the Life Science Industries: A Twentieth Century History*, Ashgate Publishing (2003) 50.

35 Jan Brinkhof, 'Chapter 8. On Patents and Human Rights', in Willem Grosheide (ed.), *Intellectual Property and Human Rights: A Paradox*, Edward Elgar (2010) 140–54, 145–6.

36 Schiff (n 33) 77–81.

37 Dutfield (n 34) 49–50. This part is heavily indebted to the work of Dutfield.

38 Ibid., 49.

39 Ibid.

were another area of variation. In many countries, if patentees did not locally manufacture or use patented products or processes, this could lead to issuing a compulsory licence to other manufacturers or even revocation of the patent. In some countries, for example the US, there was no such requirement. What might be unpatentable depended on statute or the policy of courts and patent offices in each country. Nevertheless, there appeared to be a widely shared view in European countries such as France and Germany that medicines and foods should not be patented. The underlying reasoning was that allowing private monopoly for essentials, such as medicines and foods, would endanger the public interest. Diverse national approaches to patents make it clear that patent systems were adopted as a matter of public policy, the objective of which involved encouraging as well as facilitating maximum access to technological progress. The scope and the level of patent protection generally depended on the extent of industrial development of countries and the perspectives of interest groups.[40]

A number of things can be learned from the brief description of patent laws in the territorial period. Firstly, industrial revolution, technological development and the expansion of international trade motivated most countries in Europe and North America to design public policies for migrating foreign technology and encouraging technological advancement. Patent laws were adopted to fulfil such policies. Secondly, this period saw a variation of national patent systems which reflected different industrial conditions, the perspectives of interest groups, and prevalent ideas on knowledge of countries. Such diversities in national patent systems provided room for manoeuvre for countries, in particular technological followers. Thirdly, the way of perceiving patents had shifted from the Crown giving privileges to a product of legal instrument. Nevertheless, controversy over patents did not disappear. One of the main concerns was the implications patents had for free trade. In addition, fears of monopoly led to the exclusion of foods and medicines from patentability in many European countries.

The International Period

The Paris Convention

Growing interests in international cooperation in intellectual property law in the late nineteenth century were situated within the context of an explosion of international trade as well as increasing intensive competition between countries, based on technological development. States, in particular net exporters, began to seek international cooperation on intellectual property which would provide adequate protection for their companies in foreign markets.[41] Anti-patent mood weakened along with a retreat from free trade and a resurgence of protectionism in economic policies of governments. Demand for an international framework for the regulation of intellectual property manifested itself in the form of two multilateral agreements, the Paris Convention for the Protection of Industrial

40 Ibid., 50–51; May and Sell (n 5) 111.
41 Dutfield (n 34) 54–5.

Property (1883) (Paris Convention) and the Berne Convention for the Protection of Literary and Artistic Works (1886) (Berne Convention). Here, the Paris Convention only is to be dealt with as it concerns the protection of patents.

The 1873 World Exposition of Vienna served as momentum for the adoption of an international industrial property convention. As US and German inventors expressed concern that their inventions would not be adequately protected at the Exposition, the Austro-Hungarian government adopted a temporary measure providing protection for foreign intellectual property in order to attract foreign inventors to the Exposition. In addition, the government sponsored an international patent congress, the 1873 Vienna Congress, during the conference. While anti-patent views were expressed during the Congress, the majority view was in favour of patent protection.[42] The first public call for an international industrial property convention was made during the Congress, and preparatory meetings for the convention were held in 1878 and 1880, culminating in the adoption of the Paris Convention in 1883.

The Convention addressed important issues, such as 'national treatment, the right of priority, and rules relating to local manufacture'.[43] National treatment is a principle that foreign patent applicants should be treated the same as nationals with respect to legal rights and remedies. In negotiating the content of the Convention, there was little controversy over the principle of national treatment.[44] The first filing of an application for a patent (the priority date) in one Member country gave a priority right to the applicant. During a six-month period from its filing date, the applicant was allowed to file for patents in other countries and to prevent third parties from applying a patent on the same invention. While the Convention required Member States not to revoke patents only on the grounds of importation, Members were able to grant compulsory licensing in the case of non-working, i.e. using a patent process or manufacturing a patented product, within the patent-granting country. Nonetheless, the Convention left many areas of variation among national patent laws untouched.[45] The three most important ones were whether or not prior examination of patent applications was required, the term of a patent, and exceptions from patentability. The Convention established an international organisation to administer the issues arising from the Convention, the Paris Union for the Protection of Industrial Property, whose present form is the World Intellectual Property Organization (hereinafter, WIPO), which covers not only industrial property, but also other forms of intellectual property. This international period was characterised by Drahos as being one where States sought international frames for regulations of intellectual property, yet 'retained enormous sovereign discretion over intellectual property standard setting'.[46]

---

42 Ibid., 55.

43 Ibid., 56.

44 Ibid.

45 Ibid., 57.

46 Drahos (n 2) 354. Since the adoption of the Paris Convention and the Berne Convention in the late nineteenth century, multilateral treaties on a diversity of intellectual property flourished in the twentieth century and WIPO administered 24 multilateral treaties by 1992. Nevertheless, the international period of intellectual property by no means brought a harmonisation of rules.

Patents and the Antitrust Policy in the US

The US, which currently champions the strict protection of intellectual property, was not always supportive of the patent system in the twentieth century. This section discusses anti-patent sentiments that permeated US policy until the mid-1970s.

Scepticism about the patent system and monopoly power heightened with the emergence of patent-based cartels in the late nineteenth century.[47] Corporate consolidation escalated in the 1890s and 1900s and patents were effectively used by big businesses to control competition in the market. Edwin J. Prindle, a highly influential patent attorney at the time, observed that patents were 'the best and most effective means of controlling competition. They occasionally give absolute command of the market, enabling their owner to name the price without regard to cost of production'.[48] Based on patent licensing, big companies were able to divide markets, set prices and reap vast financial rewards. The patent system became subject to critical scrutiny by all three branches of the US government.[49]

Congress passed antitrust legislation: the Interstate Commerce Act in 1887, the Sherman Antitrust Act in 1890[50] and the Clayton Antitrust Act in 1914.[51] However, the antitrust acts were not actively used until Franklin D. Roosevelt took power in 1933. More resource allocation allowed the Justice Department's Antitrust Division to initiate numerous antitrust actions between 1938 and 1942. Congressional hearings during the same period were also marked by 'condemnations of patents and calls for the rights to be rolled back such as through compulsory licensing'.[52] However, the antitrust movement weakened with the US entry into World War II in 1941 as politicians saw the merits of big business in winning the war.[53]

Nonetheless, the US court's distrust towards the patent system, which began with the Supreme Court overruling the *A.B. Dick* case in 1917,[54] continued until the 1980s. In the case of *A.B. Dick* (1912),[55] the Supreme Court condoned the tie-in practice[56] of the A.B. Dick Company, which sold its patented mimeograph machine on the condition of restricting its use to ink purchased from the patentee.[57] However, in 1917 the Supreme

---

47 May and Sell (n 5) 133–40.

48 Quoted in Peter Drahos and John Braithwaite, *Information Feudalism Who Owns the Knowledge Economy?*, The New Press (2002) 44.

49 Lawrence Kastriner, 'The Revival of Confidence in the Patent System' (1991) 73(1) *Journal of the Patent and Trademark Office Society* 5–23, 6.

50 The Sherman Antitrust Act, which regulates acts of restraining trade and forming of monopolies, gives the Justice Department the mandate for enforcement, such as by stopping illegal behaviour through orders of the federal court.

51 May and Sell (n 5) 133–40.

52 Dutfield (n 34) 113.

53 Ibid.

54 243 U.S. 502, 518 (1917).

55 *Henry v. A.B. Dick Company*, 224 U.S. 1 (1912).

56 Tie-in arrangements refer to sellers' practices of requiring a purchaser of a patented item (tying product) to buy an unpatented item (tied product) with it.

57 Kastriner (n 49).

Court struck down tie-ins as hampering free competition under the 1914 Clayton Act.[58] The Court held that 'tie-ins allowed patent owners to obtain de facto "monopolies" over non-patented claims by extending their patents to cover non-claimable items'.[59] Throughout most of the twentieth century, since the concept of misuse first emerged in 1917, 'patents were considered to be monopolies rather than necessary incentives for innovation'[60] in the eyes of the US judiciary. Patents were subordinate to the antitrust policy and the courts often presumed patents to be invalid. The concept of patent misuse 'reached its zenith in a series of cases in the 1940s'.[61] In general, the concept of misuse can be applied when the patentee has either been involved in a violation of the antitrust laws or attempted to expand the scope of the patent to unpatented material.[62]

This antitrust, anti-patent view that permeated the judiciary began to change in the 1980s. Patents became no longer construed as a bar to free competition in US public policy. This will be dealt with in later sections.

Patents and Developing Countries: Search for More Access to Technology

As of 1986, the majority of the Members of the Paris Convention[63] were from developing countries. Out of 97 Member countries of the Paris Convention, about 64 countries were developing countries.[64] While there was an apparent belief among developing countries that patents could be a medium that would assist the transfer of technology, there also existed considerable pressure from developed countries and transnational corporations on developing countries to have a patent system and to join the Paris Union by adopting the Paris Convention. The provisions of the Paris Convention (1883) were revised several times, the latest in Stockholm in 1967 which was before developing countries joined in large numbers. The Paris Convention set the international minimum standard for patent protection, the core of which was the elimination of discrimination against foreign inventors and the protection of their rights through the priority provisions.[65]

---

58 James B. Kobak, Jr, 'The Misuse Defense and Intellectual Property Litigation' (1995) 1 *Boston University Journal of Science and Technology Law* 1–43.

59 Ibid., para. 5.

60 Susan K. Sell, *Private Power, Public Law: The Globalization of Intellectual Property Rights*, Cambridge University Press (2003) 65.

61 May and Sell (n 5) 139.

62 In the case of *Morton Salt Co. v. G.S. Suppinger Co.*, the Court held that 'misuse rendered a patent unenforceable against anyone until the misuse was purged'. *Morton Salt Co. v. G.S. Suppinger Co.*, 314 U.S. 488 (1942). Kobak, Jr. (n 58) para. 7. Two years later, in the *Mercoid* cases, the Court reaffirmed that 'the owner of a patent may not employ it to secure a limited monopoly of an unpatented material used in applying the invention'. *Mercoid*, 320 U.S. 661; *Mercoid Corp. v. Minneapolis-Honeywell Regulator Co.*, 320 U.S. 680 (1944); *Mercoid Corporation v. Mid-Continent Inv. Co.*, 320 U.S. 661 (1944).

63 See 'The Paris Convention' above for the origin of the Paris Convention.

64 This part draws upon the work of Susan Sell. S. Sell, 'Intellectual Property as a Trade Issue: From the Paris Convention to GATT' (1989) XIII(4) *Legal Studies Forum* 407–22.

65 Under the Paris Convention, the first filing of an application for a patent (the priority date) in one Member country gave a priority right to the applicant. See 'The Paris Convention' above.

However, developing countries found such provisions did not take account of the vast inequities in technological development and wealth. Patents of developing countries were predominantly owned by foreigners. Edith Penrose's research in 1973 demonstrated that in developing countries 'foreigners typically take from three-fourths to well over 90% of the patents granted, and these may be highly concentrated in the hands of a very few companies'.[66] Moreover, the patents owned by foreign companies facilitated market dominance by those companies. This was particularly true of the pharmaceutical industry. More than three-quarters of 160 pharmaceutical laboratories in Venezuela were owned by foreign companies, which also controlled more than 90 per cent of the pharmaceutical market.[67] The level of market dominance by foreign companies was similar in the Brazilian pharmaceutical industry. In Colombia 32 foreign companies controlled more than 74 per cent of the pharmaceutical market.[68]

In developing countries, the effects of patents on domestic inventive activity per se were minimal, and patents were largely owned by foreign companies or foreign nationals, as described above.[69] The question was rather over whether or not patents facilitated the transfer of technology.[70] In this respect, it was argued that patents were of little importance for the transfer of technology since the patented processes were not used and the patented products were not manufactured in the patent-granting developing countries. This view is in stark contrast to one of the classical justifications of patents as 'a means or vehicle for technology transfers'.[71] Even worse, foreign-owned patents were mostly used to protect markets from other potential producers and thus prevented developing countries from seeking the goods from alternative sources at cheaper prices.[72] For instance, in a situation where no antibiotics were locally produced, the Andean countries sought to import available technology from various resources, but the patent holders blocked the imports.[73] While distrust of the patent system per se increasingly grew among developing countries, compulsory licensing was considered as a means for addressing 'abuses' of patents, including restricting imports from alternative sources or blocking other potential manufacturers.

An important attempt to address the perspective of developing countries in this regard was the 'Model Law for Developing Countries on Inventions' prepared in 1965 by BIRPI (the Secretariat for the International Bureaux of Intellectual Property, the predecessor of WIPO).[74] The Model Law for Developing Countries on Inventions (hereafter, the Model Law) provided three grounds for granting compulsory licences: 'the importance of the patented invention for the defence or the economy of the country or for public

---

66 Edith Penrose, 'International Patenting and the Less-Developed Countries' (1973) 83(331) *The Economic Journal* 768–86, 769.

67 Constantine Vaitos, 'Patents Revisited: Their Function in Developing Countries' (1972) 9(1) *Journal of Development Studies* 71–97, 79.

68 Ibid.

69 Ibid., 75; Penrose (n 66) 770.

70 Vaitos (n 67) 75; Penrose (n 66) 770.

71 Vaitos (n 67) 80–81.

72 Penrose (n 66) 776.

73 Vaitos (n 67) 81.

74 Penrose (n 66) 779–82.

health, the need to exploit an invention patented earlier in order to use a later invention, and inadequate working'.[75] Although the Model Law also restricted the extensive use of compulsory licensing without specifying the relevant categories in which such licensing may be justified, it was believed that a rigorous enforcement of compulsory licensing could adequately address most abuses that patents may cause.[76]

At the time, a different way of conceiving intellectual property was entrenched in the gulf between developed countries and developing countries. Developing countries viewed intellectual property as a part of the 'common heritage' belonging to all human beings, whereas developed countries conceived it as private property.[77] As a prominent example of the former, India considered that the notion of common heritage, when applied to patents, involved the free flow of information and technology, something considered essential for their economic and social development.[78] The common heritage principle guided 'a measure that required limitations on the extent of patentability, and emphasized the need to exclude certain fields from patent protection'.[79] The Indian Patent Law of 1970 was a reflection of this principle: it granted patents only for processes and not for the production of food, pharmaceuticals and chemicals; it restricted both the extent of patentability and the term of patents (pharmaceuticals for only seven years); and it included a detailed measure to ensure an adequate local working of patents.[80] As a result, India managed to lower drug prices which had reached their highest prices under the old patent laws formulated during colonial times.[81] In addition, it succeeded in preventing foreign companies from enjoying market dominance in India. India was not the only country that redesigned its patent law to serve public interests. Other countries, like Brazil, Argentina, Mexico and the Andean Pact countries, also limited the scope of patentability in the pharmaceutical industry.[82]

Developing countries' search for a free flow of technological information led to serious attempts to revise the international patent protection system provided in the Paris Convention. This was meant to address the disparity existing between developing countries and developed countries. Conferences for the revision of the Paris Convention[83] were held between 1980 and 1984. Among developing countries, Latin American States (Brazil, Mexico and the Andean Pact countries) and India were particularly active in the

---

75 Ibid., 780.

76 Ibid.

77 Sell (n 64) 410.

78 Anitha Ramanna, 'Chapter 5. Shifts in India's Policy on Intellectual Property: The Role of Ideas, Coercion and Changing Interests', in *Death of Patents*, Queen Mary Intellectual Property Institute and Lawtext Publishing Limited (2005) 150–74.

79 Ibid., 154.

80 Ibid., 155.

81 Drahos (n 2).

82 Peter Drahos, 'Negotiating Intellectual Property Rights: Between Coercion and Dialogue', in Peter Drahos and Ruth Mayne (eds), *Global Intellectual Property Rights Knowledge, Access and Development*, Palgrave Macmillan (2002) 161–82.

83 The Diplomatic Conference for the Revision of the Paris Convention for the Protection of Industrial Property.

conferences.[84] The developing countries put forward the idea of intellectual property as a common heritage and sought 'provision that would give developing countries more and more access to technology that had been locked up by means of patents'.[85] Specifically, the developing countries tried to incorporate exclusive compulsory licensing[86] in cases where patent holders failed to work the invention in the national territory. Such proposals by developing countries were rejected by developed countries, in particular the US. The differences in views between developing countries and developed countries were insurmountable and consequently the negotiations ended in 1984 without agreement.[87] In the meantime, shifts in the international system of patent protection were about to take place in the opposite direction to the wishes of developing countries, as will be seen in the following section.

The Global Period

In 1994, the TRIPS Agreement was made binding on all Member countries of the WTO as the Uruguay Round concluded with the signing of the Final Act embodying the Result of the Uruguay Round of Multilateral Trade Negotiations. TRIPS represents the beginning of the globalisation of intellectual property.[88] In the past, States had more space for determining policies regarding intellectual property. Previously, States had been able to make reservations to clauses in treaties or to refuse to adopt certain protocols or conventions concerning intellectual property.

The Road to TRIPS

The US industrial interests and TRIPS

TRIPS is said to largely reflect the interests of US corporations for raising the level of intellectual property protection worldwide.[89] Tracing the process towards TRIPS may show the validity of this claim.

The globalisation of intellectual property protection may be better understood against the backdrop of a broader trend of contemporary capitalism and, more specifically, the development of the US economy. According to Drahos's account,[90] increasing competition led businesses to seek out sources of innovation and to develop the desire for controlling

---

84 Sell (n 64) 409.

85 Drahos (n 2).

86 Exclusive compulsory licences refer to a practice that authorises a third party or the State to use a patented process or manufacture a patented product and excludes the patent holder from exploiting the patented process or product.

87 Sell (n 64) 407.

88 Drahos (n 2).

89 James Thuo Gathii, 'Construing Intellectual Property Rights and Competition Policy Consistently with Facilitating Access to Affordable AIDS Drugs to Low-end Consumers' (2001) 53 *Florida Law Review* 727–88, 753; Drahos and Braithwaite (n 48) 61–73.

90 Drahos (n 3) 95–117.

knowledge as a new area of industry. Creative labour came to be increasingly integrated into commodity production. Drahos argues that through this process, intellectual property has not only gained its status but also changed 'the ethos of science'.[91] As creative labour comes to be governed by intellectual property norms, the exchange of ideas and information is no longer encouraged to the degree that it used to be. The trend of US industry is particularly crucial in understanding the emergence of TRIPS. Between 1980 and 1987, the US trade deficit had increased from US $31 billion to US $170 billion, and the manufacturing trade balance had moved from a US $27 billion surplus to a US $4,138 billion deficit.[92] The growing US trade deficit increased concerns about US competitiveness and the need for a new approach to trade policy, decidedly protectionist.[93]

US businesses played a major role in the reformulation of US trade policy, significantly elevating intellectual property protection to the top of the trade agenda.[94] The US competitive advantage now largely lies with products and services with a market value which is greatly dependent on international intellectual property protection, such as software, pharmaceuticals, chemicals and the entertainment industries.[95] As some developing States began not only to acquire technological capacity but also to make patent laws that fostered a local industry, the US companies felt threatened. Among them was pharmaceutical company Pfizer, which initiated the strategy for intellectual property.[96] Intellectual property-related companies began lobbying for more vigorous protection of their intellectual property abroad, redefining weak protection of intellectual property as a barrier to trade. Increased competitive concerns in the US have dramatically changed attitudes towards the relationship between trade and intellectual property among administrators and within the courts.[97] As discussed under 'Patents and the Antitrust Policy in the US' above, the US courts used to hold the view that a patent right should be carefully reviewed with regard to its possible effect of restraining trade and its compatibility with antitrust law. No longer is the protection of intellectual property considered to conflict with trade. The US corporations also effectively employed the notion of 'individual property rights' in reframing the issue of intellectual property; more aggressive metaphors, such as 'piracy', were used to denounce copying activities, many of which were in fact legal in national and international law.[98] The way that the US business environment framed the issue of intellectual property was effective in reshaping the US trade law and policy, with explicit intellectual property protection embedded in its provisions.

---

91 Ibid., 113.
92 Drahos and Braithwaite (n 48) 85–107.
93 Gathii (n 89); ibid.
94 Sell (n 60) 75–95.
95 Gathii (n 89) 753.
96 Drahos and Braithwaite (n 48) 61–73.
97 Sell (n 60) 60–74.
98 Robert Weissman, 'A Long Strange TRIPS: The Pharmaceutical Industry Drive to Harmonize Global Intellectual Property Rules, and the Remaining WTO Legal Alternatives Available to Third World Countries' (1996) 17 *University of Pennsylvania Journal of International Economic Law* 1069–125; Drahos and Braithwaite (n 48) 61–73; Sell (n 60) 30–59.

The outcome was a series of bilateral enforcement mechanisms against countries whose intellectual property standards were lower than US standards and therefore were considered 'inadequate' by the US.[99] A system known as the General Special Preferences (GSP)[100] was used as a lever to raise the protection of intellectual property in other countries.[101] In 1984 the protection of US intellectual property became a criterion for determining the GSP status. In the same year, the US also amended its Trade Act to include an intellectual property consideration in 'section 301', which is 'a national trade enforcement tool that allows the US to withdraw the benefits of trade agreements or impose duties on goods from foreign countries'.[102] In 1985, the first targets of the US bilateral action were South Korea and Brazil.[103] With regard to patents, South Korea did not provide product patents on foods, chemicals and drugs; Brazil excluded pharmaceutical products and processes from patentability from 1969. The 301 actions against South Korea and Brazil brought about changes in legislation on intellectual property in both countries. In 1988 the 301 process was further strengthened through the Omnibus Trade and Competitiveness Act of 1988 which added more processes, referred to as 'Super 301' or 'Special 301'. Under these provisions, the United States Trade Representative (USTR) was required to 'identify those countries that denied adequate and effective protection of intellectual property rights, or deny fair and equitable market access' to the US intellectual property owners, and to negotiate with those countries to address the problems. Countries identified as 'priority foreign countries' could be subject to US trade retaliation. In so far as countries considered access to the US market critical, the US trade tools, such as the 301 process, were effective in raising the level of intellectual property protection in other countries.

In the meantime, US companies sought to obtain a strong multilateral agreement on intellectual property as a long-term strategy, while maintaining the use of unilateral trade tools and bilateral negotiations.[104] Edmund Pratt, the CEO of Pfizer from 1972 to 1991, and John Opel, a chairman of IBM in the 1980s, both played a key role in the strategic Advisory Committee on Trade Negotiations (ACTN), the committee that advised the US president on trade policy. A small number of individuals in the US business community, particularly Pratt and Opel, saw the possibility of utilising the General Agreement on Tariffs and Trade (GATT) as a forum for the international regulation of intellectual property. The US began to argue that the issue of intellectual property should be dealt with as a subject related to trade within the GATT. In 1986 Pratt and Opel created the Intellectual Property Committee (IPC) with other corporate executives of US-based multilateral corporations.[105] The IPC declared itself as 'dedicated to the negotiation of a comprehensive agreement on intellectual

---

99 Drahos and Braithwaite (n 48) 85–107; Sell (n 60) 97–120; Dutfield (n 34) 195–205.

100 The GSP is a programme which allows designated beneficiary countries to export eligible products to the US on a duty-free basis.

101 Drahos and Braithwaite (n 48) 85–107.

102 Drahos (n 82) 169.

103 See, for the details, Drahos and Braithwaite (n 48) 102–5; Dutfield (n 34) 202–3.

104 Drahos and Braithwaite (n 48).

105 Such corporations included Bristol-Myers, DuPont, FMC Corporation, General Electric, General Motors, Hewlett-Packard, IBM, Johnson & Johnson, Merck, Monsanto, Pfizer, Rockwell International and Warner Communications.

property in the current GATT round of multilateral trade negotiations'.[106] Seeking its allies in Europe and Japan, the IPC crafted a proposal based on the existing laws of industrialised countries, and by 1994 saw the final agreement incorporate most of what it wanted.[107]

Democratic deficit in the negotiation process of TRIPS

One might wonder why a large majority of countries that would not benefit from the global intellectual property regime signed the TRIPS Agreement. Was there any gain for importer countries in accepting a regime of intellectual property rights that could offset the costs? Apparently, many importer countries of intellectual property held the belief that there would be a net gain for them, for instance in agriculture or other sectors, which could justify concessions in intellectual property, including those that would restrict access to medicines. Nevertheless, while possible higher exports in other sectors may benefit some parts of the population, it may not lead to improvements in the overall capacity of citizens to afford the high price of patented products under the new global regime of intellectual property.

Drahos observed that the lack of a democratic process in the formulation of the intellectual property regime at both the national and international levels may better explain the reason why States signed TRIPS, which would narrow their sovereignty to determine appropriate levels of intellectual property, thus affecting the basic rights of their citizens.[108] One might argue that TRIPS was subject to a negotiating process among sovereign nations and was thus adequately democratically arrived at. However, a question remains as to whether the negotiating process was genuinely democratic.

Drahos specifies three conditions that must be met in order to qualify as a democratic process.

> (1) All relevant interests must be represented in the negotiation of the property rights; (2) all involved in the negotiation must have full information about the consequence of various possible outcomes; and (3) one party must not coerce the others.[109]

It is argued that these three conditions have not been met in the process of forming TRIPS.[110] Firstly, genuine negotiations took place only within a narrow circle which is mainly comprised of the US, Europe and Japan, extending up to, at most, 20 countries. Secondly, most developing countries were not exactly aware of what was going on; a positive message about TRIPS sent by developed countries succeeded in preventing developing countries from realising the real cost that their citizens would have to bear. Finally, the US bilaterally threatened trade sanctions in order to make opponent countries soften their opposition to TRIPS and accept increased protection of intellectual property. Throughout the 1980s, developing countries vehemently challenged the inclusion of intellectual property in a

---

106 Intellectual Property Committee, 'Accomplishments and Current Activities of the IP Committee', 14 June 1988.

107 Sell (n 60) 97–120.

108 Drahos and Braithwaite (n 48) 187–97.

109 Ibid., 190.

110 Ibid., 190–91.

new round of multilateral trade negotiations.[111] India, Brazil, Argentina, Cuba, Egypt, Nicaragua, Nigeria, Peru, Tanzania and Yugoslavia were particularly active in opposition to the US initiative. However, even these countries could not stand up to the increasing pressure from the US through section 301 and GSP actions as many of them were put on the list for US trade actions. In short, while a caveat should be entered about 'the complex nature of the negotiation and the wide diversity of interests being pursued',[112] whether TRIPS is an outcome of a democratic process remains a legitimate question to ask.

TRIPS: Globalising a Minimum Level of Intellectual Property Protection

With the adoption of TRIPS,[113] all WTO Member countries became obliged to harmonise their national intellectual property systems with the minimum standards laid down by TRIPS. This chapter confines itself to a brief account of distinctive features of TRIPS. More rigorous discussions over flexibilities of TRIPS are dealt with in Chapter 3.

In the pre-TRIPS era, each country retained latitude in determining its patent system, as long as it treated foreign nationals in the same manner as nationals with respect to legal rights and remedies. As discussed previously, not only developing countries but also developed countries adopted patent systems that reflected different stages of their development process. TRIPS is unprecedented in that it binds all WTO Members to provide the same level of intellectual property protection independently of their level of development. The only concession given to developing countries, including Least Developed Countries (LDCs), is 'the possibility of applying transitional periods, all of which have expired so far except for LDCs'.[114] Another distinctive feature of TRIPS is that it provides an enforcement mechanism for countries' obligations with regard to the provision of minimum intellectual property rights standards, something absent in the pre-existing conventions on intellectual property. Any dispute relating to compliance with TRIPS may be brought to a trade tribunal according to the rules of the Dispute Settlement Understanding (DSU), one of the WTO Agreements. This is one main reason why the proponents of TRIPS moved a forum for intellectual property from WIPO to the WTO.

---

111 Sell (n 60) 97–120; Drahos and Braithwaite (n 48) Drahos (n 82) 161–82.

112 Dutfield draws attention to the fact that neither interest groups such as corporations nor developing countries are monolithic in terms of their interests in intellectual property. He also acknowledges that coercion of the South by the North played a significant role in the TRIPS negotiations. See Dutfied (n 34) 195–205.

113 See, generally, Agreement on Trade-Related Aspects of Intellectual Property Rights, April 15, 1994, Marrakesh Agreement Establishing the World Trade Organization, Annex 1C, Legal Instruments – Results of the Uruguay Round vol. 31, 33 ILM 81 (1994) (TRIPS).

114 Carlos Correa, *Trade Related Aspects of Intellectual Property Rights: A Commentary on the TRIPS Agreement*, Oxford University Press (2007) 8. The transition period for LDCs for the provisions on pharmaceuticals was extended to 2016, in accordance with Paragraph 7 of the Doha Declaration on the TRIPS Agreement and Public Health, WT/MIN(01)/DEC/2, 20 November 2001. The Council for TRIPS formally adopted a decision to implement this in 2002. In 2013, the transition period for all LDC countries for implementation of TRIPS was further extended until 1 July 2021. See Decision of the Council for TRIPS of 12 June 2013.

TRIPS places specific obligations on WTO Members in relation to patents. Section 5 of the Agreement dealing with patents requires patent protection to be available for any invention in all fields of technology, defines the exclusive rights conferred to patent owners, and determines the term of patent protection. Each is discussed below in turn, alongside the relevant provision of the Agreement.

> 27.1 Subject to the provisions of paragraph 2 and 3, patents shall be available for any inventions, *whether products or processes, in all fields of technology*, provided that they are new, involve an inventive step and are capable of industrial application. Subject to paragraph 4 of Article 65, paragraph 8 of Article 70 and paragraph 3 of this Article, patents shall be available and patent rights enjoyable without discrimination as to the place of invention, the field of technology and whether products are imported or locally produced. (Emphasis added)

Before TRIPS, many countries did not grant patents on medicines or agrochemicals. At the time the Uruguay Round started, the number of countries that did not grant pharmaceutical patents was estimated to be nearly 50.[115] This meant that pharmaceuticals or agrochemicals as such could be made, used, sold or imported without exclusive rights being conferred on the 'inventor'. In some countries, patents were not provided for the product but only for the process of producing an invention. Therefore, the same product could be made and sold as long as it was produced without using a patented process. However, TRIPS requires patents to be granted if claimed inventions satisfy the criteria of novelty, inventive step, and industrial application, 'whether products or processes, in all fields of technology' (Article 27.1).

> 28.1 Patent shall confer on *its owner the following exclusive rights*:
>
> (a) where the subject matter of a patent is a product, to prevent third parties not having the owner's consent from the acts of: making, using, offering for sale, selling, or importing for these purposes that product;
>
> (b) where the subject matter of a patent is a process, to prevent third parties not having the owner's consent from the act of: using the process, and from the acts of: using, offering for sale, selling, or importing for these purposes at least the product obtained directly by that process.
>
> 28.2 Patent owners shall also have the right to assign, or transfer by succession, the patent and to conclude licensing contracts. (Emphasis added)

Article 28 establishes the exclusive rights that a patent confers on its patent holder. Such provision drew a comment that 'it … deeply interferes with national discretion in establishing rights that can be claimed by private parties in national jurisdictions'.[116]

---

115 Correa (n 114) 271.
116 Ibid., 10.

33. The term of protection available shall not end before the expiration of a period of twenty years counted from the filing date.

Before TRIPS, the term of patent protection was not harmonised. For instance, India granted a patent for food or medicines for seven years from the date of filing the application or five years from the date of sealing, whichever was shorter.[117] In the US and Canada, patents were granted for 17 years, calculated from the date of grant.[118] Article 33 determines the duration of patents for at least 20 years from the date of filing the patent application, which obliged many Member countries to amend their legislation.

At first glance, TRIPS appears to foreclose the patent policy alternatives open to countries. However, there are still flexibilities in TRIPS that countries can use to strike a balance between patent owners' interests and other important interests. The measures to meet public needs, including public health, permitted by TRIPS include compulsory licensing, exceptions to the exclusive rights, and the incorporation of strict standards for patentability. These measures deserve more detailed discussions, which follow in Chapter 3.

Post-TRIPS

The Doha Declaration on the TRIPS Agreement and Public Health

After the adoption of TRIPS, its potential impact on public health became a serious concern. Multinational pharmaceutical companies, backed by the US and the EU, initiated aggressive campaigns to frustrate countries' efforts to utilise TRIPS flexibilities for public health reasons. The most visible cases involved the US and pharmaceutical companies' challenges to South Africa and Brazil.

In 1997, the South African National Assembly passed the Medicines and Related Substances Control Amendment Act.[119] This Act amended the Medicines and Related Substances Control Act, No. 101 of 1965 and provided a range of measures designed to ensure the supply of more affordable medicines. Particularly, section 15C of the amended Medicines Act granted the Health Minister the power to prescribe conditions for the parallel imports of patented drugs[120] so as to reduce the prices of the drugs. In February 1998,

---

117 Article 53, the 1970 Indian Patents Act, available at http://ipindia.nic.in/ipr/patent/patAct1970-3-99.html, last accessed 30 July 2007.

118 Correa (n 114) 343.

119 The Medicines and Related Substances Control Amendment Act, No. 90 of 1997.

120 Section 15C of the amended Medicines and Related Substances Control Act:

The Minister may prescribe conditions for the supply of more affordable medicines in certain circumstances so as to protect the health of the public, and in particular may—

(a) notwithstanding anything to the contrary contained in the Patents Act, 1978 (Act. No. 57 of 1978), determine that the rights with regard to any medicine under a patent granted in the Republic shall not extend to acts in respect of such medicine which has been put onto the market by the owner of the medicine, or with his or her consent;

(b) prescribe the conditions on which any medicine which is identical in composition, meets the same quality standard and is intended to have the same propriety name as

39 global pharmaceutical companies, represented by the Pharmaceutical Manufacturers Association of South Africa (hereinafter, the PMA), initiated legal action in the South African High Court against the South African government alleging various violations of TRIPS and the South African Constitution.[121] The US government also began to pressure South Africa to withdraw or modify section 15C for fear that it would undermine the interests of the US pharmaceutical industry.[122] The US government put South Africa on the 301 'Watch list' and announced a suspension of South Africa's GSP benefits. A year later the US government withdrew the trade pressure on South Africa as a result of rigorous public criticism. Nevertheless, the PMA did not drop the lawsuit until 2001. This led to a long delay in the implementation of the amended Medicines Act. As their legal claims were rigorously rebuted by affidavits filed by Treatment Action Campaign (TAC), as amicus curiae,[123] the PMA conceded that parallel importation was not inconsistent with TRIPS.[124] Moreover, the language of section 15C of the amended Medicines Act, subject to criticism from the PMA, turned out to be taken from the WIPO Committee of Experts drafts for a Patent Harmonization Treaty (1990)[125] consistently approved by the US and EU delegations.[126] Finally, the PMA withdrew their lawsuit against the South African government.

---

that of another medicine already registered in the Republic, but which is imported by a person other than the person who is the holder of the registration certificate of the medicine already registered and which originates from any site of the manufacture of the original manufacturer as approved by the council in the prescribed manner, may be imported.

(c) prescribe the registration procedure for, as well as the use of, the medicine referred to in paragraph (b).

121 Case No. 4183/98.

122 Sell (n 60) 151–3; Mark Heywood, 'Debunking "Conglomo-talk": A Case Study of the Amicus Curiae as an Instrument for Advocacy, Investigation and Mobilisation' (2001) 5(2) *Law, Democracy and Development Law* 133; Frederick M. Abbott, '11 The TRIPS-legality of Measures Taken to Address Public Health Crises: Responding to USTR-State-industry Positions that Undermine the WTO', in Daniel L.M. Kennedy (ed.), *Political Economy of International Trade law: Essays in Honor of Robert E. Hudec*, Cambridge University Press (2002) 311–48; Frederick M. Abbott, 'IV. Government and Private Operators' *Study Paper 2a: WTO TRIPS Agreement and Its Implications on Access to Medicines in Developing Countries*, The Commission on Intellectual Property Rights (UK) (2002) 51–4.

123 The TAC's Founding Affidavit was filed on 16 February 2001 and the Heads of Argument of the TAC was submitted in April 2001. See www.tac.org.za/Documents/MedicineActCourtCase/MedicineActCourtCase.htm, last accessed 2 April 2011.

124 *PMA v. President*, Applicant's answering affidavit to the affidavits filed by the amicus curiae, sworn 28 March 2001, para. 9.1.14. Referenced at Abbott (n 122) 'IV. Government and Private Operators', 52.

125 WIPO, Committee of Experts on the Harmonization of Certain Provisions in Laws for the Protection of Inventions, Eighth Session, Geneva, June 11 to 22, 1990, Draft Treaty on the Harmonization of Patent Laws; Draft Regulations Under the Draft Treaty (Arts. 9 to 24; Rule7), Document prepared by the International Bureau of WIPO, HL/CE/VIII/3, 15 February 1990.

126 See, for the more detailed account, Abbott (n 122) 'IV. Government and Private Operators' 53–4.

In June 2001, the US initiated a WTO dispute settlement proceeding against Brazil claiming that Brazil's compulsory licensing legislation was incompatible with Article 27(1) of TRIPS. The Brazilian Industrial Property Law[127] permits the granting of a compulsory licence for goods that are not manufactured locally.[128] This legislation enabled the Health Ministry to mobilise the local manufacture of generic drugs and to lower the prices of drugs patented by multinational pharmaceutical companies.[129] While generics may mean a pharmaceutical product which does not have a trademark, 'generics (generic drugs/medicines)' in this book is used mostly to refer to 'copies of patented drugs or drugs whose patents have expired'.[130] The legality of generics may depend on the status of the patent and the existence of voluntary licence or compulsory licence. The procurement of cheap antiretroviral drugs was critical for the government in pursuing its universal, free HIV/AIDS treatment programme, which was initiated from 1996. As a result of this treatment programme, Brazil observed a drastic reduction in morbidity and mortality rates by 50–70 per cent.[131] The USTR ultimately withdrew its WTO proceeding against Brazil in the face of criticisms from the international community.

This series of events reinforced concerns among developing countries and citizen groups that TRIPS would be invoked to frustrate countries' efforts to address their public health needs. Developing countries sought 'an official confirmation that measures to protect public health would not make them subject to dispute settlement procedures in the WTO'.[132] In response to the request of Zimbabwe on behalf of the African Group,

---

127 Article 68(1) of the Brazilian Industrial Property Law No. 9,279 of 14 May 1996:

A patent shall be subject to compulsory licensing if the owner exercises his rights therein in an abusive manner or if he uses it to abuse economic power under the terms of an administrative or judicial decision.

(1) The following may also be grounds for compulsory licensing:

I. Failure to work the subject matter of a patent on the territory of Brazil, failure to manufacture or failure to completely use a patented process, except for failure to work due to the lack of economic viability, in which case importing shall be admitted; or

II. Marketing that does not satisfy the needs of the market.

128 Brazil – Measures Affecting Patent Protection, WT/DS199/3, 9 January 2001; Sell (n 60) 136; Duncan Matthews, 'WTO Decision on Implementation of Paragraph 6 of the Doha Declaration on the TRIPS Agreement and Public Health: A Solution to the Access to Essential Medicines Problem?' (2004) 7(1) *Journal of International Economic Law* 73–107, 80; Paul Champ and Amir Attaran, 'Patent Rights and Local Working Under the WTO TRIPS Agreement: An Analysis of the U.S.–Brazil Patent Dispute' (2002) 27 *Yale Journal of International Law* 365–93; Holger Hestermeyer, *Human Rights and the WTO: The Case of Patents and Access to Medicines*, Oxford University Press (2007) 242–4.

129 Commission on Intellectual Property Rights (UK), 'Chapter 2: Health', *Integrating Intellectual Property Rights and Development Policy*, Commission on International Property Rights (2002) 29–56, 43.

130 WTO, 'What does "Generic" Mean', in Fact Sheet on TRIPS and Pharmaceutical Patents, available at http://www.wto.org/english/tratop_e/trips_e/factsheet_pharm03_e.htm, last accessed 16 March 2015.

131 WHO, 'Chapter Two: The Treatment Initiative', *The World Health Report 2004*, WHO (2004) 21–41.

132 Sell (n 60) 158.

the TRIPS Council decided to convene a special session on access to medicines in June 2001, which ultimately led to the process that yielded the Doha Declaration on the TRIPS Agreement and Public Health (hereinafter, Doha Declaration).[133] The US 'essentially took the position of US pharmaceutical industry that patents were not an obstacle to access to medicines since price is only one factor in the public health',[134] and advocated the value of strong intellectual property protection that further restricts the flexibilities of TRIPS. Nevertheless, the anthrax threat in September 2001, in which several people became seriously ill or died after being exposed to anthrax-tainted mail in the US, damaged the claim persisted in by the US. The government of Canada announced that it would override the Bayer patent on ciprofloxacin (Cipro), an antibiotic known to be effective against anthrax and allow another company to produce a generic version of the drug to ensure prompt access to low-cost supplies in October 2001. The US threatened its use of compulsory licensing when negotiating with the pharmaceutical company Bayer for the price of Cipro. The anthrax-Cipro case clearly showed that 'no responsible government with a choice would place the public health of its citizens below the interests of a few patent holders'.[135] On 14 November 2001, the text of the Doha Declaration was adopted by the Ministerial Conference.

The Doha Declaration aims to clarify the relationship between TRIPS and public health policies of WTO Member countries. The significance of the Declaration lies with the confirmation of 'the rights that Members have retained under the Agreement, particularly by defining the flexibility allowed in certain key areas'.[136] This will be analysed in detail in Chapter 3.

'TRIPS-Plus' world and public health

While the Doha Declaration marked an important step forward in rethinking the intellectual property system in light of public health, developed countries, particularly the United States, the European Free Trade Association (EFTA) and the European Union, began to seek new bilateral and regional free trade agreements (FTAs) that mandate a higher level of intellectual property protection than required by TRIPS. This is often referred to as 'TRIPS-Plus'.[137] A range of studies warn that the new intellectual property protection requirements under the FTAs not only narrow the policy space allowed under TRIPS, but also impose a number of additional obligations on States that would further reduce their capacity to ensure access to medicines within their countries.[138] A 2013 joint study

---

133 WT/MIN(01)/DEC/2, adopted on 14 November 2001.

134 Frederick M. Abbott, 'The Doha Declaration on the TRIPS Agreement and Public Health: Lighting a Dark Corner at the WTO' (2002) 5 *Journal of International Economic Law* 469–505, 485.

135 Ibid., 488.

136 Carlos Maria Correa, *Implications of the Doha Declaration on the TRIPS Agreement and Public Health*, World Health Organization (2002) 48.

137 Peter Drahos, 'Bilateralism in Intellectual Property', Oxfam Policy Paper, December 2001. Available at http://policy-practice.oxfam.org.uk/publications/bilateralism-in-intellectual-property-111967, last accessed 15 March 2015.

138 See Cynthia M. Ho, '8. An Overview of "TRIPS-Plus" Standards', in *Access to Medicine in the Global Economy: International Agreements on Patents and Related Rights*, Oxford University Press

conducted by the World Health Organization (WHO), WIPO and the WTO provides an analysis of the heightened intellectual property standards in FTAs concluded by the US, the EFTA and the EU.[139] Those FTAs include more than one of the 'TRIPS-Plus' features affecting pharmaceutical sectors, which include 1) eliminating possible exclusions from patentability; 2) providing patents for 'new uses' of a known product; 3) restricting parallel importation; 4) limiting the grounds for compulsory licences; 5) extending the term of patent; and 6) providing data exclusivity.

Some FTAs[140] require mandatory patent protection for plants and animals and thus eliminate the flexibility in Article 27.3(b) of TRIPS, which excludes this subject matter from patentability. A number of FTAs also require the grant of patents for the 'second indication' or 'new uses' of a pharmaceutical product.[141] A pharmaceutical compound known to be effective for one disease may be found to treat another disease; this 'new use' may be patented under provisions in those FTAs. Protection of 'new uses' will encourage a trend of patent application for modified versions of older drugs. This feature not only expands the scope of patents, but also has a significant implication for the innovation of new medicines.[142] Some FTAs permit the patent owner to prevent parallel imports through the use of contracts or other means, restricting the possibility of parallel importation which is allowed under the regime of international exhaustion.[143] A limited number of FTAs restrict the grounds for compulsory licences to cases of anti-competitive practices, public non-commercial use, national emergency or other circumstances of extreme urgency.[144]

A large number of FTAs require the partner countries to provide an extension of the patent term to 'compensate' for delays in marketing approval processes and in the

---

(2011) 223–52; Drahos (n 137); Frederick Abbott, *The Doha Declaration on the TRIPS Agreement and Public Health and the Contradictory Trend in Bilateral and Regional Free Trade Agreements, Occasional Paper No. 14*, QUNO (2004); Frederick Abbott, 'Toward a New Era of Objective Assessment in the Field of TRIPS and Variable Geometry for the Preservation of Multilateralism' (2005) 8(1) *Journal of International Economic Law* 77–100; Carlos M. Correa, 'Implications of Bilateral Free Trade Agreements on Access to Medicines' (2006) 84(5) *Bulletin of the World Health Organization* 399–404; Duncan Matthews, 'TRIPS Flexibilities and Access to Medicines in Developing Countries: The Problem with Technical Assistance and Free Trade Agreements' (2005) 27(11) *European Intellectual Property Review* 420–27; Sisule F. Musungu and Cecilia Oh, *The Use of Flexibilities in TRIPS by Developing Countries: Can They Promote Access to Medicines? Study 4C*, Commission on Intellectual Property Rights, Innovation and Public Health (CIPIH), WHO (August 2005).

139 WHO, WIPO and WTO, *Promoting Access to Medical Technologies and Innovation: Intersections between Public Health, Intellectual Property and Trade* (2013) 186–90.

140 For example, US-Chile (2004), CAFTA (US-Central America and the Dominican Republic) (2006–2009) and US-Morocco (2006). Abbott (n 138) 88; Musungu and Oh (n 138) 65; Drahos (n 137) 8.

141 For example, US-Morocco (2006), US-Australia (2005), US-Bahrain (2006), US-Chile (2004), US-Korea (2012) and US-Oman (2009).

142 Correa (n 138) 401; Abbott (n 138) 88; Musungu and Oh (n 138) 66.

143 See US-Morocco FTA (2006) and US-Australia (2005).

144 See US-Australia (2005), US-Singapore (2004) and US-Jordan (2001).

examination of patent applications.[145] As a result, patents on pharmaceuticals may last longer than the 20-year term provided by TRIPS. Such extension will delay the introduction of generic versions of medicines with a negative implication for access to medicines.[146] Data exclusivity is one of the main TRIPS-Plus features in FTAs.[147] Article 39.3 of TRIPS requires the protection of undisclosed test data from unfair commercial use but does not oblige Members to confer exclusive rights over test data for a fixed period.[148] However, the provisions of test data protection under the recent FTAs require the grant of exclusive rights for clinical data associated with pharmaceutical products for a certain period of time (five years under most FTAs but eight years under some), counted from the date of approval of the product. During the period of exclusivity, no other company is allowed to use the data in seeking approval of a generic drug. Notably, test data exclusivity is applied to all pharmaceutical products, irrespective of whether such products are patented or not. This provision would deter competition from generics, since the registering of generic drugs would be delayed until the expiration of data exclusivity, even where a product is off-patent, unless generic manufacturers replicate a full set of test data necessary for market approval.[149] Data exclusivity would also indirectly limit the use of compulsory licences since even if a compulsory licence is granted, generic manufacturers may be prevented from using the test data originally submitted for regulatory approval of the product.[150] It is observed that these TRIPS-Plus requirements included in the FTAs are 'designed to inhibit the marketing of generic products'.[151]

Overall, TRIPS-Plus requirements may erode the flexibilities available to developing countries in creating their policies taking into account their public health needs and development plans. It has been cautioned that TRIPS-Plus standards on patentability criteria and test data exclusivity in particular are highly likely to lead to significant price increases for medicines in developing countries, delaying access to lower-cost generics.[152] As the earlier concluded FTAs are implemented, the impact of 'TRIPS-Plus' on the price of medicines is brought into light. A 2007 Oxfam study estimated that data exclusivity, required under the US-Jordan FTA, had delayed market entry of 79 per cent of generic

---

145 See, EFTA-Albania (2010), EFTA-Chile (2004), EFTA-Korea (2006), EFTA-Singapore (2003), US-Australia (2005), US-Bahrain (2006), CAFTA-DR (2006–2009), US-Chile (2004), US-Jordan (2001), US-Korea (2012), US-Oman (2009), US-Panama (2011), US-Peru (2009), US-Singapore (2004) and US-Morocco (2006).

146 Correa (n 138) 400–401.

147 See, for example, CAFTA-DR (2006–2009), US-Australia (2005), US-Bahrain (2006), US-Chile (2004), US-Morocco (2006), US-Singapore (2004), US-Korea (2012), US-Panama (2011), US-Peru (2009), EFTA-Tunisia (2005), EFTA-Serbia (2010–2011), EFTA-Peru (2011), EFTA-Lebanon (2007), EFTA-Egypt (2007).

148 Correa (n 114) 374–92.

149 Correa (n 138) 401; Musungu and Oh (n 138) 57–61; Matthews (n 138) 426.

150 Matthews (n 138) 426.

151 Abbott (n 138) 92.

152 Mohammed K El Said, *Public Health-related TRIPS-Plus Provisions in Bilateral Trade Agreements: A Policy Guide for Negotiators and Implementers in the WHO Eastern Mediterranean Region*, ICTSD and WHO (2010).

versions of new medicines by 21 multinational pharmaceutical companies between 2002 and 2006, resulting in the increase of medicine prices by 20 per cent since the conclusion of the agreement.[153]

Intellectual property, public health and development

While the heightening of intellectual property protection beyond TRIPS is pursued by primarily developed countries through bilateral and regional FTAs, important discussions on intellectual property in relation to public health and development are taking place in WIPO and the WHO among other international organisations. In October 2007, the WIPO General Assembly adopted a Development Agenda for WIPO, consisting of 45 recommendations to enhance WIPO's work in a manner that takes more into account the concerns of developing countries. The recommendations cover six main areas of activities, including technical assistance and capacity-building; norm-setting, flexibilities, public policy and public knowledge; technology transfer, information and communication technology (ICT) and access to knowledge; assessments, evaluation and impact studies; institutional matters including mandate and governance; and other issues.[154] The Committee on Development and Intellectual Property was established with the mandate of discussing a work programme of implementing the Development Agenda in 2008 and since then has made recommendations to the WIPO General Assembly annually.

Particularly for the discussion on intellectual property and public health, the WHO became a key forum in the post-TRIPS era. As a specialised agency of the UN mandated with the promotion of international public health, the WHO has been requested to play an adequate role in the debates over patent law and access to medicines.[155] In response, the Commission on Intellectual Property Rights, Innovation and Public Health was established by the Director-General of the WHO in 2004 and published its report on *Public Health, Innovation, and Intellectual Property Rights* in 2006.[156] The report highlighted that intellectual property may not provide an effective incentive system for health problems predominantly affecting developing countries due to their small market demand, and thus there is a need for other incentive and financial mechanisms in this field.[157] Two years later, in May 2008, the WHO's Intergovernmental Working Group on Public Health, Innovation and Intellectual Property (IGWG) adopted a Global Strategy and Plan of Action to promote new incentives for research and development into diseases disproportionately affecting developing countries.[158] The WHO Global Strategy recognised the core value of human rights: 'the enjoyment of the highest attainable standard of health is one of the fundamental

---

153 Oxfam, *All Costs, No Benefits: How TRIPS-plus Intellectual Property Rules in the US-Jordan FTA Affect Access to Medicines*, Oxfam Briefing Paper, May 2007, available at http://donttradeourlivesaway. files.wordpress.com/2011/01/all-costs-no-benefits.pdf, last accessed 15 March 2015.

154 See http://www.wipo.int/policy/en/cdip/, last accessed 15 March 2015.

155 Thomas Pogge, Matthew Rimmer and Kim Rubenstein (eds), *Incentives for Global Public Health: Patent Law and Access to Essential Medicines*, Cambridge University Press (2010) 18.

156 WHO, *Report of the Commission on Public Health, Innovation and Intellectual Property Rights* (2006).

157 For further discussion, see the following chapters.

158 WHA Res 61.21, *Global Strategy and Plan of Action on Public Health, Innovation and Intellectual Property*, World Health Assembly 61st meeting (2008).

rights of every human being without distinction of race, religion, political belief, economic or social condition'.[159] Importantly, it echoed with the Doha Declaration that 'intellectual property rights do not and should not prevent Members from taking measures to protect public health'.[160] Emphasising the strong need for 'the development of new products to fight diseases where the potential paying market is small or uncertain',[161] the WHO Global Strategy encouraged all parties to 'explore and where appropriate, promote a range of incentive schemes for research and development including addressing, where appropriate, the delinkage of the costs of research and development and the price of health products, for example through the award of prizes, with the objective of addressing diseases which disproportionately affect developing countries'.[162] Further consideration will be given to the WHO Global Strategy in discussing a human rights framework for intellectual property and access to medicines in chapters 6 and 7.

Conclusion

The historical account of patent rules shows that norms regulating knowledge, such as patent laws, have been contingent upon various factors, including the level of technological development, international trade, and public needs. The grant of exclusive rights was not perceived as the only way to respond to changing economic environments. Ownership in knowledge often invited debates regarding a tension between private interests in ideas and public access to ideas. The French Revolution, known to spread the notion of natural rights in ideas, was also laden with such debate. An argument that public access to ideas would accelerate the progress of enlightenment led to the recognition of the public domain. In the nineteenth century, many European countries, including the UK, saw strong opposition to patents, primarily concerned with the negative impact of patents on free trade. Developing countries viewed intellectual property as a common heritage and thus promoted patent systems that could encourage the free flow of information and technology.

The modern patent system was established as a legal instrument for achieving social objectives, such as the stimulation of technological development and the diffusion of knowledge. Each country had freedom to determine the scope and level of patent protection, reflecting each country's industrial development and public interests, as long as they treated foreign nationals in the same manner as nationals with respect to legal rights and remedies. Technological followers, for instance the Netherlands and Switzerland in the late nineteenth century, benefited from weak levels of national patent protection. Medicines and foods were excluded from patentability in several European countries and in developing countries, based on a view that essentials should not be subject to exclusive rights. However, the adoption of TRIPS has significantly reduced countries' policy space

---

159 Ibid., Art. 16.
160 Ibid., Art. 20.
161 Ibid., Art. 25.
162 Ibid., Art. 36(5.3).

regarding intellectual property, including patents, by obliging all WTO Member countries to extend the scope and term of patent protection. The post-TRIPS era has witnessed intensified debates over intellectual property and public health among other social concerns in a number of international and national forums. While the Doha Declaration on the TRIPS Agreement and Public Health is an outcome of global efforts to rebalance the intellectual property system with the needs of public health, the introduction of TRIPS-Plus provisions through bilateral and regional FTAs represents a setback.

Inquiry into the rationales of patents may help to critically examine the regulation of knowledge production and provide insights into how States can find the right balance between the different social objectives that patents are designed to pursue. For this reason, different perspectives on patents are discussed in the following chapter.

Chapter 2
Perspectives on Patents

Introduction

The history of patents shows that patent systems were created as public policy for promoting social progress. The scope, strength, and life of patent protections were determined according to the economic and social environment of the country to which they were to apply. Public interests and anti-monopoly concerns also informed the enactment and enforcement of patent laws. However, recent decades have seen a global move towards the harmonisation of stronger standards of patent protection. It is important to understand the underlying justifications for patents and explore what approach might play a better role in informing policy makers and judges with regard to patents.

All justifications for property in knowledge must surmount a distinctive feature of abstract objects: non-excludability. Unlike most physical objects, knowledge does not necessarily occupy only one place but can be at many places concurrently. While one's effective use of a physical object requires the exclusive right over that object, one's use of a piece of information does not preclude others from possessing and using it. Even if I tell you a formula for a particular substance, that does not deprive either me or anyone else of the formula, although sharing knowledge may keep the original possessor from making a profit from selling that particular knowledge. Prior to the creation of exclusive rights in knowledge, the nature of knowledge itself does not give rise to disputes over who can have access to knowledge. As Edwin C. Hettinger argues, this non-exclusive characteristic of abstract objects provides 'a strong prima facie case against the wisdom of private and exclusive intellectual property rights'.[1] Anyone who proposes strong or extensive patent protection must provide good reasons for why the grant of exclusive rights over abstract objects is necessary when abstract objects, by their nature, do not restrict the simultaneous possession of and use by a multiple number of people.

Numerous arguments have been put forward to justify or guide the development of patent systems. Such theories and perspectives can stimulate useful conversation among participants shaping and enforcing patent law, not only between legislators and judges, but also between policy makers and citizens, thereby enhancing accountability regarding patent policy.[2] What kind of ownership in knowledge is appropriate? With a view to fostering conversation regarding such a critical question, this chapter, in the first two sections, reviews

---

1 Edwin C. Hettinger, 'Justifying Intellectual Property' (1989) 18(1) *Philosophy and Public Affairs* 31–52, 35.

2 For a discussion about the value of theory regarding intellectual property, see William Fisher, 'Theories of Intellectual Property', in Stephen R. Munzer (ed.), *New Essays in the Legal and Political Theory of Property*, Cambridge University Press (2001) 194–9.

two of the most prevalent perspectives; a natural rights perspective and an economic incentive perspective. Each section discusses the reasoning behind each perspective. The chapter does not, however, deal with personhood or personality justifications for intellectual property that are more pertinent to discussion of copyrights. The final section argues that making and reading a patent law should be informed by moral values as well as economic concerns. It submits that international human rights instruments can provide a global normative framework for institutions that govern property in knowledge.

Natural Rights Perspective

The 'natural rights' argument implies that individuals have a natural property right in their ideas. Thus, society has a moral duty to recognise and protect that natural right. The use of the word 'stealing' or 'theft' in the context of patents reflects the natural property right approach to ideas, which is well captured by Edith Penrose's following passage.

> [T]he loose use of the word "stealing" remains in most patent discussions to remind us of the natural property right conception of patents. Stealing ... is used in a wider and vaguer sense to include the use by another of a man's ideas even though they are not in fact patented or patentable under the law applying to him who uses them. Upon this concept all charges of "piracy" are based when they are leveled against nations who permit their nationals to use freely inventions patented elsewhere but which are not patentable under their own laws.[3]

The 'natural rights' argument, by definition, indicates that intellectual property rights are a pre-societal entity and therefore their existence does not depend on positive law. For proponents of the 'natural property right' in ideas, the task of positive law would be to secure this natural right of individuals and to condemn the use of ideas by others without authorisation of the owner. This view was reflected in the preamble of the French Patent Law of 1791 which stated:

> That every novel idea whose realization or development can become useful to society belongs primarily to him who conceived it, and that it would be a violation of the rights of man in their very essence if an industrial invention were not regarded as the property of its creator.[4]

Fritz Machlup and Edith Penrose view the entry of the natural property conception to the evolution of patent law as an attempt to 'substitute a word with a respectable connotation, "property", for a word that had an unpleasant ring, "privilege"'.[5] In fact, the French law

---

3   Edith Tilton Penrose, *The Economics of the International Patent System* (Originally published by the Johns Hopkins University Press, 1951; 2nd edn, Greenwood Press, 1973) 24–5.

4   French Patent Law of 7 January 1791, cited in Fritz Machlup and Edith Penrose, 'The Patent Controversy in the Nineteenth Century' (1950) 10(1) *Journal of Economic History* 11.

5   Machlup and Penrose (n 4) 16.

of 1791, which recognised the natural property right in ideas, was rather an exception than a norm in the development of modern patent law.[6] In most other countries, patents were seen as a privilege granted by the Crown in the medieval era, and then as a legal tool to enhance social utility in the modern era. In addition, we can also see that even the French law of 1791 qualified the natural rights argument by adding a utilitarian requirement that the idea must be useful to society. Nevertheless, recent decades have seen the natural rights argument regain its strength in a drive for raising patent protection globally.[7]

The purpose of this section is to examine whether the natural rights argument can convincingly support a case for strong patent rights. This section starts with John Locke's theory of property, which is claimed to provide a foundation for the natural property right not only in material objects, but also in intellectual objects. What follows is the application of Locke's theory to intellectual objects. This section suggests that the natural rights argument does not provide a strong justification for the grant of patents. Serious consideration of natural rights might lead to common ownership of ideas or a far more moderate form of patent system than the existing one.

John Locke's Writing on Property and its Application to Patents

Do individuals have a natural property right in ideas? Those who argue for the natural right in intellectual objects derive their justification from Locke's theory of property. Locke's theory is commonly considered to provide a justification for private property based on labour. Locke's ideas on property are scattered in Chapter 5 of the Second Treatise in his book on a theory of civil government.[8]

1. The world is initially held in common by all people.
2. People have to make use of the common to fulfil the right to self-preservation.
3. Every person has a property in his/her own person and an individual's labour also belongs to that individual.
4. By mixing the individual's labour with existing resources he or she makes it his/her property.
5. Property can only be appropriated where there is 'enough and as good' left in common for others (sufficiency condition).
6. A person cannot appropriate more than he or she can make use of to the advantage before it spoils (non-waste condition).

---

6 Ibid.

7 The following excerpt from the speech by Ken Adelman, the former US Ambassador to the United Nations and currently executive director of USA for Innovation, shows how the idea of natural rights is employed to criticise a policy of a foreign government which is not illegal in view of international patent law: '... the new government of Thailand is proving stealing of American property, our intellectual property. How did that happen? It happened when the minister Health of Thailand announced so-called compulsory licensing of American and European health products'. Available at http://www.youtube.com/watch?v=8rjkODLQpPw, last accessed 15 March 2015.

8 John Locke, *Two Treatises of Government* [1698] Peter Laslett ed., 2nd edn, Cambridge University Press (1994).

Standard accounts of Locke's theory of property consider statements (3) and (4) to firmly ground the proposition that a person who labours upon resources held in common is entitled to the natural property right to the fruits of his/her labour.[9] However, there are two conditions on private appropriation (often referred to as the Lockean provisos): people have to leave a sufficient number of the same or similar things for others (5); people are not allowed to take more than enough, so as to prevent waste (6). As long as these two conditions are met, according to the standard accounts, private appropriation of what one labours upon is justified.

When applied to intellectual objects, this account of Locke's theory apparently sees little problem in supporting intellectual property as a natural right. Although Locke did not seem to have in mind intellectual objects in his writing on property, some believe that intellectual property is even better suited to Locke's theory than real property. Justin Hughes provides the following reasons for which intellectual property rights are well grounded by an appeal to Locke: 'first, that the production of ideas requires a person's labor; second, that these ideas are appropriated from a "common" which is not significantly devalued by the removal of ideas; and third, that ideas can be made property without breaching the non-waste condition'.[10] For Hughes, since the value of an idea originates from mental labour of human persons, ideas are susceptible to Locke's theory linking property to the product of one's labour.[11] He contends that a seemingly inexhaustible stock of ideas is most similar to Locke's common and, furthermore, that propertisation of ideas even expands the intellectual common by adding new ideas. Thus, private appropriation of ideas surmounts the Lockean sufficiency condition.[12] Lastly, ideas are less subject to waste because they are not perishable as, for instance, foods are.[13] Robert Nozick, in his analysis of Locke's theory of property, contends that patents are an example of private appropriation that do not violate the Lockean 'enough and as good' proviso (sufficiency condition).[14] Nozick interprets the Lockean proviso as prohibiting worsening others by depriving them of what they previously had.[15] In his view, patents do not worsen others' situations as the invention subject to patents would not exist if not for the inventor.[16]

Lockean theory discussed so far seems to support a claim that: 'I invented it. So it's mine and no one else's'. However, it seems unclear why the fruits of one's labour upon the common become the private property of an individual person rather than a part of the common. It is also unclear as to the underlying motivation behind which private appropriation is justified, as a matter of a natural right. Can any sort of thing be subject to private property? These questions redirect attention to Locke.

---

9   Justin Hughes, 'The Philosophy of Intellectual Property' (1988) 77 *Georgetown Law Journal* 287–366; Adam Moore, 'Toward a Lockean Theory of Intellectual Property', in Adam Moore (ed.), *Intellectual Property*, Rowman and Littlefield (1997) 81–103.

10   Hughes (n 9) 300.

11   Ibid.

12   Ibid., 315–25.

13   Ibid., 328.

14   Robert Nozick, *Anarchy, State, and Utopia*, Basil Blackwell (1974) 182.

15   Ibid., 175.

16   Ibid., 182.

Ideas and Intellectual Commons

Contrary to the preceding discussion, Seana Valentine Shiffrin argues that Locke's view does not support all sorts of propertisation, in particular, intellectual property.[17] She stresses the importance of common ownership in Locke's theory of property and qualifies the kind of things susceptible to private appropriation. In her view, intellectual objects, such as ideas, inventions and expressions, are unlikely to be justified by the Lockean theory of private property.

If the world is initially owned in common by all people,[18] in other words the common ownership of resources is a default situation of people,[19] it would be fair that private appropriation is qualified by specific conditions enough to change the default position.

The Lockean justification for private appropriation originates from the right of self-preservation.[20] All human beings have a right of self-preservation, which is discovered by natural reason.[21] People have to make use of the world given to people in common to fulfil the natural right to subsistence.[22] Yet the use of some items can be meaningful only by exclusive appropriation. For instance, a pear nourishes a person only when she takes it and incorporates it into her body. As such, appropriation seems the only way that one can make beneficial use of materials that one has in common with others. This explains what motivates Locke to endorse private appropriation. Following this line of reasoning, Shiffrin argues that private property is justified where the exclusive use of an article is necessary for the beneficial use of the common and to fulfil the right to self-preservation.[23] On her reading, labour enters into the process of appropriation as 'an appropriate means to stake a claim'[24] over a thing by improving the value of the thing or making it beneficial. She considers that the 'enough and as good' and non-waste conditions of the Lockean provisos function to

---

17 Seana Valentine Shiffrin, 'Lockean Arguments for Private Intellectual Property', in Stephen R. Munzer (ed.), *New Essays in the Legal and Political Theory of Property*, Cambridge University Press (2001) 138–67.

18 Locke (n 8) the Second Treatise, paras 25–7.

19 While common property, in a strict sense, only refers to a property regime where members of a clearly defined group control access to resources, it may be used to describe 'open access', where there are no limits on who can have access to resources. See, for these differences, Charlotte Hess and Elinor Ostrom, 'Ideas, Artifacts, and Facilities: Information as a Common-Pool Resource' (Winter/Spring 2003) 66 *Law and Contemporary Problems* 121–2. In Locke's writing on property, commons, as an initial situation, may indicate either open access or common control of resources.

20 Locke (n 8) the Second Treatise, para. 26, which states 'God, who has given the World to Men in common, hath also given them *reason to make use of it to the best advantage of Life and convenience* ... [its fruits and animals] belong to Mankind in common ... and no body has originally a private Dominion, exclusive of the rest of Mankind ...' (emphasis added).

21 James Tully, *A Discourse on Property: John Locke and His Adversaries*, Cambridge University Press (1980) 4.

22 Locke (n 8) the Second Treatise, para. 26. 'God, who hath given the world to men in common, hath also given them reason to make use of it to the best advantage of life, and convenience. *The earth, and all that is therein, is given to men for the support and comfort of their being*' (emphasis added).

23 Shiffrin (n 17).

24 Ibid., 147.

make sure that private appropriation does not undermine the equal rights of everyone to self-preservation and the duty to make effective use of the common for human benefit.[25]

Is appropriation of intellectual objects justifiable by Lockean theory according to this line of reasoning? Intellectual objects, in comparison to physical objects, have distinctive features.[26] Unlike physical objects, intellectual objects can be used simultaneously by a multiple number of people. One's use of an intellectual object does not prevent others from using the same object, in the absence of artificial restrictions. Ideas do not require exclusive use for their value to be fully realised. In addition, while one can appropriate and use a physical object by a private act, exclusive possession of an intellectual object and its enforcement requires public intervention by a granting authority and/or a court. Furthermore, an intellectual property right is, by nature, not a right to use but a right to prevent others from using the idea. Accordingly, Shiffrin argues that restricting the use of intellectual works to specific individuals is against the 'presumption of common ownership and the concomitant concern to make full use of resources'.[27]

However, one may object to this common ownership of intellectual objects, arguing that there is no such thing as the intellectual common in the first place. The underlying assumption behind this objection is that ideas, methods, and processes are all pure creations of individual labour and, therefore, they are the property of the individual labourer. Robert Nozick's treatment of patents comes close to this view by attributing an invention solely to the inventor.[28] However, it seems unreasonable to claim that intellectual products involve nothing but a single mind. For instance, most (if not all) subject matter of patents draws upon facts about the physical world, and is most often the result of a process, building on others' ideas over time. Seeing an invention as something attributable solely to the inventor is therefore extreme. It is also extreme in view of the implication that flows from it that may lead to an absolute right of the inventor to control the availability of the invention in any manner.[29]

It seems widely acknowledged that there are intellectual commons comprising a range of ideas, facts and propositions among other intellectual products.[30] Here, a less absolutist objection to the common ownership of intellectual objects would be that even if an intellectual product involves using common resources, the product belongs to the realm of private property. Nozick seems to support this view in his example of where a medical researcher discovers a new substance using materials in the common.[31] In his view, the researcher's propertisation of the substance does not matter as long as the raw materials are still available to others in common.

However, Shiffrin counter-argues that the crucial question for a Lockean justification for private appropriation is whether a specific thing in question requires exclusive use or

---

25 Ibid.

26 Hettinger (n 1) 34–5; Hughes (n 9) 315; Robert Merges, Peter S. Menell and Mark A. Lemley, *Intellectual Property in the New Technological Age*, Aspen Publishers, 2nd edn (2000) 2.

27 Shiffrin (n 17) 157.

28 Nozick (n 14) 182.

29 Merges, Menell and Lemley (n 26) 4.

30 Drahos, *A Philosophy of Intellectual Property*, Ashgate (1996) 49; Shiffrin (n 17).

31 Nozick (n 14) 181.

control in order to be made useful.[32] It follows that even though intellectual products are only partly based on the intellectual common, the non-excludable nature of intellectual products renders a natural right to intellectual property groundless. Intellectual products have little reason to depart from the common ownership presumption. Moreover, in her view, the presumption of common ownership, importantly, is a reflection of 'the equal moral status of individuals'.[33] Therefore, unless the nature of a given thing requires exclusive use or control, moral reasons tell us that the thing should become part of the common so that it can be available to everyone.

This view presents a contrast to Nozick's interpretation, which gives primacy to private appropriation as long as no one is worsened by being deprived of what they had previously. But why do we have starkly different interpretations of Locke's theory of property? Perhaps the difficulties inevitably arise from the fact that Locke's writing on property itself entails elements that are not easy to reconcile. On the other hand, it is fascinating that Nozick's view on patents presents a contradiction with his libertarian belief,[34] considering that the exclusive rights of the patent holder exist only by State action that artificially restricts the availability of ideas.

Apparently, Locke's theory of property does not support one single form of intellectual property. However, even if the exclusive use or control of intellectual products is not justified as a matter of natural right, a need to reward intellectual workers for their work deserves separate attention. In that context, a question of whether the exclusive right over intellectual products is an appropriate form of reward may be raised. A related question is discussed under 'The Right to Benefit from the Protection of the Moral and Material Interests Resulting from any Scientific, Literary or Artistic Production of which He is the Author (Art. 15.1(c) of ICESCR)' in Chapter 5.

So far, a serious doubt has been cast on the use of Locke's theory of property to ground the exclusive rights over intellectual objects as a natural right. Nevertheless, it might be worthwhile exploring whether the natural rights argument remains helpful for guiding legislators and judges with regard to patents. What follows is an examination of the difficulties the natural rights argument for patents might encounter.

Boundaries of the Natural Property Right

According to the natural rights argument, labour creates the property right. In other words, an inventor has the natural right to the fruits of his/her labour, the invention. However, it may not be easy to identify who gets what as a natural right. We need to address issues such as: first, to distinguish the different components of value of the resulting invention

---

32   Shiffrin (n 17) 145, 158–66.

33   Ibid., 164, 167.

34   Nozick cherishes 'the free operation of a market system' and abhors 'a de facto monopoly'. See Nozick (n 14) 182. In addition, he does not count as worsening the situation of others the activity of making what someone is selling and entering into competition with the seller, although it may limit her opportunity to appropriate by diminishing the sales that she could make. See 178.

with a view to identifying the owner(s); second, to define what sort of property right the inventor is entitled to.

First, identifying the natural right holder to a given intellectual product requires an investigation of who added what portion of value of the product because what the labourer would be entitled to, as a natural right, is the value he or she added. An initial distinction should be made between 'the value attributed to the object of the labour and the value attributed to the labour itself'.[35] For instance, there is a new substance made of existing chemicals. The question is over the portion of value attributable to the labour, separately from the value residing in the chemicals, which was exerted to discover a new way of synthesising the chemicals.

One might assume that the distinction is made between the value added by the inventor and the value that the object has on its own. Nevertheless, the inevitably cumulative process of invention poses another difficulty. The inventive idea of an inventor is built on the ideas of others.[36] Therefore, even though we succeed in separating out the value that is attributable to human labour from the total value of an intellectual product, we have another task to determine each share of value that is attributable to not only the last contributor, but also every other contributor. However difficult this task may be, being faithful to the natural property right would not tolerate any contributor being missed out from their entitlement. Otherwise, the natural right argument would find it hard to avoid the sort of criticism raised by an editorial in *The Economist* as early as 1850:

> Before … [the inventors] can … establish a right of property in their inventions, they ought to give up all the knowledge and inventions of others. That is impossible, and the impossibility shows that their minds and their inventions are, in fact, parts of the great mental whole of society, and that they have no right of property in their inventions, except that they can keep them to themselves if they please and own all the material objects in which they may realize their mental conceptions.[37]

Under modern patent law, innovators who build on an earlier patented invention have to buy the earlier patent or get a licence from the patentee. The amount of reward that each innovator gets depends on the market value of each patent.

More complication would follow if several persons (or groups) independently come up with the same idea and apply it either at the same time or subsequently. The Lockean labour-based theory of property would mandate the recognition of the natural property right of all the parties. Nozick also permits other independent inventors to make and sell their own invention.[38] From this point of view, the natural rights argument would require a

---

35 Sigrid Sterckx, 'The Ethics of Patenting – Uneasy Justifications', in Peter Drahos (ed.), *Death of Patents*, Queen Mary Intellectual Property Research Institute (2005) 181.

36 Hettinger (n 1) 37–8; Sterckx (n 35) 182.

37 *The Economist* (London), (28 December 1850) 1434, cited in Machlup and Penrose (n 4) 15.

38 '[T]hese independent inventors, upon whom the burden of proving independent discovery may rest, should not be excluded from utilizing their own invention as they wish (including selling it to others)'. Nozick (n 14) 182.

reform of current global patent standards that do not recognise the right of independent inventors but only the right of the first applicant of a patent. However, this is not the only inconsistency in current patent law with the natural rights argument, suggesting that patent law is not based on natural rights.

Secondly, assuming that we succeed in separating out each labourer's own contribution to the intellectual product, we need then to ask what sort of property rights the inventor(s) is entitled to. According to the natural rights argument, one's labour entitles the labourer to the fruits of his/her labour. The right to the fruits of the labour seems legitimately to entail a right to possess and personally use what the labourer created to the advantage of his/her own benefit.[39] In most cases, however, the exclusive right over the intellectual works seems unnecessary as the inventor can enjoy the personal possession and use of the invention without exerting an exclusive right.

However, the intriguing question is whether the market value of the product of labour also constitutes what the labourer is naturally entitled to. Current international patent law is designed to allow a patent holder to sell a patented invention in the market and reap profits by excluding others from using and selling it, without authorisation of the patentee, for a limited period of time. But is this a matter of a natural right? Edwin C. Hettinger argues that it is not.[40] Market value is 'a socially created phenomenon'.[41] Market value of a product depends on varying social factors, such as other producers, the conditions of consumers, the government's related regulations and so on. Nozick appears to believe that meeting the conditions of just acquisition in the first place justifies its transfer in the market.[42] However, there seems to be a huge gap between a moral right to the fruits of one's labour and a right to receive the market value of the product. Peter Drahos also pays attention to a similar point, raising the question 'how can labour ground a natural right to market value if that value is determined not by individual labour but by the demand activity of others?'.[43] As Hettinger puts it, 'to what extent individual laborers should be allowed to receive the market value of their products is a question of social policy'.[44] Although it is often neglected, Locke himself stated that civil law and government has to regulate the property relations in a monetary world.[45]

Limitations upon Propertisation of Ideas

As briefly touched upon before, for Locke, private appropriation is justified when it satisfies two conditions (referred to as Lockean provisos): the first condition requiring enough and as good to be left for others to use to their benefit (sufficiency condition);[46] and the second

---

39   Hettinger (n 1) 39–40.
40   Ibid., 38–40.
41   Ibid., 38.
42   Nozick (n 14) 150–82.
43   Drahos (n 30) 52.
44   Hettinger (n 1) 39.
45   Locke (n 8) the Second Treatise, 50; Tully (n 21) 150–53.
46   Locke (n 8) the Second Treatise, 27.

condition prohibiting taking more than enough that results in waste (non-waste condition).[47] Earlier, this section has questioned whether intellectual objects can be susceptible to private property, departing from the presumption of initial common ownership. Here, however, it assumes that intellectual objects as such are not prevented from private appropriation at the outset, and asks whether patents satisfy the Lockean provisos. More specifically, the question might be whether the rights to exclude others from using or making a patented invention or process satisfy the test that the Lockean provisos place before any private appropriation. The examination would tell us whether the rights granted by patents are justified as a matter of a natural right, and, further, what the Lockean provisos can inform patent law making if one wants to see a justifiable patent system in light of natural rights.

Some argue that intellectual property is not restrained by the Lockean provisos because intellectual objects are abundant enough not to leave others worsened by private appropriation, and do not spoil in the way, for example, that agricultural products do.[48] This line of argument would justify the existing patent system or promote the grant of an even wider range of exclusive rights in ideas. Is it a valid argument however? The next section will examine whether patents easily surmount the Lockean provisos on legitimate private appropriation.

Sufficiency condition

While Nozick acknowledges that one's ownership affects the situation of others, he argues that ownership does not necessarily worsen the situation of others.[49] His example is that although one's appropriation of a grain of sand from an island removes others' liberty to act on that grain of sand, plenty of other grains of sand or different objects would remain for others.[50] However, as Sigrid Sterckx points out, 'this is not valid for anything covered by a patent' as patent law would exclude others from using a product or process covered by patents.[51] A sufficient number of other objects may be an irrelevant factor if others need the specific one that falls into someone else's private property.[52] Therefore, the situation of others is arguably worsened by the fact that they no longer hold the same liberty to do with an object as before the object became subject to a patent.

However, Nozick contends that patents do not deprive others of anything that they had before as the invention would not exist if not for the inventor.[53] Therefore, according to him, patents do not breach the sufficiency condition. Nevertheless, as discussed earlier, it is clear that inventions do not come out of a single genius mind but exist through building on preceding ideas. Without the grant of an exclusive right to the first inventor, others could have a liberty to use the existing ideas, including making something comparable to the invention and benefiting from the outcome. Nozick concedes that independent

---

47 Ibid., 31.
48 Hughes (n 9) 315–25, 328.
49 Nozick (n 14) 175.
50 Ibid.
51 Sterckx (n 35) 185.
52 Ibid.
53 Nozick (n 14) 182.

(or subsequent) inventors are deprived by patents and suggests that independent inventors should not be excluded from using and selling their own invention, and that there should be a time limit placed on patents.[54]

Apart from independent inventors, a patent may prevent further development of the first invention. Also, other users may also be worse off as patents limit their liberty to ideas that otherwise could have been freely available to them. Consider Hughes's remark that 'such distribution problems are not found in pre-property uses of the field of ideas'[55] that are in the physical common. Hughes, however, contents himself with extraordinarily important ideas or widely used ideas not being propertised, holding an optimistic expectation that patents would augment the common.[56] As to the concern about other users, Nozick would insist that people could still buy the patented products and processes in the market, and their loss of liberty may be counter-balanced by increased social welfare.[57] However, whether patents increase social welfare and expand the common is a typically utilitarian question,[58] and may not critically determine whether private property in ideas is a natural right.

The sufficiency condition becomes particularly pertinent in relation to the right to self-preservation. Although Nozick appears to acknowledge the importance of the Lockean proviso in cases where a person's life is at stake,[59] his treatment of patents fails to fully reflect the ideas embedded in the sufficiency condition.

In short, the claim that patents do not deprive others of anything seems weak. If patents are to survive the sufficiency condition, a substantial change should be made in existing patent law. The following seem at least required by the sufficiency condition: (a) independent inventors should retain their liberty to use and sell their own invention; (b) a term of protection of patents should not be long, considering that someone else may well have come up with the same idea had it not been for patents; and (c) food and pharmaceutical products that are necessary for self-preservation should not, in principle, be subject to exclusive patent rights.

Non-waste condition

Locke's second proviso on the legitimate acquisition of property prohibits spoilage caused by appropriating more than one needs. Taking more than one can use and letting it spoil is considered wrong because it is wasteful. Thus, it is also referred to as the non-waste condition. Obviously, ideas are not perishable in an absolute sense. However, in a social sense, the value of an idea can perish as it becomes obsolete. If an idea is left unused while someone needs it, there can be said to be waste.

Edwin C. Hettinger points out that the non-exclusive nature of ideas makes it hard for patents to meet the non-waste condition since everyone could simultaneously use and benefit

---

54   Ibid.

55   Hughes (n 9) 315.

56   Ibid., 319–25.

57   Nozick (n 14) 177, 180.

58   This subject will be further discussed in the next section on the economic theory of patents.

59   'A theory of appropriation incorporating this Lockean proviso will handle correctly the cases (objections to the theory lacking the proviso) where someone appropriates the total supply of something necessary for life'. Nozick (n 14) 179.

from ideas were it not for patents.[60] Therefore, it seems legitimate to say that 'those who appropriate ideas with a view to doing nothing with them arguably infringe Locke's spoilage proviso'.[61] Even if an invention is used by the owner, the restriction of its beneficial use by high royalties or other conditions may amount to a violation of the non-waste proviso.[62] The more people cannot access the invention that they need, the more waste the patent in question may cause.[63] What are the devices that patent law can have for tempering waste induced by the exclusive rights of patent holders? (a) Patent law should have appropriate standards for patentability, especially regarding inventive step, so as to grant a patent to genuine innovations only; (b) a patent holder should be required to work their invention (working requirement); (c) using a patented invention or process should be made possible without authorisation from the patent holder for socially beneficial innovations whose usage is being prevented by high fees or non-exploitation (compulsory licensing).

Conclusion

It is questionable that Locke's theory of property supports the exclusive rights over ideas as a natural right. Rather than endorsing an absolute right of a patent holder, Lockean theory guides us to pay particular attention to the subsistence right of everyone and the beneficial use of resources in shaping the institution of property. In so far as an exclusive right in ideas is made possible only by State action, the argument for the pre-societal status of patent rights is weak.

Thomas Jefferson, the first administrator of the US patent system, was critical of natural rights argument over inventions although he is known to have been a Lockean sympathiser. His following passage leads us to explore other theories of patents as well as providing insights regarding the natural right argument for intellectual property.

> It has been pretended … that inventors have a natural and exclusive right to their inventions … If nature has made any one thing less susceptible than all others of exclusive property, it is the action of the thinking power called an idea … Its peculiar character … is that no one possesses the less, because every other possesses the whole of it. He who receives an idea from me, receives instruction himself without lessening mine; as he who lights his taper at mine, receives light without darkening me. That ideas should be freely spread from one to another over the globe, for the moral and mutual instruction of man, and improvement of his condition, seems to have been … designed by nature … Inventions then cannot, in nature, be a subject of property. Society may give an exclusive right to the profits arising from them, as an encouragement … to pursue ideas which may produce utility, but this may or may not be done, according to the will and convenience of the society, without claim or complaint from anybody.[64]

---

60 Hettinger (n 1) 44.
61 Drahos (n 30) 51.
62 Sterckx (n 35) 183.
63 Hettinger (n 1) 44–5.
64 Thomas Jefferson, 'The Invention of Elevators' (Letter, 1813), in Saul K. Padover (ed.), *The Complete Jefferson*, Dell, Sloan & Pearce (1943) 1015, cited in Shiffrin (n 17) 138.

Economic Incentive Perspective

The economic rationale of a patent system is that patents are an efficient method of stimulating socially valuable works and economic progress. The idea has been the most prevalent justification for patents throughout the history of patent law, as discussed in Chapter 1. In England, the Statute of Monopolies of 1623 allowed, as an exception to the proscription of monopoly, temporary monopolies in the exploitation of innovations.[65] The US also located the foundation of patent law in its role of stimulating the production of socially valuable works.[66] Modern patent laws in Europe and North America in the nineteenth century, despite variations in the level of patent protection, shared the view that patents were adopted as a public policy to encourage technological progress and increase access to knowledge. This idea is also embedded in TRIPS, which manifests 'the promotion of technological innovation and to the transfer and dissemination of technology' as the objectives of the protection and enforcement of intellectual property rights.[67] To this point, it is important to note that the focus of the economic approach to intellectual property is not to reward creators for their labour but 'to enrich the public at large'[68] by generating more knowledge. Patent law is a means to provide incentives to spur inventive activities.

It is necessary to inquire into why exclusive rights in inventions are needed as a stimulus to knowledge creation. The necessity of an incentive scheme stems from economic analysis of the market and the public-good characteristic of knowledge. The argument follows these lines: inventive activity requires the investment of resources. In a market economy, rational actors, based on self-interest, will invest in knowledge creation when they can economically benefit from the use or sales of the invention. In other words, they will be dissuaded from allocating resources unless they can reap a sufficient return exceeding their costs. However, the creation of knowledge in free unregulated competition will not guarantee investors profit opportunities since knowledge has characteristics of a public good.[69] Knowledge, by its nature, can be used by several people simultaneously without depletion. However expensive it is to create new knowledge, the cost of its reproduction is generally low.[70] Furthermore, once knowledge is created, it is hard to exclude others from using and benefiting from it. Therefore, the self-interest of each company would tell them not to invest in the production of knowledge, but rather let others do so and then to take advantage of it.[71] For these reasons, there is a danger of undersupply of new knowledge if

---

65 Machlup and Penrose (n 4) 1–29.

66 Article I, Section 8, Clause 8 of the United States Constitution empowers Congress 'to promote the Progress of Science and useful Arts, by securing for limited Times to Authors and Inventors the exclusive Right to their respective Writings and Discoveries'.

67 Article 7 of TRIPS.

68 Merges, Menell and Lemley (n 26) 16.

69 Ibid., 11–13; Drahos (n 30) 120–2.

70 Kenneth J. Arrow, 'Economic Welfare and the Allocation of Resources for Invention', in *The Rate and Direction of Inventive Activity: Economic and Social Factors: A Report of the National Bureau of Economic Research*, Universities-National Bureau (1962) 609–26, 609.

71 Merges, Menell and Lemley (n 26) 11–13; Drahos, (n 30) 120–22.

the production of knowledge is left to the market.[72] It follows, therefore, that the optimal investment and supply of public goods, including information, requires intervention of government.[73] Having the government fund public goods is one way to correct this sort of market failure. Classical examples of a public good, such as lighthouses and national defence, are funded by the general revenue of government. Knowledge creation may also be financed by the government. However, information policy is attracted by a different incentive scheme, which is the creation of intellectual property in knowledge, although it also relies on government intervention.[74]

According to the economic rationale, the main objective of patents is to stimulate the creation of more knowledge, thereby promoting social progress. However, the creation of knowledge induced by patents does not come without costs. While the benefit is increased knowledge, the cost is exclusive rights that curtail widespread access to knowledge. It is paradoxical that patents aim to create more knowledge by restricting the diffusion of knowledge.[75] Thus, striking an optimal balance between the costs and benefits of patents is essential for patents to function as an efficient incentive scheme. The notion of efficiency in economic analysis is determined by overall net utility. As to knowledge, efficient incentive schemes are expected to encourage investment in creating new knowledge with the lowest possible costs.[76] In this sense, the aim of a patent system is to stimulate 'the optimal level, not the maximum level, of innovation'.[77] A patent system is nor about the maximisation of profit.

The economic incentive perspective on patents invites such questions as: whether the benefit of the current patent system outweighs the costs; whether there is any other better incentive system for invention and innovation?[78] Both questions require empirical research which is beyond the scope of this chapter. What this section will do is to sketch the economic and legal literature on these questions.

Economic Justifications for Patents

Economic studies identify four major economic justifications for the grant of a patent.[79] Note that these justifications are not mutually exclusive.

---

72 Arrow (n 70).

73 Drahos (n 30) 122.

74 Ibid.

75 Merges, Menell and Lemley (n 26) 11–13.

76 Stephen M. Maurer and Suzanne Scotchmer, 'Procuring Knowledge', National Bureau of Economic Research Working Paper 9903, (2003) available at http://www.nber.org/papers/w9903.pdf, last accessed 15 March 2015.

77 Rochelle Cooper Dreyfuss, 'Varying the Course in Patenting Genetic Material: A Counter Proposal to Richard Epstein's Steady Course', Public Law and Legal Theory Research Paper Series, Research Paper No. 59 (April 2003) 7.

78 Nancy Gallini and Suzanne Scotchmer, 'Intellectual Property: When is it the Best Incentive System?' (2002) 2 *Innovation Policy and the Economy* 51, 52; Sterckx (n 35) 195.

79 Penrose (n 3) 31–41; William Nordhaus, *Invention, Growth and Welfare: A Theoretical Treatment of Technological Change*, MIT Press (1969); Edmund W. Kitch, 'The Nature and Function of the Patent

1. Patents stimulate more invention.
2. Patents induce investments in developing and commercialising the invention.
3. Patents encourage the disclosure of the information underlying the new invention.
4. Patents help to reduce duplicative investment in the innovation of the same prospect.

The incentive to invent theory

The most conventional thesis is that a patent system provides an incentive to invent, which is supported by the following line of reasoning.[80]

Industrial progress is desirable to society. Inventions are essential to promote industrial progress. An adequate extent of inventions will be secured when inventors have the prospect of yielding a return from their time and efforts put into the invention. The free market will not secure that inventors appropriate the value of the invention because knowledge has public-good characteristics. It is necessary to have special incentive mechanisms for stimulating inventions, among which the most effective is the grant of an exclusive patent right in inventions.

However, this rationale inevitably has to deal with the problem of welfare losses associated with monopoly, such as high prices and lower output.[81] In addition, increasing recognition has been given to other costs a proliferation of patents might bring, for example that patenting an invention may deter other inventors from undertaking the follow-on inventive work.[82] The problem of slowing down further innovation will be further discussed in under 'Patents as an impediment to future innovation' below. These social costs stem from the nature of the patent system, which is meant to increase inventions by subjecting new knowledge to the exclusive control of the patent holder. The underlying assumption of this rationale is that patents bring forth a greater amount of invention, offsetting the costs caused by the temporary exclusive rights.[83] Nevertheless, it is not clear that the level of current patent protection reflects an optimal balance between the costs and benefits. This intrinsic problem of patents has induced a growing body of studies[84] on alternative incentive schemes, as well as on the optimal form of a patent. This is further discussed later in this section.

System' (1977) 20(2) *Journal of Law and Economics* 265–90; Merges, Menell and Lemley (n 26) 16–17; Robert Mazzoleni and Richard R. Nelson, 'The Benefits and Costs of Strong Patent Protection: A Contribution to the Current Debate' (1998) 27 *Research Policy* 273–84; William M. Landes and Richard A. Posner, *The Economic Structure of Intellectual Property Law*, The Belknap Press of Harvard University Press (2003) 294–333.

80 Penrose (n 3) 34–5.

81 Arrow (n 70) 609; Nordhaus (n 79) 88.

82 Michael A. Heller and Rebecca S. Eisenberg, 'Can Patents Deter Innovation? The Anticommons in Biomedical Research' (1998) 280 *Science* 698–701.

83 Mazzoleni and Nelson (n 79) 275.

84 Nordhaus (n 79); Suzanne Scotchmer, 'Standing on the Shoulders of Giants: Cumulative Research and the Patent Law' (1991) 5(1) *The Journal of Economic Perspectives* 29–41; Mazzoleni and Nelson (n 79) 273–84; Steven Shavell and Tanguy van Ypersele, 'Rewards versus Intellectual Property Rights' (2001) 44 *Journal of Law and Economics* 525–47; Gallini and Scotchmer (n 78) 51–77; Maurer and Scotchmer (n 76).

The incentive to commercialise theory

The rationale that patents in an invention induce the companies to allocate additional resources to the development and marketing of the invention is closely related to the preceding argument. A company would be dissuaded from investing in development of a new product if competitors could duplicate the product without incurring the cost of the development. Competition would bring the price down to marginal costs and the original firm would be unable to recoup the costs of invention.[85] Free-riding, or benefiting without contributing to the cost of development, would not necessarily be a problem as 'it contributes to the diffusion of information and so adds to the productive potential of an economy'.[86] However, free-riding is considered to constitute a problem since the market cannot ensure that sufficient resources be allocated to innovation. Thus, the economic rationale suggests that granting exclusive patent rights is necessary to stimulate the additional investments necessary for inventions to be put into commercial use. Allowing the patent holders to set proprietary prices and appropriate returns from the investment is the means to this end.

The distinction between this theory and the preceding theory – the incentive to invent theory – lies in whether it concerns the attitude of business or the attitude of inventors.[87] The difference becomes clear in circumstances where inventions would have been made without patents.[88] In these circumstances, patents are sought not for the invention itself, but for the needed investment in the commercialisation of the invention. This rationale was, for instance, an impetus to the Bayh-Dole Act of the US, which encouraged government-sponsored researchers, including universities, to apply for patents on the results of their work.[89] This argument shares the same problems with the incentive to invent theory: whether society pays costs exceeding the benefits from the patents in order to provide an incentive to the development and commercialisation of the invention; whether natural market forces, such as a head start on commercialisation, would not be enough to induce the needed investment; whether there are better incentive schemes for the development and marketing of inventions. These questions need further consideration.

The incentive to disclose information theory

While the preceding two theories justify a patent system as inducement for more innovation, this rationale concerns the diffusion of new knowledge.[90] Under this theory, patents encourage inventors to disclose full information underlying new inventions, some of which would be kept secret otherwise. As a result, someone else will be able to work on an improvement to the invention. In principle, the disclosure of full information is a

---

85 Landes and Posner (n 79) 13.

86 Drahos (n 30) 121.

87 Penrose (n 3) 35.

88 Mazzoleni and Nelson (n 79) 277.

89 For a legislative analysis of the Bayh-Dole Act of 1980, see Rebecca S. Eisenberg, 'Public Research and Private Development: Patents and Technology Transfer in Government-Sponsored Research (1996) 82 *Virginia Law Review* 1663–727.

90 Mazzoleni and Nelson (n 79) 278; Penrose (n 3) 31–4.

prerequisite for obtaining a patent in inventions according to the provisions of standard patent law. However, William Nordhaus lamented,

> Unfortunately, the disclosure regulations of the patent system are often evaded. It is well known that a firm tries not to disclose key parts of the invention in order to reduce the chance of imitation, thereby reducing the effective diffusion of knowledge.[91]

Nordhaus suggests that a patent system may be better at increasing the flow of information than a laissez-faire system, but he questions whether the patent system also compares favourably with research subsidy plans that require full disclosure of results as a condition of the subsidy.[92] In addition, it is worthwhile considering criticisms of the incentive to disclose theory made in the earlier days of the modern patent system:[93] patents would rather deter inventors from publishing their ideas at an early stage to get them ready for the application of a patent. Were it not for patents, researchers would make their ideas publicly available earlier to seek recognition and fame, which would result in accelerating technological progress. Another criticism was that even if, without patents, some inventors prefer to keep their new ideas secret, other new ideas, whether similar or not, would be developed by others. In short, the diffusion of knowledge may not be a strong reason for the granting of a patent.

The prospect theory

This view of a patent system was first articulated by Edmund Kitch.[94] Under this theory, the merit of patents lies with the function of promoting an orderly investment in innovation. The term 'prospect' is used by Kitch to mean 'a particular opportunity to develop a known technological possibility'.[95] If there was no controlling patent in an early invention, he argues, many people would see the same prospects from a certain invention and chase them at the same time, which may result in a 'wasteful mining of the prospect'.[96] Once a patent is issued over an invention, other firms would learn of it and redirect their resources into other work so as to avoid duplicative investment, or seek to obtain a licence from the patent holder to develop the prospect of the invention.

This theory puts forward the patent system which grants earlier inventors a broad patent right so that they can become a controller of the prospects emanating from the invention. However, the theory is contested in that, despite the intended objective, the broader patent on earlier invention might generate patent races to be the first to obtain the patent, due to a desire for a greater reward.[97] Furthermore, it might block or delay follow-on inventions, thereby retarding technological progress in the long run.[98] These points are further explored under 'Patents as an impediment to future innovation' below.

---

91 Nordhaus (n 79) 89.
92 Ibid.
93 Machlup and Penrose (n 4) 26–7.
94 Kitch (n 79) 265–90.
95 Ibid., 266.
96 Mazzoleni and Nelson (n 79) 279.
97 Landes and Posner (n 79) 319–20.
98 Mazzoleni and Nelson (n 79) 279–80; Landes and Posner (n 79) 319.

The Costs of Patents

The preceding discussions sketched economic arguments for patents. It is, however, important to consider that the economic incentives induced by patents do come at costs. Economic arguments want more intellectual products to be available to the public. Patents are justified as a means to increase the production of knowledge. However, economic arguments for patents entail a paradox.[99] As economist Joan Robinson states, '[t]he justification of the patent system is that by slowing down the diffusion of technical progress it ensures that there will be more progress to diffuse'.[100] The very means to increase products of knowledge impedes the diffusion of knowledge. Acknowledging such a paradox, economic theories of patents neither take patent rights as having absolute status nor seek to maximise innovation. The key to the economic argument is maximising efficiency, which can be achieved by the optimal balance between the costs and benefits.[101] In the view of economic theories of patents, what law makers and judges should do is to strike an optimal balance between the economic incentive benefits and the social costs associated with the exclusivity. In order to do this job, the social costs imposed by patents should be identified.

Proprietary prices and restricted use of knowledge

One of the fundamental premises of modern economics is that free market competition will ensure the efficient allocation of resources.[102] In a perfectly competitive market, the price of a good would be set at a marginal cost of supply, where the supply and the demand curves intersect. However, the exclusive rights allow the patent holder to set the highest price that the market can bear, which results in a higher price than the marginal cost of reproducing it, and restricted access to the intellectual product. This leads to the exclusion of those who are willing to pay higher than the marginal cost of supply but lower than the proprietary price. This is referred to as a 'deadweight loss' in economics. In other words, proprietary pricing by the patent holder raises the cost of obtaining the intellectual product and fewer people will access the intellectual product than if it was supplied in a competitive environment.[103]

Efficiency concerns expect society to reduce such social costs by imposing limitations on the rights granted by a patent system.[104] Thus patent law should have the appropriate criteria for patentability as well as well-calibrated standards for the length and scope of rights.[105] In order for efficiency concerns to guide the fine-tuning of patent rules, we need

---

99 Drahos (n 30) 122; Hettinger (n 1) 47.

100 Joan Robinson, *The Accumulation of Capital*, Richard D. Irwin (1956) 87, cited in Sterckx (n 35) 197.

101 Nordhaus (n 79) 76. Economic analysis of efficiency does not consider the issue of distribution as its direct concern.

102 Merges, Menell and Lemley (n 26) 13.

103 Ibid.

104 Landes and Posner (n 79) 21.

105 Merges, Menell and Lemley (n 26) 15; Gallini and Scotchmer (n 78) 70.

to know what the optimal breadth and life of a patent is and whether current patent laws are appropriately designed to reflect the optimal rules.

Important work on the optimal patent rule has been done by William Nordhaus.[106] He links the amount of innovation with the appropriability of the value arising from information. According to his model analysing the duration of a patent, a longer life of a patent allows the patent holder to appropriate more value and generates a larger amount of invention.[107] If the only concern is to increase innovation, the life of a patent should last without limit. However, Nordhaus observes that 'a longer life means that the monopoly on information lasts longer and thus there are more losses from inefficiencies associated with monopoly'.[108] Thus, he suggests the optimal life of a patent should be set at the point where the costs and benefits of patents balance.

Nordhaus's work on patent design inspired further discussions on how to optimise patent life and scope. But the outcomes are by no means consistent.[109] While Richard Gilbert and Carl Shapiro suggest a narrow and long patent protection as the optimal,[110] Nancy Gallini reverses this conclusion.[111] Stephen Maurer and Suzanne Scotchmer recover the model by Gilbert and Shapiro.[112] The differences lie in whether the cost of imitation is considered along with the deadweight loss and whether the possibility of licensing to avoid wasteful duplication constitutes an assumption. What seems agreed by all three studies is that 'a narrow patent reduces market price', although each bases it on different arguments.[113] The foregoing discussions, although helpful to understand the role of patent scope and duration, stop short of providing policy makers with practical guidance on the optimal patent rules. In addition, the above literature assumes a single independent innovation in isolation and analyses the trade-off between the incentive benefit and the costs. However, later studies uncover that the innovative process is cumulative and a patent has an impact on a future line of innovation.

Patents as an impediment to future innovation

We have seen that patents raise prices and limit the use of knowledge. The cumulative nature of the knowledge creation process implies that patents also create complex obstacles to the further advancement of knowledge. For the past decades, many studies have enriched the understanding of the innovation process: research activities are highly

---

106 Nordhaus (n 79).

107 Ibid., 76.

108 Ibid.

109 For a good summary, see Gallini and Scotchmer (n 78) 63–5.

110 Richard Gilbert and Carl Shapiro, 'Optimal Patent Length and Breadth' (1990) 21 *RAND Journal of Economics* 106–12.

111 Nancy Gallini, 'Patent Length and Breadth with Costly Imitation' (1992) 44 *RAND Journal of Economics* 52–63.

112 Stephen Maurer and Suzanne Scotchmer, 'The Independent Invention Defense in Intellectual Property', John M. Olin Working Paper No. 98-11, Boalt Hall School of Law, University of California (1998).

113 Gallini and Scotchmer (n 78) 64.

interdependent; innovations build upon each other.[114] Suzanne Scotchmer articulates this important feature of the innovation process using a distinguished scientist, Isaac Newton's phrase:

> Sir Isaac Newton himself acknowledged, "If I have seen far, it is by standing on the shoulders of giants". Most innovators stand on the shoulders of giants, and never more so than in the current evolution of high technologies, where almost all technical progress builds on a foundation provided by earlier innovators.[115]

It is equally true that subsequent inventions further advance knowledge through improving or applying previous invention and thus are as important in increasing social benefit as the early invention.[116] Such findings on the innovation process direct our attention to another cost of patents, which is that patents can stifle further innovation. Early patent controversies in the nineteenth century did not pass by without observing the danger patents imposed on others' efforts to improve previous inventions. In 1851, *The Economist* criticised patents on the ground that:

> The privileges granted to inventors by patent laws are prohibitions on other men, and the history of inventions accordingly teems with accounts of trifling improvements patented, that have put a stop, for long period, to other similar and much greater improvements … The privileges have stifled more inventions than they have promoted, and have caused more brilliant schemes to be put aside than the want of them could ever have induced men to conceal. Every patent is a prohibition against improvements in a particular direction, except by the patentee, for a certain number of years; and, however, beneficial that may be to him who receives the privilege, the community cannot be benefited by it.[117]

Contrary to this kind of criticism, Edmund Kitch, in his prospect theory of patents, suggests that patents, especially broad initial patents, would be beneficial.[118] His theory suggests that the initial invention opens up the prospect of further development, and that granting broad and strong patent rights on the initial patent would promote orderly follow-on developments, avoiding duplicative investment in innovation. Suzanne Scotchmer also takes a view in favour of broad patents in early innovations.[119] This view derives from her concern about adequate reward to early innovators for their contribution to valuable

---

114 Paul David, 'New Technology, Diffusion, Public Policy, and Industrial Competitiveness', in Ralph Landau and Nathan Rosenberg (eds), *The Positive Sum Strategy: Harnessing Technology for Economic Growth*, Washington, D.C.: National Academy Press (1986) 373–392; Richard Nelson and Steven Winter, *An Evolutionary Theory of Economic Change*, Belknap Press of Harvard University Press (1982); Scotchmer (n 84); Robert Merges and Richard R. Nelson, 'On the Complex Economics of Patent Scope' (1990) 90(4) *Columbia Law Review* 839–916.

115 Scotchmer (n 84) 29.

116 Merges, Menell and Lemley (n 26) 15–16.

117 *The Economist*, 1 February 1851, 114–15, cited in Machlup and Penrose (n 4) 24.

118 Kitch (n 79) 265–90.

119 Scotchmer (n 84) 29–41.

subsequent technologies which, she thinks, can be done by seeking appropriate ways to divide profit among sequential innovators.

However, Robert Merges and Richard Nelson contend that broad early patents do more harm than good to society in that the number of further diverse innovations would be cut down as later innovators are constrained by the risk of litigation and cost of obtaining a licence from the earlier patent holder.[120] These blockage issues are particularly salient in the context of cumulative innovation[121] where the creation of one useful invention requires multiple inputs that are already developed.[122] In such a context, subsequent innovators would need licences from multiple predecessor innovators to pursue their research projects. In particular, the proliferation of patents on biomedical research tools has been a considerable source of concern.[123] Research tools refer to initial inventions whose primary value is to help further research.[124] This area of knowledge is normally regarded as 'science', which belongs in the public domain. However, the Bayh-Dole Act of 1980 in the US has changed the landscape, encouraging universities to patent their outcomes of federal-funded research. Michael Heller and Rebecca Eisenberg fear that this tendency of privatisation of outcome in basic research in the US would engender what they call 'the tragedy of anticommons'.[125] The term, 'the tragedy of anticommons' refers to the tendency of underuse of valuable resources 'when too many owners each have a right to exclude others from a scarce resource and no one has an effective privilege of use'.[126] They see this danger in biomedical research where research results are increasingly subject to patent rights. Heller and Eisenberg warn that too many patents in biomedical research may be deterring life-saving innovations, due to the high costs to bundle licences.[127]

The preceding discussions show that the costs of patents in a cumulative research environment include not only the restricted access to inventions by end-users, but also the deterrent effect on the further development of knowledge. How does this change the optimal patent design? Robert Mazzoleni and Richard Nelson recommend that in a research environment, where an invention is considered to contribute to further innovation potential or a new improved product for use, the breadth of patent rights should be kept relatively narrow so that subsequent improvements would not be blocked as infringement of prior patent.[128] Also, the criteria of 'novelty' and 'inventive step'

---

120   Merges and Nelson (n 114) 839–916.

121   Mazzoleni and Nelson (n 79) 280; Rebecca S. Eisenberg, '9 Bargaining over the Transfer of Proprietary Research Tools: Is This Market Failing or Emerging?', in Rochelle Dreyfuss, Diane L. Zimmerman, and Harry First (eds), *Expanding the Boundaries of Intellectual Property: Innovation Policy for the Knowledge Society*, Oxford University Press (2001) 223–49.

122   Merges and Nelson (n 114).

123   See The US National Research Council of the National Academies (ed.), *Reaping the Benefits of Genomic and Proteomic Research: Intellectual Property Rights, Innovation, and Public Health*, National Academies Press (2006).

124   Eisenberg (n 121) 228.

125   Heller and Eisenberg (n 82).

126   Ibid.

127   Ibid., 699.

128   Mazzoleni and Nelson (n 79) 281–2.

should be strictly applied in evaluating the patentability of subject matter to avoid a proliferation of patents. Furthermore, embryonic invention, in their view, has to be publicly funded and be kept in the public domain.[129] In contrast, Suzanne Scotchmer argues that relatively broad patents may be efficient to avoid wasteful duplication of R&D costs and to help the division of profit between the pioneer inventor and the subsequent inventors.[130]

Nevertheless, the validity of broad patents depends on whether licensing prior to follow-on inventions works efficiently.[131] Eisenberg discusses specifically 'bargaining over proprietary research tools' in the biomedical field on the basis of her experience as chair of the (US) National Institutes of Health (NIH) Working Group on Research Tools (1997–1998).[132] According to Eisenberg, researchers, either in universities or in the pharmaceutical and biotechnology industries, encounter difficulties in accessing proprietary research tools, and negotiations over the transfer of the research tools often cause delays in biomedical research and product development or sometimes even abandonment of the research plans.[133] Heller and Eisenberg argue, on the basis of their observations about the biomedical field, that licensing apparently fails to surmount 'the tragedy of anticommons' as researchers have to bargain with multiple patent owners and the transaction costs are high.[134] Mazzoleni and Nelson are also pessimistic about the success of the licensing market, pointing out the evidence of considerable costs of litigation conflicts and transactions.[135] Even if licensing works, as Nancy Gallini and Suzanne Scotchmer note, licensing among innovators to increase joint profit might be adverse to consumers' welfare since such licensing may 'stifle noninfringing follow-on products that would detract from joint profit' and thus reduce product market competition.[136] The probability of this worst case scenario is supported by non-negligible cases where firms seek patents to prevent others from obtaining a patent that might erode their own competitiveness in the market.[137] Consider Stephen Glazier's remark: 'Invention is not the point of most valuable patents. Instead, most patents are obtained for the proper business purpose of keeping competitors away from the market for a new product or service.'[138]

Have we reached the answers to key questions: whether the benefits of the existing level of patent protection exceed the costs, and what the optimal scope and duration of patent protection would be? An important message from the foregoing discussions is that a caveat should be given to any change towards expanding or strengthening patent

---

129 Ibid.
130 Scotchmer (n 84); Gallini and Scotchmer (n 78) 67–9.
131 Gallini and Scotchmer (n 78) 68–9.
132 Eisenberg (n 121).
133 Ibid.
134 Heller and Eisenberg (n 82) 700–701.
135 Mazzoleni and Nelson (n 79) 280–82.
136 Gallini and Scotchmer (n 78) 69.
137 Landes and Posner (n 79) 320–21.
138 Stephen C. Glazier, *Patent Strategies for Business* 1, 3rd edn, Law and Business Institute (2000) cited in Landes and Posner (n 79) 321–2.

protection. Beyond that, it seems that present developments in empirical research do not settle the above questions.[139] The remaining uncertainty about efficiency of patents leads economists to explore alternative mechanisms.

Other Incentive Mechanisms: Public Sponsorship

In the beginning, we have discussed that the public-good characteristic of knowledge requires some sort of incentive scheme for knowledge creation on the assumption that an unregulated competitive market would not provide adequate incentive for innovators. However, a number of empirical studies reveal that in a wide range of 'high-tech' industries, patents were not a particularly effective means for these industry players to reap the returns from their R&D.[140] According to studies, the firms considered 'a head-start, establishment of effective production sales and service facilities, and rapid movement down the learning curve' more important than patents to their R&D. Nevertheless, these studies focused on typically large firms, and thus may not address the interests of small and medium-sized firms, the competitiveness of which lies with their R&D activity.[141] These studies do not cover pharmaceutical sectors either.

Even though the market is not, on its own, sufficient to stimulate adequate innovation, patents are not the only mechanism available for this purpose. In fact, public sponsorship of R&D remains strong, although its extent has declined. In 2012 about 30 per cent of research in the US was sponsored by the federal government,[142] down from the percentage in the 1960s which was two-thirds of the total R&D,[143] but significant nonetheless. According to the Organisation for Economic Co-operation and Development (OECD), industry was responsible for only 55 per cent of R&D in the EU in 2012.[144] In Latin

---

139 Gallini and Scotchmer (n 78) 71–2; Mazzoleni and Nelson (n 79) 280; Landes and Posner (n 79) 310. It is even doubted that the economic analysis of patents can guide the optimal patent design. Economist George Priest argues that what lawyers and policy makers can learn from economic analysis is significantly restricted because of inadequate empirical studies for evaluating the theoretical models of innovation. George Priest, 'What Economists Can Tell Lawyers About Intellectual Property' (1986) 8 *Research in Law and Economics* 19–21.

140 Mazzoleni and Nelson (n 79) 275–6. It refers to a range of studies: Christopher T. Taylor and Aubrey Silberston, *The Economic Impact of the Patent System. A Study of the British Experience*, Cambridge University Press (1973); Edwin Mansfield, 'Patents and Innovation: an Empirical Study' (1986) *32 Management Science* 173–81; R.C. Levin, A.K. Klevorick, R.R. Nelson and S.G. Winter, 'Appropriating the Returns from Industrial Research and Development' (1987) 3 *Brookings Papers on Economic Activity* 783–820; Wesley Cohen, Richard Nelson and John Walsh, 'Appropriability Conditions and Why Firms Patents and Why They Do Not', Manuscript (1997).

141 Mazzoleni and Nelson (n 79) 276.

142 Organisation for Economic Co-operation and Development, Main Science and Technology Indicators (2012) available at http://stats.oecd.org/Index.aspx?DataSetCode=MSTI_PUB last accessed 19 March 2015; Gallini and Scotchmer (n 78) 53.

143 Darren E. Zinner, 'Medical R&D at the Turn of the Millennium', *Health Affairs*, September–October 2001.

144 Organisation for Economic Co-operation and Development (n 142).

American countries such as Mexico and Argentina, government remains the predominant source of R&D funding, with 59 per cent and 71 per cent respectively.[145]

Public sponsorship is used here as a generic term for a system where R&D is funded by a government from general revenue.[146] Knowledge created by this system would, as a norm, immediately be put into the public domain and made freely available to all. Public sponsorship may include in-house development, procurement through competitive bidding, and research grants to universities and researchers.[147] While the profits through proprietary pricing are the incentive for innovation under the patent system, public sponsorship provides innovators incentives through either prizes or grants.

From the viewpoint of economic analysis, an efficient incentive mechanism would induce knowledge creation at the lowest possible cost.[148] The costs include resource costs and the social costs associated with proprietary pricing (deadweight loss). Public sponsorship has strong merits in that there is no deadweight loss from proprietary pricing:[149] a public sponsor determines the projects with the largest social values, and finances for them with funds from the public general revenue, avoiding the deadweight loss.

However, a major difficulty with public sponsorship is whether a public sponsor can verify the cost of a particular R&D and the value of the resulting invention.[150] This information asymmetry between innovators and public sponsors has justified patents as the second best incentive system since patents are, to a certain extent, linked with social value, despite having high social costs. However, some recent studies argue that this defect with public sponsorship is not insurmountable. Steven Shavell and Tanguy van Ypersele suggest that the government can determine the size of rewards based on *ex post* sales data.[151] Stephen M. Maurer and Suzanne Scotchmer offer two compelling examples of where prizes can be linked to the value of an invention.[152] One is targeted prizes for an achievement of a verifiable performance standard. One of the most famous targeted prizes was for inventing a means to preserve food, which was awarded in 1810 to Nicolas Appert, and the information was put in the public domain.[153] The other is a prize as a patent buyout, the assumption behind which is that the size of prize would reflect the value of invention, without which the inventor would not have sold the patent rights.[154] Under this scheme, the government purchases the patent at a price reflecting the social

---

145 Ibid.

146 Shavell and van Ypersele (n 84) 525. Shavell and van Ypersele, instead, use 'reward systems'; Maurer and Scotchmer (n 76) 33. Maurer and Scotchmer seem to use 'public procurement' and 'public sponsorship' interchangeably.

147 Ibid.

148 Ibid., 2.

149 Under either public sponsorship or patents, the cost of failures as well as successes should be counted as part of the cost. Ibid., 5–6.

150 Shavell and van Ypersele (n 84); Maurer and Scotchmer (n 76).

151 Shavell and van Ypersele (n 84) 541.

152 Maurer and Scotchmer (n 76) 8–12.

153 Ibid., 10.

154 For historical examples of patent buyouts, see Michael Kremer, 'Patent Buyouts: A Mechanism for Encouraging Innovation' (1998) 113(4) *Quarterly Journal of Economics* 1137–68.

value and puts it in the public domain. Michael Kremer suggests a patent buyout as a way to meet social needs, such as with regard to pharmaceuticals, without jeopardising the incentive to innovate.[155]

Another difficulty with public sponsorship is administrative costs associated with the process of reviewing and determining the grant of rewards.[156] Litigation costs would also be incurred when there is a dispute between public sponsors and innovators or among innovators. However, patents are not free from administrative costs. Although the administrative costs involved in granting a patent are likely to be less than those incurred by a government under public sponsorship, a patent system incurs other costs arising from patent protection, not to mention litigation costs.[157] Efforts should be made to exclude and detect unauthorised uses, which is neither easy nor cheap, given the public-good characteristic of information.

While a patent system imposes the costs of an invention on its users, public sponsorship pays for an invention out of general revenue, which means the costs are borne by taxpayers in general. Which is better may depend on the kind of invention. If the invention is a game machine, it might be wise to ensure that only the users pay its costs. However, if it is an agricultural product or a medicine that is important in light of public health, public sponsorship might be more appealing. Maurer and Scotchmer argue that 'although raising funds for general revenue is not cost free, the associated inefficiencies are usually thought to be less onerous than taxing a single market, as proprietary pricing does'.[158] Even if each invention is used by different groups of people, each user group would be better off by cross-contributing their tax towards the inventions for other groups so that no one is excluded by proprietary pricing.[159]

There are typical areas where patents cannot provide adequate incentive because the social value of invention cannot be appropriated by private firms and therefore there is no alternative to public sponsorship to stimulate R&D.[160] Where social needs cannot be translated into effective market demand, patents provide little incentive for private companies to carry out R&D into those areas. This point is illustrated by insufficient medical research and development into diseases occurring exclusively in developing countries.[161] Tropical diseases and tuberculosis account for 11.4 per cent of the global diseases burden but only around 1 per cent of the new medicines developed from 1975 to 2004 were for these diseases.[162] This trend is contrasted with active medical research into diseases that are present in both high-income and low-income countries.

155　Ibid.

156　Shavell and van Ypersele (n 84) 543–4.

157　Landes and Posner (n 79); ibid.

158　Maurer and Scotchmer (n 76) 2.

159　Ibid., 34.

160　Ibid.

161　WHO, *Report of the Commission on Public Health, Innovation and Intellectual Property Rights* (2006) 25–8; Commission on Intellectual Property Rights (UK), *Integrating Intellectual Property Rights and Development Policy* (2002) 32–3.

162　Pierre Chirac and Els Torreele, 'Global Framework on Essential Health R&D' (2006) 367(9522) *The Lancet* 1560–61; Patrice Touiller, Piero Olliaro, Els Torreele, James Orbinski, Richard

Research on space, military hardware or pure basic research provides another example. In these research areas, it is difficult or impossible to exclude some from benefiting from an invention and thus impossible to charge a price for each use. For most science research, neither patents nor prizes are the primary source of funding. Researchers are directly hired by sponsors or given up-front grants for undertaking research. One way to elicit new knowledge at a high rate may be by making future funding conditional upon current performance. However, such performance-related rewards may cause researchers to focus on the 'easiest' problems. As Maurer and Scotchmer observe, what is fundamental to enriching ideas in the minds of researchers is promoting an environment of 'open science'.[163] In other words, a research environment where each discovery is widely shared can stimulate researchers to come up with more ideas at a high rate.

Maurer and Scotchmer argue that no single innovation incentive system prevails and which system is efficient can be determined by specific reference to an environment of knowledge creation.[164] Shavell and van Ypersele suggest that public sponsorship would be especially beneficial where the difference between patent price and the marginal cost of supply is large, an example being in the area of pharmaceuticals.[165] In their view, public sponsorship can be an option to provide an incentive to invest in innovation and enhance the diffusion of knowledge without the social losses associated with proprietary pricing.

Global Perspective

In a global setting, the quest for an efficient incentive system for innovation seems far more difficult. The spillover of knowledge creation, due to its public-good characteristic, does not remain within one national economy, and tends to generate benefits accruing to foreign consumers as well as domestic consumers. If a model to support R&D is efficient when worldwide consumers' net surplus is maximised, international knowledge spillover is not a problem but a salutary contribution to the diffusion of knowledge. That is unless it jeopardises incentives to invest in innovation.[166] Thus, a world efficiency concern would not necessarily require cross-border externalities to be recaptured as profits. However, since policy making tends to be based on the national interests of each State, it seems difficult to establish an optimal system for international patent protection, not to mention public sponsorship.

A world efficiency analysis would ask whether a particular area of innovation is better funded by patents or public sponsorship.[167] From a global efficiency perspective, Scotchmer argues that public sponsorship is superior to patents in many areas of knowledge creation where the premium costs of public sponsorship are smaller than the deadweight loss

---

Laing, Nathan Ford, 'Drug Development for Neglected Diseases: A Deficient Market and a Public Health Policy Failure' (2002) 359(9324) *The Lancet* 2188–94.

163   Maurer and Scotchmer (n 76) 25.
164   Ibid.
165   Shavell and van Ypersele (n 84) 543–4.
166   Scotchmer (n 145) 422.
167   Ibid.

caused by proprietary pricing.[168] This is applicable to three types of subject matter in two countries model:

1. innovations whose cost is relatively low, so that the cost efficiency of the private sector does not outweigh the deadweight loss even in the smallest market;
2. high-cost subject matter for which cost cannot be covered by revenue even in both markets; and
3. innovations whose cost cannot be covered in a single market, but for which the deadweight loss in both markets would be more burdensome than the inefficiency of public sponsorship.

What remain are:

4. innovations whose cost can be covered in a single market, and the deadweight loss in one market is smaller than the costs of public sponsorship;
5. innovations whose cost cannot be covered in a single market, and for which the deadweight loss in both markets would be less than the inefficiency of public sponsorship.

For the subject matter described in (4), patent protection in one country is optimal and, only for the subject matter in (5), patent protection in both countries is efficiency enhancing.

The above analysis shows that in many areas of knowledge creation, public spending might be the most efficient way of funding R&D, avoiding the deadweight loss. However, policy makers of each country may not be keen to provide public sponsorship, even if efficient. This may be explained by the fact that public sponsors would not count the benefits enjoyed by the public in other countries, which renders the incentive to public sponsorship inadequate. The benefits conferred upon the public abroad would be considered uncompensated externalities by trade policy makers and thus something that should be recouped as profit. For this reason, policy makers of a country would prefer a patent system as it can repatriate the benefits generated abroad. In short, in a global setting mostly governed by national interests, public sponsorship is likely to be underestimated and discouraged even when it is the most efficient incentive system for innovations.[169]

If patents are provided as a 'second best' incentive system,[170] patent protection in one country (or a small number of countries) would be efficiency enhancing in many cases.[171] In this case, the country(ies) should bear the burden of the deadweight loss and an outflow of profit. No country(ies) would be keen to be the one(s). Therefore, its feasibility seems to depend on whether other countries can agree to compensate this country(ies).[172] Instead, countries opt for a harmonisation, where all countries are required to grant patents for

---

168   The premium costs of public sponsorship may include the costs incurred when determining the most efficient firms, monitoring the use of public funds, and taxing for general revenues. Scotchmer (n 145) 423.

169   Ibid., 422.

170   Ibid., 424.

171   Phillip McCalman, 'National Patents, Innovation and International Agreements' (2002) 11(1) *The Journal of International Trade & Economic Development* 1–14, 4, 10.

172   Ibid.

foreign innovations as well as domestic ones. Such harmonisation results in stronger patent protection than optimal, both nationally and globally, even without considering the adverse effect on the cumulative research environment.[173] Scotchmer observes that TRIPS shares such characteristics.[174] Patents become 'a tool by which cross-border externalities can be recaptured by the innovating country',[175] given 'the incredible divide in the world between the technology innovators and the noninnovators'.[176] This trend of overprotective patents bears two important implications. One is that worldwide consumers are worse off due to more extensive proprietary pricing. The other is that it has an adverse distributional effect on countries that have asymmetric innovative capacities.[177] In other words, the universal raising of patent protection disadvantages most countries except for a small number of innovating countries. In fact, patent harmonisation resulting from TRIPS leads to a large flow of profits to very few countries. Phillip McCalman's study on the transfers induced by harmonisation shows that:

[O]nly six countries stand to benefit from TRIPS: US, Germany, France, Italy, Sweden, and Switzerland. All other countries experience a net loss from raising their standards of patent protection. The US stands out as the major beneficiary, gaining nearly 6 times as much as the second largest beneficiary.[178]

Nevertheless, the so-called losers from TRIPS might also benefit from patents-mediated information flows. There may be potential gains from the globalisation of patents, such as more technology transfer through foreign direct investment (FDI) or more licensing of

---

173   Note that national difference gives rise to different optimal patent policies in each country since the equilibrium point of the deadweight loss and the incentive benefit in one country depends on its market size, its capacity for innovation, etc. Ibid.; Gene M. Grossman and Edwin L.C. Lai, 'International Protection of Intellectual Property' (2004) 94(5) *The American Economic Review* 1635–53; Scotchmer (n 145). While the former two studies discuss the length of patent protection, the last one discusses its scope.

174   Scotchmer (n 145) 416.

175   Ibid.

176   Jeffery Sachs points out huge gaps between countries: 'if we consider the country of origin of U.S. utility patents (determined by the country of origin of the lead inventor on each utility patent), the top ten innovating countries account for around 94% of all of the patents taken out in the U.S. in the year 2000, yet these countries have a combined population of only around 14% of the world's population. ... If we look at the bottom 128 countries (with population of at least 1 million) ..., each of those countries has fewer than 150 patents. Those countries have 63% of the world's population, but only 1174 patents in the year 2000, or just 0.75% of all the patents taken out in the U.S. that year'. Jeffrey Sachs, 'The Global Innovation Divide' (2003) 3 *Innovation Policy and the Economy* 131–41, 132.

177   Grossman and Lai (n 173).

178   Phillip McCalman, 'Reaping What You Sow: an Empirical Analysis of International Patent Harmonization' (2001) 55(1) *Journal of International Economics* 161–86, 178. He infers the international redistribution of income due to the TRIPS agreement by identifying the relationship between patent institutions and the rents associated with patent protection.

high-quality technologies.[179] However, as Keith E. Maskus emphasises, such gains depend on the underlying circumstances of each nation: innovation capacity, the structure and funding of R&D, human and/or infrastructure capacity, etc.[180] According to Maskus, 'the least-developed countries attract virtually no FDI (except in extractive sectors) due to extremely low productivity, education, and skills'.[181]

The global environment of innovation presents a challenge to efficiency analysis. Although public sponsorship is, in many areas, a more efficient way of funding R&D than patents, global incentive for public sponsorship seems deficient. The above discussion indicates that the globalisation of patent protection under TRIPS has more connection with repatriating knowledge spillovers as profits rather than efficiency concerns. The resulting stronger patent protection is not optimal from an economic perspective, but also seems to distribute the costs and benefits disproportionately, with the major beneficiaries being the innovating industries in a limited number of countries. This poses a question about distributive issues.

Conclusion

Patents have commonly been considered to be essential for stimulating innovations, thereby enhancing the progress of technology. Nonetheless, recent economic literature indicates that different environments of knowledge creation demand different incentive systems for innovation, and patents do not always prevail as the most efficient incentive system. Alternatively, some form of public sponsorship for R&D may be better in some cases in that it can stimulate innovations, avoiding the restricted use associated with proprietary pricing. When patents are adopted, efficiency concerns require policy makers and judges to seek the optimal rules for patent protection with a view to balancing between the incentive benefits and the social costs of limiting the diffusion of knowledge.

The globalisation of patent protection under TRIPS has made all fields of technology subject to patentability, and has provided patent holders a broader and longer patent protection than most national patent laws previously provided. The global trend of proliferation of patents causes a growing concern about not only the worsening situation of consumers due to higher prices of innovation prohibiting the wide use of innovations, but also a chilling effect on follow-on innovations. It is observed that in a global setting, patents are often employed as a tool to recapture the benefits conferred upon consumers abroad and, as a result, a large sum of income is transferred to a small number of innovating countries. This raises moral issues, which are not seriously considered from an economic incentive perspective.

---

179   Keith E. Maskus, *Intellectual Property Rights in the Global Economy*, Institute for International Economics (2000).

180   Ibid., 199–232.

181   Ibid., 122. Even if some developing countries experience some benefits from a stronger patent regime, it is doubtful whether the large flow of profits to some innovating countries is the right amount of costs for such technology transfer. On top of that, developing countries have to bear the costs of administration and human resources for a tighter patent system, the negative effects on local companies and the associated loss of employment, and higher prices for consumers.

Towards an Alternative Normative Framework

The foregoing sections have suggested that patents do not have a pre-societal existence but are created to serve social functions. What social functions should patents have? An economic incentive perspective sees patents as a mechanism to induce investment in innovations, thus encouraging technological progress. Efficiency concerns tend to claim moral neutrality. However, the institutional design of a patent may have a significant impact on such areas as agriculture, health and the diffusion of knowledge, giving rise to distributive effects. In this sense, patents matter not only economically but also morally. Stimulating the optimal level of innovation is obviously an important objective that a patent system pursues. But, nonetheless, it is not the only end. This raises a question: what human values should guide the patent system?

This section first discusses the effect of patents on the life of other persons in relation to access to vital resources. Secondly, it argues that human dignity and freedom should be the core human values that a patent system should serve, suggesting that international human rights law can provide a global normative framework for this purpose.

Patents and Freedom

Property as a form of power

The analytical tradition originated from Wesley Newcomb Hohfeld established that property structures a relationship between persons in relation to an object.[182] According to Hohfeld, property involves a bundle of entitlements: privileges, rights, immunities and powers. Privileges mean the liberty to do something on or with your property. Rights indicate the entitlements to control others' behaviour with regard to the property, i.e. the entitlement to keep others from interfering with your use or possession of your property. Immunities are the security of the owners from having their property taken away without their consent. Powers describe the freedom to transfer ownership rights to someone else. Each legal advantage has its correlative legal disadvantage on the part of others: right/duty, privilege/no-right, power/liability and immunity/disability. If A has a property right over a piece of land against B, B is under a duty to stay off the land.[183] These bundles of entitlements give a property holder a considerable capacity to control other people's conduct.

Morris Cohen likened the power carried by property to one of sovereignty.[184] He saw the right to exclude others as the most distinctive feature of private property and argued that property law confers on a property owner a power over others. If the things are essential for others, the owner would have even greater power over others.

> [T]he law of property helps me directly only to exclude others from using the things which it assigns to me. If then somebody else wants to use the food, the house, the land, or the

---

182 Wesley Newcomb Hohfeld, *Fundamental Legal Conceptions* [1919] David Campbell and Philip Thomas (eds), Ashgate Publishing (2001).

183 Ibid., 13.

184 Morris R. Cohen, 'Property and Sovereignty' (1927–1928) 13 *Cornell Law Quarterly* 8–30.

plow which the law calls mine, he has to get my consent. To the extent that these things are necessary to the life of my neighbour, the law thus confers on me a power, limited but real, to make him do what I want.[185]

Linking property to power allows us to notice its resulting impact on freedom. Here, freedom is meant by the capacity and opportunity of individuals to lead their lives in their own way. As seen above, property may impose duties upon other individuals requiring them to do or not to do certain things. In this way, one's exercise of private property limits another's freedom to do what they please without interference.[186] Not all limitations on others' freedom are illegitimate. This is reflected in international human rights instruments where limitation clauses are commonly found. Thus, the question might be to what extent one's exercise of private property limits others' freedom and whether it is justifiable.

It has been discussed so far that property confers upon the owner a certain power and has an effect on the life of others. However, property is not one fixed form but a dynamic institution whose distributive pattern of power may vary depending on norms regulating property and social conditions within which property rights are exercised.[187]

> Different rules will distribute power differently, impose obligations differently, shape expectations differently, and order social relations differently. Our choice of a particular property regime alters the social world.[188]

The power of patents on the life of people

The function of a property system as a mechanism of distributing power can be observed also in the area of intellectual property, including patents. Drahos provides an analysis of intellectual property, as a distinctive form of power, and its effect on the social life of others.[189] According to Drahos, intellectual property law creates control over abstract objects.[190] Not all abstract objects create a power effect. Where abstract objects function as a gateway to valuable resources that many people depend upon, the ownership over such abstract objects would confer upon the owner enormous power.[191] Examples include chemical compounds used for medicines, agricultural seeds and information on genes for medical treatment. In these examples, the resulting ownership in the abstract objects allows the owner to control access to even physical objects that are either important in the process of production or the end-result of such processes. Intellectual property in the abstract objects generates a dependent relationship between persons, not only a dependent relationship between persons and the valuable things.[192]

---

185 Ibid., 12.

186 Jeremy Waldron, 'Chapter 13 Homelessness and the Issue of Freedom', *Liberal Rights*, Cambridge University Press (1993) 309–38.

187 Drahos (n 30) 150.

188 Joseph Singer, *Entitlement: The Paradoxes of Property*, Yale University Press (2000) 139.

189 Drahos (n 30) 145–69. This section is heavily indebted to the work of Drahos.

190 Ibid.

191 Ibid.

192 Ibid.

A farmer, in order to plant crops, is dependent upon having seeds to plant. This we might term an object-dependent relationship. If those seeds are now the subject of a patent or plant variety right, the farmer is dependent upon the permission of the owner of the abstract object for access to those seeds. A person-dependent relationship has been added to the object-dependent relationship.[193]

Intellectual property in the seeds, in the above situation, creates a relationship of dependence between the farmer and the holder of the patent (or the plant variety right), and may result in restricting the freedom of the farmer. To what extent would the exercise of intellectual property rights of the owner over such essentials as seeds or medicines cause a loss of freedom on the part of others? While an owner of a piece of land and a patent holder over a chemical compound for medical treatment both prevent others from using what is subject to property rights without consent of the owner, Drahos argues that the simple comparison between intellectual property rights and other kinds of property rights does not tell us much about the power that each right gives to the owner.[194] Instead, he draws an analogy between 'the ownership of the abstract object and the ownership of all the land of a state by one individual'.[195] In both cases, many people depend on the object of the property and the owner is empowered to direct others' behaviour in relation to the object of property.[196]

Some may point out that the patent holder justly acquired the ownership in the seeds through either his/her own invention or voluntary transfer. Even if the farmer cannot afford to buy the seeds at the price that the patent holder set, this is a private matter. However, it should be noted that intellectual property rights are the outcome of State intervention in the first place. Intellectual property as such would not exist if not for a law creating it, as discussed in the first section of this chapter. Knowledge, by nature, can be used by a multiple number of people simultaneously. In the above situation, knowledge is artificially made scarce by State intervention through its being subjected to exclusive rights. The scope of exclusive rights over abstract objects varies depending on how the law defines intellectual property.[197] Depending on the patent rule prevailing at the time, the seeds may or may not be subject to an exclusive right, and a particular use of the patented seeds may not constitute an infringement. Patent holders may have duties to exercise their patent rights in ways that are consistent with the objective for which a patent is granted.[198] The duties may depend on the characterisation of the goals of a patent system and the desired effects of patent rights. The idea of duties falling on patent holders is not alien to the history of patent systems. The working requirement of a patent that the patented process or product must be used or produced[199] is an example. It derives from the

---

193   Ibid., 159.

194   Ibid., 212.

195   Ibid.

196   Ibid., 213.

197   Ibid., 158.

198   For more discussions on the duties of the holder of intellectual property, see Drahos (n 30) 220–23.

199   See 'A wide variation among patent systems' in Chapter 1.

necessity of making the patented knowledge available to the public, which could constitute the goal of the patent system. Another example is a reasonable use requirement imposed upon patents arising from federally funded research under the Bayh-Dole Act of 2000 in the United States.[200] While the patent system creates duties as well as rights, patentees' failures to satisfy the duties may empower the government to override the exclusivity of a patent granted to the patentee, and allow other parties to work on the patented knowledge.[201] Going back to the question of the farmer and the patent holder of the seeds, different patent rules, in terms of, for instance, objectives, patentability, the scope of patent protection and exceptions to the exclusive right, could construct the relationship between the farmer and the patent holder of the seeds differently.

From the economic efficiency perspective, some may also argue that the loss of freedom caused by the ownership in knowledge may not be a problem, as long as total net efficiency is maximised. Here it is worthwhile considering some key defects in the efficiency perspective. The efficiency perspective, based on utilitarianism, is exposed to the same criticism as that directed at utilitarian theories more generally. One critique is that utilitarianism tends to lack qualitative judgments on human interests or desires.[202] Utilitarian theory tends to see the satisfaction of whatever human interests as a positive value in itself. However, all interests do not have the same social values. For instance, one's interest in a private jet is not as significant as one's interest in an affordable place to live. Another limitation is that the main focus of utilitarianism is maximising the utility sum. From an economic perspective, economic efficiency represents the utility. Utilitarianism neither tends to be interested in the distribution of utilities nor does it attach intrinsic values to non-utility concerns such as rights, freedom and justice. However, as Rawls argued, 'the loss of freedom for some' cannot be made right 'by a greater good shared by others'.[203] Echoing Rawls's view on utilitarianism, Amartya Sen stressed that '[e]ach person deserves consideration as a person, and this militates against a distribution-indifferent view'.[204] While the economic perspective plays an important role in guiding patent law and policy through its cost-benefit analysis, its limitations should be acknowledged. This discussion leads us to consider what moral considerations should be involved in making, interpreting and implementing patent law.

Patents and Human Values

The institutional design of patents has an impact on people's freedom by regulating access to knowledge. Thus, how to govern intellectual property involves not only issues of legal

---

200 35 U.S.C. §§ 200–212 The Bayh-Dole Act. See particularly §§ 200, 201 and 209(d)(3)(A). For discussion on the pricing requirement, Peter S. Arno and Michael H. Davis, 'Why Don't We Enforce Existing Drug Price Controls? The Unrecognized and Unenforced Reasonable Pricing Requirements Imposed upon Patents Deriving in Whole or in Part from Federally Funded Research' [2001] *Tulane Law Review* 631–91.

201 Arno and Davis (n 200).

202 Jeremy Waldron, *The Right to Private Property*, Clarendon Press (1990) 12.

203 John Rawls, *A Theory of Justice*, Harvard University Press (1971), reprinted in 2005, 28.

204 Amartya Sen, 'Why Health Equity?' (2002) 11(8) *Health Economics* 659–66, 662.

technicality or economic concerns, but also human values. What human values should a patent system serve? Social institutions do not necessarily serve only one end. Promoting economic development through stimulating the optimal level of innovation is one of the important ends that a patent system should strive to achieve. Nevertheless, given the growing effect on people's lives and the globalisation of patent protection, a patent system should be guided by a set of moral values that people consider to be universal, as well as by an economic perspective. However, it may not be easy to find and agree a set of universal values that obtain wide support because individuals and societies retain diverse views on values.

Although human rights are by no means free from contestation, a human rights framework arising from key human rights treaties would be the most suitable candidate for principles that can provide moral guidance when patent law making and enforcement give rise to moral issues.[205] International human rights instruments provide a positive legal order to a set of moral values,[206] and the norms embodied in these instruments bind States through a ratification process or as international customary norms. The UN Committee on Economic, Social and Cultural Rights states that a human rights approach 'encourages the development of intellectual property systems and the use of intellectual property rights in a balanced manner that meets the objective of providing protection for the moral and material interests of authors [the term includes inventors], and at the same time promotes the enjoyment of these and other human rights'.[207] The role of the economic perspective remains important in detailed rule setting, considering the development of technology and markets. The following chapters narrow down their focus on intellectual property and access to medicines and consider human rights bearing upon this issue with a view to identifying the content of a human rights framework for intellectual property, innovation and access to medicines.

Conclusion

Why should one person have exclusive rights in knowledge while everyone can possess and use knowledge without diminishing its value? This chapter looked into this question through two often-invoked perspectives in the area of patents: the natural rights argument and the economic incentive argument.

It has been argued that the Lockean theory of property, which the natural property rights argument relies on, does not provide a firm ground for the claimed natural property rights in abstract objects. Locke's main concern, which led to a justification for private

---

205   Peter Drahos, 'An Alternative Framework for the Global Regulation of Intellectual Property Rights' (2005) 1 *Austrian Journal of Development Studies* 16, available at http://papers.ssrn.com/sol3/papers.cfm?abstract_id=850751, last accessed 15 March 2015.

206   UN Committee on Economic, Social and Cultural Rights, Statement on 'Human Rights and Intellectual Property' – Follow-up to the Day of General Discussion on Art. 15.1(c) (26 November 2001) UN Doc. E/C.12/2001/15.

207   Ibid., para. 4.

property, lies with the subsistence right of human beings and the beneficial use of resources. However, in the case of knowledge, one does not need to exclude others from possessing and using a particular piece of knowledge for the effective use of it. Even if we assume that knowledge may be susceptible to the natural right to the fruits of one's labour, the exclusive rights in knowledge should be adjusted by Lockean provisos: the sufficiency condition and the non-waste condition. Most of all, the natural rights argument for patents is weakened in the face of the fact that patent rights are made to exist only by the enactment of law, due to the non-exclusive feature of abstract objects.

The crucial question for economic analysis is what system can effectively stimulate the creation of knowledge while minimising the restriction on access to knowledge. For this purpose, it is crucial to calibrate the optimal length, scope or strength of patent rights. That patents may have a stifling effect on follow-on innovation in cumulative research environments is another cost that patent policy makers and judges should be aware of. Public sponsorship for intellectual works deserves fresh attention as an alternative in certain areas of innovation in that it does not involve the social loss associated with proprietary pricing that afflicts the patent system. Economic studies warn that the globalisation of the patent system may drive standards beyond the economically optimal, with the patent system becoming a tool to recoup the externality that the production of knowledge generates abroad.

The final section discussed the situation where patented knowledge is linked with valuable resources, such as medicines or agricultural seeds. In such situations, the exclusive rights conferred upon the patent holder may have an effect of reducing the freedom of others, by restricting their access to such valuable resources. Patents are created by law as a means to achieve certain social objectives. There is a need to rebalance the relationship between the patent holder and people who rely on the patented knowledge by evaluating and adjusting the patent rules in light of basic human values. The section argued that the international human rights instruments can provide a normative framework for institutions governing property in, and access to, knowledge.

Chapter 3
Public Health Safeguards in the TRIPS Agreement

Introduction

The historical account of patent law presented in Chapter 1 showed how the patent system was created as a legal tool to achieve social objectives, and has been adjusted in response to the level of technological development and societal needs. Theories of patents have highlighted that balancing between stimulating innovation and access to resulting knowledge is crucial in a patent system. Particularly when the subject matters for patents are necessities which people rely on for their lives, the need to make patent systems responsive to social needs becomes paramount. This chapter takes a close look at ways in which TRIPS can be interpreted and implemented in order to benefit public health.

TRIPS entered into force with the establishment of the WTO in 1995. TRIPS established a set of minimum standards for the protection of intellectual property rights and extended patent protection to all fields of technology, including pharmaceutical products. Pharmaceutical patents are likely to increase the price of medicines because the exclusive right of the patent holders enables them to set the highest prices that a market can bear. Therefore, the introduction of patent protection for pharmaceutical products can have a consequence of limiting access to patented medicines in the absence of measures that can alleviate such effects. Nonetheless, even under TRIPS, Member counties retain a degree of policy space over the implementation of TRIPS, provided they meet the minimum standards mandated by TRIPS. States may define criteria for evaluating patentability, create limited exceptions to patent rights, issue compulsory licences and undertake government use, and adopt the international exhaustion principle to facilitate parallel imports.

This chapter discusses such flexibilities in TRIPS, which can be used to increase access to affordable medicines. The objectives and principles of TRIPS pursue a balance between the promotion of technological innovation and the transfer and dissemination of technology, and the Doha Declaration on the TRIPS Agreement and Public Health reaffirms the right of States to adopt measures to promote public health. The first section considers the interpretive role of the objectives of TRIPS and of the Doha Declaration. The next section focuses on compulsory licensing (Art. 31), one of the most important flexibilities that can facilitate promoting the affordability of medicines. Since the extent to which compulsory licences can achieve the desired effects may be significantly affected by, among other things, the level of remuneration payable to the patent holder,[1] it examines

---

1 Article 31(h) states that 'the right holder shall be paid adequate remuneration in the circumstances of each case, taking into account the economic value of the authorization'.

the meaning of 'adequate remuneration' under Article 31(h) of TRIPS, focusing on a situation where a compulsory licence is authorised on the ground of promoting access to medicines. It deepens an analysis of the potential of compulsory licensing for addressing public health needs through a case study of Thailand's compulsory licensing between 2006 and 2008. It also traces the development within TRIPS in addressing the issue of countries with few manufacturing capacities. The final section briefly touches upon other flexibilities in TRIPS, such as standards for patentability (Art. 27.1), exceptions to patent rights (Art. 30), and parallel importing (Art. 6).

Interpretation of TRIPS in Accordance with the Vienna Convention on the Law of Treaties

In accordance with customary international law, TRIPS must be interpreted in good faith using the ordinary meaning of its terms in context and in light of the treaty's object and purpose. This methodology of treaty interpretation is affirmed by the WTO's Understanding on Rules and Procedures Governing the Settlement of Disputes (referred to as DSU), which requires the Dispute Settlement Body to clarify WTO provisions 'in accordance with the customary principles of treaty interpretation'.[2] These customary principles of treaty interpretation, which the WTO Dispute Settlement Body has to follow in interpreting WTO Agreements, including TRIPS, are embodied and codified in Articles 31 and 32 of the Vienna Convention on the Law of Treaties (hereinafter VCLT)[3] as confirmed in the jurisprudence of the WTO Panel and Appellate Body.[4]

Objectives and Principles of TRIPS: Articles 7 and 8

In accordance with Article 31.1 of the VCLT, text, context, and object and purpose, as well as good faith are elements for treaty interpretation[5] and these elements 'are to be

---

2 WTO Agreement, Annex 2, Understanding on Rules and Procedures Governing the Settlement of Disputes, Art. 3.2. 'The Members recognize that it [Dispute Settlement Body] serves ... to clarify the existing provisions of those agreements *in accordance with customary rules of interpretation of public international law*' (emphasis added).

3 Adopted 23 May 1969 by the United Nations and entered into force on 27 January 1980.

4 See, the first WTO Appellate Report, *United States – Standards for Reformulated and Conventional Gasoline*, 20 May 1996, WT/DS2/9, 17: 'Articles 31 and 32 of the Vienna Convention on the Law of Treaties ("Vienna Convention") have attained the status of rules of customary international law'; reaffirmed by, *inter alia*, Appellate Body report on *Japan – Taxes on Alcoholic Beverages*, WT/DS8/AB/R, 4 October 1996, 10–11, Panel report on *United States – Sections 301–310 of the Trade Act of 1974*, WT/DS152/R (22 December 1999) para. 7.21; WTO panel report on *Canada – Patent Protection of Pharmaceutical Products*, WT/DS114/R (17 March 2000), para. 7.13: 'The rules that govern the interpretation of WTO agreements are the rules of treaty interpretation stated in Articles 31 and 32 of the Vienna Convention.'

5 Article 31.1 of the VCLT states: 'A treaty is to be interpreted in good faith in accordance with the ordinary meaning to be given to the terms of the treaty in their context and in the light of its object and purpose.'

viewed as one holistic rule of interpretation rather than a sequence of separate tests to be applied in a hierarchical order'.[6] This approach echoes the view of the International Law Commission, the drafters of the VCLT, on Article 31.1 that '[t]he article, when read as a whole, cannot properly be regarded as laying down a legal hierarchy of norms for the interpretation of treaties'.[7] Therefore, the interpretation of TRIPS must be conducted in such a way that the ordinary meaning be sought in the context of the provision and also be determined taking into account the objectives and principles of TRIPS, which are embodied in Articles 7 and 8 of the text. Therefore, Articles 7 and 8 should be considered for the analysis of public health measures permitted in TRIPS.

Objectives

7. The protection and enforcement of intellectual property rights should contribute to the promotion of technological innovation and to the transfer and dissemination of technology, to the mutual advantage of producers and users of technological knowledge and in a manner conducive to social and economic welfare, and to a balance of rights and obligations.

Article 7 recognises different interests involved in the protection of intellectual property and requires a balance of different interests in the interpretation of TRIPS. It sets out 'next to the overarching goal of facilitating social and economic welfare, three sets of (competing) interests which need to be properly balanced in order to achieve that overarching aim'.[8] First, two distinctive objectives, the promotion of technological innovation on one hand and the transfer and dissemination of technology on the other, must be balanced. Secondly, the interests of users of technological knowledge, as well as its producers, must be mutually promoted. Lastly, a balance of rights and obligations must be pursued in the protection and enforcement of intellectual property rights. The wording of Article 7 presents clear evidence that Member States are required to promote a balanced approach towards distinctive societal values/interests in building and enforcing intellectual property, unlike the view of some who assert that TRIPS should exclusively aim at strengthening and harmonising the protection of intellectual property rights throughout the world.[9] For the present purpose, Article 7 suggests that the provision of incentives to medical innovation and access to medicines should be properly balanced in the implementation of TRIPS.

---

6 WTO, *Sections 301–310 of the Trade Act of 1974* (n 4) para. 7.22. See also, *Japan – Taxes on Alcoholic Beverages* (n 4) 11–12: '[I]nterpretation must be based above all upon the text of the treaty. The provisions of the treaty are to be given their ordinary meaning in their context. The object and purpose of the treaty are also to be taken into account in determining the meaning of its provisions.'

7 Yearbook of the International Law Commission, The International Law Commission's Commentary on Articles 27 to 29 of its Final Draft Articles on the Law of Treaties, vol. II (1966) 219–20.

8 Henning Grosse Ruse-Khan, 'Proportionality and Balancing within the Objectives', in Paul Torremans (ed.), *Intellectual Property and Human Rights: Enhanced Edition of Copyright and Human Rights*, Kluwer Law International (2008) 161–94, 173.

9 Ibid., 174–5; UNCTAD-ICTSD, *Resource Book on TRIPS and Development*, Cambridge University Press (2004) 125.

While Article 7 sets forth the objectives of intellectual property protection, Article 8 confirms the Members' discretion to take measures in order to satisfy public needs in relation to the protection of intellectual property.[10]

Principles

8.1 Members may, in formulating or amending their laws and regulations, adopt measures necessary to protect public health and nutrition, and to promote the public interest in sectors of vital importance to their socio-economic and technological development, provided that such measures are consistent with the provisions of this Agreement.

8.2 Appropriate measures, provided that they are consistent with the provisions of this Agreement, may be needed to prevent the abuse of intellectual property rights by right holders or the resort to practices which unreasonably restrain trade or adversely affect the international transfer of technology.

Article 8.1 makes clear that measures may be taken for the purpose of (a) protecting 'public health and nutrition' and (b) promoting 'the public interest in sectors of vital importance to their socio-economic and technological development'. Article 8.2 secures countries' freedom to adopt measures in order to prevent (a) 'the abuse of intellectual property rights by rights holders', (b) 'practices which unreasonably restrain trade' and (c) 'practices which adversely affect the international transfer of technology'. The condition for all cases is the consistency of the measures with the provisions of TRIPS. Carlos Correa comments that the test of consistency should be assessed in the light of Article 7, which mandates a balanced approach to rights and obligations and promotes social and economic welfare as an overarching objective.[11] The 'measures necessary to protect public health and nutrition' consistent with TRIPS may include exceptions to exclusive rights (Art. 30) and compulsory licences (Art. 31). The relevance of Articles 7 and 8.1 to the interpretation of the provisions of TRIPS is acknowledged in *Canada – Patent Protection for Pharmaceutical Product*, where the Panel stated that '[b]oth the goals and the limitations stated in Articles 7 and 8.1 must obviously be borne in mind when doing so [examining the words of the conditions upon Article 30] as well as those of other provisions of TRIPS which indicate its object and purposes'.[12] With regard to public health measures pertaining

---

10 Carlos Correa, *Trade Related Aspects of Intellectual Property Rights: A Commentary on the TRIPS Agreement*, Oxford University Press (2007) 108.

11 Ibid., 104.

12 *Canada – Patent Protection of Pharmaceutical Products* (n 4) para. 7.26. In this case, the Panel considered whether provisions of Canadian patent law that allow a third party to use a patented pharmaceutical product, during the patent term, in relation to an application for regulatory review, and to manufacture and stockpile for the purpose of entering the post-expiry market are a 'limited exception' within the meaning of Art. 30 of the TRIPS Agreement. The Panel rightly acknowledged the role of objectives and principles of the TRIPS Agreement in the interpretation and implementation of individual provisions. But it failed to give full effect to the objectives expressed in Arts 7 and 8.1 when it examined the provision on a limited exception

to TRIPS, the European Communities and their Member States, in their communication to the Council for TRIPS, have acknowledged that 'they [Articles 7 and 8] are important for interpreting other provisions of the Agreement, including where measures are taken by Members to meet health objectives'.[13]

The Doha Declaration on the TRIPS Agreement and Public Health

In the context of access to patented medicines, the Doha Declaration[14] constitutes an important part of the interpretive process. Paragraph 5(a) of the Declaration confirms the need to interpret each provision of TRIPS in light of the object and purpose of the Agreement set out in Articles 7 and 8 of the text.

5(a) In applying the customary rules of interpretation of public international law, each provision of TRIPS shall be read in the light of the object and purpose of the Agreement as expressed, in particular, in its objectives and principles.

4. We agree that the TRIPS Agreement does not and should not prevent members from taking measures to protect public health. Accordingly, while reiterating our commitment to the TRIPS Agreement, we affirm that the Agreement can and should be interpreted and implemented in a manner supportive of WTO members' right to protect public health and, in particular, to promote access to medicines for all.

In this connection, we reaffirm the right of WTO members to use, to the full, the provisions in the TRIPS Agreement, which provide flexibility for this purpose.

The first sentence of paragraph 4 implies that the protection of intellectual property rights should not be an obstacle to the promotion of public health.[15] The second sentence indicates that States may adopt measures to limit patent rights with a view to guaranteeing access to affordable medicines.[16] The Declaration confirms the right of countries under TRIPS to make full use of flexibilities in the Agreement to protect public health and promote access to medicines for all. Paragraph 5 of the Declaration[17] indicates policy measures to protect

---

in question. The Panel decided that the regulatory review exception was consistent with Art. 30 while the stockpiling exception was not. For critique of the Panel decision in this respect, see Ruse-Khan (n 8) 187–91.

13 IP/C/W/280, 12 June 2001. Available at http://www.wto.org/English/tratop_e/trips_e/ paper_eu_w280_e.htm, last accessed 15 March 2015.

14 WT/MIN(01)/Dec/2, adopted by consensus of all WTO Members at the fourth Ministerial Conference, 14 November 2001.

15 Correa (n 10) 105.

16 UNCTAD-ICTSD (n 9) 131.

17 Paragraph 5. 'Accordingly and in the light of paragraph 4 above, while maintaining our commitments in the TRIPS Agreement, we recognize that these flexibilities include: (a) In applying the customary rules of interpretation of public international law, each provision of the TRIPS Agreement shall be read in the light of the object and purpose of the Agreement as expressed,

public health within TRIPS, such as compulsory licensing for pharmaceutical products (Art. 31) and the discretion of States with regard to parallel importation of medicines (Art. 6). The measures permitted in TRIPS that countries may adopt to promote public health are analysed later in this chapter.

The Declaration is part of 'any subsequent agreement between the parties regarding the interpretation of the treaty or the application of its provisions' under Article 31.3(a) of the VCLT.[18] The Declaration was adopted notably in the form of an agreement[19] by the Ministerial Conference, which has 'the authority to take decisions on all matters under any of the Multilateral Trade Agreements'.[20] Therefore, it can be considered a 'decision' of the Members under Article IX:1 of the WTO Agreement.[21] On the other hand, the Declaration does not technically amount to 'interpretations' within the meaning of Article IX:2 of the WTO Agreement,[22] which are legally binding upon all Members, because the Declaration is not based on a recommendation by the General Council.[23] Nevertheless, commentators

---

in particular, in its objectives and principles. (b) Each Member has the right to grant compulsory licences and the freedom to determine the grounds upon which such licences are granted. (c) Each Member has the right to determine what constitutes a national emergency or other circumstances of extreme urgency, it being understood that public health crises, including those relating to HIV/ AIDS, tuberculosis, malaria and other epidemics, can represent a national emergency or other circumstances of extreme urgency. (d) The effect of the provisions in the TRIPS Agreement that are relevant to the exhaustion of intellectual property rights is to leave each Member free to establish its own regime for such exhaustion without challenge, subject to the MFN and national treatment provisions of Articles 3 and 4.'

18 Article 31.3(a) of the VCLT: 'There shall be taken into account, together with the context: (a) any subsequent agreement between the parties regarding the interpretation of the treaty or the application of its provisions'; for discussion of the legal status of the Doha Declaration under the VCLT, see Frederick M. Abbott, 'The Doha Declaration on the TRIPS Agreement and Public Health: Lighting a Dark Corner at the WTO' (2002) 5 *Journal of International Economic Law* 469–505, 491–3; James Thuo Gathii, 'The Legal Status of the Doha Declaration on TRIPS and Public Health under the Vienna Convention on the Law of Treaties' (2002) 15 *Harvard Journal of Law and Technology* 291–317.

19 See para. 4 of the Doha Declaration on the TRIPS Agreement and Public Health.

20 Article IV:1 of the WTO Agreement.

21 Article IX (Decision-Making) states that '1. The WTO shall continue the practice of decision-making by consensus followed under GATT 1947. (1) Except as otherwise provided, where a decision cannot be arrived at by consensus, the matter at issue shall be decided by voting. At meetings of the Ministerial Conference and the General Council, each Member of the WTO shall have one vote. ... Decisions of the Ministerial Conference and the General Council shall be taken by a majority of the votes cast, unless otherwise provided in this Agreement or in the relevant Multilateral Trade Agreement.'

22 Article IX:2 provides that '[t]he Ministerial Conference and the General Council shall have the exclusive authority to adopt interpretations of this Agreement and of the Multilateral Trade Agreements. In the case of an interpretation of a Multilateral Trade Agreement in Annex 1, they shall exercise their authority *on the basis of a recommendation by the Council overseeing the functioning of that Agreement* ...' (emphasis added).

23 Abbott (n 18) 492; UNCTAD-ICTSD (n 9) 131; Ruse-Khan (n 8) 183–4.

note that 'a decision that states a meaning of the Agreement may be considered as a very close approximation of an interpretation and, from a functional standpoint, may be indistinguishable'.[24] In any event, the Declaration should be taken into account as a 'subsequent agreement', together with the context, in accordance with Article 31.3(a) of the Vienna Convention.

In short, the objectives of TRIPS (Art. 7) make it clear that the Agreement should be interpreted and implemented in a balanced manner conducive to the transfer and dissemination of technology, as well as the promotion of technological innovation. The principles of TRIPS (Art. 8) recognise Member countries' rights to adopt measures to protect public health. In accordance with Article 31.1 of the VCLT, each provision of TRIPS must be interpreted in light of Articles 7 and 8, which set out the objectives and principles of the Agreement. In the Doha Declaration, Ministers of WTO Members reiterated the interpretive role of Articles 7 and 8. Also, the Doha Declaration clarifies that 'the Agreement can and should be interpreted and implemented in a manner supportive of WTO members' right to protect public health and, in particular, to promote access to medicines for all'.[25] The rest of this chapter examines some of the flexibilities in TRIPS that can be used to promote access to medicines.

Compulsory Licensing (Non-voluntary Licensing)[26]

Compulsory licensing usually refers to an act by a government authorising others to use the patented inventions without the consent of the patent owner. Where the patented inventions are used by the government itself without the consent of the patent owner, it is called 'government use' (or 'Crown use' under the legislation of the Commonwealth countries). In this analysis, compulsory licences are used to refer to both practices, except where 'government use' needs to be given specific attention.

Compulsory licences have long been considered a safeguard against the adverse effects that may arise from patents granting exclusive rights,[27] and an important tool for lowering prices and thus to strike a balance between the interests of the patent holders and those of the users in the diffusion of knowledge and the access to the outcomes of innovation. Particularly in the field of pharmaceuticals, compulsory licences can be used to serve public health goals where the pricing by the patent holder, among other factors, is considered to aggravate the unaffordability of medicines.

Although TRIPS does not use the term 'compulsory licensing' in its text, Article 31 on 'other use without the authorization of the right holder' stipulates a set of conditions for issuing such licences:

---

24 Abbott (n 18) 492; this same view is taken in UNCTAD-ICTSD (F.M. Abbott and C. Correa as principal consultant) (n 9) 131.

25 Paragraph 4 (n 4).

26 Both terms can be interchangeably used.

27 Edith Tilton Penrose, ch. XI, *The Economics of the International Patent System* (originally published by the Johns Hopkins University Press, 1951; 2nd edn, Greenwood Press, 1973).

31. Where the law of a Member allows for other use of the subject matter of a patent without the authorization of the right holder, including use by the government or third parties authorized by the government, the following provisions shall be respected …

Grounds for Compulsory Licences

Article 31 of TRIPS does not limit the grounds for which compulsory licences may be issued.[28] Although Article 31 mentions some of the possible grounds for compulsory licences, including 'a national emergency', 'other circumstances of extreme urgency', 'public non-commercial use', 'anti-competitive practices' and 'dependent patents', this list of grounds is by no means exhaustive.[29] Rozek and Rainey argue that 'Article 31 establishes well-defined limits on considering use of compulsory licensing' referring to such grounds stated above.[30] But, the text does not support this restrictive view since there is no specific provision that limits the grounds for compulsory licensing.[31] Such grounds as national emergency, other circumstances of extreme urgency, or public non-commercial use are mentioned in Article 31(b)[32] so as to waive certain requirements for a Member State in those circumstances. Furthermore, the Doha Declaration confirms that Article 31 does not limit the grounds for the grant of compulsory licences, providing that:

> 5(b) Each member has the right to grant compulsory licences and the freedom to determine the grounds upon which such licences are granted.[33]

Paragraph 5(c) of the Doha Declaration also added clarity with regard to the discretion of each Member to determine the circumstances constituting 'national emergency'

---

28 Article 31 of the TRIPS Agreement; Thomas Cottier, 'TRIPS, the Doha Declaration and Public Health' (2003) 6(2) *Journal of World Intellectual Property* 373–8, 386; P. Champ and A. Attaran, 'Patent Rights and Local Working Under the WTO TRIPS Agreement: An Analysis of the U.S.-Brazil Patent Dispute' (2002) 27 *Yale Journal of International Law* 365–93, 368, 384; Frederick M. Abbott, *WTO TRIPS Agreement and its Implications for Access to Medicines in Developing Countries, Commission on Intellectual Property Rights(UK) Study Paper 2a* (2002) 13.

29 UNCTAD-ICTSD (n 9) 468; Correa (n 10) 314–15; and Cynthia M. Ho, 'Patent Breaking or Balancing?: Separating Strands of Fact from Fiction under TRIPS' (2009) 34 *North Carolina Journal of International Law & Commercial Regulation* 371–469, 396–7.

30 Richard P. Rozek and Renee L. Rainey, 'Broad-Based Compulsory Licensing of Pharmaceutical Technologies: Unsound Public Policy' (2001) 4(4) *Journal of World Intellectual Property* 463–80, 468.

31 Holger Hestermeyer, *Human Rights and the WTO: The Case of Patents and Access to Medicines,* Oxford University Press (2007) 242–4; UNCTAD-ICTSD (n 9) 468.

32 See Art. 31(b) 'such use may only be permitted if, prior to such use, the proposed user has made efforts to obtain authorization from the right holder on reasonable commercial terms and conditions and that such efforts have not been successful within a reasonable period of time. This requirement may be waived by a Member in the case of a national emergency or other circumstances of extreme urgency or in cases of public non-commercial use …'.

33 Paragraph 5(b) of the Doha Declaration (n 14).

or 'other circumstances of extreme urgency'.[34] The same paragraph in the Declaration expressly recognises that public health crises can represent a national emergency or other circumstances of extreme urgency, and thus justify the grant of compulsory licences when provided under national legislation, without the obligation of prior negotiation with the patent holder:[35]

> 5(c) Each member has the right to determine what constitutes a national emergency or other circumstances of extreme urgency, it being understood that public health crises, including those relating to HIV/AIDS, tuberculosis, malaria and other epidemics, can represent a national emergency or other circumstances of extreme urgency.

According to Article 31(b) of TRIPS, 'public non-commercial use' is another possible ground for a compulsory licence to address public health needs, and is also one of such situations that do not require prior negotiation with the patent holder.[36] 'Public non-commercial use' is often equated with 'government use', whereby the government authorises a government department or a contractor to use a patented invention without the consent of the patent owner, for a non-commercial purpose.[37] A question may arise as to whether 'public non-commercial use' covers a licence granted to a commercial enterprise to exploit the patented product. No precise meaning of 'public, non-commercial use' is defined in TRIPS so there is broad room for interpretation of this term. Notably, Article 31(b), the fourth sentence, explicitly refers to 'the government or contractor' in the context of public, non-commercial use. It indicates that public non-commercial use does not prevent the government from appointing a private entity to use the patent on behalf of the government. State practice also supports this reading that public non-commercial use may cover the use of a patent by a private entity to the extent that it acts on behalf of the government for the benefit of the public.[38] For instance, in the US, under 28 U.S.C. § 1498 (2000),[39] a commercial contractor for the government may be authorised to use the patent on behalf of the government without the consent of the patent holder, subject only to subsequent payment. In the context of medicines, when a government authority uses or authorises its contractors to use a patented drug for the purpose of providing medicines as part of a public health programme, such use may be considered to fall within the scope of 'public, non-commercial use'.[40] In such circumstances, public non-commercial

---

34 Paragraph 5(c) (n 14).

35 Abbott (n 18) 494; Correa (n 10) 316. With regard to prior negotiation, see the part below for requirements.

36 Article 31(b) of the TRIPS Agreement.

37 Correa (n 10) 316.

38 UNCTAD-ICTSD (n 9) 471; Correa (n 10) 316–17; Ho (n 29) 403.

39 28 U.S.C. § 1498 (2000) '(a) … For the purposes of this section, the use or manufacture of an invention described in and covered by a patent of the United States by a contractor, a subcontractor, or any person, firm, or corporation for the Government and with the authorization or consent of the Government, shall be construed as use or manufacture for the United States …'.

40 Peter-Tobias Stoll, Jan Busche and Katrin Arend (eds), *WTO-Trade-Related Aspects of Intellectual Property Rights: Max Planck Commentaries on World Trade Law*, Martinus Nijhoff (2009) 570;

use may enable public health authorities to procure affordable drugs in the provision of public services.

Conditions on the Grant of Compulsory Licences

Article 31 of TRIPS sets forth a series of requirements for the grant of compulsory licences. Such conditions include:

- Each grant of a compulsory licence must be considered on a case-by-case basis (Art. 31(a)).
- The proposed user must first make efforts to obtain a voluntary licence (Prior negotiation: Art. 31(b)).
- The scope and duration of such use must be limited to the purpose for the authorisation of a licence (Art. 31(c)).
- The licence must be non-exclusive (Art. 31(d)) and non-assignable (Art. 31(e)).
- Production must be predominantly for the domestic market (Art. 31(f)).
- Adequate remuneration must be paid to the patent holder (Art. 31(h)).
- Review by a judicial or distinct higher authority must be available to any decisions related to the compulsory licence (Art. 31(i)).

Some key interpretive points should be made with regard to the above conditions, bearing in mind the context of compulsory licences for addressing public health needs.

Individual merits

Article 31(a) states that 'authorization of such use shall be considered on its individual merits …'.

This provision requires the grant of a licence to be decided considering the individual merits of an individual case, as to whether it meets the criteria established for that purpose. The ordinary meaning of the wording prevents a Member State from granting compulsory licences on the basis of types of subject matter or title-holder.[41] However, as commentators note, this provision does not bar national legislation from establishing specific contexts that trigger the consideration of compulsory licences, such as where a patented medicine is not adequately supplied on the local market at an affordable price.[42]

Prior negotiations

Article 31(b) states:

> such use may only be permitted if, prior to such use, the proposed user has made efforts to obtain authorization from the right holder on reasonable commercial terms and conditions

Sisule F. Musungu and Cecilia Oh, 'The Use of Flexibilities in TRIPS by Developing Countries: Can They Promote Access to Medicines' Study 4C of the Commission on Intellectual Property Rights, Innovation and Public Health (CIPIH) (2005) 20.

41 UNCTAD-ICTSD (n 9) 468; Correa (n 10) 320; Ho (n 29) 398–40.

42 UNCTAD-ICTSD (n 9) 468; Correa (n 10) 320.

and that such efforts have not been successful within a reasonable period of time. This requirement may be waived by a Member in the case of a national emergency or other circumstances of extreme urgency or in cases of public non-commercial use. In situations of national emergency or other circumstances of extreme urgency, the right holder shall, nevertheless, be notified as soon as reasonably practicable. In the case of public non-commercial use, where the government or contractor, without making a patent search, knows or has demonstrable grounds to know that a valid patent is or will be used by or for the government, the right holder shall be informed promptly.

Under this provision, the proposed licensee has to have made 'efforts to obtain authorization from the right holder on reasonable commercial terms and conditions' prior to the grant of the licence. Only after these efforts have failed 'within a reasonable period of time' may a compulsory licence be authorised. In other words, a prior negotiation with the patent holder is obligatory generally in the granting of a compulsory licence, although the terms 'reasonable commercial terms and conditions' and 'a reasonable period of time' leave room for interpretation.

Article 31(b) and (k) allows this requirement of prior negotiation to be waived in the case of a national emergency; other circumstances of extreme urgency; public, non-commercial use; or licences to remedy anti-competitive practices. As mentioned earlier, public health exigencies can represent national emergency or other circumstances of extreme urgency. Furthermore, when a government authorises its agency or contractor to use a patented drug to ensure access to the medicine within the public health service, the government can also waive a prior negotiation with the patent owner before authorising or proceeding with such government use.[43] However, it should be noted that even if the obligation of prior negotiation is waived, there remains an obligation on the government to notify the patent holder of the grant of the compulsory licence and to pay adequate remuneration in accordance with Article 31(b) and (h) respectively.

Scope and duration
Article 31(c) states that 'the scope and duration of such use shall be limited to the purpose for which it was authorized …'.

This provision implies that the purpose must be specified in the individual authorisation of a licence.

Non-exclusivity
Article 31(d) states that 'such use shall be non-exclusive'.

Under compulsory licences, a licensee cannot be granted an exclusive right to exploit a patented product in a particular territory. In other words, a patented product for which a compulsory licence has been granted may be marketed by the patent holder or other licensees as well in the same territory.

---

43 UNCTAD-ICTSD (n 9) 471.

Non-assignment

Article 31(e) states that 'such use shall be non-assignable, except with that part of the enterprise or goodwill which enjoys such use'.

This provision prevents the sale or transfer of a compulsory licence. However, the latter part of the provision indicates that it is permitted to assign and transfer the enterprise which has obtained the compulsory licence.[44]

Predominantly for the domestic market

Article 31(f) states that 'any such use shall be authorized predominantly for the supply of the domestic market of the Member authorizing such use'.

From a public health point of view, one of the most controversial conditions on a compulsory licence was Article 31(f) since this limitation may imply that a compulsory licence may not be authorised principally for export. If this is the case, countries with insufficient manufacturing capacities in pharmaceuticals could encounter a barrier to acquiring affordable medicines through importation. This limitation was eased by Article 31*bis*,[45] the first amendment to TRIPS which followed the adoption of paragraph 6 of the Doha Declaration, and was made by the WTO Decision of 30 August 2003. The section below entitled 'Compulsory Licensing: Countries with Few Manufacturing Capacities in the Pharmaceutical Sector' discusses in more detail how countries lacking manufacturing capacities in pharmaceuticals can utilise compulsory licences to ensure access to affordable medicines.

Termination of a compulsory licence

Article 31(g) states:

> [A]uthorization for such use shall be liable, subject to adequate protection of the legitimate interests of the persons so authorized, to be terminated if and when the circumstances which led to it cease to exist and are unlikely to recur. The competent authority shall have the authority to review, upon motivated request, the continued existence of these circumstances.

When there is a request that the circumstances which have triggered the grant of a compulsory licence cease to exist and are unlikely to recur, the provision stipulates that the competent authority must review the circumstances. However, even with the absence of the circumstances which a licence purports to address, the termination of the compulsory licence is subject to 'adequate protection of the legitimate interests' of the licensee. This proviso is important since if a licence could be terminated at any time, few would take the risk of undertaking the substantial investment needed in producing and marketing the product that is required if the compulsory licence is to be successful.[46]

---

44 Ibid., 473.

45 Agreed upon on 6 December 2005. The full content of Art. 31*bis* is available at http://www. wto.org/english/tratop_e/trips_e/wtl641_e.htm, last accessed 15 March 2015.

46 Correa (n 10) 322.

Adequate remuneration

Article 31(h) states that 'the right holder shall be paid adequate remuneration in the circumstances of each case, taking into account the economic value of the authorization'.

When granting a compulsory licence, adequate remuneration must be paid to the patent holder as one of the conditions.[47] The key question in this regard is what level of remuneration is 'adequate'. When a compulsory licence is pursued to promote access to medicines, the level of remuneration payable to the patent holder may affect the effectiveness of compulsory licences as a means for the stated aim. It is worthwhile examining separately this issue of adequate remuneration payable to the patent holder in a case of compulsory licensing for access to medicines. This will be done in the section entitled 'Adequate Remuneration for Compulsory Licences in the Context of Access to Medicines' below.

Review by judicial or other distinct higher authority

Article 31(i) states that 'the legal validity of any decision relating to the authorization of such use shall be subject to judicial review or other independent review by a distinct higher authority in that Member'.

Article 31(j) states that 'any decision relating to the remuneration provided in respect of such use shall be subject to judicial review or other independent review by a distinct higher authority in that Member'.

In accordance with the above provisions, a Member State has to provide the patent holder with the possibility of review by either judicial or other 'distinct higher authority' of the legal validity of any decision relating to the authorisation of a compulsory licence, as well as relating to the remuneration provided to the patent holder. These provisions have to be interpreted together with Article 44.2 of TRIPS regarding injunctions, which provides that, in the case of government use, remedies may be limited to 'payment of remuneration in accordance with sub-paragraph (h) of Article 31'. In other words, as long as a government-use licence is issued in a manner consistent with the requirements set out in Article 31 of TRIPS, it should not be subject to injunctive remedies.[48]

Adequate Remuneration for Compulsory Licences in the Context of Access to Medicines

As noted above under 'Adequate remuneration', one of the conditions for compulsory licences laid down by TRIPS is the payment of 'adequate remuneration' to the patent holder. The level of remuneration under compulsory licences generates considerable interests for all the parties involved: the patent holder, the third party or the government agency that are authorised to use the patented invention, as well as those who are intended to benefit from such use. Particularly when a compulsory licence is authorised as part of

---

47 According to Art. 31(k) of the TRIPS Agreement, if a compulsory licence is issued to remedy a situation where the patent holder has unfairly benefited, thus determined to be anti-competitive, the remuneration may accordingly be diminished. Abbott (n 28) 35.

48 UNCTAD-ICTSD (n 9) 478.

an effort to ensure access to affordable medicines for all, the level of remuneration payable to the patent holder can significantly impact on whether such an effort will achieve the desired result. The following section analyses the meaning of 'adequate remuneration' under Article 31(h)[49] of TRIPS in the context of a compulsory licence granted on the ground of promoting access to medicines.

General reading of Article 31(h) of TRIPS

According to Article 31(h), the adequacy of remuneration must be determined according to 'the circumstances of each case', and 'the economic value of the authorization' is another element of consideration. What level of remuneration can be considered 'adequate' in the circumstances of each case? What does 'the economic value of the authorization' mean and how much weight should be given to it? The ordinary meaning of the terms in the context of this provision should be sought for interpreting these requirements.

According to the *Oxford English Dictionary*, 'adequate' means 'satisfactory or acceptable in quality or quantity'.[50] The literal meaning of 'adequate', on its own, does not seem to give much guidance on the question as to when the level of remuneration is to be deemed consistent with TRIPS. '[A]dequate remuneration in the circumstances of each case' suggests that the adequate level of remuneration should be decided on a case-by-case basis. The circumstances of each case would consist of a range of factors, such as the purpose of a compulsory licence,[51] the duration and scope of the licence, the circumstances of the licensing country and of the licensee, if it is authorised to the third party.[52]

'[T]he economic value of the *authorization*' (emphasis added) also has to be taken into account in determining 'adequate remuneration'. The economic value referred to by the provision is contingent on 'the actual scope and purpose of the authorization'.[53] In order to clarify the meaning of 'the economic value of the authorization', consideration must be given to the context in which a compulsory licence is authorised, in accordance with the VCLT.[54] To be consistent with TRIPS, as discussed under 'Conditions on the Grant of Compulsory Licences', an authorisation of either a compulsory licence or government use must meet a set of conditions: it, *inter alia*, (i) must be 'limited to the purpose for which it is authorised' in terms of its scope and duration;[55] (ii) shall be non-exclusive[56] and (iii) non-assignable;[57] (iv) must be predominantly for the domestic

---

49 Article 31(h) 'the right holder shall be paid adequate remuneration in the circumstances of each case, taking into account the economic value of the authorization; …'.

50 *The Oxford English Dictionary*, Oxford University Press.

51 Antony Taubman, 'Rethinking TRIPS: "Adequate Remuneration" for Non-voluntary Patent Licensing' (2008) 11(4) *Journal of International Economic Law* 927–70, 953–4; Correa (n 10) 322.

52 Correa (n 10) 322.

53 Taubman (n 51) 954.

54 Article 31(1) of the VCLT states: 'A treaty is to be interpreted in good faith in accordance with the ordinary meaning to be given to the terms of the treaty in their context and in the light of its object and purpose.'

55 Article 31(c) of TRIPS.

56 Article 31(d) of TRIPS.

57 Article 31(e) of TRIPS.

market[58] unless it is in accordance with the Article 31*bis* procedure.[59] This means, among other things, that even in a case where a compulsory licence is granted for a patented product, the patent holder can continue to sell the patented product and economic loss incurred by the patent holder need not be significant,[60] depending on the factual situation surrounding the authorisation. As Taubman suggests, the value of the TRIPS-consistent authorisation of a compulsory licence is distinct from 'the full market value of the patent' and should be evaluated through considering the purpose, scope and duration of the authorisation.[61] In the end, 'the circumstances of each case' is significant, both in evaluating the economic value of the non-voluntary licence and ultimately in determining the level of adequate remuneration.

The ordinary meaning of the terms in Article 31(h) indicates that the adequacy of the remuneration to the patent holder should be assessed on a case-by-case basis. In other words, there is no absolute standard for determining an adequate level of remuneration applicable to every case. The adequate level of remuneration can vary depending on circumstances, including the economic value of authorisation. The purpose of the authorisation of compulsory licences necessarily constitutes the circumstances that need to be considered. The terms of Article 31(h) indicate that it is the licensing government that determines 'adequacy' of the remuneration to the patent holder, balancing societal objectives enshrined in Article 7.[62] Thus, broad discretion is permitted to WTO Member States in determining the level of remuneration, taking into account the circumstances that give rise to the need for compulsory licences and the economic value of the authorisation,[63] although the decision may be subject to review by a judicial or distinct higher authority of the country, as well as under the WTO Dispute Settlement procedure.[64]

Article 31(h) in the context of access to patented medicines

The following analysis of 'adequate remuneration' focuses on the context of compulsory licences that are granted for the purpose of increasing the availability of affordable medicines. As mentioned above, one of the factors defining 'the circumstances of each case' is the ground for compulsory licences. In this context, one of the key questions is

---

58 Article 31(f) of TRIPS.

59 Article 31*bis* of TRIPS.

60 Carlos M. Correa, 'Investment Protection in Bilateral and Free Trade Agreements: Implications for the Granting of Compulsory Licenses' (2004–2005) 26 *Michigan Journal of International Law* 331–53, 351.

61 Taubman (n 51) 954.

62 WTO Secretariat, TRIPS and Health: Frequently Asked Questions: Compulsory Licensing of Pharmaceuticals and TRIPS, available at http://www.wto.org/english/tratop_e/trips_e/public_health_faq_e.htm, last accessed 15 March 2015. Note that the note from the WTO Secretariat is not an official interpretation. Article IX:2 of the WTO Agreement states that the General Council can recommend interpretations binding upon all the Members.

63 UNCTAD-ICTSD (n 9) 475.

64 Article 31(j) of TRIPS 'any decision relating to the remuneration provided in respect of such use shall be subject to judicial review or other independent review by a distinct higher authority in that Member'.

how much weight the purpose of compulsory licences carries in determining the level of remuneration. In other words, should the level of remuneration in the case of compulsory licensing to address public health needs be different from when a compulsory licence is granted for purely economic purposes, for instance to allow domestic companies access to patented technology on more favourable terms? In order to answer this question, it is necessary to consider each factor that should be taken into account in determining the level of remuneration.

Economic value of the authorisation   The meaning of 'the economic value of the authorisation' under Article 31(h) can be understood in different ways, for instance the market value of the licence, i.e. a royalty rate that the patentee and the licensee would agree in a voluntary licence, the cost of research and development of a drug, and the medical benefit of a drug.

One approach would estimate 'the economic value of the authorisation' based on the market value of the licence, i.e. a royalty rate that the patentee and the licensee would agree in a voluntary licence. In estimating the market value of a particular licence, the scope and non-exclusive character of the licence, among other things, has to be considered. In accordance with the conditions for compulsory licensing set out in Article 31 of TRIPS, a compulsory licence does not exclude the patent holder from manufacturing and selling the patented item to a national market,[65] which indicates the existence of competitors. The size of the market for the licence is also another important factor in estimating the market value of the licence. For example, we can envisage a country where, despite significant needs for a particular drug, the demand for the drug is small because of a lack of purchasing power. Or we might find a country where there is vast income inequality among the population, and the drug produced under the compulsory licence is only made available to those who would not be able to access the drug otherwise, thus leaving the current commercial market for the patented drug intact. Therefore, the characteristics of the market for the licence are crucial in estimating the market value of the licence.

Some might estimate the economic value of the authorisation primarily based on research and development costs incurred by the patent holder, but also considering other relevant factors, such as the extent of the government funding (including tax benefits) used in the development of the medicine in question and the average revenue flowing from the medicine.[66] A significant challenge for this analysis arises from a methodological difficulty in obtaining all specific data necessary for it. The patent holder could be required to provide relevant data, although the provided information would need to be verified.

Alternatively, the economic value of the authorisation may be deduced from the benefits of new medicines. The benefits of new medicines can be measured in terms of their contribution to preventing premature death or improving the quality of life. Measuring 'the economic value of the authorisation' based on the benefits of medicines is not free from a general difficulty with valuing the benefits of medicines, e.g. the effect of new medicines on premature death or quality of life in monetary terms. Nevertheless, such cost-benefit

---

65 Article 31(d) of TRIPS; Taubman (n 51) 954.
66 UNCTAD-ICTSD (n 9) 476.

analysis of new medicines has been increasingly adopted by the governments of high-income countries as a useful decision-making tool 'to guide decisions about accepting such [pharmaceutical] products for reimbursement under their public programme, or to inform negotiations about pricing'.[67]

So far, different approaches to the meaning of 'the economic value of the authorisation' have been examined. This does not suggest that each approach is exclusive. A country may estimate 'the economic value of the authorisation' based on multiple factors, such as the market value of the licence, i.e. a royalty rate that the patentee and the licensee would agree in a voluntary licence, the cost of research and development of a drug, and the medical benefit of a drug. The text of TRIPS does not seem to favour one interpretation, leaving broad latitude to the WTO Member States in interpreting 'the economic value of the authorisation'. In any event, it has to be borne in mind that the economic value of the authorisation need only be 'taken into account'; it is not the sole factor in assessing adequate remuneration.

The circumstances of each case   The wording of Article 31(h) indicates that the level of remuneration deemed adequate may vary depending on the circumstances of each case. The economic value of the authorisation discussed above constitutes part of the circumstances of each case. Other factors that deserve consideration include the purpose of the compulsory licence, and the circumstances of the country where such non-voluntary use is authorised.

The WHO recommends a non-exhaustive list of factors that may be considered in determining the level of remuneration as follows:

> therapeutic value of the medicine, including the extent to which it represents an advance over other available products; the ability of the public to pay for the medicine; actual, documented expenditures on development of the medicine; the extent to which the invention benefited from publicly funded research; the need to respond to public health exigencies; the importance of the patented invention to the final product; cumulative global revenues and profitability of the invention; the need to remedy anti-competitive practices.[68]

This list reflects the economic value of the authorisation which can be represented by such factors as the benefits of the medicine in question, the costs of R&D, and the size of the particular market relative to the global one. But also it recommends that due regard be given to the ability to pay and to the public health needs existing in the licensing country. Although not every factor needs to be considered in any given situation, in general this formula suggests that while the costs of R&D for needed medicines should be shared via

---

67 See Michael Dickson, Jeremy Hurst and Stéphane Jacobzone, *Survey of Pharmacoeconomic Assessment Activity in Eleven Countries*, OECD Health Working Papers No. 4, DELSA/ELSA/WD/HEA (2003) para. 2.

68 WHO, Remuneration Guidelines for Non-voluntary Use of a Patent on Medical Technologies, WHO/TCM/2005.1, 83, available at http://www.who.int/medicines/areas/technical_cooperation/WHOTCM2005.1_OMS.pdf, last accessed 15 March 2015.

paying the remuneration to the patent holder, the level of remuneration should be adjusted to account for the income level of the licensing country and the relative burden of disease in the country.

Weight of public health needs and the ability to pay   This raises the question, how much weight should be given to such factors as the income level of the country and public health needs? A clue is provided by the Doha Declaration confirming that 'the Agreement can and should be interpreted and implemented in a manner supportive of WTO Members' right to protect public health and, in particular, to promote access to medicines for all'.[69] Therefore, the remuneration payable to the patent holder has to be set at a level which does not undermine access to essential medicines. The WHO remuneration guidelines pronounce that 'the policy objective of promoting access to medicines is central to the decision regarding the general level of remuneration and proposals for royalties that undermine access goals should be rejected'.[70] In other words, where access to medicines is restricted by the price and a compulsory licence is used to address pressing public health needs, 'the government could justify the payment of a minimal royalty on grounds that the public interest in the circumstances of the case warrants a reduced royalty'.[71]

In addition, the 'adequacy' of remuneration should vary in accordance with the income level of countries, in a manner conducive to an equitable sharing of the costs of R&D. As mentioned earlier, this factor should also be reflected in considering 'the economic value of the authorisation' since low-income countries are likely to represent a small percentage of the global market of the patented medicine and a voluntary licensee has little chance to make much profit in low-income countries. It is inconceivable that the level of remuneration is determined with no account of the income level of countries.

This reading of Article 31(h) places significant weight on the public health ground for compulsory licences, as well as the relative ability to pay, among other factors in determining the level of remuneration. Conversely, in cases where a compulsory licence is issued to achieve an industrial policy objective, 'the economic value of the authorisation' might carry more weight than in the case of a public health purpose-compulsory licence.[72]

Practical implications
There are a number of remuneration guidelines on compulsory licensing.[73] The 2001 UNDP Human Development Report suggests that a base royalty rate be set at 4 per cent of the price of the product under the licence and be increased or decreased by as much as up to two percentage points, depending on factors such as the particular therapeutic value of the product and the role of public funds in research and development.[74] The 2005

---

69 Paragraph 4 (n 14).

70 WHO (n 68) 63.

71 UNCTAD-ICTSD (n 9) 477.

72 UNCTAD-ICTSD (n 9) 477; Taubman (n 51) 962–3.

73 WHO (n 68) 68–74.

74 UNDP, *Human Development Report 2001: Making New Technologies Work for Human Development* (2001) 108.

Canadian government royalty guidelines for compulsory licences for international humanitarian purposes provide a sliding scale of 0.02 per cent to 4 per cent of the price of the product under the licence, based on the ranking of importing countries on the UN Human Development Index.[75] The Tiered Royalty Method (TRM) proposes a standard royalty rate of 4 per cent based on the price of the patented product in high-income countries, and that this base royalty be adjusted for each country upwards or downwards, considering 'relative per capita income or, where there is an unusually high incidence of a disease, the relative national income per person needing treatment'.[76] All the above guidelines take account of the ability of the public to pay in a particular country, regardless of different methods employed for this purpose. The differences among the above guidelines lie in whether and to what degree each formula considers factors such as the therapeutic value of the medicine, the degree of burden of diseases for the country, the role of public funds in R&D for the medicine, and the importance of the patented invention to the final product.

The actual practice undertaken within national jurisdictions can also provide some indications over how 'adequate remuneration' under Article 31(h) is interpreted and implemented.[77] Recent State practice of compulsory licensing on HIV/AIDS drugs shows that the royalty rates range between 0.5 per cent (Indonesia and Thailand), 1.5 per cent (Brazil), 2 per cent (Mozambique), 2.5 per cent (Zambia) and 4 per cent (Malaysia).[78] When exporting HIV/AIDS drugs to Rwanda, Canada set the royalty at 2 per cent.[79] For compulsory licensing on several cancer drugs, Thailand set the royalties at 3–5 per cent.[80] There was no reported protest by other States at these decisions of the licensing countries, nor complaint under the WTO procedure. It suggests that varying levels of 'adequate' remuneration payable to the patent holder across countries, taking into account the income level of the country and the public health grounds, are generally validated.

---

75 Section 21.8 of the Bill C-9 – An Act to Amend the Patent Act and the Food and Drugs Act (The Jean Chrétien Pledge to Africa), assented to 14 May 2004 and entered into force in May 2005; Section 8 of SOR/2005-143, Use of Patented Products for International Humanitarian Purposes Regulations, May 10, 2005, *Canada Gazette*, vol. 139, No. 11. Available at http://laws-lois.justice. gc.ca/eng/regulations/sor-2005-143/index.html last accessed 15 March 2015.

76 WHO (n 68) 73–4.

77 It may not be considered as a formal source of law, constituting 'subsequent practice in the application of treaty which establishes the agreement of the parties regarding its interpretation', since the WTO Dispute Settlement Body tends to set a comparatively high threshold for State practice as a source of law; in *Japan – Taxes on Alcoholic Beverages*, the Appellate Body stated that '[a]n isolated act is generally not sufficient to establish subsequent practice; it is a sequence of acts establishing the agreement of the parties that is relevant'. Article 31.3(b) of the VCLT. *Japan – Taxes on Alcoholic Beverages* (n 4) 13.

78 WHO, Briefing Note: Country Experiences in Using TRIPS Safeguards (February 2008) 3, available at http://searo.who.int/entity/intellectual_property/IPT_Briefing_note_country_ experiences.pdf last accessed 15 March 2015.

79 Ibid.

80 Ibid.

Sub-conclusion

Striking a fair balance between the private interests of the patent holder and the unmet health needs of the public is crucial in determining the level of 'adequate remuneration'. Interpretive insights in the balancing exercise can be sought from Articles 7 and 8.1 of TRIPS, and the Doha Declaration. It is clear from the text of TRIPS that this balancing exercise has to take place at the national level. In this sense, wide discretion is given to national authorities in determining remuneration payable to the patent holder when issuing a compulsory licence, although it is subject to potential review by means of the WTO Dispute Settlement mechanism. The WTO Secretariat also notes that 'the authority in the country concerned' 'decides whether the payment is "adequate"', subject to the right to appeal of the patent owner in that country.[81]

In a circumstance where a compulsory licence is issued for the purpose of increasing access to affordable medicines, the national authority should exercise discretion in determining the level of remuneration in a manner that facilitates fulfilling the purpose of the licence. Therefore, in this context, public health needs and the ability of the public to pay for the medicine should be regarded as the most important factors for determining the level of remuneration payable to the patent holder.

A Case Study: The Grant of Compulsory Licence (Government Use) in Thailand

According to a 2012 study, there were 24 attempts to issue compulsory licences to increase access to medicines by WTO Member States from 2001 to 6 June 2011.[82] The large majority brought about price reduction of the relevant pharmaceutical product for the State in question, whether by means of resultant compulsory licence, negotiated voluntary licence or discount. Those countries that issued compulsory licences include Brazil, Egypt, Malaysia, Zimbabwe, Zambia, Ghana, Indonesia, Thailand and Ecuador.[83] While most countries issued their compulsory licences for drugs for treating HIV/AIDS, Thailand took a more broad approach by authorising compulsory licences on not only HIV/AIDS treatments, but also drugs for heart disease and cancers.[84] Thailand's broad use of compulsory licences carries significant importance in promoting public health in developing countries, given a major epidemiological transition that has taken place in low- and middle-income countries. Recent data show that non-communicable or chronic diseases, such as cardiovascular disease, diabetes, cancer, and mental and neurological conditions, account for almost as large a share of the burden of diseases in developing countries as do communicable diseases and maternal, perinatal and nutritional conditions, exposing developing countries to the double burden of disease.[85]

---

81 See WTO Secretariat (n 62).

82 Reed Beall and Randall Kuhn, 'Trends in Compulsory Licensing of Pharmaceuticals Since the Doha Declaration: A Database Analysis' (2012) 9(1) *PloS Medicine.*

83 Ibid. WHO (n 78).

84 Brent Savoie, 'Thailand's Test: Compulsory Licensing in an Era of Epidemiologic Transition' (2007) 48(1) *Virginia Journal of International Law* 211–48; Ho (n 29).

85 Dele O Abegunde et al., 'The Burden and Costs of Chronic Diseases in Low-Income and Middle-Income Countries' (2007) 370 *The Lancet* 1029–38; Stephen Matlin, 'Introduction: Poverty,

While efforts have to be made to encourage health behaviours that prevent chronic diseases, the importance of treatment using medicines cannot be underestimated.[86] However, the price of medicines for chronic diseases often places a barrier to access to such medicines in developing countries due to 'the constraints on public funds available for pharmaceutical therapies for chronic diseases and the limited purchasing power of consumers'.[87] It is widely known that patents play a critical role in the pricing of medicines. In this context, the examination of Thailand's experiences can shed light on the extent of opportunities to enhance access to medicines that compulsory licences under TRIPS can provide.[88]

Access to medicines in Thailand

According to the World Bank's criteria, Thailand is a lower middle-income country with a GNI (Gross National Income) per capita of US $3,670 in 2008.[89] In 2001, the Thai government introduced health care reforms, including the '30 Baht treat all' scheme (later, the Universal Health Coverage Scheme) under which registered members pay 30 Baht (£0.50, $0.86) each time they access health care services.[90] As a result of this health care reform, the coverage of health care insurance extended from about 40 per cent of the population (25 million people) in 2001 to 95.5 per cent (59.8 million) by 2004.[91] Ensuring universal access to health care is mandated by the Thai Constitution, which provides that '[a] person shall enjoy an equal right to receive standard public health service, and the indigent shall have the right to receive free medical treatment

---

Equity and Health Research' in *Global Forum Update on Research for Health*, vol. 2: Poverty, Equity and Health Research, 10–3, available at http://announcementsfiles.cohred.org/gfhr_pub/assoc/ s14810e/s14810e.pdf, last accessed 15 March 2015; Alan Lopez and Colin Mathers, 'Inequities in Health Status: Findings from the 2001 Global Burden of Disease Study', *Global Forum Update on Research for Health, vol. 4: Equitable Access: Research Challenges for Health in Developing Countries*, 163–75, 167–9; WHO, *Report of the Commission on Public Health, Innovation and Intellectual Property Rights* (2006) 3.

86 WHO, *Preventing Chronic Diseases: A Vital Investment* (2005) 48–9, 108, available at http:// www.who.int/chp/chronic_disease_report/en/, last accessed 15 March 2015.

87 Savoie (n 84) 223–4.

88 For related issues that are not limited to the case of Thailand, see Kevin Outterson, 'Should Access to Medicines and TRIPS Flexibilities be Limited to Specific Diseases?' (2008) 34 *American Journal of Law & Medicine* 279–301.

89 See country classifications by the World Bank, available at http://data.worldbank.org/ about/country-classifications/country-and-lending-groups#Lower_middle_income, last accessed 15 March 2015. The 2008 world GNI per capita is US $8,654. See the World Bank data, available at http://databank.worldbank.org/data/home.aspx, last accessed 15 March 2015.

90 Adrian Towse, Anne Mills and Viroj Tangcharoensathien, 'Learning from Thailand's Health Reforms' (2004) 328 *British Medical Journal* 103–5, 103.

91 David Hughes and Songkramchai Leethongdee, 'Universal Coverage in the Land of Smiles: Lessons from Thailand's 30 Baht Health Reforms' (2007) 36(4) *Health Affairs* 999–1008, 1001. The data cited in this article is based on P. Jongudomsuk (ed.), *NHSO Annual Report 2004: Implementation of Universal Health Care Coverage*, S.P.S. Printing Co. Ltd. (2004).

from the State's infirmary'.[92] Furthermore, section 5 of the National Health Security Act of 2002 states that '[t]he Thai population shall be entitled to a health service with such standards and efficiency as prescribed in this Act'[93] and stipulates such entitlements in the subsequent sections of the Act. The Thai government states that Thai citizens are entitled to access to essential medicines by way of being covered by one of the public health insurance schemes, i.e. the Civil Servant Medical Benefit Scheme, the Social Security Scheme, and the Universal Health Coverage Scheme (formerly referred to as the '30 Baht Scheme').[94]

In accordance with the constitutional right and the related provision in the National Health Security Act, every Thai citizen is entitled to access to all medications on the national essential medicines list.[95] In 2003, the Thai government also pledged to expand the provision of antiretroviral treatments (ARVs) to all eligible Thai people living with HIV/AIDS. This is the origin of the National Access to Antiretroviral Program for People living with HIV/AIDS (NAPHA).[96] The 2005 review, conducted by the WHO jointly with the Ministry of Public Health, noted that '[t]he per capita health budget allocation increased from 700 baht [£14.12] in 2001 to 1,396 Baht [£28.17] in 2005, [and] will rise further to 1,650 Baht in 2006'.[97] The Thai government in 2007 stated that the public health budget increased from about '4 per cent of the overall national budget in the 1980s to 7 per cent in the 1990s and now to more than 10 per cent'.[98] The budget for the universal access to ARVs also saw more than a tenfold increase in six years, from around US$10 million in 2001 to more than US$100 million in 2007.[99] Thailand's NAPHA enabled more

92 Article 51 of the Constitution of the Kingdom of Thailand 2007, available at http://www.asianlii.org/th/legis/const/2007/1.html#C03P09, last accessed 15 March 2015. This provision was similarly included in Art. 52 of the 1997 Constitution: 'A person shall enjoy an equal right to receive standard public health service, and the indigent shall have the right to receive free medical treatment from public health centres of the State, as provided by law.' Available at http://www.asianlii.org/th/legis/const/1997/1.html#S006, last accessed 15 March 2015.

93 Available at http://www.nhso.go.th/eng/Files/Userfiles/file/Thailand_NHS_Act.pdf, last accessed 15 March 2015.

94 Thai Ministry of Public Health and the National Health Security Office, Facts and Evidences on the 10 Burning Issues related to the Government Use of Patents on Three Patented Essential Drugs in Thailand (February 2007), available at http://www.moph.go.th/hot/White%20Paper%20CL-EN.pdf, last accessed 15 March 2015.

95 Ibid.

96 For Thailand's development of universal access to ARVs, see Sanchai Chasombat, Cheewanan Lertpiriyasuwat, Sombat Thanprasertsuk, Laksami Suebsaeng and Ying Ru Lo, 'The National Access to Antiretroviral Program for PHA (NAPHA) in Thailand' (2006) 37(4) *The Southeast Asian Journal of Tropical Medicine and Public Health* 704–15, 706.

97 WHO Regional Office for South-East Asia and the Ministry of Public Health, *External Review of the Health Sector Response to HIV/AIDS in Thailand* (2005). The bank exchange rate of 25 April 2010 is used here by this author to represent the equivalent value in British Pounds; 1 GBP is about 49.55 Thai Baht.

98 Thai Ministry of Public Health and the National Health Security Office (n 95) 2.

99 Ibid.

than 80,000 people to access ARVs by the end of 2006, and the speed with which the provision of ARVs was scaled up was considered remarkable.[100]

However, the high costs of medicines placed an obstacle in the way of the government's efforts.[101] One prominent issue concerned the provision of second-line ARV treatment, for those who have started to develop resistance to first-line treatments. According to the Thai government, around 10 per cent of the 500,000 people living with HIV/AIDS are expected to develop drug resistance.[102] A World Bank study, undertaken jointly with the Thai Ministry of Public Health, estimated that the potential financial burden that would result from the inclusion of second-line, as well as first-line, ARV treatment would be substantial: '[t]he total cost of NAPHA [National Access to Antiretroviral Programs for People living with HIV/AIDS] with second-line therapy reaches a ceiling at US$500 million (B 20 billion) per year in 2008. Beginning in 2010, expenditures on second-line therapy account for more than one-half of total ART spending'.[103] The World Bank study suggested a few policy options for the Thai government: one way to reduce the fiscal burden is to limit the NAPHA to first-line treatment only; another option is 'to grant compulsory licenses for the manufacture of patented second-line pharmaceutical products'.[104] By the grant of compulsory licences, the World Bank estimated that the cost of second-line treatment would be reduced by 90 per cent.[105]

Compulsory licensing of patented medicines
From 2006 to 2008, the Thai government authorised government use of seven patented medicines, i.e. two HIV/AIDS drugs, one anti-platelet medicine, and four cancer drugs, in accordance with section 51 of the Thai Patent Act. The rationale for the government use is to fulfil the mandate to achieve universal access to essential medicines for all Thai people under the Thai Constitution and the National Health Security Act 2002.[106] Section 51 of Thailand's Patent Act permits the government use of patents to 'carry out any

---

100 Ana Revenga, Mead Over, Emiko Masaki, Wiwat Peerapatanapokin, Julian Gold, Viroj Tangcharoensathien and Sombat Thanprasertsuk, *The Economics of Effective AIDS Treatment: Evaluating Policy Options for Thailand*, World Bank, August 2006, available at http://siteresources. worldbank.org/INTEAPREGTOPHIVAIDS/Resources/TH_economics_of_AIDS_full_report. pdf, last accessed 15 March 2015.

101 Thai Ministry of Public Health and the National Health Security Office (n 95) 2; Hughes and Leethongdee (n 91) 1000.

102 Thai Ministry of Public Health and the National Health Security Office (n 95) 14.

103 Revenga, Over, Masaki, Peerapatanapokin, Gold, Tangcharoensathien, and Thanprasertsuk (n 100) 166.

104 Ibid., 169–70.

105 Ibid., 169.

106 Thai Ministry of Public Health and the National Health Security Office (n 95) 1; Thai Ministry of Public Health and the National Health Security Office, The 10 Burning Questions on the Government Use of Patents on the Four Anti-cancer Drugs in Thailand (February 2008) 2, available at http://www.moph.go.th/hot/White%20paper%20CL%20II%20FEB%2008-ENG. pdf, last accessed 15 March 2015.

service for public consumption or which is of vital importance to the defence of the country or for the preservation or realization of natural resources or the environment or to prevent or relieve a severe shortage of food, drugs or other consumption items or for any other public service'.[107] The government use can be exercised by 'any ministry, bureau or department of the Government, by themselves or through others'.[108]

There existed a demand for compulsory licensing of patented medicines as early as 1999. In December 1999, Thai people living with HIV/AIDS (PLWHA) and NGOs took part in a massive demonstration to demand that the Thai Ministry of Public Health issue a compulsory licence on an ARV drug, *Didanosine* (ddl), the tablet form of which is patented by British Myer Squibb (BMS).[109] However, no compulsory licence was issued on any patented medicines by the Thai government until 2006.

In November 2006, the government authorised a government-use licence to the Government Pharmaceutical Organization (GPO) on a first-line antiretroviral drug, *Efavirenz*, which is patented and sold by Merck under the brand name *Stocrin*.[110] The government explained that *Efavirenz* is an ARV with very low side-effects, but, due to its high price induced by patent protection, the government could not afford to provide all eligible patients with *Efavirenz*.[111] The government use would 'significantly make the drug more accessible under the national health insurance schemes', according to a government statement.[112] In January 2007, the government announced that it authorised a government-use licence on a combined formulation of *Lopinavir* and *Ritonavir*, patented and sold by Abbott under the brand name *Kaletra*.[113] This drug is a second-line ARV drug for patients who develop resistance to basic formulations of ARVs. According to the Thai government, at least 50,000 of the 500,000 people living with HIV/AIDS in Thailand would need second-line ARVs in the near future.[114] The government justified its government-use licence on the ground that the high cost of *Kaletra* restricted access to this medicine under the National Health Security Schemes, and domestic production or importing of the medicine under the government use would increase access to this drug

---

107 Section 51 of Thailand's Patent Act B.E. 2522 (A.D. 1979) as amended by the Patent Act (No. 3) B.E. 2542 (A.D. 1999), reprinted in Thai Ministry of Public Health and the National Health Security Office (n 95) 30.

108 Ibid.

109 Jakkrit Kuanpoth, 'TRIPS-Plus Intellectual Property Rules: Impact on Thailand's Public Health' (2006) 9(5) *The Journal of World Intellectual Property* 573–91, 575.

110 Notification of the Department of Disease Control, Ministry of Public Health regarding Exercising of Right under Drugs and Pharmaceuticals Products Patent, 29 November 2006, reprinted in Thai Ministry of Public Health and the National Health Security Office (n 95) 38.

111 Ibid.

112 Ministry of Public Health, a Letter to MSD Company (a subsidiary of Merck), reprinted in Thai Ministry of Public Health and the National Health Security Office (n 95) 47–8.

113 Notification of the Department of Disease Control, Ministry of Public Health, Re: Exercising of Right under Drugs and Pharmaceuticals Products Patent for Combined Formulation of Lopinavir and Ritonavir, 24 January 2007, reprinted in Thai Ministry of Public Health and the National Health Security Office (n 95) 14, 41–3.

114 Thai Ministry of Public Health and the National Health Security Office (n 95) 14.

so as to allow the treatment of 8,000 more people within the same budget.[115] At the same time, a government-use licence was issued for *Clopiodogrel*, an anti-platelet drug useful for treating heart disease, which is marketed in Thailand by Sanofi-Aventis under the brand name *Plavix*.[116] According to the licence, heart disease is one of the top three causes of death in Thailand, but the high price of this medicine resulted in limited access within the National Health Security Schemes.[117] High incidence of heart disease among Thai people requires medicines for treatment, as well as preventive measures for heart disease, the government argued.[118]

In January 2008, government-use licences were issued on four cancer drugs: *Docetexel* (trade name *Taxotere*), a drug for treating lung and breast cancer; *Letrozole* (trade name *Femara*), used against breast cancer; a lung cancer drug, *Erlotinib* (trade name *Tarceva*); and *imatinib* (trade name *Glivec*) for treating leukaemia and gastrointestinal cancer.[119] The government stated that the ground for the government use is 'to allow universal access to essential medicines by all the beneficiaries of the National Health Security System, which are all publicly financed schemes'.[120] According to the government, cancer is one of the leading causes of death among Thai people.[121] In particular, lung and breast cancers are the most common types of cancer in Thailand. But most new cancer drugs are patented and, due to the high price of those medicines, they were not covered by the National Health Security System. Consequently, many people, not only the poor, were not able to access those cancer drugs. Moreover, people who pay the cost out of pocket would be likely to experience serious financial difficulties. The government argued that compulsory licensing of the four cancer drugs would make these essential drugs available 'at prices ranging from 4 to more than 30 times lower than the patented products', and thus enable the National Health Security Schemes to provide the drugs to all who need them.[122] In the case of *imatinib* (trade name *Glivec*), as a result of continued negotiations, the patent holder, Novartis, agreed to provide free access to *Glivec* to patients under the Universal Health Coverage Scheme (formerly, the 30 Baht Scheme), one of the National Health Security Schemes that covers about three-quarters of the Thai population.[123]

---

115 Notification of the Department of Disease Control, Ministry of Public Health (n 113).

116 Notification of the Ministry of Public Health, Re: Exercising of Right under Drugs and Pharmaceutical Products Patent for Clopidogrel, 25 January 2007, reprinted in Thai Ministry of Public Health and the National Health Security Office (n 95) 44–6.

117 Ibid.

118 Ibid.

119 Thai Ministry of Public Health and the National Health Security Office (n 106) 2.

120 Ibid.

121 Ibid.

122 Ibid.

123 Letter from Novartis to Minister of Public Health, Mongkol Na Songkhla, Re: CML and GIST Patient Access to Glivec, 23 January 2008, reprinted in Thai Ministry of Public Health and the National Health Security Office (n 106); Notification of the Ministry of Public Health, Re: Exercising of Right on Pharmaceuticals Products Patent for Imatinib, 25 January 2008, reprinted in Thai Ministry of Public Health and the National Health Security Office (n 106) 34–5; See Ed Silverman, 'Novartis Strikes Deal With Thailand over Gleevec', *Pharmalot* (31 January 2008).

Compliance with TRIPS

While Thailand's compulsory licences met criticisms from pharmaceutical companies[124] and pressure from the United States Trade Representative (USTR) and the European Commission,[125] no legal dispute in this respect was brought to the WTO dispute mechanism. Instead, the US placed Thailand on the Priority Watch List, referring to 'an overall deterioration in the protection and enforcement of intellectual property rights'.[126] The USTR explicitly acknowledged 'a country's ability to issue such licenses in accordance with WTO rules' in the 2007 Special 301 report.[127] Nevertheless, the report claimed that 'the lack of transparency and due process exhibited in Thailand represents a serious concern'. In July 2007, Peter Mandelson, the European Trade Commissioner, sent a letter to Thailand's Minister of Commerce, Krirk-krai Jirapaet, stating that '[n]either TRIPS nor the Doha Declaration appear to justify a systematic policy of applying compulsory licenses wherever medicines exceed certain prices' referring to the government use on *Clopiodogrel* (an anti-platelet drug, trade name *Plavix*).[128] In a letter dated 21 February 2008, Mandelson expressed concerns over the decision to authorise the government-use licences on cancer drugs, and urged the Thai government to review this policy.[129] In contrast, in July 2007, the European Parliament passed a resolution on TRIPS and Access to Medicines that '[e]ncourages the developing countries to use all means available to them under TRIPS, such as compulsory licences ...'.[130]

Are the criticisms of Thailand's compulsory licences grounded in TRIPS? Article 31, the provision on compulsory licences, has been discussed in earlier sections. It is worthwhile examining the compliance of Thailand's compulsory licences with Article 31.

Grounds for compulsory licences   Thailand's compulsory licences were issued in accordance with section 51 of the Thai Patent Act, which permits the government use of patents for public non-commercial use. 'Public non-commercial use' is explicitly

---

124 See PhRMA Press Release, Protecting Patent Rights in Thailand, 1 December 2006; PhRMA Press Release, PhRMA Response to 2007 Special 301 Report, 30 April 2007, available at http://phrma.org, last accessed 7 April 2014.

125 Office of the United States Trade Representative, 2007 Special 301 Report, at 27, available at http://www.ustr.gov/sites/default/files/asset_upload_file230_11122.pdf, last accessed 15 March 2015; Letter from Commissioner for External Trade, Peter Mandelson, to Thai Minister of Commerce Krirk-krai Jirapaet (10 July 2007), available at http://www.wcl.american.edu/pijip/thai_comp_licenses.cfm, last accessed 15 March 2015.

126 Office of the United States Trade Representative (n 125).

127 Ibid.

128 Letter from European Commissioner for External Trade, Peter Mandelson, to Thai Minister of Commerce Krirk-krai Jirapaet (n 125)

129 Letter from European Commissioner for External Trade, Peter Mandelson to Thai Minister of Commerce, Mingkwan Saengsuwan (21 February 2008), available at http://www.ip-watch.org/files/Peter_Mandelson_letter_Febr_21_2008_to_Thai_Minister_of_Commerce.pdf, last accessed 15 March 2015.

130 See http://www.europarl.europa.eu/sides/getDoc.do?pubRef=-//EP//TEXT+TA+P6-TA-2007-0353+0+DOC+XML+V0//EN, last accessed 15 March 2015.

acknowledged as an example of grounds for compulsory licences in Article 31 of TRIPS. The government stated that the decisions to authorise the government use of the patented medicines are to help achieve universal access to essential medicines for all Thai people through its National Health Security Schemes.[131] Under the licences, the Ministry of Public Health authorised the GPO to exercise the public use of the aforementioned patented medicines.[132] The GPO is entrusted to procure all the medicines under the government-use provision and to supply them to hospitals contracted with the National Health Security System.[133] Neither TRIPS nor section 51 of the Thai Patent Act requires the existence of an emergency situation as a prerequisite for a compulsory licence.[134]

Subject matter   Another question may be whether compulsory licences have to be restricted to particular diseases. In other words, are Thailand's compulsory licences on an anti-platelet drug or four anti-cancer drugs in breach of TRIPS? No restriction on the subject matter for compulsory licences is found in the text. Abbott and Reichman note that '[t]he suggestion that treatments for heart disease exceed a state's right to grant a compulsory license conflicts directly with TRIPS, the Doha Declaration and the August 30 Decision [2003 WTO Decision]'.[135] Kevin Outterson also finds it clear that 'the controlling legal texts do not limit the use of TRIPS flexibilities to any particular set of diseases'.[136]

Individual merit   According to the Thai government, the individual merit of each drug was examined against a set of criteria: the price of a drug has to be too high for the government to provide it to the beneficiaries of the National Health Security Schemes, and the drug has to be on the national essential medicines list, or should be necessary for any of the following situations, e.g. important public health problems; emergency or extreme urgency; the prevention and control of outbreaks/epidemic/pandemics; life saving.[137] Such practice is consistent with Article 31(a) of TRIPS, which requires authorisation of such use to be considered on its individual merits.

Prior negotiations   Article 31(b) of TRIPS and section 51 of the Thai Patent Act waive an obligation of prior negotiation with the patent holder in the case of public,

---

131 Thai Ministry of Public Health and the National Health Security Office (n 95) 1–2; Thai Ministry of Public Health and the National Health Security Office (n 106) 2.

132 Notification of the Department of Disease Control (nn 110, 113); Notification of the Ministry of Public Health (n 116); Thai Ministry of Public Health and the National Health Security Office (n 106) 14.

133 Thai Ministry of Public Health and the National Health Security Office (n 106) 14.

134 Article 31 of the TRIPS Agreement; section 51 of the Thai Patent Act; See also Sean Flynn, *Analysis of Thai Law on Government Use Licenses*, available at http://www.wcl.american.edu/pijip/thai_comp_licenses.cfm, last accessed 15 March 2015.

135 Frederick M. Abbott and Jerome H. Reichman, 'The Doha Round's Public Health Legacy: Strategies for the Production and Diffusion of Patented Medicines under the Amended TRIPS Provisions' [2007] *Journal of International Economic Law* 921–87, 956.

136 Outterson (n 88) 283.

137 Thai Ministry of Public Health and the National Health Security Office (n 95) 11.

non-commercial use, as well as in the case of a national emergency or other circumstances of extreme urgency.[138] Instead, the government is required to 'notify the patentee in writing without delay' under section 51 of the Thai Patent Act and to inform the patent holder promptly 'where the government or contractor, without making a patent search, knows or has demonstrable grounds to know that a valid patent is or will be used by or for the government' under Article 31(b) of TRIPS. As all seven compulsory licences were issued for public, non-commercial purpose under section 51 of the Patent Act, the government was not required to conduct prior negotiations.

The first three compulsory licences in 2006 and 2007 were issued without prior negotiation. Although there had been unsuccessful attempts to negotiate price reductions from the patent holders between 2005 and 2006, no specific reference had been made to the possibility of compulsory licensing.[139] With regard to the 2008 compulsory licences on cancer drugs, the Committee to Negotiate for the Price of Essential Patented Drugs, upon the request of the Minister of Public Health, undertook a series of negotiations with the patent holders of each drug prior to the announcement of the government use.[140]

Scope and duration   Article 31(c) requires the scope and duration of a compulsory licence to be limited to the purpose for the authorisation of a licence. Each of Thailand's compulsory licences states its scope and duration, which is specifically limited to the authorised purpose, and which is consistent with TRIPS. According to the government, all the drugs licensed under the government use are procured by the GPO and only supplied to hospitals contracted to the National Health Security Schemes.[141] The government stressed that the medicines supplied under the government-use licences would not be used for commercial purposes.[142]

What follows is the scope and duration of each compulsory licence. The licence on *Efavirenz* is to provide an effective ARV drug having fewer side-effects to all who need

---

138   Article 31(b) states that 'such use may only be permitted if, prior to such use, the proposed user has made efforts to obtain authorization from the right holder on reasonable commercial terms and conditions and that such efforts have not been successful within a reasonable period of time. This requirement may be waived by a Member in the case of a national emergency or other circumstances of extreme urgency or in cases of public non-commercial use. … In the case of public non-commercial use, where the government or contractor, without making a patent search, knows or has demonstrable grounds to know that a valid patent is or will be used by or for the government, the right holder shall be informed promptly.'
Section 51 of the Thai Patent Act provides that 'any ministry, bureau or department of the Government … shall notify the patentee in writing without delay, notwithstanding the provisions of Section 46, 47 and 47*bis*'. In the case of compulsory licences for commercial purposes, section 47 of the Thai Patent Act requires the application for a licence to 'show that he has made an effort to obtain a license from the patentee having proposed conditions and remuneration reasonably sufficient under the circumstances but unable to reach an agreement within a reasonable period'.
139   Thai Ministry of Public Health and the National Health Security Office (n 95) 5–7, 69–83.
140   Thai Ministry of Public Health and the National Health Security Office (n 106) 4–5.
141   Ibid., 14.
142   Ibid.

it within the public health system. For this purpose, the licence is limited to no more than 200,000 patients who are covered by either the National Health Security System Act, B.E. 2545 (2002), the Social Security Act, B.E. 2533 (1990) or the Medical Benefits for Civil Servants and Government Employees Scheme. It was due to expire in December 2011, and extended until August 2013[143] The number of people living with HIV/AIDS in Thailand is more than 500,000.[144] The compulsory licence on a combined formulation of *Lopinavir* and *Ritonavir* is to increase access to an effective second-line ARV for patients who develop resistance to first-line HIV/AIDS drugs. Accordingly, the licence is for no more than 250,000 patients who are entitled to access to essential medicines under any of the three above-mentioned National Health Security Schemes, and is due to expire in 2021 after an extension in 2010.[145] The compulsory licence on *Clopidogrel (Plavix)* is to increase access to this medicine so as to fulfil the mandate to ensure universal access to essential medicines. The licence is limited to the provision of this medicine to those who are covered by the three National Health Security Schemes, and is valid until the patent expires or no essential need for this medicine exists.[146]

The compulsory licences on four cancer drugs are to enable the National Health Security Schemes to provide universal access to these drugs without undue financial burden. Each of the licences stated that the scope is limited to the provision of the drug in question to those who are covered by one of the three National Health Security Schemes, and it is valid either until the patent expires or until the essential need ceases to exist, as with the licence on *Clopidogrel*, an anti-platelet drug.[147] In fact, in the case of the licence on *imatinib*, since the patent holder, Novartis, agreed to provide its product at no cost for all patients under the Universal Health Coverage Scheme, and thus no further essential need was considered to exist any longer, the government amended the licence so that it would be given effect only when the offer from Novartis is terminated.[148]

Adequate remuneration   Article 31(h) of TRIPS requires adequate remuneration to be paid to the patent holder. As discussed under 'Conditions on the Grant of Compulsory Licences' and 'Adequate Remuneration for Compulsory Licences in the Context of Access to Medicines', the licensing country determines the level of remuneration in the case of

143 Notification of the Department of Disease Control (n 110); *The Nation*, 'NHSO wants licence extended for two Aids drugs' (15 June 2010).

144 Notification of the Department of Disease Control (n 110).

145 Notification of the Department of Disease Control (n 113); *The Nation* (n 143).

146 Notification of the Ministry of Public Health (n 116).

147 Notification of the Ministry of Public Health, Re: Exercising of Right on Pharmaceuticals Products Patent for Docetaxel, 4 January 2008; Notification of the Ministry of Public Health, Re: Exercising of Right on Pharmaceuticals Products Patent for Letrozole, 4 January 2008; Notification of the Ministry of Public Health, Re: Exercising of Right on Pharmaceuticals Products Patent for Erlotinib, 4 January 2008; Notification of the Ministry of Public Health, Re: Exercising of Right under Drugs and Pharmaceuticals Products Patent for Imatinib, 4 January 2008, reprinted in Thai Ministry of Public Health and the National Health Security Office (n 106) 34–5.

148 Notification of the Ministry of Public Health, Re: Exercising of Right on Pharmaceuticals Products Patent for Imatinib (n 147).

compulsory licences, subject to independent review in the country following an appeal by the patent holder and under the WTO Dispute Settlement procedure. Section 51 of the Thai Patent Act also states that 'paying a royalty to the patentee or his exclusive licensee' is a condition upon the government use. It also provides that '[t]he royalty rate shall be as agreed upon by the ministry or bureau or department and the patentee or his licensee ...'.[149] Section 50 requires 'the remuneration fixed shall be adequate for the circumstances of the case'.[150] It states that '[i]f no agreement has been reached by the parties within the period prescribed by the [Department of Disease Control], the [Department] shall fix the royalty ...'.[151] Royalties were set at 0.5 per cent of the total sale value of the drug under the licence for the first set of compulsory licences on two HIV/AIDS drugs and a drug for heart disease[152] and raised to 3 per cent for the compulsory licences on the three cancer drugs.[153]

Review by judicial or other distinct higher authority   Article 31(i) and (j) of TRIPS require Member countries to give the patent holder the possibility of independent review in the country regarding the legal validity of any decision relating to the authorisation of a compulsory licence, including the issue of remuneration payable to the patent holder. Section 50 of the Thai Patents Act states that the decision of the Department of Intellectual Property on the terms and conditions of the compulsory licence is appealable to the Board of Patents, within a period of 60 days.[154] Under section 70 of the Thai Patent Act, the patent holder may also appeal the Board's decision to the Intellectual Property and International Trade Court, again within a period of 60 days.[155] Therefore, the patent holder is given the possibility to appeal the terms of any licence, including its remuneration.

Legal and policy implications

Thailand's compulsory licences (government use) on seven drugs appear to fall within the framework established by Article 31 of TRIPS. All the licences were issued as a measure

---

149 Section 51 of Thailand's Patent Act B.E. 2522 (A.D. 1979) as amended by the Patent Act (No. 3) B.E. 2542 (A.D. 1999) (n 107).

150 Section 50 (n 107).

151 Ibid.

152 Notification of the Department of Disease Control (nn 110, 113); Notification of the Ministry of Public Health (n 116); Thai Ministry of Public Health and the National Health Security Office (n 95).

153 Notifications of the Ministry of Public Health on Docetaxel, Letrozole, and Erlotinib (n 147).

154 Section 50 (n 107).

155 WHO, Improving Access to Medicines in Thailand: The Use of TRIPS Flexibilities (31 January to 6 February 2008) 16. In Thailand, the Intellectual Property and International Trade Court was established by the Act for the Establishment of and Procedure for Intellectual Property and International Trade Court B.E. 2539 (1996). See Vichai Ariyanuntaka, 'Intellectual Property and International Trade Court: A New Dimension for Intellectual Property Rights Enforcement in Thailand' (2010), available at http://www.wipo.int/wipolex/en/details.jsp?id=6822, last accessed 15 March 2015.

to enable the national health authority to fulfil its mandate to ensure universal access to essential medicines under its Constitution B.E. 2550 and the National Health Security Act B.E. 2545. Furthermore, Thailand is a State Party to the International Covenant on Economic, Social and Cultural Rights entailing an obligation to ensure access to essential medicines as a core obligation,[156] although the Thai government did not invoke it in the process of compulsory licensing. In accordance with TRIPS and the Doha Declaration, the government has wide discretion in determining the grounds for compulsory licensing. Also, there is no restriction on the type of drugs that can be subject to compulsory licensing, as discussed under 'Grounds for Compulsory Licences' above. Public, non-commercial use, for which Thailand's licences were issued, waives a requirement of prior negotiations with the patent holder. The Thai government satisfied other conditions upon compulsory licensing under TRIPS, e.g. issuing each licence based upon individual merit; limiting the scope and duration of a compulsory licence to the stated purpose of the licence. In accordance with TRIPS, the Thai Patents Act also provides the patent holder with a right to appeal the terms of the licences, including over the remuneration. However, no appeal by the pharmaceutical companies concerned was filed.

Thailand used compulsory licences to address not only HIV/AIDS but also chronic diseases, such as cardiovascular disease and cancer because the latter increasingly constitute leading causes of mortality in Thailand. While wide consensus has been built on compulsory licensing of HIV/AIDS medications, the potential of TRIPS flexibilities in ensuring access to medicines for addressing chronic diseases has not been much explored as yet. Developing countries suffer from the double burdens of both chronic diseases and communicable, maternal, perinatal and nutrition-related diseases. When there are no alternatives with similar effects, high costs of patented medications, whether for chronic diseases or for infectious diseases, can easily deplete the already constrained health care budgets of many developing countries. Under such circumstances, individual citizens have to bear the burden of paying for needed medications out of pocket, which may lead to or aggravate the poverty of the household. In this respect, Thailand's compulsory licences have tested the potential of the compulsory licence provision of TRIPS for alleviating problems in addressing the health needs in developing countries. In 2012, India followed the Thai example, issuing a compulsory licence for a cancer drug, *sorafenib*, which is a treatment for liver and kidney cancer.[157]

Compulsory Licensing: Countries with Few Manufacturing Capacities in the Pharmaceutical Sector

From paragraph 6 of the Doha Declaration to the adoption of Article 31bis

As discussed, Article 31 of TRIPS provides important policy space for WTO Members in adjusting their patent systems to the health needs of their populations. However, Article

---

156 How the International Covenant on Economic, Social and Cultural Rights relates to this issue is discussed in further detail in the following chapters.

157 See http://ipindia.nic.in/ipoNew/compulsory_License_12032012.pdf, last accessed 15 March 2015.

31(f), requiring Member countries to grant a compulsory licence 'predominantly for the supply of the domestic market', placed a barrier to many developing countries in making effective use of the compulsory licence provision of TRIPS. The crux of the problem, which has led to Article 31*bis*,[158] the first amendment to TRIPS agreed upon on 6 December 2005, lies with the fact that only a few developing countries have substantial manufacturing capacities in pharmaceutical fields.[159] Even if a country is willing to issue a compulsory licence for the production of a patented medicine to increase access to affordable medicines, few or no local manufacturing capacities might make it futile. In order to ensure the supply of needed medicines, importing them from other countries is necessary. Until 1 January 2005, when a 10-year transitional period under Article 65 of TRIPS came to an end,[160] some countries, like India, were able to produce and export low-cost generic drugs[161] since developing countries were not required to introduce patent protection for pharmaceutical products before that date. Thus, countries without sufficient manufacturing capacities, if the price of a patented product was too high, had an option to issue a compulsory licence to import generic medicines from other countries, most notably India, 'a thriving generic drug manufacturer and exporter'.[162] However, after 1 January 2005, India was obliged to provide patent protection for pharmaceutical products. Even if India can issue a compulsory licence to manufacture patented medicines and export them to other countries, under Article 31(f) the exports must be restricted to a 'non-predominant' part of the production.[163] Due to such restrictions on compulsory licences for exports, it was anticipated that many developing countries lacking manufacturing capacities in pharmaceutical products were likely to face difficulties in obtaining access to affordable medicines, and this problem led to the inclusion of paragraph 6 of the Doha Declaration:

---

158 WT/L/641, available at http://www.wto.org/english/tratop_e/trips_e/wtl641_e.htm, last accessed 15 March 2015.

159 Graham Dutfield, 'Delivering Drugs to the Poor: Will the TRIPS Amendment Help?' (2008) 34 *American Journal of Law & Medicine* 107–24, 121; Correa (n 10) 321.

160 The transition period for least-developed countries for the provisions on pharmaceuticals was extended to 2016 in accordance with para. 7 of the Doha Declaration on the TRIPS Agreement and Public Health (n 14). The Council for TRIPS formally adopted a decision to implement this in 2002. See Decision of the Council for TRIPS of 27 June 2002. In 2013, upon the request by the LDC group, the transition period for all LDC countries for implementation of TRIPS was further extended until 1 July 2021. See Decision of the Council for TRIPS of 12 June 2013.

161 While generics can mean a pharmaceutical product which does not have a trademark, 'generics (generic drugs/medicines)' in this book are used mostly to refer to 'copies of patented drugs or drugs whose patents have expired'. The legality of generics may depend on the status of the patent and the existence of a voluntary licence or compulsory licence. See WTO, 'What does "Generic" Mean', in Fact Sheet on TRIPS and Pharmaceutical Patents, available at http://www.wto.org/english/tratop_e/trips_e/factsheet_pharm03_e.htm, last accessed 15 March 2015.

162 Frederick M. Abbott, 'The WTO Medicines Decision: World Pharmaceutical Trade and the Protection of Public Health' (2005) 99(2) *The American Journal of International Law* 317–58, 320.

163 Ibid., 319.

6. We recognize that WTO members with insufficient or no manufacturing capacities in the pharmaceutical sector could face difficulties in making effective use of compulsory licensing under TRIPS. We instruct the Council for TRIPS to find an expeditious solution to this problem and to report to the General Council before the end of 2002.[164]

Following up on paragraph 6 of the Doha Declaration, on 30 August 2003 the General Council of the WTO adopted a decision[165] waiving the obligations under Article 31(f) in accordance with certain conditions. Paragraph 2 of the Decision stipulates that '[t]he obligations of an exporting Member under Article 31(f) of TRIPS shall be waived with respect to the grant by it of a compulsory licence to the extent necessary for the purposes of production of a pharmaceutical product(s) and its export to an eligible importing Member(s) …'. This Decision was adopted as a provisional measure that would provide an 'expeditious solution' to the problem relating to Members lacking manufacturing capacities in the pharmaceutical sector.[166] On 6 December 2005, the General Council of the WTO adopted the Protocol amending TRIPS[167] so as to formally incorporate the waiver Decision of August 2003 into the Agreement. According to the Amendment, TRIPS added Article 31*bis*, the Annex to TRIPS, and the Appendix to the Annex to TRIPS. The waiver Decision of August 2003 will continue to take effect[168] until two-thirds of the WTO Members (106 Members out of the 160 Members as of 26 June 2014[169]) have formally accepted this Amendment so that the Amendment will replace the 2003 Decision for those Members in accordance with paragraph 3 of Article X of the WTO Agreement.[170] As of September 2014, the Amendment has been accepted by 79 Member countries, including the US, Switzerland, India, Japan, the European Union (27 countries), Brazil and Canada.[171]

A waiver of Article 31(f) obligations The 2003 Decision and the Amendment (hereinafter, the 'Paragraph 6' system) provide for a waiver of the obligations under Article 31(f) and thus enable medicines produced under compulsory licences to be imported to countries without sufficient manufacturing capacities. It applies to 'any least-developed

---

164 See n 14.

165 Decision of the General Council of 30 August 2003, 'Implementation of paragraph 6 of the Doha Declaration on the TRIPS Agreement and Public Health', WT/L/540 and Corr.1, available at http://www.wto.org/english/tratop_e/trips_e/implem_para6_e.htm, last accessed 15 March 2015.

166 Ibid., paragraph 11: '[t]his Decision, including the waivers granted in it, shall terminate for each Member on the date on which an amendment to the TRIPS Agreement replacing its provisions takes effect for that Member'.

167 WT/L/641.

168 Paragraph 11 (n 165).

169 Last checked on 15 March 2015. http://www.wto.org/english/thewto_e/whatis_e/tif_e/org6_e.htm.

170 Decision of the General Council of 6 December 2005, 'Amendment of the TRIPS Agreement', WT/L641; Marrakesh Agreement Establishing the World Trade Organization.

171 For the list of Members that have accepted the Amendment, see http://www.wto.org/english/tratop_e/trips_e/amendment_e.htm, last accessed 19 March 2015.

country Member, and any other Member that has made a notification to the Council for TRIPS of its intention to use the system as an importer'.[172] Thus, countries other than least-developed countries have an obligation of general notification of intent. In a given case, a country other than a least-developed county must confirm that 'it has insufficient or no manufacturing capacities in the pharmaceutical sector for the product(s) in question'.[173] As Abbott and Reichman noted, this 'applies to the specific product in question, and not generally to the country's pharmaceutical industry'.[174] Most high-income countries have made a notification of their intention not to use the system as importing Members, or if they use the system, it would be only in a limited way to address a national emergency or other circumstance of extreme urgency.[175]

Terms and conditions   Further, the current 'Paragraph 6' system has provided a set of requirements for the grant of compulsory licences by eligible importing and exporting countries. Some of the requirements are as follows. An importing Member has to issue a domestic compulsory licence when there is an applicable patent, and make a notification to the Council of its intent to issue or its issuance of the licence,[176] as well as of 'the names and expected quantities of the product(s) needed'.[177] An exporting Member has to issue a compulsory licence for exports that is subject to conditions such that 'only the amount necessary to meet the needs of the eligible importing Member(s) may be manufactured' and the products for export must be identifiable as well as distinguishable through labelling and marking.[178] These conditions were established to address concerns about a risk of diversion.[179] The exporting Member is required to notify the Council for TRIPS of the grant of the licence and its conditions, including the quantities being supplied to each destination.[180] Anti-diversion measures are required of importing Member countries as well; technical and financial cooperation by developed country Members may be provided to importing Members in implementing such measures.[181] As to the remuneration requirement under Article 31(h) of TRIPS, the current 'Paragraph 6' system requires adequate remuneration to be paid only in the exporting country 'taking into account the economic value to the importing Member of the use that has been authorized in the exporting Member'.[182]

One of the practical issues concerning the current 'Paragraph 6' system is whether it allows economies of scale, so as to provide incentives for pharmaceutical companies to

172 Paragraph 1 (n 166).

173 Paragraph 2(a)(ii) (n 166).

174 Abbott and Reichman (n 135) 939.

175 For the list of countries that have made such notifications, see paragraph 4 of General Council Chairperson's Statement, WT/GC/M/82, 13 November 2003, available at http://www. wto.org/english/tratop_e/trips_e/gc_stat_30aug03_e.htm, last accessed 15 March 2015.

176 Paragraph 2(a)(iii) (n 166); para. 2(iii) (n 167).

177 Paragraph 2(a)(i) (n 166); para. 2(i) (n 167).

178 Paragraph 2 (n 166); para. 2 (n 167).

179 Correa (n 10) 334–5.

180 Paragraph 2(c) (n 166); para. 2 (n 167).

181 Paragraph 4 (n 166); para. 3 (n 167).

182 Paragraph 3 (n 166); para. 2 (n 167).

produce and export generic drugs under this system, and also to bring prices down.[183] Médecins Sans Frontières (MSF), an international humanitarian organisation which has worked to improve access to medicines across many countries, criticised that the conditions attached to compulsory licences under this system 'ignores the fact that economies of scale are needed to attract interest from producers'.[184] This is with reference to the requirements that importing Members have to specify the expected quantities of the product and notify that to the Council for TRIPS,[185] and the prospective exporters have to manufacture on a case-by-case, licence-by-licence basis.[186] Such conditions may act as disincentives to prospective producers from seeking compulsory licences for export under the 2003 Decision[187] since those companies are 'just as much in the business of making a profit as the research-based ones'.[188] As a measure to harness economies of scale, in case of Members of regional trade agreements, of which at least half the Members are presently least-developed countries, pharmaceutical products imported into one of the parties to the group, in accordance with the 2003 Decision and the Amendment, may be re-exported to the markets of those other developing or least-developed country parties to this group.[189] However, this qualification is so restrictive that countries in South America, Central America, the Caribbean and Asia are not able to make use of this provision so as to realise economies of scale.[190] With regard to this problem, Abbott and Reichman suggest that a number of countries pool their single compulsory licences in a consortium so as to 'afford greater buying power and offer suppliers sounder incentives to invest in production'.[191]

The case of Canada–Rwanda

Rwanda has been the first and only country to make a notification to the WTO Council for TRIPS under the 'Paragraph 6' system of its intent to import a pharmaceutical product as of December 2014. Rwanda notified that it intends 'to import during the next two years 260,000 packs of *TriAvir*, a fixed-dose combination product of *Zidovudine*, *Lamivudine* and *Nevirapine* manufactured in Canada by Apotex, Inc'.[192] In Canada, Apotex applied

---

183 Dutfield (n 159) 123; Mike Gumbel, 'Is Article 31*bis* Enough? The Need to Promote Economies of Scale in the International Compulsory Licensing System' (2008) 22 *Temple International and Comparative Law Journal* 161–85.

184 Médecins Sans Frontières (MSF), Neither Expeditious, Nor a Solution: The WTO August 30th Decision is Unworkable (2006), available at http://www.msfaccess.org/content/neither-expeditious-nor-solution-wto-august-30th-decision-unworkable, last accessed 15 March 2015.

185 Paragraph 2(a)(i) (n 166); para. 2(i) (n 167).

186 Paragraph 2 (n 166); para. 2 (n 167).

187 Médecins Sans Frontières (MSF) (n 184).

188 Dutfield (n 159).

189 Paragraph 6 (n 166); para. 3 (n 167).

190 Abbott and Reichman (n 135) 945; Gumbel (n 183) 178–9.

191 Abbott and Reichman (n 135) 969.

192 Notification under paragraph 2(a) of the Decision of 30 August 2003 on the Implementation of Paragraph 6 of the Doha Declaration on the TRIPS Agreement and Public Health, Rwanda, WTO Doc, IP/N/9/RWA/1, 19 July 2007, available at http://www.wto.org/english/tratop_e/trips_e/public_health_notif_import_e.htm, last accessed 15 March 2015.

for and obtained a compulsory licence to export *TriAvir* to Rwanda and it was followed by Canada's notification to the WTO Council for TRIPS of such authorisation.[193] Nine Canadian patents are related to this fixed-dose combination product and are held by GlaxoSmithKline (GSK), Shire and Boehringer Ingelheim.[194] The designated quantities of *TriAvir* arrived in Rwanda in September 2008 and September 2009.[195]

The compulsory licence for export was implemented in accordance with Canada's amended patent law (Canada's Access to Medicines Regime: CAMR)[196] as compulsory licences are granted under national law. CAMR was adopted in May 2004 to implement the 2003 Decision. CAMR permits the granting of compulsory licences for export to Canadian pharmaceutical companies that are willing to supply countries lacking manufacturing capacities in pharmaceuticals with medicines patented in Canada at low cost. In addition to the conditions of the 2003 Decision, CAMR entails a number of requirements for compulsory licences for export, such as restricting the application of this mechanism to a limited list of drugs[197] and obliging a prior negotiation with the patent holder without acknowledging a waiver of this obligation, permitted in Article 31(b) of TRIPS in situations of national emergency, extreme urgency or public non-commercial use.[198] Also, there is a two-year time limit for the compulsory licence.[199]

The producer, Apotex, expressed its view on the process that 'it is unnecessarily complex and does not adequately represent the interests of those who require treatment' and therefore 'the Canadian Federal Government must change the process to get quality affordable medicines to those who have no access'.[200] NGOs also criticised the current CAMR for including a number of significant restrictions that limit its impact and thus

---

193 Notification under paragraph 2(c) of the Decision of 30 August 2003 on the Implementation of paragraph 6 of the Doha Declaration on the TRIPS Agreement and Public Health, Canada, WTO Doc, IP/N/10/CAN/1, 8 October 2007, available at http://www.wto.org/english/tratop_e/trips_e/public_health_notif_export_e.htm, last accessed 15 March 2015.

194 Frederick M. Abbott, 'Introductory Note to World Trade Organization Canada First Notice to Manufacture Generic Drug for Export' (2007) 46 *International Legal Materials* 1127–31, 1127; Holger Hestermeyer, 'Canadian-made Drugs for Rwanda: The First Application of the WTO Waiver on Patents and Medicines' (2007) 11(28) *The American Society of International Law Insights*, available at http://www.asil.org/insights/volume/11/issue/28/canadian-made-drugs-rwanda-first-application-wto-waiver-patents-and, last accessed 4 March 2015.

195 See the information posted by Apotex on its website, available at http://www.apotex.com/apotriavir/product/rwanda_shipments.pdf, last accessed 15 March 2015.

196 Bill C-9, an Act to Amend the Patent Act and the Food and Drug Act (known as the 'Jean Chrétien Pledge to Africa'), available at http://www2.parl.gc.ca/Sites/LOP/LegislativeSummaries/Bills_ls.asp?Parl=37&Ses=3&ls=C9, last accessed 15 March 2015. For more information, see http://www.camr-rcam.gc.ca/index_e.html, last accessed 15 March 2015.

197 § 21.02 Patent Act, available at http://laws.justice.gc.ca/eng/P-4/index.html, last accessed 15 March 2015.

198 Abbott (n 194).

199 § 21.09 Patent Act (n 197).

200 Press Release of Apotex, Life Saving AIDS Drug for Africa Gets Final Clearance, 20 September 2007, available at https://www.apotex.com/ca/en/about/press/20070920.asp, last accessed 15 March 2015.

make the 2003 waiver mechanism even more unworkable.[201] A new Bill (C-393) that proposed streamlining the process of CAMR was passed in the House of Commons on 9 March 2011 but died in the Senate as the Parliament dissolved on 25 March 2011.[202] The main reforms proposed in this Bill included 'providing a pharmaceutical producer with the opportunity to obtain a "single license" from the Commissioner of Patents that will authorize it to make and use a patented pharmaceutical invention or inventions for purposes of export to eligible countries that identify public health needs'.[203]

Other Public Health Safeguards

While compulsory licensing is one of the most important public health safeguards contained in TRIPS, there are other flexibilities that Member countries can use in promoting public health and access to medicines. Within the framework of TRIPS, Member countries can, for example, define the standards for patentability, i.e. novelty, inventive step and industrial applicability, permit limited exceptions to the patent rights, and use parallel importation in order to benefit public health. This section examines them in turn.

Standards for Patentability

Patentability criteria and public health
Evergreening: Patenting of incrementally modified drugs   While the protection of patents provides incentives to develop new pharmaceutical products, a proliferation of patents may, by its nature, have a negative impact on access to medicines. Calibrating appropriate patentability criteria is one of the crucial elements when striking the right balance between the provision of incentives to innovation and access to knowledge. Particularly in pharmaceutical fields, ways in which the criteria for patentability are designed and applied are highly important in addressing the issue of so-called 'evergreening'. The term 'evergreening' refers to 'the use of IP [intellectual property] rights in order to extend the monopoly or at least market dominance of a drug beyond the life of the original patent protecting it'.[204] Innovator pharmaceutical companies, when relying on a small number of

---

201 Médecins Sans Frontières (MSF) (n 184); Richard Elliott, 'Delivery Past Due: Global Precedent Set under Canada's Access to Medicines Regime' (2008) 13(1) *HIV/AIDS Policy & Law Review*.

202 The text and relating debate in the Parliament is available at http://openparliament.ca/bills/2080/, last accessed 15 March 2015. See Statement by concerned civil society organisations working for health and human rights, 'Parliament Fails to Fix Law to Save Lives – BILL C-393 Stalled to Death in Senate' (25 March 2011) available at http://www.aidslaw.ca/site/parliament-fails-to-fix-law-to-save-lives-bill-c-393-stalled-to-death-in-senate/, last accessed 15 March 2015.

203 Frederick Abbott, Prepared Testimony before Senate Banking, Trade and Commerce Committee, Parliament of Canada, 19 November 2009, available at http://www.parl.gc.ca/Content/SEN/Committee/402/bank/14evb-e.htm?Language=E&Parl=40&Ses=2&comm_id=3, last accessed 15 March 2015

204 Graham Dutfield, *Intellectual Property Rights and the Life Science Industries: A Twentieth Century History*, Ashgate Publishing (2003) 109. See also Rochelle Cooper Dreyfuss, 'Patents and Human

highly profitable drugs, are motivated to seek to extend their exclusive rights over those drugs for as long as possible by patenting modified versions of the original invention, for example new delivery methods for the drug, reduced dosage regimens,[205] changes in salts, esters, ethers, isomers, polymorphs of known molecules, and combinations of a known drug with other known drugs.[206] The decline in the number of new chemical entities for pharmaceutical use amid the proliferation of patents[207] also highlights the importance of setting the appropriate standards for patentability in domestic law so as to encourage genuine pharmaceutical innovation.

There are rebuttals to charges against strategic patenting of improvements on existing drugs. Parker and Mooney argue that incremental improvements upon existing drugs may lead to significantly enhanced therapeutic benefits and thus incentives to such improvements should not be removed.[208] They also consider that the issue of 'weak' patents which should not have been granted would be minimised if countries had set the patentability criteria at the right level and had an appropriate examination process.[209] On the former point, undoubtedly, some of the modified versions of existing chemical entities may accompany benefits. Nevertheless, it is necessary to consider whether those variations sufficiently depart from prior art, i.e. all existing information which has been disclosed to the public, thereby deserving the protection of patents. The latter point is precisely what Member countries have to pay attention to. Strategic patenting of minor variations of existing drugs is possible when rules on patentability are lax. For example, in the US, where there is a presumption in favour of the applicant in the examination process of patentability,[210] the National Institute for Health Care Management Research and Educational Foundation observed that '[d]rug manufacturers patent a wide range of inventions connected with incremental modifications of their products, including minor features such as inert ingredients and the form, color, and scoring of tablets. In some cases, these patents may discourage generic companies from trying to develop a competitive product'.[211] Companies other than the one holding a patent on the

---

Rights: Where is the Paradox?', in Willem Grosheide (ed.), *Intellectual Property and Human Rights: A Paradox*, Edward Elgar (2010) 72–96, 83.

205 Dutfield (n 204), 109.

206 Carlos Correa, *Guidelines for the Examination of Pharmaceutical Patents: Developing a Public Health Perspective*, WHO-ICTSD-UNCTAD (2007).

207 Ibid., footnote 9. 'The number of new molecular entities (NMEs) approved by the US Food and Drug Administration drastically declined since the mid-1990s (from 53 in 1996 to a minimum of 17 in 2002)'.

208 Scott Parker and Kevin Mooney, 'Is "Evergreening" a Cause for Concern? A Legal Perspective' (2007) 13(4) *Journal of Commercial Biotechnology* 240.

209 Ibid., 240–42.

210 Margaret Llewelyn, 'Schrodinger's Cat: An Observation on Modern Patent Law', in Peter Drahos (ed.), *Death of Patents*, Lawtext Publishing Limited and Queen Mary Intellectual Property Research Institute (2005) 11–66, 32.

211 The National Institute for Health Care Management Research and Educational Foundation, *Changing Patterns of Pharmaceutical Innovation*, May 2002, at 16, available at http://www.nihcm.org/pdf/innovations.pdf, last accessed 15 March 2015.

original substance may also seek a patent for such minor modifications. However, the strong market position of the first company may make it difficult for other companies to commercially use the original patent. Thus, it is observed that in many cases these other companies rather choose to license their patents to the first company.[212] More importantly, it has to be borne in mind that the proliferation of patents protecting minor variations of existing drugs, whether sought by the first company or other companies, broadens zones of exclusion around pharmaceutical development and may thus lead to situations where high costs of relevant drugs remain for an extended period. Therefore, it is desirable that patentability standards in domestic law are designed and implemented in a manner which provides patents for genuinely non-obvious pharmaceutical innovation and prevents excessive restrictions from being placed upon access to existing medicines and their variations.[213]

Patentability standards of TRIPS   Article 27.1 of TRIPS lays out the requirements for patentability: novelty, inventive step and industrial applicability.

> 27.1 Subject to the provisions of paragraphs 2 and 3, patents shall be available for any inventions, whether products or processes, in all fields of technology, provided that they are *new*, involve *an inventive step* and are *capable of industrial application*. (Emphasis added)

The novelty criterion is meant to prevent the patentability of material which belongs to prior art.[214] However, Article 27.1 does not provide guidance on how to determine what inventions are considered to be 'new', thereby permitting WTO Member countries flexibilities in applying the novelty requirement within their domestic systems.[215] Another criterion is 'an inventive step'. The official footnote 5 of the text of TRIPS clarifies that the term 'inventive step' can be considered by a Member to be synonymous with the term 'non-obvious'.[216] A commentator notes that the inventive step criterion is 'to ensure that monopoly rights are not granted over obvious, or too simple or incremental, developments within a given technological sphere'.[217] The question is whether the developments or departures that have taken place for the invention in question are not obvious for an expert in the relevant field.[218] 'The extent to which it must not be obvious' involves a judgment.[219] There can be variations in how to determine the level of 'non-obviousness/inventive step' among Members. A strict standard can be adopted with a view to 'rewarding substantive departures from the prior art'; others may adopt

---

212 Dutfield (n 204) 109.

213 Correa (n 206) 3–4.

214 Stoll, Busche and Arend (eds) (n 40) 482; Correa (n 10) 275.

215 Stoll, Busche and Arend (eds) (n 40) 483; Correa (n 10) 275–6.

216 See the text of the TRIPS Agreement, footnote 5. 'For the purposes of this Article, the terms "inventive step" and "capable of industrial application" may be deemed by a Member to be synonymous with the terms "non-obvious" and "useful" respectively.'

217 Llewelyn (n 210) 26.

218 Stoll, Busche and Arend (eds) (n 40) 484; Llewelyn (n 210) 26.

219 Llewelyn (n 210) 26.

a low standard of inventive step, allowing the grant of patents to a broad range of minimal developments.[220] The text of TRIPS leaves considerable flexibilities to Members in establishing the level of non-obviousness/inventive step required for patents within their domestic patent system. The third criterion for patentability relates to the industrial applicability of the invention. Again, the scope of this requirement is open to interpretation and thus Members can determine how to apply the industrial applicability criterion under their national patent laws.[221]

TRIPS does not establish what degree of each patentability criterion is required. It is important that Members set the threshold of novelty, inventive step and industrial applicability at a proper level. Patents confer exclusive rights over the patented product and thus have the consequence of restraining competition and reducing access to the product. Such costs can be justified only when patents are granted to genuine innovations. In this regard, it would be desirable for Members to adopt a strict standard of novelty, inventive step and industrial applicability so as to reward genuine innovations and prevent unnecessary limitations to competition.[222] From the public health perspective, the application of stringent criteria of patentability may help to prevent the proliferation of patents on incrementally modified versions of drugs, thereby enhancing a fair balance between the provision of incentive to innovations and access to existing drugs. The bottom line in establishing the level of patentability standards is that patents are 'a system intended to provide a public benefit through an actual contribution'.[223]

The Case of India

India: 'The pharmacy of the developing world'[224]   India has been 'a world leader in high-quality generic drug manufacturing'.[225] Until 2005, India had not provided patent protection to pharmaceutical products. There was no restriction on making generic versions of pharmaceutical products patented outside India under the India Patents Act of 1970,[226] as long as the process by which the products were produced did not infringe an Indian process patent. Generic medicines produced in India could also be exported to

---

220 Correa (n 10) 276–7.

221 Stoll, Busche and Arend (eds) (n 40) 485; Correa (n 10) 278.

222 Correa (n 10) 4.

223 Llewelyn (n 210), 27–8.

224 This expression is borrowed from Tido von Schoen-Angerer, 'India: Will Pharma, Trade Agreements Shut Down the Pharmacy of the Developing World?', *The Huffington Post*, 19 April 2010, available at http://www.huffingtonpost.com/tido-von-schoenangerer/india-will-pharma-trade-a_b_543572.html, last accessed 15 March 2015.

225 Janice M. Muller, 'The Tiger Awakens: The Tumultuous Transformation of India's Patent System and the Rise of Indian Pharmaceutical Innovation' (2007) 68, Spring, *University of Pittsburgh Law Review* 491–641, 495.

226 Section 5 of India Patents Act (1970) '(a) claiming substances intended for use, or capable of being used, as food or as medicine or drug, or … no patent shall be granted in respect of claims for the substances themselves, but claims for the methods or processes of manufacture shall be patentable'. Available at http://www.wipo.int/wipolex/en/details.jsp?id=2393, last accessed 15 March 2015.

other developing countries without violating any foreign patent law, provided that, first, those importing countries did not provide pharmaceutical product patents, and second, that the processes used for the generic medicines were not ones protected by process patents in the importing countries.[227] Domestic generic drug manufacturing thrived and the price of medicines experienced a sharp decline under the India Patents Act of 1970.[228] The strong generic manufacturing capacity enabled India to become one of the largest suppliers of low-cost generic medicines to the world market.[229] For instance, MSF obtains 80 per cent of its AIDS medicines from India,[230] and generic AIDS medicines from India have also played a significant role in the US President's Emergency Plan for AIDS Relief.[231]

India Patents Act (Amendment) of 2005 The introduction of pharmaceutical product patents in India's patent law generated concerns that a major source of affordable generic medicines for poor people around the world would cease to exist.[232] Under TRIPS, India was required to provide patents for pharmaceutical products from 1 January 2005 when the 10-year transition period for developing countries in implementing TRIPS ended.[233] India also had to start reviewing the pharmaceutical patent applications that were filed in its 'mailbox' between 1 January 1995 and 31 December 2004.[234] Accordingly, the India Patents Act (Amendment) of 2005,[235] which was adopted following intense debate,[236] recognises patentability of pharmaceutical products by deleting the provision in the Patent Act of 1970 which prohibited product patents for pharmaceuticals. At the same time, the India Patents Act (Amendment) of 2005 contains provisions that can be used for public health safeguards, such as compulsory licensing for the export of patented pharmaceutical products in accordance with the 2003 WTO waiver Decision (the 'Paragraph 6' system),[237] and pre- and post-grant opposition.[238] Pre-and post-grant opposition is a mechanism for challenging the validity of patents. Even where a national patent office is well equipped

---

227 Muller (n 225) 514.

228 Ibid.

229 Abbott and Reichman (n 135) 928.

230 Schoen-Angerer (n 224).

231 Kaiser Daily HIV/AIDS Report, Politics and Policy, President Bush Signs PEPFAR Reauthorization Bill, 31 July 2008, available at http://kaiserhealthnews.org/morning-breakout/dr00053609/, last accessed 15 March 2015.

232 Patralekha Chatterjee, 'India's New Patent Law Still Hurt Generic Drug Supplies' (2005) 365(9468) *The Lancet* 1378, Radhika Bhattacharya, 'Are Developing Countries Going Too Far on TRIPS? A Closer Look at the New Laws in India' (2008) 34 *American Journal of Law & Medicine* 395–421, 404.

233 Abbott and Reichman (n 135) 934.

234 Muller (n 225) 519–20.

235 Available at http://www.wipo.int/wipolex/en/details.jsp?id=2407, last accessed 15 March 2015.

236 For the process that led to the India Patents Act (Amendment) of 2005, see Bhattacharya (n 232) 397–405; Muller (n 225).

237 Section 92(A) of the India Patents Act (Amendment) of 2005 (n 235).

238 Section 25(2) (n 235).

with expertise and capable of substantive examination, wrong patents, e.g. lack of novelty or inventive step, may be granted so as to unduly block competition and reduce access to the subject matter. Therefore, it is important to have effective mechanisms for challenging the validity of patents, both before and after the time of grant.[239]

Section 3(d), a provision on patent eligibility, is also one of the public health safeguards. Section 3 of the India Patents Act regulates 'patent eligibility' and lists non-patentable subject matter. Section 3(d) aims to ensure that only truly innovative technical contributions be patented, 'by limiting the scope of protection available for derivatives and new uses of a known substance'[240] Section 3(d) states the non-patentability of:

> the mere discovery of a new form of a known substance which does not result in the enhancement of the known efficacy of that substance or the mere discovery of any new property or new use for a known substance or of the mere use of a known process, machine or apparatus unless such known process results in a new product or employs at least one new reactant.

> Explanation – For the purposes of this clause, salts, esters, ethers, polymorphs, metabolites, pure form, particle size isomers, mixtures of isomers, complexes, combinations and other derivatives of known substance shall be considered to be the same substance, unless they differ significantly in properties with regard to efficacy.[241]

As discussed above, WTO Member countries have flexibilities to fashion the degree of inventive step required for patents within their domestic law. In order to curtail 'evergreening', which attempts to patent minor variations of old patents, the first clause of section 3(d) restricts the patenting of modifications of previously known pharmaceutical substances by requiring significant enhancement in 'efficacy' for them to be patentable.[242] This provision does not exclude the patentability of incremental pharmaceutical innovation as such. If modifications to a known substance demonstrate improved efficacy, they can be patentable.[243] In this way, the provision aims at promoting incremental innovation with enhanced efficacy, while preventing the patenting of mere variations of the existing invention.[244]

The second clause of section 3(d), 'the mere discovery of any new property or new use for a known substance or of the mere use of a known process, machine or apparatus

---

239 For further discussions, see Correa (n 206) 24–5.

240 Linda L. Lee, 'Trials and TRIPS-ulations: Indian Patent Law and *Novartis AG v. Union of India*' (2008) 23 *Berkeley Technology Law Journal* 281–313, 304.

241 Section 3(d) (n 235).

242 *Novartis AG v. Union of India*, W.P. Nos. 24759 and 24760 of 2006, High Court of Madras (India), decided 6 August 2007, para. 12; Janice M. Muller, 'Taking TRIPS to India – Novartis, Patent Law, and Access to Medicines', *The New England Journal of Medicine* (8 February, 2007) 541–3, 542; Muller (n 225) 550–56; Abbott and Reichman (n 135) 959; Bhattacharya (n 232) 403.

243 Shamnad Basheer and T. Prashant Reddy, 'The "Efficacy" of Indian Patent Law: Ironing out the Creases in Section 3(d)' (2008) 5(2) *SCRIPTed* 232–66, 239; Muller (n 242) 542.

244 Basheer and Reddy (n 243) 239.

unless such known process results in a new product or employs at least one new reactant', codifies the non-patentability of a 'new use' claim in the absence of the development of a new product. TRIPS requires the grant of patents over products and processes that are novel, involve inventive step, and are industrially applicable. TRIPS makes no specific reference to medical use claims, leaving Member countries the discretion to decide whether a new medical use of an existing substance is patentable.[245] In the standard understanding of novelty, product patents based on a new use lack novelty.[246] Even if novelty of the use, separately from the product, is recognised, the use lacks industrial applicability, another requirement for patentability. For 'what is new [the use] is an identified effect on the body, not the product as such or its method of manufacture'.[247] Therefore, allowing a use claim of a known product has an effect of 'expand[ing] patent protection beyond the general principles of patent law'.[248]

Approaches to the patentability of a new medical use of a known product vary across different jurisdictions. Depending on whether the product had an existing pharmaceutical use, a new therapeutic use of a known product can be termed as a 'first indication' or a 'second indication'.[249] Article 54(4) of the European Patent Convention (1973 and 2000) provides a product patent ('purpose-limited-product patent') for the first indication of a known product.[250] Article 54(5) of the 2000 European Patent Convention permits a product claim for the subsequent medical use (the second indication) of a known substance.[251] In the US, a new use of a known product can be treated only as a process

---

245 Article 27.1 of TRIPS: '1. Subject to the provisions of paragraphs 2 and 3, patents shall be available for any inventions, whether products or processes, in all fields of technology, provided that they are new, involve an inventive step and are capable of industrial application'; Lee (n 240) 310; Carlos Correa, 'Public Health and Patent Legislation in Developing Countries' (2001) 3 *Tulane Journal of Technology and Intellectual Property* 1–53, 16.

246 Correa (n 245) 14. Allowing claims for known substances for a new medical use or the subsequent medical use is 'derivatives to the law of novelty'. William Cornish and David Llewelyn, *Intellectual Property: Patents, Copyright, Trade Marks and Allied Rights*, 5th edn, Sweet & Maxwell (2003) 216 (5-69).

247 Correa (n 206) 21.

248 Correa (n 245) 15–16; Philip Grubb, *Patents for Chemicals, Pharmaceuticals and Biotechnology: Fundamentals of Global Law, Practice and Strategy*, Clarendon Press (1999) 221. Grubb comments that the Swiss formula is susceptible to 'the logical objection that it lacks novelty, since it claims the use of the compound for preparation of a medicament, and normally the medicament itself will be the same as that already used for the first pharmaceutical indication'.

249 Correa (n 245) 14–15.

250 Article 54(4) of the European Patent Convention (2000) 'Paragraphs 2 and 3 shall not exclude the patentability of any substance or composition, comprised in the state of the art, for use in a method referred to in Article 53(c), provided that its use for any such method is not comprised in the state of the art.'

251 Article 54(5) 'Paragraphs 2 and 3 shall also not exclude the patentability of any substance or composition referred to in paragraph 4 for any specific use in a method referred to in Article 53(c), provided that such use is not comprised in the state of the art.' For a critique, see Sigrid Sterckx and Julian Cockbain, 'Purpose-limited Pharmaceutical Product Claims under the Revised European Patent Convention: A Camouflaged Attack on Generic Substitution?' (2010) 1 *Intellectual*

patent claim, and the patent protection on use is confined to a particular 'method-of-use', not the product.[252] On the other hand, there are countries that do not provide patent protection for use claims of a known pharmaceutical product. For instance, the Andean Community of Nations, comprising Bolivia, Colombia, Ecuador and Peru, shares such a stance with India. Article 21 of Decision 486 of the Andean Community of Nations, titled Common Intellectual Property Regime, states that '[p]roducts or processes already patented and included in the state of the art within the meaning of Article 16 of this Decision may not be the subject of new patents on the sole ground of having been put to a use different from that originally contemplated by the initial patent'.[253]

Section 3(d) and Novartis This issue of the degree of inventive step required for a patent was brought to the fore when Novartis challenged section 3(d) of the Amended Patents Act of 2005.[254] What follows is a brief chronicle of the events relating to a legal dispute over the inventive step requirement between Novartis and the Indian Patent Office, which ended with the decision of the Supreme Court of India on a case concerning interpretation of section 3(d) and thus an assessment of enhanced efficacy of a patent claim for a modification of a known compound in April 2013.[255] In 1993, Novartis claimed a patent for a free base compound of Glivec (or Gleevec), *imatinib*, in many countries,[256] but not in India where no patent protection for pharmaceutical products was provided.[257] Glivec is a drug used for treating chronic myeloid leukaemia (CML). Novartis filed another patent on the beta crystalline form of *imatinib mesylate* in over 50 countries and obtained patents in 35 of those countries.[258] Also in India, Novartis filed a mailbox application in 1998 for the beta crystalline form of *imatinib mesylate* to obtain a patent once India introduced pharmaceutical products patents following the expiration of the 10-year transition period for the implementation of TRIPS.[259] In 2003, Novartis was granted

---

Property Quarterly 88–107. From 1984 to the time when the 2000 European Patent Convention came into force, the European Patent Office granted a process patent for the second indication in 1984, which is called a Swiss-type claim. Correa (n 245) 15. EPO, Enlarged Board of Appeal, 19 February 2010, Decision No. G 02/08 – ABBOT RESPIRATORY/*Dosage regime* (19 February 2010).

252 United States Code Title 35 – Patents (35 U.S.C.) 100. 'Definitions. … (b)The term "process" means process, art, or method, and includes *a new use* of a known process, machine, manufacture, composition of matter, or *material*' (emphasis added). Available at http://www.uspto.gov/web/offices/pac/mpep/consolidated_laws.pdf, last accessed 15 March 2015. Correa (n 245) 15.

253 Available at http://www.sice.oas.org/trade/junac/decisiones/DEC486ae.asp last accessed 15 March 2015.

254 *Novartis AG v. Union of India* (n 242).

255 *Novartis v. India*, Supreme Court of India, Civil Appeal Nos. 2706–2716 of 2013 (Arising out of SLP(C) Nos. 20539–20549 of 2009), decided 1 April 2013.

256 US Patent Number 5521184 titled 'Pyrimidine Derivatives and Processes for the Preparation Thereof' (filed in April 1993 and issued on 28 May 1996).

257 Novartis, History of Glivec in India, available at http://www.novartis.com/downloads/about-novartis/glivec-history-india.pdf, last accessed 3 June 2010.

258 Basheer and Reddy (n 243) 236.

259 Novartis (n 257).

exclusive marketing rights (EMR) for *imatinib* which is 'a short-term quasi-patent right …
during the transition period for certain mailbox applications'.[260] It brought to a halt the
production of the generic version of Glivec and one month's dose of Glivec cost £1,400,
which was 10 times higher than the cost of its generic version.[261] In January 2006, the
Office of the Indian Controller of Patents and Designs at Chennai examined the mailbox
application for Glivec (*imatinib mesylate*, a beta crystalline form of the free base *imatinib*) and
rejected the claim.[262] In its decision, the Controller of Patents considered the application
of Novartis and found that it did not meet the requirements of novelty and inventiveness
because the beta crystalline form of *imatinib mesylate* was already included in Novartis'
earlier US patent on the free base *imatinib*,[263] thereby falling within the prior art.[264] Further,
the Indian Patent Office was of a view that the claim did not demonstrate improved
'efficacy' under section 3(d).[265]

Subsequently, Novartis challenged the validity of section 3(d) on the ground that it is
inconsistent with TRIPS as well as with Article 14 (equality before law) of the Constitution
of India.[266] It also appealed against the decision of the Patent Controller, which rejected
a patent for Glivec.[267] On the validity of section 3(d), the High Court of Madras asserted
that it did not have jurisdiction in relation to the compliance of domestic legislation
with TRIPS and such issues should be addressed by the WTO Dispute Settlement
Body.[268] The Court rejected Novartis' claim on unconstitutionality of section 3(d) on
the ground of its vagueness, arbitrariness and conferring of uncontrolled power to the
Patent Controller.[269] The Court observed that the meaning of 'efficacy' under section
3(d) can be well understood as the 'therapeutic effect' of a drug in the pharmaceutical
field[270] and this general term should be interpreted in the context on a case-by-case basis
in light of the object and purpose of the provision.[271] The Court observed that the
legislature did not arbitrarily enact the provision in question, but did so with the aim 'to
prevent evergreening; to provide easy access to the citizens of this country to life saving

---

260 For the exclusive marketing rights regime in India, see Muller (n 225) 519–25.

261 Ganapati Murdur, 'Indian Patients Go to Court Over Cancer Drug' (2004) 329 (21 August)
British Medical Journal 419.

262 Novartis (n 257); C.R. Sukumar, 'Novartis Loses Patent Claim on Cancer Drug – Patents
Controller Upholds Natco Contention', The Hindu Business Line, 25 January 2005, available at http://
www.thehindubusinessline.in/bline/2006/01/26/stories/2006012601150500.htm, last accessed 15
March 2015; Shamnad Basheer, 'First Mailbox Opposition (Gleevec) Decided in India' Spicy IP,
11 March 2007, available at http://spicyipindia.blogspot.com/2006/03/first-mailbox-opposition-
gleevec.html, last accessed 15 March 2015.

263 US Patent No. 5521184 (1993).

264 Sukumar (n 262); Basheer (n 262); Lee (n 240) 298–9.

265 Ibid.

266 *Novartis AG v. Union of India* (n 242); Novartis (n 257).

267 Novartis (n 257); Lee (n 240) 299–300.

268 *Novartis AG v. Union of India* (n 242) para. 8.

269 Ibid., para. 11; for comments, see Lee (n 240) 301–2.

270 *Novartis AG v. Union of India* (n 242) para. 13.

271 Ibid., para. 14.

drugs and to discharge their Constitutional obligation of providing good health care to its citizens'.[272]

The latter part of the case that challenges the denial of Novartis' patent was transferred to the Intellectual Property Appellate Board (IPAB), a body in charge of patent review in India.[273] In June 2009, the IPAB upheld the decision of the Patent Controller that a claim for the beta crystalline form of *imatinib mesylate* is not patentable, while it allowed Novartis to proceed with certain process claims.[274] The IPAB asserted that, first, the beta form of *imatinib mesylate* did not demonstrate the enhancement of the efficacy of *imatinib*, which is a known substance, and thus failed to meet the inventive step standard under section 3(d) of the Act. The IPAB viewed that the 30 per cent enhanced bio-availability of the beta form of *imatinib mesylate* claimed by Novartis was obvious and did not constitute 'therapeutic efficacy' following the High Court of Madras' understanding of the term 'efficacy' being 'therapeutic efficacy'.[275] On 1 April 2013, the Supreme Court of India confirmed the rejection by the Patent Controller of a production patent for the beta crystalline form of *imatinib mesylate*, clarifying that efficacy under section 3(d) is therapeutic efficacy and Novartis' patent claim for a modified version of Glivec 'fails in both the tests of invention and patentability'.[276]

This *Novartis* patent case has highlighted the function of section 3(d) requiring a higher standard of inventive step as 'one of the different public interest provisions adopted in the patent law at the pre-grant level'.[277] As the IPAB (India) noted, calibrating the degree of inventiveness required for a patent within domestic law is 'permissible under TRIPS and to accommodate the spirit of the Doha Declaration which gives to the WTO member states including India the right to protect public health and, in particular, to promote access to medicines for all'.[278] How India manages to achieve a balance between the provision of incentives to innovation and the promotion of access to medicines in the implementation of the TRIPS standards can have a significant impact on the availability of affordable essential medicines in other developing countries, given that India presently remains a major source of affordable generic drugs to developing countries.[279]

Exclusions to Patentability

Article 27.2 of TRIPS states:

---

272 Ibid., paras 12 and 19.

273 Lee (n 240) 299, 303.

274 *Novartis AG v. The Controller General of Patents, Designs and Trade Marks*, M.P. Nos 1 to 5/2007 in TA/1 to 5/2007/PT/CH, M.P. No. 33/2008 in TA/1/2007/PT/CH, TA/1 TO 5/2007/PT/CH, IP Appellate Board (India), available at http://www.i-mak.org/storage/Gleevec%20IPAB%20decision%2026%20June%202009.pdf last accessed 15 March 2015.

275 Ibid.

276 *Novartis v. India* (n 255); See Frederic M. Abbott, 'The Judgment in *Novartis v. India*: What the Supreme Court of India Said', *Intellectual Property Watch* (Inside Views), 3 April 2013.

277 *Novartis AG v. The Controller General of Patents, Designs and Trade Marks* (n 274).

278 Ibid.

279 Abbott and Reichman (n 135) 959–60.

Members may exclude from patentability inventions, the prevention within their territory of the commercial exploitation of which is necessary to protect *ordre public* or morality, including to protect human, animal or plant life or health or to avoid serious prejudice to the environment, provided that such exclusion is not made merely because the exploitation is prohibited by domestic law.

Under Article 27.2, countries may exclude some inventions from patentability and prevent the commercial exploitation thereof, based on the grounds of, '*ordre public* or morality' which includes the protection of human, animal or plant life or health and the prevention of serious prejudice to the environment. This provision may allow countries to consider the impacts of an invention on human, animal or plant life or health, or the environment as a ground for denying patentability. However, patentability can only be excluded if the commercial exploitation of the invention is prevented in the territory of the Member country. In the context of patents and access to medicines, the issue is the unaffordable price arising from patents, not the commercialisation of pharmaceuticals as such.[280] This provision does not seem to provide a way to exclude pharmaceuticals from patentability for public health purposes unless the pharmaceuticals are provided there solely for non-commercial purposes.

Exceptions to Patent Rights

Article 30 of the TRIPS provides:

Members may provide limited exceptions to the exclusive rights conferred by a patent, provided that such exceptions do not unreasonably conflict with a normal exploitation of the patent and do not unreasonably prejudice the legitimate interests of the patent owner, taking account of the legitimate interests of third parties.

Countries may establish in their domestic laws limited exceptions to a patent owner's right to exclude others from making, using, selling or importing an invention. There are three conditions to be satisfied: the exceptions must be limited; they should not 'unreasonably prejudice the legitimate interests of the patent owner', taking into account 'the legitimate interests of third parties'; and they should not 'unreasonably conflict with a normal exploitation of the patent'. Given the general wording of Article 30, the exceptions to the patent rights seem to require a case-by-case assessment of their validity.[281] Also, some emphasis should be placed on 'the legitimate interests' as this concept indicates 'the need to balance diverse social and economic interests'.[282]

As the Panel noted in *Canada – Patent Protection of Pharmaceutical Products*, Article 30 of TRIPS makes reference to 'the legitimate interests of third parties', differently from

---

280 Hestermeyer (n 31) 56–7.

281 Correa (n 10) 303.

282 Robert Howse, 'The Canadian Generic Medicines Panel: A Dangerous Precedent in Dangerous Times' (2000) 3(4) *Journal of World Intellectual Property* 493–507, 501.

Article 9(2) of the Berne Convention and Article 13 of TRIPS.[283] The Panel interpreted this as 'the instruction that account must be taken of "the legitimate interests of third parties"'.[284] In understanding the meaning of this rather broad term, objectives (Art. 7) and principles (Art. 8) of the Agreement should play a role.[285] Therefore, an appropriate reading of Article 30 should include not only patent holders' economic interests, but also 'the mutual advantage of producers and users of technological knowledge' (Art. 7); 'public health and nutrition' (Art. 8); and 'the public in sectors of vital importance to socio-economic and technological development' (Art. 8).[286]

Bearing in mind that a case-by-case assessment of exceptions remains required, some of the exceptions deemed permissible within the scope of Article 30 can be indicated: the so-called Bolar exception, which is the use of a pharmaceutical invention to conduct tests and obtain approval from the health authority during the patent term for commercialisation of a generic version just after such expiry; experimental use;[287] preparation of medicines for individual cases according to prescription; and private non-commercial use by individuals.[288]

Parallel Importing

Parallel importing refers to the practice of importing into a country a product protected by patents within that country without authorisation of the patent holder after the product has been placed in a foreign market by the patent holder or with the patent holder's consent. Parallel importing is considered to be one of the measures that countries may adopt to meet public health needs in that parallel imports may allow consumers to buy products from a foreign country at lower prices than those locally charged by the intellectual property owner.[289]

Legality of parallel imports

The legality of parallel imports depends on the policy regarding 'exhaustion of rights'.[290] Under the first sale doctrine, once a patented product has been first placed on a market by the patent holder or with its consent, the patent holder's right to control the subsequent disposition is exhausted. In other words, the purchaser of the product can resell it without restraint. While the application of the first sale doctrine at the national level (national exhaustion) is established as a rule, the question is whether the commercialisation of a patented product in another country by the patent holder or with its consent is also

---

283 WT/DS114/R.17 March 2000, para. 7.71.

284 Ibid.

285 Ruse-Khan (n 8) 189.

286 Howse (n 282) 501–5.

287 Daniel Gervais, *The TRIPS Agreement: Drafting History and Analysis*, 3rd edn, Sweet & Maxwell (2008) 382.

288 Hestermeyer (n 31) 238–9; Correa (n 10) 303.

289 Correa (n 10) 80.

290 Frederick M. Abbot, 'The TRIPS-Legality of Measures Taken to Address Public Health Crisis: Responding to USTR-State Industry Positions that Undermine the WTO', in Daniel L.M. Kennedy and James D. Southwick (eds), *Political Economy of International Trade Law: Essays in Honor of Robert E. Hudec*, Cambridge University Press (2002) 311–12, 329; Correa (n 10) 78–9.

deemed to have exhausted the patent holder's rights (international exhaustion). Where the principle of exhaustion of rights reaches the international level, the patent holder may no longer retain the right to consent to importation. Article 6 of TRIPS leaves freedom to countries in adopting the policy for exhaustion that they consider appropriate:

> Article 6. For the purposes of dispute settlement under this Agreement, subject to the provisions of Articles 3 and 4 nothing in this Agreement shall be used to address the issue of the exhaustion of intellectual property rights.

Nevertheless, some authors, particularly multinational pharmaceutical companies, contest the legality of international exhaustion arguing that Article 28.1[291] of TRIPS grants patent holders the exclusive right to ban the importation of their patented products even after the products have been first placed into market by or with the consent of the patent holder.[292] However, the exclusive right that patent holders have under Article 28.1 regarding importing is applied to imports of products placed in other countries without their consent, that is, imports of infringing products, but not extended to the imports of products first put on the market by the patent holders themselves or with their consent. In addition, the footnote to this provision indicates that the exclusive rights of a patent holder are subject to Article 6 concerning the principle of exhaustion.[293] Therefore, a reading of Article 28 with Article 6 leads to the conclusion that TRIPS does not prohibit parallel imports, allowing the discretion of countries to adopt the exhaustion policy that suits them. Moreover, such an interpretation of TRIPS is clearly confirmed by the Doha Declaration: paragraph 5(d) provides that:

> The effect of the provisions in the TRIPS Agreement that are relevant to the exhaustion of Intellectual Property Rights is to leave each member free to establish its own regime for such exhaustion without challenge, subject to the MFN [most-favoured-nation] and national treatment provisions of Articles 3 and 4.[294]

Role of parallel imports

What would be the role of parallel imports in enhancing access to medicines, particularly for people with low income? For this purpose, it is important to purchase products from the cheapest sources possible. It is suggested that if parallel imports are permitted, consumers would be able to get patented drugs at lower prices than those locally charged by the patent holders.[295]

---

291 Article 28.1: 'A patent shall confer on its owner the following exclusive rights: (a) where the subject matter of a patent is a product, to prevent third parties not having the owner's consent from the acts of: making, using, offering for sale, selling, or importing for these purposes that product.'

292 Harvey E. Bale Jr., 'The Conflicts Between Parallel Trade and Product Access and Innovation: The Case of Pharmaceuticals' (1998) 1 *Journal of International Economic Law* 637–53, 641.

293 Abbott (n 290) 329; Correa (n 10) 297–8.

294 See n 14.

295 Keith Maskus and M. Ganslandt, 'Parallel Trade in Pharmaceutical Products: Implications for Procuring Medicines for Poor Countries', in Brigitte Granville (ed.), *The Economics of Essential Medicines*, Royal Institute of International Affairs (2002) 57–80, 57, 78.

However, opponents of parallel imports argue that parallel imports would reduce R&D expenditures in multinational pharmaceutical companies, and that if parallel imports are not allowed, the companies could set different prices according to per capita income, which is more beneficial to people in low-income countries.[296] Firstly, however, economic studies show that there is no strong empirical evidence to support a negative relationship between R&D activities and the policy allowing parallel imports.[297]

Secondly, as to price discrimination, classic economic theory claims that if firms can separate national markets, prices would be inversely charged proportional to demand elasticity.[298] In other words, where demand is most sensitive to prices, companies would charge the lowest price, although even that price cannot go below the level at which a company is willing to sell. It thus follows that prices would be lower in developing countries with low purchasing power than in developed countries. Such price discrimination is clearly desirable to maintain. However, empirical research shows that multinational pharmaceutical companies do not necessarily set prices according to per capita income.[299] Even in low-income countries, if the market is internally segmented due to skewed income distribution, companies may decide to sell low volumes at high prices, only targeting high-income consumers.[300] In those circumstances, parallel imports may contribute to bringing prices down for the purpose of improving access to the products.

Nevertheless, there remains a risk that a regime of parallel imports may engender the leakage of low-priced products to high-income markets and thus multinational companies might raise the price in previously low-priced markets to prevent parallel imports for fear of leakages. Therefore, to the extent that the supply of medicines relies on the activities of multinational companies, market segmentation between developing and developed countries seems desirable.

What would be the optimal policy of parallel imports? The (UK) Commission on Intellectual Property Rights[301] recommended that developing countries should adopt a policy of international exhaustion so that they can import the low-priced patented products from cheaper sources anywhere whenever the patentee's rights have been exhausted in the foreign country. On the other hand, it is desirable that developed countries prevent

---

296 Bale Jr. (n 292) 641.

297 Maskus and Ganslandt (n 295) 77.

298 Ibid., 59; F.M. Scherer and Jayashree Watal, 'The Economics of TRIPS Options for Access to Medicines', in B Granville (ed.), *The Economics of Essential Medicines*, Royal Institute of International Affairs (2002) 32–56, 41.

299 Maskus and Ganslandt (n 295) 62–8; Scherer and Watal (n 298) 43–5.

300 Sean Flynn, Aidan Hollis and Mike Palmedo, 'An Economic Justification for Open Access to Essential Medicine Patents in Developing Countries' [2009] *Journal of Law, Medicine & Ethics* 2–25. This research found that 'at high levels of inequality within a country, a monopolist will maximize its revenue by selling at a high price affordable to few people. In countries with more equitable income distribution, a monopolist will maximize revenue by selling at a lower price to a great number of consumers.' It illustrates this point with examples of 14 countries with varying degrees of income equality, including South Africa, Mexico, Brazil, Norway, the US and France.

301 Commission on Intellectual Property Rights (UK), *Integrating Intellectual Property Rights and Development Policy* (2002) 41–2.

imports of the low-priced products originating from developing countries. This would enable multinational pharmaceutical companies to engage in a system of differential pricing according to per capita income differences. These recommendations are in compliance with TRIPS since TRIPS leaves countries free to adopt an exhaustion policy best suited to them.

Conclusion

The adoption of TRIPS has given rise to increased concerns about access to affordable medicines because TRIPS requires all WTO Members to provide the protection of intellectual property rights in all fields of technology, including pharmaceuticals. At the same time, it should be borne in mind that TRIPS provides flexibilities for Members to adopt measures necessary to promote access to medicines for all. This chapter has examined ways in which TRIPS can be interpreted and implemented in a manner conducive to the promotion of public health. Also, some State practices in this regard have been looked into. In Chapter 6, the role of these TRIPS flexibilities in resolving potential conflicts between TRIPS and international human rights is discussed.

The objectives and principles of TRIPS make it clear that the protection of intellectual property is not an end in itself. The Doha Declaration reaffirms that Member countries should be able to use, to the full extent, the flexibilities of TRIPS with a view to promoting access to medicines for all. Therefore, TRIPS has to be read and enforced in a way supportive of access to medicines for all. The TRIPS flexibilities include standards for patentability, exceptions to patent rights, compulsory licensing and parallel importing.

The use of TRIPS flexibilities by States has provided a pool of examples of balancing between the protection of interests of the patent holders and the promotion of access to medicines for all. The compulsory licensing of the Thai government between 2006 and 2008 was not restricted to AIDS medications but was broadened in scope to include medicines to address chronic diseases, such as cancer and heart disease, calling attention to the double burden of diseases that developing countries face. The issue of countries with little or no pharmaceutical manufacturing capacity was addressed by the 2003 WTO Decision and the subsequent 2005 Amendment to the WTO Agreement, which waives the requirement under Article 31(f) of TRIPS. However, the case of *Canada–Rwanda* has exposed limitations resulting from the cumbersome requirements imposed by either the 2003 WTO waiver Decision or relevant domestic law. Amid post-TRIPS fears of the declining prospect of the production of low-cost generic medicines, India's Amended Patents Act of 2005 has incorporated some provisions that can support the promotion of access to medicines. Among other things, the introduction of strict standards for patentability in terms of inventive step is considered to be helpful in addressing the issue of extending exclusive rights over drugs by patenting modified versions of the original invention.

Chapter 4
Human Right to Access to Medicines

Introduction

About 30 per cent of the world's population remains without regular access to essential medicines.[1] Most countries with low access to essential medicines have very low health outcomes.[2] Many people are not only suffering from poor health but also dying due to a lack of access to medicines. A widely known, but not isolated, example indicating the problem of access to medicines is HIV/AIDS. Despite progress in access to HIV treatment in the past decade, in 2012 the HIV treatment coverage in low- and middle-income countries was only 34 per cent of all eligible for treatment under the 2013 WHO HIV treatment guidelines and 1.6 million people died from AIDS-related causes worldwide in the same year.[3] This is a human rights problem. As Alicia Yamin observes, seeing access to medicines as a human right 'forces us to face the momentous suffering and loss of life that is occurring in developing countries due to HIV/AIDS, tuberculosis, malaria, and other diseases as not just a tragedy; it forces us to recognize it as a horrific injustice'.[4]

Access to medicines is a human right. Access to medicines constitutes one of the essential conditions for one's life and health in the event of sickness, as well as for prevention and treatment of diseases. This chapter examines the human right to access to medicines as a legally binding norm that flows from the right to health, the right to life, and customary international law respectively. It offers an analysis of the obligations of States with respect to the right to access to medicines. This analysis categorises the obligations of States in four different ways: access to essential medicines under the right to health; access to non-essential medicines under the right to health; access to essential medicines under the right to life; access to medicines in the context of pandemics as a customary rule. They are not exclusive of each other, but are regulated by different norms. Furthermore, it also discusses the responsibility of pharmaceutical companies to ensure access to medicines as an emerging norm.

---

1 WHO, *The World Medicines Situation 2011: Access to Essential Medicines as Part of the Right to Health* (2011) 1.

2 WHO, *The World Medicines Situation* (2004) 64.

3 Joint United Nations Programme on HIV/AIDS (UNAIDS), Global Report: UNAIDS Report on the Global AIDS Epidemic 2013 (2013) 4–6.

4 Alicia Yamin, 'Not Just a Tragedy: Access to Medications as a Right under International Law' (2003) 21 *Boston University International Law Journal* 325–71, 370.

Access to Medicine: An Element of the Right to Health

The Right to Health

The right to health is generally used as a shorthand expression for the right of everyone to the enjoyment of the highest attainable standard of physical and mental health. The Constitution of the WHO,[5] adopted in 1946, provided the foundations for the right to health for most international human rights instruments by laying down that 'the enjoyment of the highest attainable standard of health is one of the fundamental rights of every human being …'.[6] Article 25.1 of the Universal Declaration of Human Rights (hereinafter UDHR), adopted in 1948, affirms health as a subject of human rights.[7] The right to health, since then, has been firmly embedded in a myriad of legally binding international and regional human rights treaties, as well as numerous national Constitutions.

One of the most comprehensive provisions on the right to health is found in Article 12 of the International Covenant on Economic, Social and Cultural Rights (hereinafter ICESCR),[8] which requires States parties to recognise 'the right of everyone to the enjoyment of the highest attainable standard of physical and mental health'. In addition, the right to health is provided for in a number of other human rights treaties for particular vulnerable groups that include Article 5(e)(iv) of the International Convention on the Elimination of All Forms of Racial Discrimination,[9] Articles 11.1(f) and 12 of the Convention on the Elimination of All Forms of Discrimination against Women,[10] Article 24 of the Convention on the Rights of the Child,[11] Articles 25, 28, 43(1)(e), 45(1)(c) of the International Convention on the Protection of the Rights of Migrant Workers and Members of their Families,[12] and Article 25 of the Convention on the Rights of Persons with Disabilities.[13] Furthermore, the right to health is recognised in several regional human rights instruments, including Article 11 of the revised European Social Charter,[14] Article 16 of the African Charter on Human and Peoples' Rights (known as the 'Banjul Charter': ACHPR)[15] and Article 10 of the Additional

---

5 Adopted on 22 July 1946 and entered into force on 7 April 1948.

6 Preamble of the WHO Constitution.

7 Adopted on 10 December 1948 by the General Assembly of the United Nations. Article 25.1 of the UDHR states: 'Everyone has the right to a standard of living adequate for the health of himself and of his family, including food, clothing, housing and medical care and necessary social services.'

8 Adopted on 16 December 1966 and entered into force on 3 January 1976.

9 Adopted on 21 December 1965 and entered into force on 4 January 1969.

10 Adopted on 19 December 1979 and entered into force on 3 September 1981.

11 Adopted on 20 November 1989 and entered into force on 2 September 1990.

12 Adopted on 18 December 1990 and entered into force on 1 July 2003.

13 Adopted on 13 December 2006 and entered into force on 3 May 2008.

14 Adopted in 1961 and revised in 1996. The European Committee of Social Rights (ECSR) is the monitoring body regarding compliance of State parties.

15 Adopted on 27 June 1981 and entered into force 21 October 1986.

Protocol to the American Convention on Human Rights in the Area of Economic, Social and Cultural Rights (known as the 'Protocol of San Salvador').[16] More than 60 national Constitutions include provisions on the right to health or the right to health care.[17]

The linkages between human rights and health have increasingly been examined by academic commentators and practitioners.[18] There have been remarkable efforts made to elaborate the normative content of the right to health, particularly regarding the right to health provision in the ICESCR. The ICESCR binds 164 counties as of March 2015. General Comment No. 14[19] of the UN Committee on Economic, Social and Cultural Rights (CESCR), the primary body responsible for the interpretation and implementation of the ICESCR, and numerous reports of the Special Rapporteur on the Right to Health[20] significantly contributed to the normative development of the right to health. General Comments issued by the CESCR are not legally binding but provide authoritative guidance in clarifying the content of specific rights and delineating the correlative obligations. The normative evolution and implementation of the right to health has been subject to an in-depth analysis by several authors in recent years.[21] Before analysing access to medicine under the right to health, it is necessary to identify the contours of the right to health enshrined in the ICESCR.

Article 12 of ICESCR states:

(1) The States Parties to the present Covenant recognize the right of everyone to the enjoyment of the highest attainable standard of physical and mental health.

(2) The steps to be taken by the State Parties to the present Covenant to achieve the full realization of this right shall include those necessary for:
   (a) The provision of the reduction of the stillbirth-rate and of infant mortality and for the healthy development of the child;

---

16 OAS Treaty Series No. 69 (1988), entered into force 16 November 1999.

17 See Report of the first Special Rapporteur on the Right to Health, Paul Hunt (2003) UN Doc. E/CN.4/2003/58; the WHO notes that at least 135 national Constitutions recognise health as a human right. See WHO, MDG Gap Taskforce Report 2008 'Delivering on the Global Partnerships for Achieving the Millennium Development Goals' (2008) 42.

18 See, for example, Jonathan Mann et al. (eds), *Health and Human Rights: A Reader*, Routledge (1999); Sofia Gruskin and Michael A. Grodin (eds), *Perspectives on Health and Human Rights*, Routledge (2005); and Paul Farmer, *Pathologies of Power: Health, Human Rights and the New World on the Poor*, University of California Press (2005). See also articles in *Health and Human Rights: An International Journal* and in *BMC International Health and Human Rights*.

19 Adopted at 22nd session of the CESCR on 11 August 2000. UN Doc. E/C.12/2000/4.

20 The reports of the Special Rapporteur (Paul Hunt, 2002–2008; Anand Grover, 2008–) are available at http://www.ohchr.org/EN/Issues/Health/Pages/SRRightHealthIndex.aspx, last accessed 15 March 2015.

21 John Tobin, *The Right to Health in International Law*, OUP (2012); Jonathan Wolff, *The Human Right to Health*, W. W. Norton & Company (2012); Jose M. Zuniga, Stephen Marks and Lawrence O. Gostin, *Advancing the Human Right to Health*, Oxford University Press (2013).

(b) The improvement of all aspects of environmental and industrial hygiene;

(c) The prevention, treatment and control of epidemic, endemic, occupational and other diseases;

(d) The creation of conditions which would assure to all medical service and medical attention in the event of sickness.

The right to health, as mentioned earlier, is a shorthand expression of the right to the highest standard of health that a person can achieve given his/her biological preconditions. The CESCR comments that this definition of the right to health takes into account an 'individual's biological and socio-economic preconditions and a State's available resources'.[22] In order to ensure for everyone the enjoyment of the highest attainable standard of health, the right to health has to guarantee not only 'timely and appropriate health care', but also 'the underlying determinants of health, such as access to safe and potable water and adequate sanitation, and adequate supply of safe food, nutrition and housing, healthy occupational and environmental conditions, and access to health-related education and information, including on sexual and reproductive health'.[23] The right to health has both elements of freedom and entitlements. The freedom includes the right to control one's health and body and to be free from interference.[24] Entitlements include the right to a system of health protection (health care and underlying determinants of health) that provides equal opportunity for people to enjoy the highest attainable standard of health.[25]

Access to Medicines

Medicines are an indispensable part of any medical service, both in the event of sickness and in the prevention, treatment and control of diseases,[26] although access to medicines alone is not sufficient to ensure everyone an equal opportunity for good health. The CESCR considers the provision of essential drugs to be part of the measures necessary for 'the creation of conditions which would assure to all medical service and medical attention in the event of sickness (Article 12.2(d))'.[27] Numerous resolutions of the UN Human Rights Council (and its predecessor, the Commission on Human Rights) also confirm that 'access to medicines is one of the fundamental elements in achieving progressively the full realization of the right of everyone to the enjoyment of the highest attainable standard of

---

22 CESCR, GC No. 14 The Right to Health (Art. 12 of the ICESCR), adopted in 22nd session (2000) UN Doc. E/C.12/2000/4, para. 9.

23 Ibid., para. 11.

24 Ibid., para. 8.

25 Ibid., para. 9; Report of the first Special Rapporteur on the Right to Health, Paul Hunt (2003, n 17) para. 24.

26 Report of the first Special Rapporteur on the Right to Health, Paul Hunt (13 September 2006) UN Doc. A/61/338, para. 40.

27 CESCR, GC No. 14 (n 22) para. 9; Report of the first Special Rapporteur on the Right to Health, Paul Hunt (2003, n 17) para. 17.

physical and mental health'.[28] In short, access to medicines is an integral part of the right to health.[29]

The Responsibilities of States

The general obligations of the State parties to the ICESCR, to which the right to health is also subject, are set out in its Article 2(1), which reads:

> Each State Party to the present Covenant undertakes to take steps, individually and through international assistance and co-operation, especially economic and technical, to the maximum of its available resources, with a view to achieving progressively the full realization of the rights recognized in the present Covenant by all appropriate means, including particularly the adoption of legislative measures.

Understanding of the obligations of the State parties with respect to access to medicines is enhanced by the CESCR's interpretative comments on the nature of States parties' obligations (General Comment No. 3)[30] and on the Right to Health (General Comment No. 14).[31] More specifically as to access to medicines, the Special Rapporteur on the Right to Health fleshed out the obligations of States.[32] What follows are the key elements of the content of the right to access to medicines.

Progressive realisation
The wording of 'achieving progressively the full realization of the rights' in Article 2(1) reflects the reality that 'full realization of all economic, social and cultural rights will

---

28 See the UN Human Rights Council Resolutions on 'Access to Medicine in the Context of the Right of Everyone to the Enjoyment of the Highest Attainable Standard of Physical and Mental Health (13 June 2013, A/HRC/RES/23/14; 12 October 2009, A/HRC/RES/12/24). See also the UN Commission on Human Rights Resolutions on 'Access to Medication in the Context of Pandemics such as HIV/AIDS, Tuberculosis and Malaria' (E/CN.4/2003/29, E/CN.4/2004/26, E/CN.4/2005/23); and the UN Commission on Human Rights Resolutions on 'Access to Medication in the Context of Pandemics such as HIV/AIDS' (23 April 2001, E/CN.4/RES/2001/33; 22 April 2002, E/CN.4/RES/2002/32).

29 Report of the second Special Rapporteur (Anand Grover) on the Right to Health (1 May 2013) UN Doc. A/RHC/23/42, para. 3; Report of the first Special Rapporteur on the Right to Health, Paul Hunt (2006, n 26) para. 40; Yamin (n 4) 336; Danwood Mzikenge Chirwa, 'The Right to Health in International Law: Its Implications for the Obligations of State and Non-State Actors in Ensuring Access to Essential Medicine' (2003) 19 *South African Journal on Human Rights* 541–66, 548.

30 CESCR, GC No. 3: The Nature of States parties' obligations (Art. 2, para. 1 of the Covenant), adopted in fifth session (1990) UN Doc. E/1991/23.

31 CESCR, GC No. 14 (n 22).

32 Report of the first Special Rapporteur on the Right to Health, Paul Hunt (2006, n 26) paras 47–81; Report of the second Special Rapporteur on the Right to Health, Anand Grover (31 March 2009) UN Doc. A/HRC/11/12.

generally not be able to be achieved in a short period of time'.[33] The duty of progressive realisation obliges States to 'move as expeditiously and effectively as possible' towards the full realisation of economic, social and cultural rights without 'any deliberate retrogressive measures' which would require a high level of justification.[34] Nevertheless, Article 2(1) imposes an immediate obligation to 'take steps … to the maximum available resources'. The principle of non-discrimination in Article 2(2) and Article 3 of the ICESCR is also an obligation of immediate effect.[35]

Limited resources are one major factor that gives rise to the concept of progressive realisation of many human rights, including the right to health. That everyone has the right to health does not imply that everyone is entitled to access to every treatment that may improve their health. The provision of health care and underlying determinants of health, such as access to water and sanitation, involves resources and thus inevitably requires priority setting even in high-income countries, let alone in low-income countries.[36] Limited resources have to be allocated with careful consideration of competing claims to different human rights and interests, as well as competing claimants to the same right.

In relation to the right to health, decisions have to be made about the amount of resources to be allocated for health care and underlying determinants of health, and how these resources are spent. As the CESCR states, '[t]he right to health is closely related to and dependent upon the realization of other human rights, … including the rights to food, housing, work, education, human dignity, life, non-discrimination, equality, the prohibition against torture, privacy, access to information, and the freedoms of association, assembly and movement'.[37] Resources for health care cannot be allocated in isolation from these other areas.

Once the health budget is determined, it has to be utilised in full knowledge of the fact that granting some people access to a particular treatment might have the effect of denying other people access to the same or other treatments that benefit them. While there is no one firm answer to this difficult task of priority setting, the Special Rapporteur provided a useful starting point for the discussion from the right-to-health perspective.[38] What is necessary is to make the process of priority setting consistent with key human

---

33 CESCR, GC No. 3 (n 30) para. 9.

34 Ibid., para. 9.

35 Article 2(2) of ICESCR states: 'The States Parties to the present Covenant undertake to guarantee that the rights enunciated in the present Covenant will be exercised without discrimination of any kind as to race, colour, sex, language, religion, political or other opinion, national or social origin, property, birth or other status'. Article 3 requires the State parties to 'ensure the equal right of men and women to the enjoyment of all economic, social and cultural rights set forth in the present Covenant'.

36 Norman Daniels, *Just Health: Meeting Health Needs Fairly*, Cambridge University Press (2008) 318; Eugene B. Broady, *Biomedical Technology and Human Rights*, UNESCO Series, Ashgate Publishing (1993) 233, cited in *Thiagraj Soobramoney v. Minister of Health (Kwazulu-Natal)*, Constitutional Court of South Africa, Case CCT 32/97, 27 November 1997, § 53.

37 CESCR, GC No. 14 (n 22) para. 3.

38 Report of the first Special Rapporteur on the Right to Health, Paul Hunt (8 August 2007) UN Doc. A/62/214, paras 11–32.

rights elements, such as equality, participation and accountability, each of which is further discussed later. A human rights approach requires the full consideration of the totality of human rights, the analysis of the potential impact of any given option on the right to health of different groups of people with special attention to people in vulnerable situations, the participation of those affected in the priority-setting process, and the accountability of government and relevant organisations. Such a process would also help to distinguish between States' unwillingness and inability to promote the right to health.

The jurisprudence of national courts sheds light on the principle of progressive realisation in relation to access to medicines. The *Bermúdez* case of the Venezuelan Supreme Court addressed the issue of progressive realisation, including the adequacy of the allocated health budget.[39] In this case, the Ministry of Health defended its failure to provide antiretroviral treatment for people living with HIV/AIDS on the ground of its financial constraints and argued that it was progressively making improvements in relation to HIV/AIDS.[40] The Court also acknowledged that 'the budgetary capacities of the [Ministry] have been insufficient to fulfil the duty to assist the HIV/AIDS patients'.[41] Nevertheless, the Court observed that the government did not comply with its duty under the right to health in that the Ministry had not sought additional funds available under Venezuelan law.[42] As this case suggests, the principle of progressive realisation does not legitimise all failures of the government on the basis of a lack of financial resources. On the contrary, it requires a government to prove that it has taken all the steps available to fulfil its duty. In relation to the right to health, consideration should be given to the question of whether the overall allocation of resources to health is reasonable and equitable, rather than taking for granted the given resources to health.

The *Soobramoney* case in the Constitutional Court of South Africa[43] dealt with one of the difficult but quite commonly raised issues: whether everyone is entitled to access to

---

39 *Cruz Bermudez et al. v. Ministerio de Sanidad y Asistencia Social, Sala Polico Administrativa.* Corte Suprema de Justica, Republica de Venezuela, Expediente Numero: 15.789 (1999). The analysis of the case in this paragraph is based on Mary Ann Torres, 'The Human Right to Health, National Courts, and Access to HIV/AIDS Treatment: A Case Study from Venezuela', in Gruskin and Gordin (n 18) 507–18.

40 Torres (n 39) 511.

41 Ibid., 513.

42 Ibid.

43 *Soobramoney v. Minister of Health (Kwazulu-Natal)* (n 36). Soobramoney, who suffered from chronic renal failure, sought kidney dialysis treatment from a State hospital but was not provided the treatment. The policy of the hospital was that only patients that met a set of criteria were given access to dialysis treatment due to limited resources, and Soobramoney did not meet the criteria. In this case, the Court, while acknowledging section 27 of the South African Constitution 'entitles everyone to have access to health care services provided by the state "within its available resources"'(§ 22 of the decision), did not find a violation of the right to health care (§ 36). Section 27(1) of the Constitution reads '[e]veryone has the right to have access to (a) health care services, including reproductive health care'. Section 27(2) states that '[t]he state must take reasonable legislative and other measures, within its available resources, to achieve the progressive realisation of each of these rights'.

expensive treatment or drugs regardless of the limits of available resources. In this case, the Court stressed that 'the State has to manage its limited resources in order to address all these claims [to access to health care, housing, food and water, employment opportunities and social security]' and 'this requires it to adopt a holistic approach to the larger needs of society rather than to focus on the specific needs of particular individuals within society'.[44] Research by Octavio Luiz Motta Ferraz about right-to-health litigation in Brazil illustrates how the lack of such a holistic approach that takes into account the health needs, health system and resources in society has led to the reallocation of health budgets in favour of the better off in society, worsening inequalities in health outcome.[45]

Core obligations

The CESCR's interpretative comment states that the rights in the Covenant give rise to *'a minimum core obligation* to ensure the satisfaction of, at the very least, minimum essential levels of each of the rights is incumbent upon every State party' (emphasis added).[46] The CESCR provides an illustration that 'a State party in which any significant number of individuals is deprived of essential foodstuffs, of essential primary health care, of basic shelter and housing, or of the most basic forms of education is, prima facie, failing to discharge its obligations under the Covenant'.[47] According to the CESCR, without imposing a minimum core obligation, the Covenant would lose 'its raison d'etre'.[48] Minimum core obligations are, according to the definition given in General Comment No. 3, not subject to progressive realisation. Such an approach echoes with a general concept of rights, that each right, however vague the scope of a right may be, has a core that is, if not absolute, resilient to permissible infringement.[49] Nevertheless, there may be circumstances beyond the control of States, such as natural catastrophes, where States fail to meet even minimum core obligations. The CESCR, in its General Comment No. 3, envisages such circumstances, in which case the State has to prove that it has committed 'all resources that are at its disposition in an effort to satisfy, as a matter of priority, those minimum obligations'.[50] However, the concept of minimum core obligations does not entirely remove the task of priority setting even at the level of minimum core obligations because the precise scope of these obligations has to be determined contextually. In any event, the concept of minimum core obligations must inform the priority setting and helps to prevent the concept of progressive realisation from becoming a convenient excuse for States' unwillingness to take measures to realise human rights.

---

44 Ibid., para. 31.

45 Octavio Luiz Motta Ferraz, 'The Right to Health in the Courts of Brazil: Worsening Health Inequities?' (2009) 11(2) *Health and Human Rights* 33–45.

46 CESCR, GC No. 3 (n 30) para. 10.

47 Ibid.

48 Ibid.

49 Joel Feinberg, *Social Philosophy*, Prentice-Hall (1973) 79–83.

50 CESCR, GC No. 3 (n 30) para. 10; Craig Scott and Philip Alston, 'Adjudicating Constitutional Priorities in a Transnational Context: A Comment on Soobramoney's Legacy and Grootboom's Promise' (2000) 16 *South African Journal on Human Rights* 206–68, 250.

The provision of essential medicines is among the minimum core obligations of States parties to the ICESCR, in accordance with General Comment No. 14.[51] The WHO defines essential medicines as 'those that satisfy the priority health care needs of the population'. Essential medicines are selected considering 'disease prevalence, evidence on efficacy and safety, and comparative cost-effectiveness'.[52] It is a national responsibility to prepare a national essential medicines list, guided by the WHO Model Lists of Essential Medicines.[53] A State must, as a minimum core obligation, make the essential medicines on its national list available and accessible throughout its jurisdiction.[54] Access to non-essential medicines is subject to progressive realisation.[55] As discussed above, in General Comment No. 14, the CESCR has stressed the normative supremacy of minimum core obligations by stating that 'a State party cannot, under any circumstances whatsoever, justify its non-compliance with the core obligations ... which are non-derogable'.[56]

There has been scant national jurisprudence on a minimum core content of the right to health. The Colombian Constitutional Court has adopted the approach of distinguishing an essential minimum core of the right to health and other elements to be progressively realised in its recent decision regarding the country's health system.[57] Contrary to this approach, the South African Court did not accept the minimum core approach in the *Minister of Health v. Treatment Action Campaign* case.[58] The Court has taken a view that the test under its Constitution is whether the measures adopted by the government were reasonable.[59] However, the Court has suggested that a minimum core content of a specific right could be taken into account in assessing the reasonableness of the measures taken by the government.[60]

---

51 CESCR, GC No. 14 (n 22) para. 43(d) 'to provide essential drugs, as from time to time defined under the WHO Action Programme on Essential Drugs'. Report of the first Special Rapporteur (Paul Hunt) on the Right to Health (2006, n 26) para. 56.

52 WHO, The Selection and Use of Essential Medicines, Technical Report Series 920 (2003) 54. See Hans V. Hogerzeil, 'Essential Medicines and Human Rights: What can They Learn from Each Other?' (2006) 84(5) *Bulletin of the World Health Organization* 371–5.

53 The WHO Model Lists of Essential Medicines has been updated from time to time since 1977. Latest version is available at http://www.who.int/medicines/publications/essentialmedicines/en/, accessed 15 March 2015. See Richard Laing, Brenda Waning, Andy Gray, Nathan Ford and Ellen't Hoen, '25 Years of the WHO Essential Medicines Lists: Progress and Challenges' (2003) 361 *The Lancet* 1723–29.

54 Report of the Special Rapporteur on the Right to Health, Paul Hunt (2006, n 26), para. 57.

55 Ibid., para. 58.

56 CESCR, GC No. 14 (n 22) para. 47.

57 Alicia Ely Yamin and Oscar Parra-Vera, 'How do Courts Set Health Policy? The Case of the Colombian Constitutional Court' (2009) 6(2) *PLoS Medicine* 1–4. Corte Constitucional de Colombia (2008) Sala Segunda de Revision, Sentencia T-760. 31 July 2008.

58 *Minister of Health and Others v. Treatment Action Campaign and Others*, CCT 8/02, SA 721 (5 July 2002). For a critique of the Constitutional Court's view on the minimum core content of a right, see David Bilchitz, 'Towards a Reasonable Approach to the Minimum Core: Laying the Foundations for Future Socio-economic Rights Jurisprudence' [2003] *South African Journal on Human Rights* 19.

59 *Minister of Health v. Treatment Action Campaign and Others* (n 58) paras 33–35.

60 Ibid., para. 34.

Availability, accessibility, acceptability and good quality

The CESCR sets out four elements of the right to health that have to be ensured; that is, all health care facilities, goods, and services, including medicines, shall be (1) available in sufficient quantity within the State party; (2) accessible to everyone without discrimination economically as well as physically; (3) acceptable culturally and in light of medical ethics; and (4) of good quality.[61] The first Special Rapporteur on the Right to Health has elaborated these four elements in relation to medicines as follows:[62] (a) not only should existing medicines be available in sufficient quantity within the territory of States parties, but also States have to take reasonable measures to develop new medicines addressing priority health needs of people and thus make them available within a framework of international assistance and cooperation.[63] The issue of availability of medicines is acute regarding diseases predominantly affecting people in developing countries, known as 'neglected diseases', 'poverty-related diseases', or 'tropical diseases';[64] (b) medicines must be accessible in all parts of the country, economically affordable to all, and without discrimination; reliable information about medicines has to be accessible; (c) medicines must be respectful of medical ethics and of the culture of individuals and communities, which bears upon, for instance, the treatment of traditional medicine or clinical trials; (d) safety and good quality of medicines must be ensured; thus effective medicine regulation has to be in place to ensure the safety, efficacy and quality of medicines.[65] Similarly, the UN Human Rights Council requested States 'to ensure access to all, without discrimination, of medicines, in particular essential medicines, that are affordable, safe, effective and of good quality'.[66]

The following cases highlight the issue of availability and accessibility of medicines, albeit that each case does not involve exclusively one element. The Argentinean case of *Mariela Viceconte v. Ministry of Health and Social Welfare*[67] concerns availability of a vaccine for addressing an endemic disease.[68] Three-and-a-half million inhabitants of the Pampa

---

61 CESCR, GC No. 14 (n 22) para. 12.

62 Report of the first Special Rapporteur on the Right to Health, Paul Hunt (2006, n 26) paras 47–51.

63 Ibid., para. 47. The obligation of international assistance and cooperation under the ICESCR is discussed in Chapter 7.

64 Report of the first Special Rapporteur on the Right to Health, Paul Hunt: Mission to Uganda (19 January 2006), UN doc. E/CN.4/2006/48/Add.2, paras 4–9 and 62–66.

65 Report of the Special Rapporteur on the Right to Health, Paul Hunt (2006, n 26) paras 71–73.

66 See UN Human Rights Council Resolutions on 'Access to Medicine in the Context of the Right of Everyone to the Enjoyment of the Highest Attainable Standard of Physical and Mental Health' (n 28).

67 *Viceconte v. Ministry of Health and Social Welfare*, National Court of Appeals for the Federal Contentious-Administrative Jurisdiction of Argentina Poder Judicial de la Nación Causa no 31.777/96, 2 June 1998.

68 Report of the Special Rapporteur on the Right to Health, Paul Hunt (17 January 2007), UN Doc. A/HRC/4/28 para. 70; Christian Courtis, 'Socio-economic Rights before the Courts in Argentina', in Fons Coomans (ed.), *Justiciability of Economic and Social Rights: Experiences from Domestic Systems*, Intersentia (2006) 330.

region of Argentina were potentially exposed to Argentine haemorrhagic fever. However, a WHO-certified vaccine (Candid-1) for this disease was not sufficiently available due to interruption of the production by the government. The Argentinean Federal Court of Appeal ordered the government to produce Candid-1 and make it available. On the other hand, in the South African case of *Minister of Health v. Treatment Action Campaign*, a central issue was accessibility of the antiretroviral drug Nevirapine, which had proved to be effective in the prevention of mother-to-child transmission of HIV.[69] Although the drug had been offered to the public health system free of charge by the manufacturers, the South African government limited the provision of Nevirapine to only two research and training sites per province. The Constitutional Court found that such a policy 'fails to address the needs of mothers and their newborn children who do not have access to these sites',[70] and is thus unreasonable and in contravention of the State's obligations under the Constitution.[71]

The duties to respect, protect and fulfil[72]

States have duties to respect, to protect and to fulfil the right to access to medicines as they have with regard to other rights.[73] The duty to respect requires States to refrain from action that interferes with the right to access to medicines. For example, discriminating against women, ethnic minorities or other disadvantaged people in terms of access to medicine and raising prices to the level that the medicine becomes unaffordable would be in breach of the duty to respect.[74] The duty to protect obliges States to ensure that third parties do not hinder access to medicine.[75] States have to adopt legislation or measures that safeguard availability, accessibility, acceptability and quality of medicines from any limitation by third parties. The adoption of a stringent form of pharmaceutical patent law that allows private companies to impose high prices on medicines without alleviating economic burdens placed on people could constitute a violation of the duty to protect the right to access to medicines. The duty to fulfil requires States to adopt appropriate legislative, administrative, budgetary and other measures towards the realisation of access to medicines.[76] For example, States have to provide adequate information on essential medicines. The duty to fulfil includes a duty to provide people living in poverty with essential medicines when

---

69 *Minister of Health v. Treatment Action Campaign* (n 58).

70 Ibid., para. 67.

71 Bilchitz (n 58) 4.

72 The typology of obligations was proposed by Henry Shue and developed by Asbjorn Eide. Henry Shue, *Basic Rights: Subsistence, Affluence, and U.S. Foreign Policy*, Princeton University Press (1980); Asbjorn Eide, 'Realisation of Social and Economic Rights and the Minimum Threshold Approach' (1989) 10 *Human Rights Law Journal* 1–2.

73 For the duty to respect, protect and fulfil the right to access to medicine in the context of pandemics, see UN Commission on Human Rights Resolutions 'Access to medication in the context of pandemics such as HIV/AIDS, tuberculosis and malaria' (16 April 2004) 2004/26, para. 7; (15 April 2005) 2005/23, para. 7.

74 CESCR, GC No. 14 (n 22), para. 34; Report of the Special Rapporteur on the Right to Health, Paul Hunt (2006, n 26) para. 59.

75 Ibid.

76 CESCR, GC No 14 (n 22) paras 33, 36, 37.

the medicines would not be affordable otherwise.[77] Furthermore, States have to ensure the availability of new essential medicines addressing the unmet primary health needs of people through the promotion of relevant medical research and development.[78]

Access to Essential Medicines: An Element of the Right to Life

The Right to Life

The right to life is one of the most basic human rights, and it is a prerequisite to the realisation of all other human rights. The right to life is firmly embedded in international human rights instruments.[79] Article 3 of the UDHR sets forth the right to life[80] and Article 6(1) of the International Covenant on Civil and Political Rights (ICCPR)[81] states that '[e]very human being has the inherent right to life. This right shall be protected by law. No one shall be arbitrarily deprived of his life.' The right to life is also enshrined in numerous regional human rights instruments: Article 4 of the ACHPR,[82] Article 2 of the European Convention on Human Rights (ECHR),[83] and Article 4 of the American Convention on Human Rights (ACHR).[84] The right to life is a non-derogable right under Article 4 of the ICCPR, Article 15 of the ECHR, and Article 4 of the ACHR.[85] Even in times of public emergency, no derogation to the right to life is permitted.

The right to life is not limited to prohibiting the State from killing persons and protecting individuals from murder. It also encompasses protection against deprivation of life by lack of access to the means essential for survival.[86] The Human Rights Committee, in its interpretative comment on the right to life, states:

---

77 Report of the Special Rapporteur on the Right to Health, Paul Hunt (2006, n 26) para. 59.

78 Report of the Special Rapporteur on the Right to Health, Paul Hunt: Mission to Uganda (n 64) paras 62–63.

79 Bertrand G. Ramcharan, 'I. The Concept and Dimensions of the Right to Life', in Bertrand Ramcharan (ed.), *The Right to Life in International Law*, Martinus Nijhoff (1985) 1–32, 2–3.

80 Article 3 of UDHR reads '[e]veryone has the right to life, liberty and security of person'.

81 ICCPR, adopted by General Assembly Resolution 2200A(XXI) on 16 December 1966, entered into force on 23 March 1976.

82 African Charter on Human and Peoples' Rights (ACHPR), adopted on 27 June 1981 and entered into force 21 October 1986.

83 European Convention for the Protection of Human Rights and Fundamental Freedoms (ECHR), adopted by the Council of Europe on 4 November 1950 and entered into force on 3 September 1953.

84 American Convention on Human Rights (ACHR), adopted by the nations of Americas meeting on 22 November 1969 and entered into force on 18 July 1978.

85 The ACHPR has no express clause regulating derogation. However, Bertrand Ramcharan interprets that even under the African Charter no derogation is allowed with respect to the right to life since when derogation is allowed it is stated so in the article; such derogation is not expressly stated in Article 4 (the right to life). Ramcharan (n 79) 15–16.

86 Ramcharan (n 79) 4–6; F. Menghistu, 'III. The Satisfaction of Survival Requirements', in Bertrand Ramcharan (ed.), *The Right to Life in International Law*, Martinus Nijhoff (1985) 63–83, 63–5.

… the right to life has often been too narrowly interpreted. The expression "inherent right to life" cannot properly be understood in a restrictive manner, and the protection of this right requires that states adopt positive measures. In this connection, the Committee considers it would be desirable for States parties to take all possible measures to reduce infant mortality and to increase life expectancy, especially in adopting measures to eliminate malnutrition and epidemics.[87]

Such interpretation of the right to life is also found in the jurisprudence of the regional human rights bodies. The former European Commission of Human Rights considered that the right to life in Article 2 of the ECHR imposes on the State not only a duty to refrain from taking life 'intentionally', but also a 'positive duty to take appropriate steps to safeguard life'.[88] According to the Commission, the obligation to protect the right to life includes the provision of adequate and appropriate medical care. The broad interpretation of the right to life is reiterated by the Commission in the case of *Tavares v. France*.[89] The African Commission on Human and Peoples' Rights has also reasoned that, inter alia, pollution and environmental degradation 'to a level humanly unacceptable' constituted violations of the right to life.[90] Further, the Inter-American Court, in the case of *Morales v. Guatemala*, has affirmed that the right to life requires not only negative obligations but also a positive obligation 'to take all necessary measures to protect and preserve the right to life.[91] Two judges of the Inter-American Court, in a joint concurring opinion on the same case, clarify that the language 'arbitrary deprivation of life' in Article 4 of the ACHR extends to 'the deprivation of the right to live with dignity'.[92]

---

87 Human Rights Committee, GC No. 6: The Right to life (Art. 6), Adopted at the 16th session in 1982.

88 *Association X v. United Kingdom*, Application No. 7154/75 14 Decision and Reports 31 (1978) European Commission of Human Rights, 32.

89 *Tavares v. France*, Application No. 16593/90, 12 September 1991, European Commission of Human Rights, cited in Rebecca J. Cook and Bernard M. Dickens, 'Human Rights Dynamics of Abortion Law Reform' (2003) 25 *Human Rights Quarterly* 1–59.

90 *Social and Economic Rights Action Centre and the Centre for Economic and Social Rights v. Nigeria*, Communication No. 155/1996, ACHRP/COMM/A044/1 (27 May 2002) para. 67.

91 *Villagran-Morales et al. v. Guatemala* (Street Children Case), Judgment of 19 November 1999 *(Merits)* Inter-American Court of Human Rights, para. 139. Available at http://www.corteidh.or.cr/docs/casos/articulos/seriec_63_ing.pdf, last accessed 11 April 2014.

92 Ibid. Joint Concurring Opinion of Judges A.A. Cancado Trinidade and A. Abreu-Burelli (19 November 1999) Inter-American Court of Human Rights, para. 4: 'The duty of the State to take positive measures is stressed precisely in relation to the protection of life of vulnerable and defenseless persons, in situation of risk, such as the children in the streets. The arbitrary deprivation of life is not limited, thus, to the illicit act of homicide; it extends itself likewise to the deprivation of the right to live with dignity. This outlook conceptualizes the right to life as belonging, at the same time, to the domain of civil and political rights, as well as economic, social and cultural rights, thus illustrating the interrelation and indivisibility of all human rights.'

Access to Essential Medicines

The jurisprudence of the UN Human Rights Committee and regional human rights bodies confirms that the right to life encompasses access to minimum conditions necessary for survival. F. Menghistu argues that '[s]urvival requirements [for the right to life] are minimum requirements which are related to the concept of basic needs'.[93] Following this line of argument, access to essential medicines, defined earlier in this chapter, constitutes one of the minimum conditions for survival, and thus a part of the right to life. The scope of access to essential medicines is narrower than the scope of access to life-saving medicines. Life-saving medicines entail very expensive ones that can be made accessible to only a small number of people even in resource-rich countries.

In a number of national courts, the right to life has been successfully invoked, along with the right to health, in cases where a particular treatment was potentially life saving or life sustaining. The Constitutional Court of Colombia has held that denial of antiretroviral treatment under the social security system of the country violates the constitutional right to life.[94] The Indian Supreme Court, in *Samity v. State of West Bengal*, affirmed that '[a]rticle 21 (of the Constitution) imposes an obligation on the State to safeguard the right to life of every person.[95] ... Failure on the part of a Government hospital to provide timely medical treatment to a person in need of such treatment results in violation of his right to life guaranteed under Article 21.'[96] In short, the State's obligations to safeguard the right to life include the obligation to ensure everyone has access to essential medicines.

The Right to Access to Medicines as Customary International Law

Customary International Law

Custom is a source of international law. According to the Statute of the International Court of Justice (ICJ), customary international law is 'a general practice accepted as law'.[97] While treaty law binds only the parties to it, customary international law binds all States regardless of their express consent, with the exception of a persistent objector.[98] Is the right to access to medicines a norm of international customary law, as well as of treaty law?

---

93 Menghistu (n 86) 68–9, 80–81.

94 The Constitutional Court of Colombia, Protection Writ, Judgment of Fabio Moron Diaz, Magistrado Ponente, T-328/98 (Corte Constitucional de Colombia 1998), cited in Yamin (n 4).

95 Note that this case was not about access to medicines but about emergency health care.

96 *Paschim Banga Khet Samity v. State of West Bengal*, Case No. 169, Judgment of 6 May 1996, Indian Supreme Court, para. 9.

97 Article 38(b) of the Statute of the International Court of Justice.

98 *North Sea Continental Shelf Cases (Federal Republic of Germany v. Denmark; FRG v. The Netherlands)* ICJ Report 1969 3, International Court of Justice (20 February 1969) paras 70, 71. Concerning the theory of the persistent objector, the dissenting State, see Jonathan Charney, 'The Persistent Objector Rule and the Development of Customary International Law' (1985) 56 *British Yearbook of International Law* 1.

It is generally considered that, in order for a norm to be a rule of customary international law, it has to have two elements: an objective element – consistent State practice – and a subjective element known as *opinion juris sive necessitates*. In this regard, the ICJ stated in the *North Sea Continental Shelf* cases that '[n]ot only must the acts concerned amount to a settled practice, but they must also be such, or be carried out in such a way, as to be evidence of a belief that this practice is rendered obligatory by the existence of a rule of law requiring it'.[99] There have been debates among scholars about what acts of States count as State practice, and the relationship between practice and *opinio juris*.[100]

State practice

This book takes the view that both physical and verbal acts of States constitute State practice. Verbal acts include national legislation, national case law, statements made by governments, and positions taken by governments with regard to resolutions of international organisations or international treaties.[101] This approach is based on the view taken by leading bodies in the field of international law, including the ICJ, the International Law Commission, the International Law Association, and the International Committee of the Red Cross.[102] The ICJ looked for evidence of custom in official statements in numerous cases, including the *North Sea Continental Shelf* cases,[103] the *Fisheries Jurisdiction* cases,[104] the *Nicaragua* case,[105] and the *Gabčíkovo-Nagymaros Project* case.[106] The International Law Commission has also considered verbal acts to contribute to the formation of custom by listing the following categories as evidence of customary international law: international instruments; decisions of national and international courts; national

99 *North Sea Continental Shelf* cases (n 98) para. 77.

100 See Anthony A. D'Amato, *The Concept of Custom in International Law*, Cornell University Press (1971); Michael Akehurst, 'Custom as a Source of International Law' (1974–75) 47 *British Year Book of International Law* 1–53; Bruno Simma and Philip Alston, 'The Sources of Human Rights Law: Custom, Jus Cogens, and General Principles' (1988–1989) 12 *Australia Year Book of International Law* 82–108; Oschar Schachter, 'New Custom: Power, Opinio Juris and Contrary Practice', in Jerzy Makarczyk (ed.), *Theory of International Law at the Threshold of the 21st Century*, Kluwer Law International (1996) 531–2; Anthea Elizabeth Roberts, 'Traditional and Modern Approaches to Customary International Law: A Reconciliation' (2001) 95 *American Journal of International Law* 757–91.

101 Akehurst (n 100) 1–10.

102 International Committee of the Red Cross (ICRC), *Customary International Humanitarian Law, Volume I Rules*, Cambridge University Press (2004) XXXii.

103 *North Sea Continental Shelf* cases (n 98) 3, 32–3, 47 and 53.

104 *Fisheries Jurisdiction* case (*United Kingdom v. Iceland*) (25 July 1974) ICJ Reports 1974, 47, 56–8, 81–8, 119–20, 135, 161; *Fisheries Jurisdiction* case (*Federal Republic of Germany v. Iceland*) (25 July 1974) ICJ Reports 1974, 175.

105 *Military and Paramilitary Activities in and against Nicaragua* case (*Nicaragua v. United States*), Merits, Judgment (27 June 1986) ICJ Reports 1986, 100, § 190. In examining the customary law nature of the principle of the prohibition of the use of force expressed in Art. 2(4) of the UN Charter, the Court considered 'statements by State representatives' along with other evidence.

106 *Gabčíkovo-Nagymaros Project* case (*Hungary v. Slovakia*), Judgment, 25 September 1997, ICJ Reports 1997, 39–46, §§ 49–58. The Court used many official statements in declaring the validity as customary law of the concept of a 'state of necessity'.

legislation, including the regulations and declarations promulgated by executive bodies; diplomatic correspondence; opinions of national legal advisers; and the practice of international organisations.[107] The International Law Association has stated that 'verbal acts, and not only physical acts, of States count as State practice'.[108]

Density of State practice

One of the requirements for State practice to contribute to the formation of customary international law is that the practice has to be uniform, extensive and representative.[109] A long period of time is not necessarily required for a norm to solidify into a rule of customary international law. The ICJ stated in the *North Sea Continental Shelf* cases that

> the passage of only a short period of time is not necessarily, or of itself, a bar to the formation of a new rule of customary international law ... an indispensable requirement would be that within the period in question, short though it might be, State practice, including that of States whose interests are specially affected, should have been both extensive and virtually uniform in the sense of the provision invoked ...[110]

The requirement of uniformity or consistency does not require State practice to be identical or perfect with a rule in question. If the State practice is in general similar or consistent with the rule in question, it suffices.[111] The ICJ observed in the *Nicaragua* case that '[i]n order to deduce the existence of customary rules, the Court deems it sufficient that the conduct of States should, in general, be consistent with such rules, and that instances of State conduct inconsistent with a given rule should generally have been treated as breaches of that rule, not as indications of the recognition of a new rule'.[112] As extensive and representative participation has to be demonstrated, the number of States taking part in a practice is important. However, there can be no precise criterion regarding how many States participate in a practice. The important question is, as the ICJ states in the *North Sea Continental Shelf* cases, whether the practice includes 'that of States whose interests are specially affected'.[113]

Opinio juris

The other requirement for State practice to create customary international law is that it has to be coupled with evidence of *opinio juris*; a sense that the practice is undertaken by

---

107 International Law Commission (1950) II *Yearbook* 368–72.

108 International Law Association, *Final Report of the Committee on the Formation of Customary (General) International Law, Statement of Principles Applicable to the Formation of General Customary International Law*, International Law Association Conference, London, 2000, Principle 4.

109 Ibid., Principles 12, 13, 14.

110 *North Sea Continental Shelf* cases (n 98) 3, 43.

111 ICRC, *Customary International Humanitarian Law, Volume I Rules*, Cambridge University Press (2004) XXXVii.

112 *Military and Paramilitary Activities in and against Nicaragua (Nicaragua v. United States)* (n 105) § 186.

113 *North Sea Continental Shelf* cases (n 98) 43.

States as a legal duty. In the words of the ICJ, *opinio juris* plays a role in distinguishing legal obligations from obligations out of 'courtesy, convenience or tradition'.[114] This subjective element, however, does not have to exist separately from State practice.[115] State practice itself may include, within that practice, legal conviction indicating that 'certain conduct is permitted, required, or forbidden by international law'.[116]

The Right to Access to Medicines in the Context of Pandemics

This section analyses the customary nature of the right to access to medicines, but it confines the scope of the analysis to the right to access to medicines in the context of pandemics. It does not suggest any conclusion about the customary nature of the right to access to medicines in general, as that requires separate research. In order to assess whether the right to access to medicines in the context of pandemics forms part of customary international law, this chapter assesses the following sources of State practice: resolutions and declarations adopted by the UN General Assembly, human rights bodies, World Health Assembly, multilateral treaties, national Constitutions, national case law, and policy documents made by governments.

State practice
There are numerous declarations and resolutions adopted by representatives of States or governments which recognise the right to access to medicines in the context of pandemics, such as HIV/AIDS, tuberculosis and malaria. The UN General Assembly adopted a resolution titled 'Declaration of Commitment on HIV/AIDS' in 2001, without a vote.[117] In the resolution, representatives of States recognised that 'access to medication in the context of pandemics such as HIV/AIDS is one of the fundamental elements to achieve progressively the full realization of the right [to health]'[118] and declared their commitment to make every effort to provide progressively and in a sustainable manner, the highest attainable standard of treatment for HIV/AIDS, including the prevention and treatment of opportunistic infections'.[119] This resolution emphasised the obligation of conduct by States in relation to access to medicines in the context of pandemics. Although the full realisation of the right to access to medicines can be ensured only progressively, steps towards fulfilling the commitment must be taken. This approach is in line with Article 2(1) of the ICESCR, which sets out the obligations of States parties.[120]

---

114 Ibid., 3, 44.

115 International Committee of the Red Cross (n 102) xl.

116 Akehurst (n 100) 53.

117 GA, Declaration of Commitment on HIV/AIDS, 26th special session, 2 August 2001, UN Doc. A/RES/S-26/2.

118 Ibid., para. 15.

119 Ibid., para. 55.

120 Art. 2, para. 1 of the ICESCR 'Each State Party to the Covenant undertakes to take steps, … with a view to achieving progressively the full realization of the rights recognized in the present Covenant …'.

In 2003, the UN General Assembly adopted resolution 58/179, which extended the scope of the commitment to tuberculosis and malaria, beyond that of HIV/AIDS, and reaffirmed that access to medication in the context of pandemics is 'one fundamental element for achieving progressively the full realization of the right of everyone to the enjoyment of the highest attainable physical and mental health essential to ensuring the right to health'.[121] This resolution called upon States to 'develop and implement national strategies … to progressively realize access for all to prevention-related goods, services and information as well as access to comprehensive treatment, care and support for all individuals infected and affected by pandemics such as HIV/AIDS, tuberculosis and malaria'.[122] It comprehensively incorporates human rights elements of access to medicines and accordingly requires States to ensure the availability, accessibility, affordability and good quality of pharmaceutical products and medical technologies used to treat pandemics.[123] States are required to refrain from taking measures that would deny or limit equal access to medicines, to safeguard access to medicines from any limitations by third parties, and to take all appropriate measures, to the maximum available resources, to promote effective access to medicines in the context of pandemics.[124] This resolution was adopted by a vote of 181 to 1 against. The US was the only country that voted against. While one vote against this resolution does not change the fact that it was adopted with a wide acceptance, the position of the US with regard to this issue is separately considered below.

In 2006, the General Assembly, in its resolution 60/262, explicitly reiterated the right to health commitment of States that was expressed in the Declaration of Commitment on HIV/AIDS (2001) and pledged to move towards the goal of universal access to comprehensive prevention programmes, treatment, care and support by 2010.[125] The States committed themselves 'to finding appropriate solutions to overcome barriers in pricing, tariffs and trade agreements, and to making improvements to legislation, regulatory policy, procurement and supply chain management in order to accelerate and intensify access to affordable and quality HIV/AIDS prevention products, diagnostics, medicines and treatment commodities'.[126] The right-to-health commitments continued to be centred at the 2011 UN General Assembly resolution 65/277 on HIV and AIDS.[127]

The Millennium Development Goals (hereinafter MDGs),[128] the most prominent initiative on global development, also include a commitment of States that is related to the right to access to medicines in the context of pandemics by setting a goal to halt and begin to reverse the spread of HIV/AIDS, malaria and other major diseases (goal 6).

---

121 GA Resolution 58/179, para. 1, 58th session (22 December 2003) UN Doc. A/RES/58/179, adopted by 181 votes to 1 (US).

122 Ibid., para. 4.

123 Ibid., para. 6. See 'Availability, accessibility, acceptability and good quality' above.

124 Ibid., para. 7. See 'The duties to respect, protect and fulfil' above.

125 GA Resolution 60/262, 60th session, 2 June 2006, UN Doc. A/RES/60/262, adopted without a vote, para. 49.

126 Ibid., para. 42.

127 GA Resolution 65/277, 95th session, 8 July 2011, UN Doc. A/RES/65/277, para. 32.

128 UN Millennium Development Goals (MDG), available at www.un.org/millenniumgoals, last accessed 10 April 2014.

The MDGs also include a target specifically related to access to essential drugs (8e).[129] The MDGs derive from the Millennium Declaration, which was adopted by the UN General Assembly on 8 September 2000, at a Millennium Summit attended by 147 heads of State or government.[130] States repeatedly reaffirmed their commitments to these goals at various UN meetings.[131]

The Human Rights Council and its predecessor, the Commission on Human Rights, also adopted a series of resolutions reaffirming access to medicine as constituting a fundamental element for achieving the right to health and stressing the responsibility of States to ensure access to all, without discrimination, of medicines, in particular essential medicines, that are affordable, safe, effective and of good quality.[132] A number of resolutions concerned particularly access to medicines in the context of pandemics and emphasised the importance of enhancing availability, accessibility and affordability of medicines for treating pandemics and calling upon States to meet all three human rights obligations – the duty to respect, protect and fulfil.[133] At the WHO, Member States adopted several resolutions on HIV/AIDS,[134] on malaria, on intellectual property rights, on innovation and public health,[135] and on ensuring accessibility of essential

---

129 Target 8(e) of the UN MDG is to 'in cooperation with pharmaceutical companies, provide access to affordable essential drugs in developing countries'.

130 United Nations Millennium Declaration, adopted 8 September 2000, GA Resolution A/55/L.2, UN Doc. A/RES/55/2 (2000), available at http://www.un.org/millennium/declaration/ares552e.htm, last accessed 11 April 2014.

131 For example, see the outcome document of the 2010 High-Level Plenary Meeting of the General Assembly on the Millennium Development Goals, entitled 'Keeping the Promise: United to Achieve the Millennium Development Goals', paras 73 and 76, adopted at the 65th session (22 September 2010) UN Doc. A/RES/65/1; the Johannesburg Declaration on Sustainable Development adopted at the Johannesburg World Summit on Sustainable Development, para. 20 (26 August–4 September 2002), available at http://www.un-documents.net/jburgdec.htm, last accessed 15 March 2015, and the Monterrey Consensus on Financing for Development, adopted by the International Conference on Financing for Development, at Monterrey, Mexico, 18–22 March 2002, available at http://www.un.org/esa/ffd/monterrey/MonterreyConsensus.pdf, last accessed 15 March 2015.

132 See UN Human Rights Council Resolutions (n 28); in the context of pandemics, see (2005, n 73).

133 Human Rights Council, Decision 2/107 Access to Medication in the Context of Pandemics such as HIV/AIDS, Tuberculosis and Malaria, 27 November 2006, adopted without a vote; Commission on Human Rights Resolutions on access to medication (see n 28, 2005/23, 2004/26, 2003/29, 2002/32, 2001/33).

134 WHA Resolution 53.14 'HIV/AIDS: Confronting the Epidemic' (May 2000), Resolution 54.10 'Scaling up the Response to HIV/AIDS' (21 May 2001), Resolution 56.30 'Global Health-Sector Strategy for HIV/AIDS' (28 May 2003) and Resolution 57.14 'Scaling Up Treatment and Care within a Coordinated and Comprehensive Response to HIV/AIDS' (22 May 2004).

135 WHA Resolution 56.27 'Intellectual Property Rights, Innovation and Public Health' (28 May 2003), Resolution 59.24 'Public Health, Innovation, Essential Health Research and Intellectual Property Rights: Towards a Global Strategy and Plan of Action' (27 May 2006), Resolution 60.30 'Public Health, Innovation and Intellectual Property' (23 May 2007), Resolution 61.21 'Global Strategy and Plan of Action on Public Health, Innovation and Intellectual Property' (24 May 2008),

medicines,[136] although the framework of human rights, specifically the right to health, was not used explicitly.

All these resolutions and declarations are sufficiently similar to satisfy the requirement of uniformity in the sense that all of the documents call upon States to take appropriate measures in order to progressively realise access to medicines in the context of pandemics for all. Another question is whether physical acts of States are consistent in general with the verbal acts. The Secretary-General of the UN reviewed progress in implementing the 2011 United Nations General Assembly Political Declaration on HIV and AIDS based on the reports of 186 Member States (96 per cent of the UN Member States) on national progress in response to HIV.[137] The report shows that, as a result of significant expansion of antiretroviral treatment coverage, more than 8 million people in low- and middle-income countries have access to HIV treatment in 2011. However, still about 46 per cent of people who need antiretroviral treatment in those countries did not have access to it.[138] The Joint United Nations Programme on HIV/AIDS (UNAIDS) stated that 101 countries had set targets for universal access to treatment, prevention and care relating to HIV/AIDS.[139] While most States are fulfilling the duty to progressively realise access to medicines for all in the context of pandemics (obligation of conduct), many States have not yet met the goal of universal access to medicines in the context of pandemics (obligation of result). That most of the States act upon the commitments suggests that the physical practice of States is in general consistent with the verbal practice of States. The fact that the goal of universal access has not been fulfilled does not constitute a bar to the formation of a rule to impose States' obligations to ensure the right to access to medicines in the context of pandemics.

All the documents were adopted by States with a wide, if not universal, acceptance. The position of the US deserves additional attention since the US is one of 'the specially affected states' as a home for many multinational pharmaceutical companies. The ICJ in the *North Sea Continental Shelf* cases considered that the practice must 'include that of States whose interests are specially affected'.[140] Notably, even the US, whose antipathy towards economic, social and cultural rights is widely known, participated, under both Republican and Democrat administrations, in the adoption of most of the documents that set out the commitments to ensure access to medicines in pandemics discussed above.[141] Furthermore, President Clinton of the US on 1 December 1999 stated that the US would 'implement its health care and

---

Resolution 65.22 'Follow-up of the report of the Consultative Expert Working Group on Research and Development: Financing and Coordination' (26 May 2012), and Resolution 66.22 'Follow up of the report of the Consultative Expert Working Group on Research and Development: Financing and Coordination' (27 May 2013).

136 WHA Resolution 55.14 adopted on 18 May 2002; WHA Resolution 60.20 'Better Medicines for Children' adopted on 23 May 2007.

137 Report of the Secretary-General, Accelerating the AIDS Response: Achieving the Targets of the 2011 Political Declaration, 3 April 2013, UN Doc. A/67/822.

138 Ibid., para. 8.

139 UNAIDS, The Road Towards Universal Access (1 August 2008).

140 *North Sea Continental Shelf* cases (n 98) 43.

141 Holger Hestermeyer, *Human Rights and the WTO: The Case of Patents and Access to Medicines*, Oxford University Press (2007) 132.

trade policies in a manner that ensures that people in the poorest countries won't have to go without medicine they so desperately need'.[142] In May 2000, he issued an executive order which declared that the US should not obstruct the legitimate attempts of Sub-Saharan African countries that promote access to HIV/AIDS treatment.[143] Section 2012(b)(4)(C) of the 2002 Trade Act of the US (Bipartisan Trade Promotion Authority Act of 2002) commits the US government to respecting the Doha Declaration.[144] It can be concluded that the State practice also satisfies the requirement of an extensive and widespread participation.

Opinio juris

Also, the question of *opinio juris* should be examined. In other words, is the State practice promoting access to medicines in the context of pandemics accompanied by a sense of legal obligation? The ICJ in the *South West Africa* case stated that the court 'can take account of moral principles only in so far as these are given a sufficient expression in legal form'.[145] In this respect, all the three General Assembly resolutions discussed above, not to mention all the resolutions adopted by the UN human rights bodies, recognise that access to medicines in the context of pandemics is one of the fundamental elements of the right to health.[146] The right to health is provided in the ICESCR,[147] to which 161 States had become party as of February 2014. The US has not ratified, but has signed the Covenant. The right to health is also enshrined in the Convention on the Rights of the Child,[148] to which 193 countries are parties as of February 2014. The ICJ, in its advisory opinion on the legal consequences of the construction of a wall in the occupied Palestinian territory, made a reference to the right to health as a relevant legal norm.[149] Therefore, the States' commitments and follow-up measures to progressively realise access to medicines for all in the context of pandemics are, arguably, based on a legal obligation under the right to health so as to satisfy the requirement of *opinio juris*. Nevertheless, further assessment is needed as to State practice at the national level on the right to access to medicines in the context of pandemics.

The reference to the right to health or health care in national Constitutions can also constitute evidence. The existing research presents disparities in answering this question. This seems due to the fact that the different research has used different criteria for the

---

142 Available at http://www.essentialdrugs.org/edrug/archive/199912/msg00015.php, last accessed 15 March 2015.

143 Section 1(a) Executive Order No 13155, Access to HIV/AIDS Pharmaceuticals and Medical Technologies (10 May 2000).

144 Section 2012(b)(4)(C) of the 2002 Trade Act: 'The principal negotiating objectives of the United States regarding trade-related intellectual property are … to respect the Declaration on the TRIPS Agreement and Public Health, adopted by the World Trade Organization at the Fourth Ministerial Conference at Doha, Qatar on November 14, 2001'.

145 *South West Africa* case (*Ethiopia v. South Africa*), Decision, 18 July 1966, ICJ Reports 1966, 34.

146 GA Resolution S-26/2, Declaration of Commitment on HIV/AIDS (2001), para. 15; Resolution 58/179 (n 121) para. 1; Resolution 60/262 (n 125), para. 12.

147 Article 12 of the Covenant.

148 Article 24 of the Convention.

149 *Legal Consequences of the Construction of a Wall in the Occupied Palestinian Territory*, Advisory Opinion (9 July 2004) ICJ Reports 2004, 189, 191, 192.

right to health. The WHO acknowledges that at least 135 national Constitutions recognise health as a fundamental human right.[150] Kinney and Clark found that 67.5 per cent of the Constitutions of Member States of the UN, as of 30 June 2003, have provisions on a right regarding health and health care.[151] Despite differences in pinning down the numbers, it can be concluded that the recognition of the right to health in national Constitutions is a widespread practice. This leads to another question as to whether access to medicines in the context of pandemics can be implemented as part of the right to health and be enforceable through the courts. In this regard, research analysing 71 court cases from 12 countries found 59 cases where access to essential medicines as part of the fulfilment of the right to health were successfully enforced through the courts.[152] Twenty-four out of 59 successful cases related to the right to access to HIV/AIDS treatment. Although this research is limited to low-income and middle-income countries with particular relevance to Central and Latin American countries, it does provide some useful evidence of State practice.

In conclusion, the analysis of State practice suggests that the right to access to medicines in the context of pandemics is emerging as a rule of customary international law. The innumerable documents adopted by States, along with the wide acceptance and follow-up measures taken by States, evince the density of the State practice. Furthermore, the reference to the right to health found in most of the relevant documents supports the existence of States' sense of obligation, which derives from international human rights law. Numerous national Constitutions also recognise the right to health or health care, and there are a number of national cases confirming that access to medicines in the context of pandemics is implemented as part of the right to health. In short, State practice in this field supports the view that access to essential medicines in the context of pandemics is emerging as part of customary international law.

Human Rights Responsibilities of Pharmaceutical Companies

A Need for the Recognition of Human Rights Responsibilities of Companies

Companies constitute powerful global actors in the current world order.[153] Companies can benefit people, but also can pose a threat like any powerful institution if its power is

---

150 See Katrina Perehudoff, Richard Laing and Hans Hogerzeil, 'Access to Essential Medicines in National Constitutions' (2010) 88(11) *Bulletin of the World Health Organization* 800; WHO, *MDG Gap Task Force Report 2008: Delivering on the Global Partnerships for Achieving the Millennium Development Goals* (2008).

151 Eleanor D. Kinney and Brian Alexander Clark, 'Provisions for Health and Health Care in the Constitutions of the Countries of the World' (2004) 37 *Cornell International Law Journal* 287.

152 Hans V. Hogerzeil, Melanie Samson, Jaume Vidal Casanovas and Ladan Rahmani-Ocora, 'Is Access to Essential Medicines as Part of the Fulfilment of the Right to Health Enforceable through the Courts?' (2006) 368, 22 July, *The Lancet* 305–11.

153 The economic and de facto political power of some transnational corporations exceeds the power of many states. See Justin Nolan, 'With Power Comes Responsibility: Human Rights and Corporate Accountability' (2005) 28 *The University of New South Wales Law Journal* 581.

insufficiently constrained.[154] In relation to the right to access to medicines, pharmaceutical companies can significantly influence availability and accessibility of medicines by their policies, such as on patents, pricing, research and development, and licensing.[155] This section briefly describes the emergence of human rights norms regulating companies and draws attention to the human rights responsibilities of patent-holding pharmaceutical companies.

International human rights law requires States to prevent abuses by private actors, including companies, in relation to all human rights. In general, the focus of this book is on the duty of States to protect the right to access to medicines. However, there is a growing concern that imposing indirect legal obligations on companies through States may not be adequate. Such a concern points to the changing relations between States and companies, that is to say, transnational companies becoming 'ever more independent of government control'.[156] Some governments are not willing to regulate companies for fear that it will discourage foreign investment, and some other governments might use companies in their own human rights abuses.[157] In other words, the globalised economy has increased the number of situations where States are unwilling, or unable, to fulfil the duties to protect people from the power exercised by companies. The inadequacy of sole reliance on State responsibility suggests it is necessary to discuss to what extent international human rights standards can be applied directly to companies.

Direct Human Rights Obligations of Companies

A major focus in the early development of international human rights law after World War II was on States, since States represented the greatest threat to people's lives.[158] However, this is not the full story of the evolution of international human rights norms. The preamble of the UDHR provides that 'every individual and *every organ of society*, keeping this Declaration constantly in mind, shall strive by teaching and education to promote respect for these rights and freedoms and by progressive measures, national and international, to secure their universal and effective recognition and observance, both among the peoples of Member States themselves and among the peoples of territories under their jurisdiction' (emphasis added). Commenting on this part of the preamble, Louis Henkin, a prominent scholar of international law, stressed that 'every individual and every organ of society excludes no one, no company, no market, no cyberspace. The UDHR applies to them

---

154 International Council on Human Rights Policy (ICHRP), *Beyond Voluntarism: Human Rights and the Developing International Legal Obligations of Companies* (2002) available at http://www.ichrp.org/en/projects/107?theme=10, last accessed 15 March 2015.

155 UK Department for International Development (DFID), Increasing People's Access to Essential Medicines in Developing Countries: A Framework for Good Practice in the Pharmaceutical Industry: A UK Government Policy Paper, March 2005 available at http://apps.who.int/medicinedocs/en/d/Js18384en/, last accessed 15 March 2015.

156 Steven Ratner, 'Corporations and Human Rights: A Theory of Legal Responsibility' (2001–2002) 111 *Yale Law Journal* 443–545, 463.

157 Ibid., 462–3.

158 Ibid., 462–3; ICHRP (n 154) 60–61.

all.'[159] From the wording, it seems logical that companies, as organs of society, are also bound to respect human rights contained in the UDHR.

Reference to non-State actors' human rights duties is also found in the preambles to the ICESCR and the ICCPR.[160] Moreover, Article 30 of the UDHR contains a reference to group or person, as well as States, in warning that the Declaration must be interpreted in ways that do not undermine any rights set forth in the Declaration.[161] Nevertheless, it is doubtful whether either preambles to the UDHR, ICESCR, ICCPR or Article 30 of the UDHR are legally binding. It is generally a rule of interpretation that preambles to international instruments do not create legal obligations by themselves. Moreover, the UDHR is not a treaty. Even if some norms contained in the Declaration have become customary international law, it remains unclear whether they include Article 30 of the Declaration. However, whether or not corporate responsibilities are legally binding, no dispute can arise over the fact that the preambles to the UDHR and both Covenants affirm that private actors, as well as States, must strive for the respect and the observance of all human rights recognised in the UDHR and the Covenants, which is not without any legal effect.[162] That private actors shall strive to promote respect for human rights should be considered in interpreting the substantive norms in the UDHR and both Covenants.

Recent decades saw a number of attempts to create standards for companies, such as the OECD Guidelines for Multinational Enterprises,[163] the International Labour Organization Tripartite Declaration of Principles Concerning Multinational Enterprises and Social Policy,[164]

---

159 Louis Henkin, 'The Universal Declaration at 50 and the Challenge of Global Markets' (1999) 25(1) *Brooklyn Journal of International Law* 25.

160 Preambles to both Covenants state that '[r]ealizing that the individual, having duties to other individuals and to the community to which he belongs, is under a responsibility to strive for the promotion and observance of the rights recognized in the present Covenant'.

161 Article 30 of the UDHR 'Nothing in this Declaration may be interpreted as implying for any State, group or person any right to engage in any activity or to perform any act aimed at the destruction of any of the rights and freedoms set forth herein.'

162 ICHRP (n 154) 61.

163 The Guidelines for Multinational Enterprises were first adopted in 1976 by the Organisation for Economic Co-operation and Development (OECD) and have been revised five times since then. The 2011 edition of the Guidelines includes a new human rights chapter, drawing upon the UN Framework for Business and Human Rights 'Protect, Respect and Remedy' (2008). Besides, the Guidelines contain standards of practice for multinational companies covering disclosure of information, employment and industrial relations, environmental protection, combating bribery, consumer interests, science and technology, ensuring competition and payment of taxation.

164 The Tripartite Declaration of Principles Concerning Multinational Enterprises and Social Policy was adopted in November 1977 by the International Labour Organization and significantly calls on multinationals as well as governments, employers and trade unions to 'respect the Universal Declaration of Human rights and the corresponding international Covenants [on civil and political rights and on economic, social and cultural rights] adopted by the General Assembly of the United Nations as well as the principles [of the ILO] according to which freedom of expression and association are essential to sustained progress' (Article 8) available at http://

and the UN Global Compact.[165] All three initiatives request companies to respect human rights as a principle. Although none of them is legally binding, they are considered useful points of reference that can guide national governments in imposing human rights obligations on companies and provide an instrument for NGOs who seek to address human rights abuses by companies.[166]

There are some important initiatives led by the UN human rights bodies to outline human rights standards for companies. One of the most comprehensive documents in this respect is the 'Norms on the Responsibilities of Transnational Corporations and Other Business Enterprises with regard to Human Rights' (hereinafter, the Norms) that was adopted by the UN Sub-Commission on the Promotion and Protection of Human Rights (the Sub-Commission) in its 2003 session.[167] The Norms assert that '[w]ithin their respective spheres of activity and influence, transnational corporations and other business enterprises have the obligation to promote, secure the fulfilment of, respect, ensure respect of and protect human rights recognized in international as well as national law, including the rights and interests of indigenous peoples and other vulnerable groups'.[168]

The obligation to 'secure fulfilment' of human rights is of particular relevance to the present context. On this, the Commentary on the Norms elaborated that '[t]ransnational corporations and other business enterprises shall further refrain from activities that would undermine the rule of law as well as governmental and other efforts to promote and ensure respect for human rights ...'.[169] Andrew Clapham considers this obligation 'an injunction which implies that companies inform themselves of the government's human rights obligations and respect the fact that there will be legal obligations on the government to ensure the enjoyment of rights'.[170] David Weissbrodt, one of the key drafters as a member of the Sub-Commission, noted that the Norms are not 'a voluntary initiative of corporate social responsibility' and thus go 'beyond the voluntary guidelines' found in

---

www.ilo.org/empent/Whatwedo/Publications/lang--en/docName--WCMS_094386/index.htm, last accessed 10 April 2014.

165 The Global Compact is a set of standards of a voluntary nature for the business sector which includes 10 principles covering human rights, labour rights, the protection of the environment and corruption. It was established in 2000 by the United Nations. Available at http://www.unglobalcompact.org/docs/news_events/8.1/GC_brochure_FINAL.pdf, last accessed 15 March 2015.

166 Sarah Joseph, *Corporations and Transnational Human Rights Litigation*, Hart Publishing (2004) 10; ICHRP (n 154) 73.

167 Available at http://www.unhchr.ch/huridocda/huridoca.nsf/(Symbol)/E.CN.4.Sub.2.2003. 12.Rev.2.En, last accessed 11 April 2014. For scholarly comments, see Nolan (n 153); David Kinley and Rachel Chambers, 'The UN Human Rights Norms for Corporations: The Private Implications of Public International Law [2006] *Human Rights Law Review* 447–97.

168 Paragraph 1 of the Norms.

169 Sub-Commission on the Promotion and Protection of Human Rights, Commentary on the Norms on the Responsibilities of Transnational Corporations and other Business Enterprises with regard to Human Rights (26 August 2003) UN Doc. E/CN.4/Sub.2/2003/38/Rev.2.

170 Andrew Clapham, *Human Rights Obligations of Non-State Actors*, Oxford University Press (2006) 231.

the aforementioned documents.[171, 172] However, in 2004, the UN Commission on Human Rights called for a study into human rights responsibilities of corporations, instead of adopting the Norms.[173]

Following upon the request by the Commission, John Ruggie was appointed as the Special Representative of the Secretary-General on the issue of human rights and transnational corporations and other business enterprises (hereinafter, the Special Representative on Business and Human Rights or the Special Representative).[174] The Special Representative has identified 'the governance gaps created by globalization – between the scope and impact of economic forces and actors, and the capacity of societies to manage their adverse consequences' as 'the root cause of the business and human rights predicament today'.[175] With a view to closing these governance gaps, the Special Representative has developed a policy framework for business and human rights – the 'Protect, Respect and Remedy' Framework – comprising three core principles: the State duty to protect against corporate-related human rights abuse, the corporate responsibility to respect human rights, and access to effective remedy.[176] The 'Protect, Respect and Remedy' Framework suggests that the responsibility to respect, 'to do no harm', is 'the baseline expectation for all companies in all situations', which is not legally binding under international law but

---

171 The UN Global Compact, the ILO Tripartite Declaration, and the OECD Guidelines for Multinational Enterprises.

172 David Weissbrodt and Muria Kruger, 'Norms on the Responsibilities of Transnational Corporations and Other Business Enterprises with Regard to Human Rights' (2003) 97(4) *The American Journal of International Law* 901–22, 913.

173 The UN Human Rights Commission, in its 2004 session, passed a resolution stating that the Norms 'has no legal standing, and that the Sub-Commission should not perform any monitoring function in this regard'. Resolution 2004/116, Responsibilities of Transnational Corporations and Related Business Enterprises with Regard to Human Rights, contained in E/CN.4/2004/L.11/Add.7, 81–2. The largely negative responses from the governments are contrasted with the support by the most active human rights NGOs, such as Amnesty International, Human Rights Watch and the International Commission of Jurists. These NGOs endorsed them 'as a major step forward in the process of establishing a common global framework' for human rights responsibilities of companies. NGO Statement of Support for the UN Human Rights Norms for Business, delivered at the 60th Session of the Commission on Human Rights (15 March–23 April 2004) http://business-humanrights.org/en/nearly-200-ngos-join-in-oral-statement-to-un-commission-on-human-rights-supporting-the-un-norms-on-business-human-rights-0#c35999, last accessed 15 March 2015; see Kinley and Chambers (n 167) 493.

174 The mandate of the Special Representative of the UN Secretary-General on the Issue of Human Rights and Transnational Corporations and other Business Enterprises was created by the UN Commission on Human Rights in its Resolution 2005/69 (20 April 2005) and John Ruggie served the mandate from 2005 to 2011.

175 Report of the Special Representative of the Secretary-General on the Issue of Human Rights and Transnational Corporations and other Business Enterprises, John Ruggie, 'Protect, Respect and Remedy: A Framework for Business and Human Rights' (The Protect, Respect and Remedy Framework) (7 April 2008) UN Doc. A/HRC/8/5, para. 3.

176 Ibid.

subject to the possibility of binding obligations under domestic law.[177] In addition, the Special Representative has acknowledged that 'there are situations in which companies may have additional responsibilities, for example, where they perform certain public functions, or because they have undertaken additional commitments voluntarily'.[178] In order to operationalise the 'Protect, Respect and Remedy' Framework, the Human Rights Council requested the Special Representative to provide recommendations for its implementation.[179] The outcome is the Guiding Principles on Business and Human Rights, submitted by the Special Representative on 21 March 2011.[180] These Guiding Principles were adopted with consensus by the UN Human Rights Council on 6 July 2011.[181] The Framework and the Guiding Principles are revisited later under 'Putting the Human Rights Guidelines for Pharmaceutical Companies into perspective' when discussing the nature of the human rights responsibilities of pharmaceutical companies in relation to access to medicines.

It is also worth noting some guidance offered by UN human rights treaty bodies as to the behaviour of non-State actors, including companies. While only the State is bound by the standards guaranteed in the human rights treaties because States are the parties to the treaties, various UN human rights treaty bodies have addressed obligations of non-State actors, as well as obligations of States.[182] The Committee on Economic, Social and Cultural Rights' General Comment No. 14 on the right to health is of particular relevance to human rights responsibilities of pharmaceutical companies. It stresses that '[w]hile only States are parties to the Covenant and thus ultimately accountable for compliance with it, all members of society – individuals, including health professionals, families, local communities, intergovernmental and non-governmental organizations, civil society organizations, as well as *the private business sector* – have responsibilities regarding the realization of the right to health'[183] (emphasis added).

---

177 Ibid., para. 54; Report of the Special Representative on Business and Human Rights: Further Steps Toward the Operationalization of the 'Protect, Respect and Remedy' framework, UN Doc. A/HRC/14/27 (9 April 2010) para. 66.

178 Report of the Special Representative (John Ruggie): The Protect, Respect and Remedy Framework, (n 175) para. 24. See also Report of the Special Representative (John Ruggie) on Business and Human Rights: Further Steps Toward the Operationalization of the 'Protect, Respect and Remedy' Framework (n 177), paras 62 and 63.

179 Human Rights Council Resolution 8/7, Mandate of the Special Representative of the Secretary-General on the Issue of Human Rights and Transnational Corporations and other Business Enterprises, adopted without a vote on 18 June 2008.

180 Report of the Special Representative (John Ruggie) on Business and Human Rights, Guiding Principles on Business and Human Rights: Implementing the United Nations 'Protect, Respect and Remedy' Framework (21 March 2011) UN Doc, A/HRC/17/31.

181 Human Rights Council Resolution 17/4, Human Rights and Transnational Corporations and Other Business Enterprises, adopted without a vote (6 July 2011) UN Doc. A/HRC/RES/17/4.

182 See e.g. CRC, GC No. 5, 'General Measures of Implementation of the Convention on the Rights of the Child' (27 November 2003) paras 43–44, in relation to the context of privatization; CESCR, GC No. 12, 'the Right to Adequate Food (Art.11)' (12 May 1999) paras 19–20; GC No. 14 (n 22) para. 42.

183 CESCR, GC No. 14 (n 22), para. 42.

To summarise, while legally binding human rights norms for companies at the international level continue to crystallise, there are numerous soft law standards requesting companies to play their part in respecting and promoting human rights. These soft law standards can be used by companies to make internal human rights policies, for States to create human rights obligations on companies at the national level, and for NGOs to monitor companies' behaviour and to push for a legally binding global human rights framework for companies. Furthermore, increasing numbers of statements and standards bearing upon the human rights responsibilities of companies confirm a widening consensus that companies must strive for the respect and promotion of human rights, and anticipate the emergence of binding human rights norms for companies. What is further needed is to elaborate the content of human rights responsibilities of companies.

Human Rights Responsibilities of Pharmaceutical Companies in Relation to Access to Medicines

The Human Rights Guidelines for Pharmaceutical Companies

In relation to access to medicines, the efforts to give more precision to the scope of pharmaceutical companies' human rights responsibilities was started by the first Special Rapporteur on the Right to Health (hereinafter, the Special Rapporteur). The Special Rapporteur has not only prepared the Human Rights Guidelines for Pharmaceutical Companies in relation to Access to Medicines (hereinafter, the Guidelines for Pharmaceutical Companies),[184] but has also undertaken a mission to a pharmaceutical company,[185] the first of its kind by a UN human rights special procedure. The Guidelines for Pharmaceutical Companies, in the preamble, affirm that '[p]harmaceutical companies, including innovator, generic and biotechnology companies, have human rights responsibilities in relation to access to medicines'.[186] The Special Rapporteur has outlined right-to-health frameworks for pharmaceutical companies, and specified some of the right-to-health responsibilities particularly relevant to patent-holding companies.[187] Here, the following discussion focuses on the right-to-health responsibility of patent-holding companies in relation to their impact on prices of medicines and their role in research and development for neglected diseases.

Research-based pharmaceutical companies contribute to enhancing access to medicines by formulating new medicines. Patents are granted as both the reward for developing a life-saving medicine and incentives for research and development. However, the patent-holding pharmaceutical companies may negatively affect people's rights to life and health, for instance by imposing excessively high prices.[188] Medicines are inherently different

---

184 Report of the Special Rapporteur on the Right to Health, Paul Hunt (11 August 2008) UN Doc. A/63/263.

185 Report of the Special Rapporteur on the Right to Health, Paul Hunt: Mission to GlaxoSmithKline (5 May 2009), UN Doc. A/HRC/11/12/Add.2.

186 Report of the Special Rapporteur on the Right to Health, Paul Hunt (2008, n 184).

187 See Report of the Special Rapporteur on the Right to Health, Paul Hunt (2009, n 185).

188 The UK Department for International Development (DFID) stated that unaffordable prices of medicines and lack of new medicines are 'significantly affected by the activities of research-based and generic pharmaceutical companies'. UK DFID (n 155).

from other commodities in that 'the consumers of prescription drugs are often a captive rather than a willing market'.[189] The control of prices by patent-holding pharmaceutical companies is enormous since a patent-holding company tends to be the sole supplier of the medicine. This issue is acute, especially in developing countries where the government does not have adequate capacity to subsidise the cost of medicines, as well as to regulate the price of medicines at an affordable level. Thus, people in developing countries are exposed to the strong influence of pharmaceutical companies.

'Society has legitimate expectations of a company holding the patent on a life-saving medicine', the Special Rapporteur notes.[190] In other words, the company that is granted the exclusive power has corresponding responsibilities. The Guidelines for Pharmaceutical Companies help to clarify and give content to these responsibilities. The Guidelines state that the patent-holding company should respect the right of countries to use TRIPS flexibilities for promoting access to medicines, including compulsory licensing and parallel importing.[191] Also, in accordance with the Guidelines, the patent-holding pharmaceutical company has a responsibility to 'take all reasonable steps to make the medicine as accessible as possible, as soon as possible, to all those in need, within a viable business model',[192] which includes differential pricing between and within countries, non-exclusive commercial voluntary licences, non-commercial voluntary licences, donation programmes, and public-private partnerships.[193] In this way, the Special Rapporteur notes, pharmaceutical patents can be worked 'for the benefit of all those who need it'[194] consistent with the right to health.

While pharmaceutical companies that develop a life-saving medicine have played an important role in the realisation of the rights to life and health, the priority health needs of developing countries have long been neglected in the market-based research and development system.[195] In this regard, the Guidelines stress that pharmaceutical companies have a responsibility to take reasonable measures to redress this historic imbalance and suggest that 'they should either provide in-house research and development for neglected diseases, or support external research and development' for such poverty-related diseases.[196] The Guidelines further recommend that companies should 'engage constructively with key international and other initiatives that are searching for new,

---

189 Sarah Joseph, 'Pharmaceutical Corporations and Access to Drugs: The "Fourth Wave" of Corporate Human Rights Scrutiny' (2003) 25(2) *Human Rights Quarterly* 425–52, 436.

190 Report of the Special Rapporteur on the Right to Health, Paul Hunt (2009, n 185) para. 36.

191 Report of the first Special Rapporteur on the Right to Health, Paul Hunt (2008, n 184) paras 26–29.

192 Ibid., para. 41.

193 Ibid., paras 30–38; Report of the first Special Rapporteur on the Right to Health, Paul Hunt (2009, n 185) para. 38.

194 Report of the first Special Rapporteur on the Right to Health, Paul Hunt (2009, n 185) para. 107.

195 Report of the first Special Rapporteur on the Right to Health, Paul Hunt: Mission to Uganda (n 64) paras 4–9 and 62–66.

196 Report of the first Special Rapporteur on the Right to Health, Paul Hunt (2008, n 184), para. 23.

sustainable and effective approaches to accelerate and enhance research and development for neglected diseases'.[197]

Putting the Human Rights Guidelines for Pharmaceutical Companies into perspective

The Guidelines for Pharmaceutical Companies constitute an important step in the elaboration of the right-to-health responsibilities of the private business sector referred to by General Comment No. 14 of the CESCR.[198] However, pharmaceutical companies have played down the normative importance of the Guidelines. GSK commented, in its response to the report of the Special Rapporteur on GSK, that the role and responsibilities of pharmaceutical companies are not well defined.[199] Merck expressed its discomfort with the Guidelines defining human rights responsibilities specific to pharmaceutical companies.[200] Some acceptance comes from Klaus M. Leisinger, President of the Novartis Foundation for Sustainable Development, who noted that 'there is basic agreement that different pricing, donations, licenses, and *pro bono* research services are important elements' of pharmaceutical companies' responsibilities[201] although his comment was not directly addressed to the Guidelines for Pharmaceutical Companies. However, there remains uncertainty as to whether practices to improve access to affordable medicines are voluntary or obligatory.[202] Furthermore, the patent-holding pharmaceutical companies seem unwilling to acknowledge their responsibilities to respect the rights of States to use TRIPS flexibilities for public health purpose, while stressing the primary responsibility of States to ensure access to medicines.[203] Clarification should be given to the nature of the responsibilities of patent-holding pharmaceutical companies, with a view to solidifying human rights norms in this context. For this purpose, it might be helpful to consider those responsibilities identified in the Guidelines for Pharmaceutical Companies with reference to the 'Protect, Respect and Remedy' Framework[204] and the Guiding Principles on Business and Human Rights.[205]

---

197 Ibid., para. 25.

198 CESCR, GC No. 14 (n 22) para. 42.

199 GlaxoSmithKline, Statement in Response to Paul Hunt's Report on GSK (A/HRC/11/12/Add.2) June 2009. Available at http://198.170.85.29/GSK-response-to-Paul-Hunt-report-June-2009.pdf, last accessed 15 March 2015.

200 Merck, Human Rights Guidelines for Pharmaceutical Companies in Relation to Access to Medicines, prepared by United Nations Special Rapporteur, Paul Hunt. Response from Merck & Co., Inc., 29 February 2008, available at http://www.merck.com/corporate-responsibility/docs/access_developing_response_feb08.pdf, last accessed 15 March 2015.

201 Klaus M. Leisinger, 'Corporate Responsibilities for Access to Medicines' (2009) 85(1) *Journal of Business Ethics* 3–23, 19.

202 Ibid., 16, 19.

203 Ibid., 7, 11; Merck (n 200).

204 See 'Direct Human Rights Obligations of Companies' above. Report of the Special Representative on Business and Human Rights (John Ruggie): The Protect, Respect and Remedy Framework (n 175).

205 Report of the Special Representative: Guiding Principles on Business and Human Rights: Implementing the United Nations 'Protect, Respect and Remedy' Framework (John Ruggie) (n 180)

The 'Protect, Respect and Remedy' Framework and the Guiding Principles on Business and Human Rights were adopted by the UN Human Rights Council without a vote[206] and provide an authoritative UN standard for human rights responsibilities of companies. The Guiding Principles on Business and Human Rights enunciates that the responsibility of business enterprises to respect human rights 'means that they should avoid infringing on the human rights of others and should address adverse human rights impacts with which they are involved'.[207] In order to implement the responsibility to respect human rights, the Guiding Principles on Business and Human Rights recommends that companies should express their commitment to meet this responsibility, carry out human rights due diligence, and put in place 'processes to enable the remediation of any adverse human rights impacts they cause or to which they contribute'.[208] Through the process of human rights due diligence, companies should assess actual and potential human rights impacts,[209] integrate and act upon the findings,[210] track how their human rights impacts are addressed,[211] and communicate how these impacts are addressed.[212]

The Guidelines for Pharmaceutical Companies affirming that companies should not impede the efforts of States to promote access to medicines, including using TRIPS flexibilities,[213] forms the corporate responsibility to respect, 'the baseline expectation' for companies.[214] Even if the patent-holding companies may see the use of TRIPS flexibilities reducing their economic interests, the companies have responsibilities to respect the rights to life and health and not to undermine the capacity of the government to ensure access to affordable medicines through legislative or administrative measures.[215]

Also, the Guidelines for Pharmaceutical Companies' call for evaluating and adjusting companies' activities, such as on patenting, licensing and pricing, in light of their impact on access to medicines. This should be understood to form part of 'a human rights due-diligence' process, elaborated in the Guiding Principles on Business and Human Rights.[216] The primary obligation to ensure access to affordable medicines under the right to

---

206 Human Rights Council Resolution 8/7 (n 179); Human Rights Council Resolution 17/4 (n 181).

207 Report of the Special Representative (John Ruggie): Guiding Principles on Business and Human Rights: Implementing the United Nations 'Protect, Respect and Remedy' Framework (n 180) para. 11.

208 Ibid., para. 15.

209 Ibid., para. 18.

210 Ibid., para. 19.

211 Ibid., para. 20.

212 Ibid., para. 21.

213 Report of the first Special Rapporteur on the Right to Health, Paul Hunt (n 184), paras 26–29.

214 Report of the Special Representative on Business and Human Rights, John Ruggie: The Protect, Respect and Remedy Framework (n 175), para. 54.

215 For a similar comment in a wider context, see Clapham (n 170) 231.

216 Report of the Special Representative (John Ruggie): Guiding Principles on Business and Human Rights: Implementing the United Nations 'Protect, Respect and Remedy' Framework (n 180) paras 17–21.

life and the right to health lies with the State. However, patent-holding pharmaceutical companies are the only entity empowered to grant a voluntary licence for and set the price of the patented medicines in a way that can impact on the right to access to affordable medicines and undermine the capacity of the State to carry out its obligations. Therefore, these companies should carry out human rights due diligence regarding their policies on patenting, licensing and pricing.

The Special Representative on Business and Human rights notes that due diligence requires companies to consider three distinctive factors: (1) 'the country contexts in which their business activities take place'; (2) the human rights impacts of their own activities; and (3) the possibility of contributing to 'abuse through the relationships connected to their activities'.[217] In the context of access to medicines, the patent-holding pharmaceutical companies should consider the country contexts, including the human rights obligations befalling the government, income level and inequalities of the country, and the existing capacity of the government to ensure access to medicines. Considering the contexts, the patent-holding pharmaceutical companies should assess any actual or potential impacts on access to medicines of their patents, pricing, licensing and lobbying,[218] and once adverse impacts are identified, take appropriate action to cease or prevent them.[219] The Guideline 33 for Pharmaceutical Companies that recommends the company to 'consider all the arrangements at its disposal with a view to ensuring that its medicines are affordable to as many people as possible'[220] should be understood as a translation of the above human rights due diligence requirements for the pharmaceutical sector.

A remaining question is whether or not companies have additional responsibilities beyond the corporate responsibility to respect. The Special Representative acknowledged that where companies perform certain public functions, 'additional corporate responsibilities may arise as a result of the specific functions the company is performing'.[221] The Institute for Human Rights and Business, an international NGO, in its Submission to the Special Representative, noted the difficulty in defining the notion of 'public functions' and suggested that 'the scope of activities of a company and their effects' can be a more helpful criterion than 'ownership or stated purpose – public or private'. Accordingly, it observed that

> where there are circumstances under which a company's activities are tied closely with the fulfilment and realization of specific rights – for example, companies running healthcare facilities, food distribution, water provision, power generation or telecommunication providers – it seems reasonable, at a minimum, to consider further whether companies

---

217 Ibid., para. 57.

218 Ibid., para. 18.

219 Ibid., para. 19.

220 Report of the Special Rapporteur on the Right to Health, Paul Hunt (2008, n 184) para. 33.

221 Report of the Special Representative on Business and Human Rights, John Ruggie: Towards Operationalizing the 'Protect, Respect and Remedy' Framework (22 April 2009) A/HRC/11/13, para. 64.

involved in these or other services have responsibilities beyond the scope of the corporate responsibility to respect human rights.[222]

In other words, where the realisation of a specific human right depends on particular industries' core activities, responsibilities to fulfil the right may be shared between States and those companies. Developing medicines for neglected diseases is such an area. The MDGs recognise that pharmaceutical companies should cooperate with States 'to provide access to affordable essential drugs in developing countries'.[223] In accordance with the Guidelines for Pharmaceutical Companies, the companies should take reasonable measures to contribute to research and development for neglected diseases, including engaging constructively with key international and other initiatives that aim to enhance research and development for priority health needs in developing countries. In order to facilitate the implementation of this shared responsibility by the companies, there is a need for further work to delineate responsibilities among States and companies.

In short, substantial parts of the responsibilities of the patent-holding companies in the Guidelines can establish their validity by applying the corporate responsibility to respect human rights[224] and its operationalising Guiding Principles of Business and Human Rights[225] in the pharmaceutical sector. Going beyond the corporate responsibility to respect, research-based pharmaceutical companies also have a shared responsibility to contribute to research and development for the priority health needs in developing countries. The responsibilities of the patent-holding pharmaceutical companies in relation to access to medicines can help clarify the meaning of 'obligations' of the intellectual property rights holder that the TRIPS Agreement has stated in its objectives, which was alluded to under 'Objectives and Principles of TRIPS: Articles 7 and 8' in Chapter 3.[226] In order to promote the effective implementation of the Guiding Principles on Business and Human Rights, the UN Human Rights Council established the Working Group in 2011.[227]

---

222 Institute for Human Rights and Business, *Setting Boundaries: Clarifying the Scope and Content of the Corporate Responsibility to Respect Human Rights*, Submission to the UN Special Representative on Business and Human Rights, December 2009. Available at http://www.ihrb.org/pdf/Setting_Boundaries-Clarifying_Scope_and_Content_of_Corporate_Responsibility_to_Respect_Human_Rights.pdf, last accessed 15 March 2015.

223 Goal 8 'Develop a Global Partnership': Target 8.E. 'In cooperation with pharmaceutical companies, provide access to affordable essential drugs in developing countries'.

224 Report of the Special Representative (John Ruggie): The Protect, Respect and Remedy Framework (n 175) paras 51–81.

225 Report of the Special Representative (John Ruggie): Guiding Principles on Business and Human Rights: Implementing the United Nations 'Protect, Respect and Remedy' Framework (n 180) paras 17–21.

226 Article 7 [Objectives] of the TRIPS Agreement states: 'The protection and enforcement of intellectual property rights should contribute to the promotion of technological innovation and to the transfer and dissemination of technology, to the mutual advantage of producers and users of technological knowledge and in a manner conducive to social and economic welfare, and to a balance of rights and *obligations*' (emphasis added).

227 See Human Rights Council Resolution 17/4 (n 181).

The evolving norms and mechanisms governing the responsibilities of companies at the UN will provide an opportunity to enhance human rights accountabilities and solidify the content of the human rights responsibilities of the patent-holding pharmaceutical companies, as well as companies in general.

Conclusion

This chapter has examined the human right to access to medicines in international law. Access to medicines is one of the fundamental elements of the right to health. States are required, as a minimum core obligation, to ensure that quality essential medicines are available in sufficient quantity, accessible and economically affordable. The right to life requires States not only to refrain from taking life intentionally but also to adopt positive measures to safeguard life with dignity, including the provision of essential medicines. Therefore, access to essential medicines is part of the right to life. Furthermore, this chapter has considered the right to access to essential medicines as an emerging customary international norm, particularly in the context of pandemics, which is evidenced by State practice in this field, including via numerous declarations and national Constitutions recognising the right, and the implementation of the right by national authorities. Based on the recent normative developments regarding human rights responsibilities of companies, this chapter has also argued that patent-holding pharmaceutical companies should carry out human rights due diligence in relation to access to medicines as part of their responsibilities to respect human rights, and furthermore contribute to enhance availability and accessibility of medicines for neglected diseases as a shared responsibility with States.

The human right to access to medicines under international law should be a cornerstone of a normative framework for addressing the issue of intellectual property and access to medicines. The role of the right to access to medicines in the interpretation and implementation of intellectual property law and rule is discussed in chapters 6 and 7.

Chapter 5
The Right to Science and Culture

Introduction

Rights relating to the development of science and culture are enshrined in international human rights instruments, notably in Article 27 of the UDHR and Article 15 of the ICESCR. These provisions recognise the right to take part in cultural life, the right to the benefit from scientific progress and its applications, as well as the right of those who contribute to the development of science, arts or culture.[1] The analysis of these provisions can contribute to developing a human rights framework within which knowledge creation, and access to it, is promoted and balanced. However, these provisions have barely received attention, either from the UN human rights mechanisms or from academic literature. The Committee on Economic, Social and Cultural Rights (CESCR) has produced interpretive comments on the right to take part in cultural life (Art. 15.1(a) of the ICESCR)[2] and on the right to the protection of moral and material interests of the author (Art. 15.1(c) of the ICESCR),[3] but not on the right to the benefit from scientific progress and its applications (Art. 15.1(b) of the ICESCR) as of the present date. The rights stipulated in Article 15.1(b) and (c) are of particular relevance to the present context of intellectual property and access to medicines. This chapter highlights some essential features of Article 15.1(b) and Article 15.1(c).

Considering that the normative contents of these rights have not yet crystallised, the first section of this chapter briefly reviews the drafting history of the relevant provisions in the UDHR and ICESCR.[4] Although the provisions must be interpreted and

---

1 What is protected under Art. 27.2 of the UDHR and Art. 15.1(c) is often misunderstood as 'intellectual property rights'. However, the scope of 'the moral and material interests resulting from any scientific, literary or artistic production of which he is the author' is different from the rights that are protected in the existing intellectual property system. Thus, here, the term, 'the author's right' or 'the right to benefit from the protection of the moral and material interests of the author' is alternatively employed unless the full phrase is used. The differences between the right to the protection of the moral and material interest of the author and the existing intellectual property rights are discussed later in this chapter.

2 CESCR, GC No. 21, Right of Everyone to Take Part in Cultural Life (Art. 15, para. 1(a) of the ICESCR) (21 December 2009).

3 CESCR, GC No. 17, The Right of Everyone to Benefit from the Protection of the Moral and Material Interests Resulting from Any Scientific, Literary or Artistic Production of Which He or She is the Author (Art. 15, para. 1(c) of the ICESCR) (12 January 2006).

4 For more detailed discussion of the drafting history, see Maria Green, 'Drafting History of the Article 15 (1) (c) of the International Covenant on Economic, Social and Cultural Rights', Background Paper submitted to UN Economic and Social Council, CESCR, 24th Session

implemented in light of current developments, the drafting history helps to clarify their origin and meaning, and provides some valuable perspectives on contemporary issues arising from intellectual property, including the issue of access to medicines. The second section provides a preliminary understanding of the normative content of the right to enjoy the benefits of scientific progress and its applications, using some key concepts of the CESCR's analytical framework, for example freedoms and entitlements, and a tripartite typology of State obligations to respect, protect and fulfil. This analysis is based on emerging discussions on this right. The third section briefly discusses the right to benefit from the protection of the moral and material interests of the author. Drawing upon the interpretive comments of the CESCR,[5] this chapter pays special attention to some of the elements of the right that often create confusion, with a view to promoting enhanced understanding.

Drafting History

Article 27 of the UDHR and Article 15 of the ICESCR both address everyone's right to the benefits of scientific progress and cultural participation on one hand and the right to the protection of moral and material interests of the author on the other. This chapter refers to the former as the 'access element' and the latter as the 'protection element', as Lea Shaver suggested.[6] While the provisions on the right of everyone to the benefits of scientific advancement and cultural participation were adopted with little dispute, the provision on the right to benefit from the protection of the moral and material interests of the author gave rise to much controversy throughout the drafting process of both the UDHR and ICESCR.

Article 27 of the Universal Declaration of Human Rights

Article 27 of the UDHR:

> 1. Everyone has the right freely to participate in the cultural life of the community, to enjoy the arts and to share in scientific advancement and its benefits.

> 2. Everyone has the right to the protection of the moral and material interests resulting from any scientific, literary or artistic production of which he is the author.

John Humphrey, Director of the Division on Human Rights, compiled a list of draft provisions for the UDHR in the First Session of the Human Rights Commission. Humphrey's draft included the provision '[e]veryone, has the right to participate in the

---

(9 October 2000) UN Doc. E/C.12/2000/15; Johannes Morsink, *The Universal Declaration of Human Rights: Origins, Drafting, and Intent*, University of Pennsylvania Press (1999).

    5 CESCR, GC No. 17 (n 3).

    6 Lea Shaver, 'The Right to Science and Culture' [2010] *Wisconsin Law Review* 121–84.

cultural life of the community, to enjoy the arts and to share in the benefits of science'.[7] According to Johannes Morsink's account, this cultural right provision holds an idea that equal opportunity shall be provided for all to participate in the cultural life.[8] It is also noteworthy that the drafters, by stressing the word 'benefits', made it clear that the benefits of scientific progress shall be available to all as a human right.[9] The French delegate René Cassin concurred that 'even if all persons could not play an equal part in scientific progress, they should indisputably be able to participate in the benefits derived from it'.[10] Following a suggestion by the Peruvian delegate, José Encinas, the word 'freely' was inserted in the final draft of what is now Article 27.1, in its first sentence. Encinas emphasised the significance of recognising 'freedom of creative thought, in order to protect it from harmful pressures which were only too frequent in recent history'.[11] His proposal was adopted by a vote of 38 to 0, with two abstentions.

The right to the protection of the moral and material interests of the author was not in Humphrey's draft article on cultural rights. Cassin introduced a provision on the author's right in his draft,[12] emphasising the 'moral rights' aspect. The Cassin provision reads that '[t]he authors of all artistic, literary and scientific works and inventors shall retain, in addition to the just remuneration of their labour, a moral right to their work or discovery which shall not disappear even after such work or discovery has become the common property of mankind'.[13] However, the proposed provision on the right to the protection of the moral and material interests of the author encountered objections. The UK and Indian delegations expressed their view that 'no special group should be singled out for attention'.[14] A similar view recurred when the UK and Australian delegations argued that this proposed right could not fit with human rights of a general nature. The US delegation contended that this right would be more properly dealt with in 'the domain of copyrights'.[15] However, the French delegation highlighted 'the special

---

7 Article 44 of the 'Humphrey Draft': A Draft Outline of an International Bill of Human Rights (prepared by the Division of Human Rights of the Secretariat), in Mary Ann Glendon (ed.), *A World Made New: Eleanor Roosevelt and the Universal Declaration of Human Rights*, Random House (2001) 271–4.

8 Morsink (n 4) 218.

9 Ibid., 219. The word 'benefits' was omitted by mistake and restored with the unanimous approval of the drafters. Pérez Cisneros, the Cuban delegate, noticed the omission and argued for the restoration of the word 'benefits' saying that 'not everyone was sufficiently gifted to play a part in scientific advancement'. The French Delegate René Cassin concurred that 'even if all persons could not play an equal part in scientific progress, they should indisputably be able to participate in the benefits derived from it'.

10 Ibid.

11 Ibid., 218.

12 Cassin was requested to make a new draft based on discussions in the Drafting Committee of the Commission on Human Rights. Ibid., 8.

13 Article 43 of the 'Cassin Draft': Suggestions Submitted by the Representative of France for Articles of the International Declaration of Human Rights, in Glendon (n 7) 275–80.

14 Morsink (n 4) 221.

15 Ibid., 221.

character of the moral interests' over mutilation and other misuse of the creation.[16] Mexican delegate Pablo Campos Ortiz claimed that all forms of work, manual as well as intellectual, should be safeguarded, and defended what is now the second paragraph of Article 27 as the one protecting the rights of the individual 'as an intellectual worker, artist, scientist or writer'.[17] The Chinese delegate, Peng-Chun Chang, offered a different perspective, in favour of the right, proposing that the moral rights provision could promote the interests of everyone, as well as of intellectual workers, by securing the integrity of the creation.[18]

There were two international events that also influenced the drafting process: the Conference on the Berne Convention for the Protection of Literary and Artistic Works (Berne Convention) and the drafting of the American Declaration on the Rights and Duties of Man (hereinafter, ADRD), both of which took place in 1948.[19] As an outcome of the Conference, the Berne Convention was revised so as to strengthen protection against actions that would be prejudicial to the author's honour or reputation. Most Latin American nations recognised the author's right by including, in the ADRD, 'the right to the protection of his moral and material interests as regards his inventions or any literary, scientific, or artistic works of which he is the author'. The ADRD offered the French delegation, as well as delegations from Latin America, a strong basis for discussion in favour of the inclusion of the right to the protection of the moral and material interests of the author in the UDHR. The provision on the right to the protection of the moral and material interests resulting from any scientific, literary or artistic production of which he is the author (Art. 27(2) of the UDHR) was adopted by 18 votes to 13, with 10 abstentions.[20]

Article 15 of the International Covenant on Economic, Social and Cultural Rights

Article 15 of the ICESCR reads that:

1. The States Parties to the present Covenant recognize the right of everyone:
   (a) To take part in cultural life
   (b) To enjoy the benefits of scientific progress and its applications
   (c) To benefit from the protection of the moral and material interests resulting from any scientific, literary or artistic production of which he is the author

---

16 Ibid.

17 Ibid.

18 Ibid., 221–2. Chang stated that the proposed moral rights provision was 'not merely to protect creative artists but to safeguard the interests of everyone. … [L]iterary, artistic and scientific works should be made accessible to the people directly in their original form. This could only be done if the moral rights of the creative artist were protected'.

19 Ibid., 220.

20 Ibid., 222.

2. The steps to be taken by the States parties to the present Covenant to achieve the full realization of this right shall include those necessary for the conservation, the development and the diffusion of science and culture.

3. The States Parties to the present Covenant undertake to respect the freedom indispensable for scientific research and creative activity.

4. The States parties to the present Covenant recognize the benefits to be derived from the encouragement and development of international contacts and cooperation in the scientific and cultural fields.

As with the drafting process of the UDHR, while there was strong support for the right to the benefits of scientific progress (Art. 15.1(b)) and cultural participation (Art. 15.1(a)), the provision on the right to the protection of the moral and material interests of the author (Art. 15.1(c)) had to overcome strong objections. The United Nations Educational, Scientific and Cultural Organization (UNESCO) presented two versions of a draft provision concerning science and culture. With regard to the right to the benefits of scientific progress, Jacques Havet from UNESCO stated:

> The right of everyone to enjoy his share of the benefits of science was to a great extent the determining factor for the exercise by mankind as a whole of many other rights … Enjoyment of the benefits of scientific progress implied the dissemination of basic scientific knowledge, especially knowledge best calculated to enlighten men's minds and combat prejudices, coordinated efforts on the part of States, in conjunction with the competent specialized agencies, to raise standards of living, and a wider dissemination of culture throughout the processes and apparatus created by science.[21]

No dissent to his proposal was presented and the text on the right to cultural participation (Art. 15.1(a)) and the benefits of scientific progress (Art. 15.1(b)) was adopted by a vote of 15 to 0, with three abstentions.[22]

The proposed text on the right to the protection of moral and material interests of the author generated heated debate. The US delegate, Eleanor Roosevelt, pointed out 'the complexities of that subject' as a reason for the inappropriateness of its inclusion in the Covenant.[23] The UK and Yugoslavia made similar points.[24] Another important concern

---

21 UN Doc. E/CN.4/SR.228, at 11–12, cited in Green (n 4) para. 20.

22 Green (n 4) para. 20. One controversial issue was whether or not the phrase 'in the interest of the maintenance of peace and cooperation among nations', as the ends that scientific research should serve, should be added. The majority of Members opposed this proposal as they feared that it could be a pretext for political interference with scientific research. Green (n 4) para. 42; William A. Schabas, '7 Study of the Right to Enjoy the Benefits of Scientific and Technological Progress and its Applications', in Yvonne Donders and Vladimir Volodin (eds), *Human Rights in Education, Science and Culture: Legal Developments and Challenges*, UNESCO, Ashgate Publishing (2007) 281.

23 Green (n 4) para. 23.

24 Ibid., para. 28.

raised by other delegates was the negative impact that the protection of an author's right might have on the under-developed countries. The Chilean delegate, Valenzuela, noted:

> [I]ntellectual production should be protected; but there was also need to protect the under-developed countries, which had greatly suffered in the past from their inability to compete in scientific research and to take out their own patents. As a result, they were in thrall to the technical knowledge held exclusively by a few monopolies. As the [inclusion of the right to the protection of the moral and material interests of the author] would perpetuate that situation, [I] would have to vote against it.[25]

It was followed by similar positions being adopted by Azmi Bey, the Egyptian delegate, and Whitiam, the Australian delegate.[26] As a result, when the Commission on Human Rights submitted the draft article to the General Assembly, the article lacked the provision on the protection of the moral and material interests of the author.

However, a provision on this right resurfaced in the General Assembly Third Committee in 1957. The Uruguayan and Costa Rican delegates submitted a proposal reinserting the provision on the right to the protection of the moral and material interests of the author. Tejera, from Uruguay, reiterated the point made by Chang in earlier discussions on the UDHR, stating that 'the right of the author and the right of the public were not opposed to but complemented each other. Respect for the right of the author would assure the public of the authenticity of the works presented to it'.[27] Responses to the proposal varied. However, the provision on the right to the protection of the moral and material interests of the author finally survived objections and was eventually adopted, as Article 15.1(c), by 39 votes to 9, with 24 abstentions.[28]

It is worthwhile to note a few points regarding the drafting history. First, while most debates concentrated on whether the provision on the right to the protection of the moral and material interests of the author should be included, neither the scope of the right nor the methods of implementing the right was delineated by the drafters. Second, given that three elements, the right to cultural participation, the right to the benefits of scientific progress, and the right to the protection of the moral and material interests of the author, constitute a single article in the UDHR and ICESCR, the drafters seemed to see these three elements as interrelated, which has to be kept in mind in interpreting the provisions.[29] Nevertheless, little consideration was given to the relationship of, and the potential tension between, the 'access element' and the 'protection element'.[30] Therefore, it is left to the human rights community of today to clarify the meaning of each right and their relationship to each other.

---

25 Ibid., para. 29.

26 Ibid., para. 30.

27 Ibid., para. 35.

28 Ibid., para. 41.

29 Audrey R. Chapman, 'Core Obligations Related to ICESCR Article 15(1)(c)', in Audrey Chapman and Sage Russell (eds), *Core Obligations: Building a Framework for Economic, Social and cultural Rights*, Intersentia (2002) 314.

30 Green (n 4) para. 45; Chapman (n 29) 315.

The Right of Everyone to Enjoy the Benefits of Scientific Progress and its Applications (Art. 15.1(b) of the ICESCR)

Background

Several international human rights instruments enshrine the right of everyone to enjoy the benefits of scientific progress and its applications. Article 27(1) of the UDHR states that 'everyone has the right ... to share in scientific advancement and its benefits'.[31] The right to enjoy the benefits of scientific progress became a legally binding norm as Article 15 of the ICESCR included it in its paragraph 1(b).[32] This right is also found in regional human rights instruments, such as Article 13 of the ADRD[33] and Article 14 of the Protocol of San Salvador.[34] As seen in the drafting history, Article 27(1) of the UDHR and Article 15.1(b) of the ICESCR were adopted with little controversy, which indicates general agreement among the drafters on recognition of the right to enjoy the benefits of scientific progress and its applications. However, since then, little work has been undertaken to elaborate the meaning of the right to enjoy the benefits of scientific progress, and authoritative interpretation of this right has yet to be adopted by the CESCR.[35] In the meantime, accelerated scientific and technological developments have increased the effects on human rights, both in positive and negative ways, giving rise to a strong need for human rights guidance in this field. The right to enjoy the benefits of scientific progress can potentially help to address normative issues arising from scientific development.

Only recently, academic literature discussing the right to enjoy the benefits of scientific progress has begun to emerge.[36] A pioneering work for developing the normative content

---

31 Article 27(1) 'Everyone has the right freely to participate in the cultural life of the community, to enjoy the arts and *to share in scientific advancement and its benefits*' (emphasis added).

32 Article 15, paragraph 1 states: 'The States Parties to the present Covenant recognize the right of everyone: ... (b) To enjoy the benefits of scientific progress and its applications ...'.

33 Article 13 of the American Declaration of the Rights and Duties of Man: 'Every person has the right to take part in the cultural life of the community, to enjoy the arts, and to participate in the benefits that result from intellectual progress, especially scientific discoveries'. OAS Res. XXX, adopted by the Ninth International Conference of America States in 1948.

34 Article 14 of the Additional Protocol to the American Convention on Human Rights in the Area of Economic, Social and Cultural Rights (the Protocol of San Salvador: 1980): '1. The States Parties to this Protocol recognize the right of everyone: ... (b) to enjoy the benefits of scientific progress and technological progress ...'.

35 Report of the Independent Expert in the Field of Cultural Rights, Farida Shaheed (22 March 2010) UN Doc. A/HRC/14/36, para. 13.

36 The few academic sources are such as Audrey Chapman, 'Towards an Understanding of the Right to Enjoy the Benefits of Scientific Progress and Its Applications' (2009) 8(1) *Journal of Human Rights* 1–36; Richard Pierre Claude, 'Scientists' Rights and the Human Rights to the Benefits of Science', in Chapman and Russell (n 29) 247–78; Schabas (n 22); Hans Morten Haugen, '6 The Right to Benefit from the Moral and Material Interests of Scientific Production and the Right to Enjoy Benefits from Scientific Progress and Its Applications', in *The Right to Food and the TRIPS Agreement*, Martinus Nijhoff (2007) 169–212; Shaver (n 6).

of this right was started under the auspices of UNESCO, which culminated with the adoption of the Venice Statement.[37] The Venice Statement, aiming to clarify the meaning of the right to enjoy the benefits of scientific progress, was the outcome of a series of meetings by a group of experts from academia, intergovernmental organisations such as UNESCO, WIPO and the WTO, and UN human rights bodies such as the Office of the High Commissioner for Human Rights and the CESCR. This initiative was followed by further efforts to elaborate the content of this right. In 2010, the Board of Directors of the American Association for the Advancement of Science (AAAS), the world's largest multi-disciplinary scientific society, adopted a statement that recognised the importance of this right, and has contributed to the relevant discussions in a significant way.[38] In the following year, the Inter-American Commission on Human Rights held a hearing on this right.[39] The UN Independent Expert in the field of Cultural Rights also undertook the work to further elaborate the normative content of the right to enjoy the benefits of scientific progress, taking into account the views of States and experts, and placed this right on the agenda of the Human Rights Council in 2012.[40]

Building upon this recent work, the following section analyses the content of the right to enjoy the benefits of scientific progress, and corresponding obligations of the State.

Scope of the Right to Enjoy the Benefits of Scientific Progress and its Applications

The Special Rapporteur in the field of cultural rights sets out that basic tenets of this right include (a) access by all without discrimination to the benefits of science and its applications, including scientific knowledge; (b) freedom indispensable for scientific research; (c) participation of individuals and communities in decision making; (d) an enabling environment for the conservation, development and diffusion of science.

The right to enjoy the benefits of scientific progress contains both freedoms and entitlements. While this section considers the general contours of this right, it pays special attention to universal access to the benefits of scientific progress as a key element of this right, and addresses the implication of this right for knowledge production.

---

37 UNESCO, The Right to Enjoy the Benefits of Scientific Progress and its Applications: the Outcome of the Experts' Meeting held on 16–17 July 2009 in Venice, Italy. Available at http://unesdoc.unesco.org/images/0018/001855/185558e.pdf, last accessed 15 March 2015. This initiative was undertaken in cooperation with the European Inter-University Centre for Human Rights and Democratisation (EIUC), the Amsterdam Center for International Law, and the Irish Centre for Human Rights.

38 See the AAAS Statement on the Human Right to the Benefits of Scientific Progress, adopted by the AAAS Board of Directors (16 April 2010) available at http://www.aaas.org/sites/default/files/migrate/uploads/Article15_AAASBoardStatement.pdf, last accessed 15 March 2015.

39 The video on the hearing can be downloaded at http://www.oas.org/es/cidh/audiencias/hearings.aspx?lang=en&session=123, last accessed 15 March 2015.

40 Report of the Special Rapporteur in the field of Cultural Rights, Farida Shaheed (14 May 2012) UN Doc. A/HRC/20/26.

Freedoms

The freedoms entail academic and scientific freedom, and freedom from potential harmful effects of science and its applications. The Venice Statement has considered academic and scientific freedom to include 'freedoms of opinion and expression, to seek, receive and impart information, and association and movement'.[41] Freedom of expression, and freedom to seek, receive and impart scientific information and ideas are inextricably related to the right to information enshrined in Article 19.2 of the ICCPR.[42, 43] The freedom of scientists to association and movement is respectively linked with Article 22.1,[44] and Article 12 of the ICCPR.[45] The freedom to scientific information and ideas not only has merit on its own, but is also a prerequisite for the realisation of the right to enjoy the benefits of scientific progress. Free access to scientific information is essential for identifying the potential benefits of scientific progress and to its enjoyment.[46]

Freedom of scientific research is directly addressed by Article 15.3 of the ICESCR, which states that '[t]he States Parties to the present Covenant undertake to respect the freedom indispensable for scientific research and creative activity'. A significant amount of

---

41 Venice Statement on the Right to Enjoy the Benefits of Scientific Progress and its Applications (2009), para. 13(a). Available at http://unesdoc.unesco.org/images/0018/001855/185558e.pdf, last accessed 15 March 2015.

42 Article 19.2 of the ICCPR 'Everyone shall have the right to freedom of expression; this right shall include freedom to seek, receive and impart information and ideas of all kinds, regardless of frontiers, either orally, in writing or in print, in the form of art, or through any other media of his choice'.

43 Schabas (n 22), 299–300; Hiroko Yamane, 'Impacts of Scientific and Technological Progress on Human Rights: Normative Response of the International Community', in Christopher Gregory Weeramantry (ed.), *Human Rights and Scientific and Technological Development*, United Nations University Press (1990) 103.

44 Article 22(1) of ICCPR states: 'Everyone shall have the right to freedom of association with others, including the right to form and join trade unions for the protection of his interests.'

45 Article 12. '1. Everyone lawfully within the territory of a State shall, within that territory, have the right to liberty of movement and freedom to choose his residence. 2. Everyone shall be free to leave any country, including his own. 3. The above-mentioned rights shall not be subject to any restrictions except those which are provided by law, are necessary to protect national security, public order (ordre public), public health or morals or the rights and freedoms of others, and are consistent with the other rights recognized in the present Covenant. 4. No one shall be arbitrarily deprived of the right to enter his own country.'

46 'There is no question that human beings have the right to benefit from scientific and technological progress. And this right logically implies that in order to make responsible qualitative judgments on how this "benefit" should be defined, people have the right to information concerning scientific and technological developments. Again it is clear that the key principle involved in making decisions about human rights in a world of rapidly advancing science and technology is the right to information. As scientific and technological developments continue to play an increasingly significant role in more and more human lives, the right to have free access to accurate, truthful, and complete information concerning these developments should be self-evident.' Yamane (n 43) 102–3.

scientific research is now undertaken by industries.[47] In this changing context, the freedom of scientific research may be interfered with not only by States, but also by private, non-State actors, which presents new challenges.[48]

Freedom from potential harmful effects of scientific progress also constitutes an element of the right to enjoy the benefits of scientific progress. Potential harmful effects of scientific advancement on human rights have been a major concern in terms of scientific progress and human rights. This is reflected in the Proclamation of Teheran (1968),[49] the Declaration on the Use of Scientific and Technological Progress in the Interest of Peace and for the Benefit of Mankind (1975),[50] and the Vienna Declaration and Programme of Action (1993),[51] although the main area of such concern has been changing according to the development of technologies and social responses to these developments. For example, while the arms race appeared a major source of concern in the 1975 Declaration,[52] the potential adverse effects of 'the biomedical and life sciences as well as … information technology' were given attention in the Vienna Declaration (1993).[53] The freedom from potential harmful effects of scientific progress indicates that the freedom of scientific research is not without limitations, but should be exercised responsibly.

Entitlements

The cornerstone of this right is that everyone should be able to share the benefits of scientific progress and its applications. The entitlements include access to scientific

---

47 See Venice Statement (n 41) para. 5. 'The relationship between human rights and science is further complicated by the fact that private and non-State actors are increasingly the principal producers of scientific progress and technological advances.'

48 See Claude (n 36) 260–61; Schabas (n 22) 280–82.

49 Proclamation of Teheran, Final Act of the International Conference on Human Rights, Teheran, 22 April to 13 May 1968, UN Doc. A/CONF. 32/41 at 3 (1968). Available at http://www1.umn.edu/humanrts/instree/l2ptichr.htm, last accessed 11 April 2014. Paragraph 18 states that 'while recent scientific discoveries and technological advances have opened vast prospects for economic, social and cultural progress, such developments may nevertheless endanger the rights and freedoms of individuals and will require continuing attention'.

50 See preamble and paras 2 and 7 of Declaration on the Use of Scientific and Technological Progress in the Interests of Peace and for the Benefit of Mankind, Proclaimed by General Assembly Resolution 3384 (XXX) of 10 November 1975, available at http://www.ohchr.org/EN/ProfessionalInterest/Pages/ScientificAndTechnologicalProgress.aspx, last accessed 15 March 2015.

51 'Everyone has the right to enjoy the benefits of scientific progress and its applications. The World Conference on Human Rights notes that certain advances, notably in the biomedical and life sciences as well as in information technology, may have potentially adverse consequences for the integrity, dignity and human rights of the individual, and calls for international cooperation to ensure that human rights and dignity are fully respected in this area of universal concern'. Paragraph 18 of the Vienna Declaration and Programme of Action, Adopted by the World Conference on Human Rights on 25 June 1993, available at http://www.ohchr.org/EN/ProfessionalInterest/Pages/Vienna.aspx, last accessed 15 March 2015.

52 See the Declaration on the Use of Scientific and Technological Progress in the Interests of Peace and for the Benefit of Mankind (n 50).

53 Paragraph 18 of the Vienna Declaration and Programme of Action (n 51).

information and education, participation in the process of setting a priority of scientific research, and access to products and services generated by scientific progress. Access to scientific information constitutes entitlement as well as freedom. The meaningful participation of people in the decision-making process on issues relating to science is also crucial to the right to enjoy the benefits of scientific progress, particularly when determining priorities for the development of science and technology.[54]

Access to the benefits of scientific progress and its applications is also linked to other human rights. Caution should be exercised when the state of scientific and technological development seems to be used as a convenient excuse for the non-realisation of human rights.[55] However, the ability to access products and services generated by scientific progress can have a significant impact on the realisation of certain human rights, such as the rights to food, health, education, and freedom of information and expression. For instance, in the area of the right to food and the right to health, scientific progress may condition the availability and quality of food and health products which are crucial to the realisation of such rights.[56] The relevance to the realisation of other human rights can be one of the criteria for evaluating what scientific development should be prioritised and equitably accessed in terms of the right to enjoy the benefits of scientific progress. For example, according to the extent in which specific products resulting from scientific development are necessary for the realisation of the right to health, their comparative importance in terms of the right to enjoy the benefits of scientific progress can rise. It can be summarised that 'innovations essential for a life with dignity should be accessible to everyone, in particular marginalized populations', which the Special Rapporteur in the field of cultural rights considers as a core principle regarding access to scientific applications.[57]

Obligations of the State

Obligation to respect
The obligation to respect requires the State not to be involved in any act which negatively affects the enjoyment of the benefits of scientific progress and its applications. The State must refrain from restricting freedom to seek, receive and impart scientific information

---

54 'The human rights principle of self-determination enumerated in the ICESCR and the various civil and political rights defined in the International Covenant on Civil and Political Rights emphasize the right of all members of society to participate in a meaningful way in deciding on their governance and common future. This translates into a right to societal decision-making on setting priorities for and major decisions regarding the development of science and technology.' Audrey R. Chapman, 'A Human Rights Perspective on Intellectual Property, Scientific Progress, and Access to the Benefits of Science' in *Intellectual Property and Human Rights*, WIPO (1998) 10. Available at http://www.oapi.wipo.net/edocs/mdocs/tk/en/wipo_unhchr_ip_pnl_98/wipo_unhchr_ip_pnl_98_5.pdf, last accessed 15 March 2015.

55 Schabas (n 22) 296–7.

56 Ibid., 296–7.

57 Report of the Special Rapporteur in the field of Cultural Rights, Farida Shaheed (2012, n 40) para. 29.

and ideas, and freedom of scientific research.[58] The obligation of the State 'to respect the freedom indispensable for scientific research and creative activity' is further confirmed by Article 15.3 of the ICESCR.[59] The obligation to respect is not exclusively a negative obligation. For instance, as the Venice Statement rightly noted, the obligation to respect includes 'to take appropriate measures to prevent the use of science and technology in a manner that could limit or interfere with the enjoyment of the human rights and fundamental freedoms',[60] which is also linked with the obligation to protect in the event of non-State actors' engagement with the abuse of scientific and technological development.

Obligation to protect

The obligation to protect requires the State to prevent third parties from using scientific developments in a way that could interfere with the human rights of individuals and peoples. The Venice Statement noted that the duty to protect requires the State to 'take measures, including legislative measures, to prevent and preclude the utilization by the third parties of science and technologies to the detriment of human rights and fundamental freedoms and the dignity of the human person'.[61] This resonates with the Declaration on the Use of Scientific and Technological Progress in the Interests of Peace and for the Benefit of Mankind.[62] In addition, the Venice Statement stressed the obligation to safeguard 'the human rights of people subject to research activities by entities, whether public or private, in particular the right to information and free and informed consent'.[63] The CESCR requests States parties to provide information in their periodic report about 'measures taken to prevent the use of scientific and technical progress for purposes which are contrary to the enjoyment of human dignity and human rights'.[64]

Obligation to fulfil

The obligation to fulfil requires the State to take appropriate legislative, administrative, budgetary, judicial, promotional and other measures towards the realisation of the right to

---

58 See para. 14 of the Venice Statement (n 41).

59 Article 15.3 of ICESCR.

60 Paragraph 14(d) of the Venice Statement (n 41). See also para. 2 of the Declaration on the Use of Scientific and Technological Progress (n 50): 'All states shall take appropriate measures to prevent the use of scientific and technological developments, particularly by the State organs, to limit or interfere with the enjoyment of the human rights and fundamental freedoms of the individual as enshrined in the Universal Declaration of Human Rights, the International Covenants on Human Rights and other relevant international instruments.'

61 Paragraph 15(a) of the Venice Statement (n 41).

62 '8. All States shall take effective measures, including legislative measures, to prevent and preclude the utilization of scientific and technological achievements to the detriment of human rights and fundamental freedoms and the dignity of the human person.' The Declaration on the Use of Scientific and Technological Progress (n 50).

63 Paragraph 15(b) of the Venice Statement (n 41).

64 Paragraph 70(b) of Guidelines on Treaty-Specific Documents to be Submitted by States parties under Articles 16 and 17 of the ICESCR (Reporting Guidelines) (24 May 2009) E/C.12/2008/2.

enjoy the benefits of scientific progress. Critically, the States must ensure that 'the benefits of science are physically available and economically affordable on a non-discrimination basis'.[65] The non-discrimination obligation demands the States to give particular attention to disadvantaged and marginalised groups such as people living in poverty and persons with disabilities, as well as the elderly, women and children. The Reporting Guidelines of the CESCR requests States parties to indicate 'the measures taken to ensure affordable access to the benefits of scientific progress and its applications for everyone, including disadvantaged and marginalized individuals and groups'.[66] Those measures encompass ensuring non-discriminatory access to the existing benefits of scientific and technological development, but also identifying the priority needs of disadvantaged and marginalised people through a participatory process and facilitating research for those unmet needs by both public and private institutions.[67] For instance, marginal medical development addressing health needs of women[68] and people living in poverty[69] calls into question whether States, individually and collectively, fulfil their obligations under this right. The obligation of non-discrimination and equality requires the State to evaluate the likely impact of the current tendency of scientific research and put into place or improve the regulatory mechanism in relation to scientific research so as to ensure non-discrimination in the end result.[70]

The right to enjoy the benefits of scientific progress is a collective right as well as an individual right. Creating an enabling environment for the conservation, development and diffusion of science constitutes an obligation of the States to fulfil this right. Article 15.2 of the ICESCR mandates the measures, *inter alia*, 'necessary for the conservation, the development and the diffusion of science and culture'.[71] Accordingly, the States parties are obliged to 'adopt a legal and policy framework and to establish institutions to promote the development and diffusion of science and technology in a manner consistent with fundamental human rights'.[72] The Venice Statement stresses that 'the relevant policies should be periodically reviewed on the basis of a participatory and transparent process, with particular attention to the status and needs of disadvantaged and marginalized

---

65 Report of the Special Rapporteur in the field of Cultural Rights, Farida Shaheed (n 40) para. 31. Paragraph 16(b) of the Venice Statement (n 41). Article 6 of the 1975 Declaration on the Use of Scientific and Technological Progress states that '[a]ll States shall take measures to extend the benefits of science and technology to all strata of the population' (n 50).

66 Paragraph 70(a) of the Reporting Guidelines (n 64).

67 Report of the Special Rapporteur in the field of Cultural Rights, Farida Shaheed (n 40) para. 31.

68 Claude (n 36) 268.

69 For neglected diseases, see Report of the first Special Rapporteur on the Right to Health, Paul Hunt (19 January 2006) UN Doc. E/CN.4/2006/48/Add.2.

70 Audrey R. Chapman, 'Development of Indicators for Economic, Social and Cultural Rights' in Donders and Volodin (n 22) 135; Chapman (n 54) 10.

71 '15.2. The steps to be taken by the States Parties to the present Covenant to achieve the full realization of this right shall include those necessary for the conservation, the development and the diffusion of science and culture.'

72 Paragraph 16(a) of the Venice Statement (n 41).

groups'.[73] A meaningful participation of individuals and communities in decision making about science and technology is possible, when effective science education is provided at all levels of the education system, which also constitutes the obligation to fulfil the right.[74]

International assistance and cooperation in the scientific fields is required for the realisation of the right to enjoy the benefits of scientific progress, which is recognised in Article 15.4 of the ICESCR.[75] The development of international collaborative models of innovation for the priority needs of people living in developing countries can be key part of international cooperation envisaged in Article 15.4. As suggested in the Summit on the Millennium Development Goals, international cooperation should be sought for facilitating 'the development and dissemination of appropriate, affordable and sustainable technology, and the transfer of such technologies on mutually agreed terms, in order to strengthen national innovation and research and development capacity'.[76]

Implications for Scientific Knowledge Production

The right to enjoy the benefits of scientific progress has significant implications for the State's role in scientific knowledge production. The public-good nature of knowledge requires the State to play a role in adequate supply of new knowledge, as discussed in Chapter 2. There are two major ways in which the government provides incentives to knowledge production. The first is to allow an innovator to appropriate a high level of returns from its innovation by granting patents. The second is direct financial support to innovation by the government.[77] This right does not direct which policy option for knowledge production is to be adopted by the State. Nonetheless, this right would become rendered meaningless unless the State assumes the responsibility 'to ensure that all relevant interests are balanced, in the advance of scientific progress, in accordance with human rights'.[78]

In the current research environment where private and non-State actors are playing an increasing role in the production of scientific progress and technological application, science has been more influenced by the profit motive.[79] As a consequence, research priorities are increasingly driven by the market rather than human needs.[80] For example,

---

73 Ibid.

74 Chapman (n 36) 25.

75 '15.4. The States Parties to the present Covenant recognize the benefits to be derived from the encouragement and development of international contacts and co-operation in the scientific and cultural fields.'

76 *Keeping the Promise: United to Achieve the Millennium Development Goals*, adopted by the High-Level Plenary Meeting of the General Assembly at its 64th session (17 September 2010) UN Doc. A/65/L.1, para. 78, u.

77 Joseph E. Stiglitz, 'Knowledge as a Global Public Good', in Inge Kaul, Isabelle Grunberg and Mare A. Stern (eds), *Global Public Goods: International Cooperation in the 21st Century*, UNDP/OUP (1999) 308–25, 311–12.

78 Paragraph 5 of the Venice Statement (n 41).

79 Chapman (n 36) 8.

80 Ibid., 8.

the Special Rapporteur on the Right to Food stated that '[o]nly 1 per cent of research and development budgets of multinational corporations is spent on crops that might be useful in the developing world'.[81] The Special Rapporteur on the right to health observed similar problems in the field of health, notably the issue of 'neglected diseases',[82] which was mentioned in chapters 2 and 4. Data shows that the total number of drugs addressing diseases that mostly affect people in the developing world represents only around 1 per cent of all new drugs (1,556) launched over the past 30 years.[83] Another noticeable trend is that more products resulting from scientific research are patented, thus rendering them often unaffordable to the majority of people.[84] Furthermore, increasing patents over scientific research itself engender the risk of blocking or delaying further research and development.[85]

The State must take appropriate measures to promote equitable access to the benefits of science and its applications for all. Those measures include investing in R&D and providing incentives for innovation with particular focus on vulnerable and marginalised groups. International cooperation of States and other actors is vital in fulfilling the right to enjoy the benefits of scientific progress, in particular, given the global public-good nature of knowledge. When knowledge is produced, the benefits of its application, with some exceptions, can be universal.[86] For instance, knowledge about how to make tuberculosis treatment is of value beyond the national border. Joseph E. Stiglitz highlighted that 'knowledge is a global public good requiring public support at the global level'.[87] As early as 1947, in discussions prior to the adoption of the UDHR, J.M. Burgers underscored the obligation of international cooperation in scientific research and sharing the benefits from it, and proposed that 'when scientific work leads to the possibility of technological applications or of other measures of importance for or affecting in any way, the whole of mankind, such applications or measures should come under the sponsorship of international bodies, deriving their status and power from international authority'.[88]

---

81 Report submitted by the Special Rapporteur on the Right to Food, Jean Ziegler, 9 February 2004, UN Doc. E/CN.4/2004/10, para. 37; the reference given by him is Prabhu L. Pingali and Greg Traxler, 'Changing Locus of Agricultural Research: Will the Poor Benefit From Biotechnology and Privatization Trends?' (2002) 27 *Food Policy* 223–38.

82 Report of the Special Rapporteur on the Right to Health, Paul Hunt: Mission to Uganda (19 January 2006) UN doc. E/CN.4/2006/48/Add.2, para. 63.

83 Pierre Chirac and Els Torreele, 'Global Framework on Essential Health R & D' (2006) 367(9522) 13 May, *The Lancet* 1560–61.

84 Chapman (n 36) 7–8.

85 See 'Patents as an impediment to future innovation' in Chapter 2 of this book. The US National Research Council of the National Academies (ed.), *Reaping the Benefits of Genomic and Proteomic Research: Intellectual Property Rights, Innovation, and Public Health*, National Academies Press (2006).

86 Stiglitz (n 77).

87 Ibid., 320.

88 J.M. Burgers, 'Rights and Duties Concerning Creative Expression in Particular in Science', in UNESCO (ed.), *Human Rights: Comments and Interpretations*, 215–20, 216.

The Right to Benefit from the Protection of the Moral and Material Interests Resulting from any Scientific, Literary or Artistic Production of which He is the Author (Art. 15.1(c) of the ICESCR)

Background

Article 15, paragraph 1(c) of the ICESCR stipulates 'the right of everyone to benefit from the protection of the moral and material interests resulting from any scientific, literary or artistic production of which he or she is the author'. Similarly, this right is recognised in Article 27, paragraph 2 of the UDHR. It is also found in regional human rights instruments, such as Article 13, paragraph 2 of the ADRD, and Article 14, paragraph 1(c) of the Protocol of San Salvador. As this rarely invoked right attracted increasing attention in the last decade, the CESCR has elaborated the normative content of the right provided in Article 15.1(c) of the ICESCR separately in its General Comment No. 17.[89] This section does not intend to provide a detailed analysis of the content of, and corresponding State obligations arising from, the right to benefit from the protection of the moral and material interests of the author provided in Article 15.1(c) of the ICESCR. Rather, it focuses on understanding the nature of the right, primarily drawing upon General Comment No. 17.

Scope of the Right to Benefit from the Protection of the Moral and Material Interests Resulting from any Scientific, Literary or Artistic Production of which He is the Author

Authors

What is the scope of the author under Article 15.1(c)? This provision does not explicitly refer to inventors, unlike the ADRD, which recognises the 'right to the protection of his moral and material interests as regards his *inventions* or any literary, scientific or artistic works of which he is the author' (emphasis added).[90] This may lead one to exclude inventors as a beneficiary of the right. However, the CESCR considers the words 'any scientific, literary or artistic production' in the provision to include 'scientific publications and innovations'.[91] Thus, inventors as well as artists and writers are, *prima facie*, within the scope of protection afforded under this provision.

The authors that are entitled to the right under Article 15.1(c) must be natural persons. The CESCR clarifies that the protection of human rights does not extend to legal entities, whereas legal entities, such as corporations, are the major beneficiary under the existing intellectual property system.[92] The view of the CESCR is consistent with the idea of a human right 'as a right grounded in interests general to humanity and in the moral standing of human beings rather than in any independent moral

---

89 CESCR, GC No. 17 (n 3).
90 Article 13 of the American Declaration of the Rights and Duties of Man (n 33).
91 CESCR, GC No. 17 (n 3), para. 9.
92 Ibid., para. 7.

standing'.[93] Corporate entities may hold certain statutory rights subject to applicable law in a given situation, but these rights are distinct from human rights in that corporate rights are 'rights held by corporate entities rather than human beings' and 'grounded in whatever gives those corporate entities their special moral status'.[94]

As Peter Yu commented, companies may bring human rights claims on behalf of individuals whose human rights have been violated, but allowing a corporation to claim its own human rights seems overstretching the concept of 'human' rights.[95] Some human rights, such as freedom of association and rights of a trade union, may entail a collective dimension, but are still grounded in the moral standing of human persons.[96] While no universal human rights instruments recognise corporations within the protection of human rights, Article 1 of Protocol 1 to the ECHR affords the protection of the right under this provision to legal persons as well as natural persons.[97] Carl J. Mayer's study of corporations and the US Bill of Rights suggests that corporations have made increasing efforts to use fundamental rights as 'a potent shield against government regulation' in changing political economy.[98] His analysis sheds light on why corporations' invocation of human rights increased, and the validity of the explanation is not confined to the US. Separate from whether Article 1 of Protocol 1 extending its protection to legal entities is morally justifiable, the question of patent holders under this provision is discussed in a positive manner in 'Patent Rights and the Human Right to Property' in Chapter 6. Here, what is crucial is that legal entities are outside the ambit of 'the author' under Article 15.1(c) of the ICESCR.

The CESCR considers that human persons who can enjoy the right under Article 15.1(c) are generally the individual authors, artists and inventors, but also include 'groups of individuals' or 'communities' as long as they contribute knowledge.[99] In other words, Article 15.1(c) recognises that indigenous peoples and traditional communities are within its scope when it comes to their knowledge, innovations and practices. Traditional knowledge commonly refers to information that has been developed and applied by traditional and indigenous communities. Traditional knowledge includes information for different functions, such as 'information on the use of biological and other materials for medical treatment and agriculture, production processes, designs, literature, music, rituals, and other techniques and arts'.[100] Such knowledge is developed in the past but is subject

---

93 Peter Jones, 'Human Rights, Group Rights, and Peoples' Rights' (1999) 21 *Human Rights Quarterly* 80–107, 90.

94 Ibid., 88.

95 Peter Yu, 'Ten Common Questions about Intellectual Property and Human Rights' (2007) 23(4) *Georgia State University Law Review* 709–53, 730.

96 Jones (n 93) 82–3.

97 Article 1 of Protocol 1 to the European Convention on Human Rights: 'Every natural or legal person is entitled to the peaceful enjoyment of his possessions ...'.

98 Carl J. Mayer, 'Personalizing the Impersonal: Corporations and the Bill of Rights' (1989–1990) 41 *Hastings Law Journal* 577–667, 661.

99 CESCR, GC No. 17 (n 3) para. 8.

100 Carlos Correa, *Traditional Knowledge and Intellectual Property – Issues and Options Surrounding the Protection of Traditional Knowledge*, Quaker United Nations Office Discussion Paper (2001) 4, available at http://www.tansey.org.uk/docs/tk-colourfinal.pdf, last accessed 11 April 2014.

to continuous development.[101] From the perspective of the CESCR, a core element that requires the protection under Article 15.1(c) is a link between authors and their creations, whether a new or existing contribution.[102] The reasons why the protection under Article 15.1(c) should be provided for traditional and indigenous communities are further discussed under 'Traditional knowledge' below.

Moral interests

The right of authors, both in the UDHR and the ICESCR, includes two different types of interests: moral interests and material interests. As the drafting history of the UDHR has shown, the primary reason for the inclusion of the provision on this right was the need for the protection of the 'moral interests' of authors. Rene Cassin, who first proposed such provision, stressed 'a moral right on their work and/or discovery'.[103] This is based on the idea that scientific, literary and artistic productions are intrinsically 'expressions of the personality of their creator'[104] and thus the link between creators and their creations must receive respect and protection. In this respect, the CESCR interprets the protection of moral interests of authors as 'safeguard[ing] the personal link between authors and their creations and between peoples, communities, or other groups and their collective cultural heritage'.[105] Although it is not obvious whether an invention can be considered a manifestation of the personality of the inventor,[106] inventors are, nevertheless, not excluded from the protection of moral interests under General Comment No. 17.

What must the State do in order to protect such a personal link between creators and their creations? The CESCR enumerates 'the right of authors to be recognized as the creators of their scientific, literary and artistic productions and to object to any distortion, mutilation or other modification of, or other derogatory action in relation to, such productions, which would be prejudicial to their honour and reputation'.[107] These two rights, the right of attribution and the right of integrity relating to the creation, are also found in Article 6*bis* of the Berne Convention for the Protection of Literary and Artistic Works.[108] These two rights constitute the essential elements of the protection of the moral

---

101 Ibid.

102 CESCR, GC No. 17 (n 3).

103 Article 43 of the 'Cassin Draft': Suggestions Submitted by the Representative of France for Articles of the International Declaration of Human Rights, in Glendon (n 7) 275–80.

104 CESCR, GC No. 17 (n 3) para. 14.

105 Ibid., para. 2.

106 Rochelle Cooper Dreyfuss, 'Patents and Human Rights: Where is the Paradox?', in Willem Grosheide (ed.), *Intellectual Property and Human Rights: A Paradox*, Edward Elgar (2010) 72–96, 80–81.

107 CESCR, GC No. 17 (n 3) para. 13.

108 Article 6*bis* of the Berne Convention for the Protection of Literary and Artistic Works, para. 1: 'Independently of the author's economic rights, and even after the transfer of the said rights, the author shall have the right to claim authorship of the work and to object to any distortion, mutilation or other modification of, or other derogatory action in relation to, the said work, which would be prejudicial to his honor or reputation.'

rights of authors, although the degree of the protection of the moral rights of authors may vary across different jurisdictions.[109]

Material interests

To what extent are the author's material interests recognised as a human right? To answer this question, it is instructive to identify the purpose of recognising the author's material interests as a human right. The CESCR states that the material interests of authors 'are not directly linked to the personality of the creator, but contribute to the enjoyment of the right to an adequate standard of living (Art. 11 [of ICESCR], paragraph 1)'.[110] This indicates that the protection of material interests of authors within a human rights context is essentially to enable authors to enjoy an adequate standard of living. This interpretation seems in line with the drafters' intention. The original Article 43 of Cassin's draft of the UDHR included the phrase 'just remuneration for [the author's] labour' in parallel with a moral right.[111] In the drafting process, while the delegates of India and the UK questioned the validity of the provision, arguing that 'no special group should be singled out for attention', this provision was defended as providing a necessary protection for intellectual workers.[112]

In light of the drafting history, the phrase 'material interests' should be understood as the limited interests that enable intellectual workers to enjoy an adequate standard of living through adequate remuneration of their work.[113] The CESCR, throughout the General Comment No. 17, restricts the protection of 'material interests' to the purpose of enabling authors to enjoy an adequate standard of living.[114] Accordingly, the obligation of the States parties in this regard is 'to respect and protect the basic material interests of authors resulting from their scientific, literary or artistic productions, *which are necessary to enable those authors to enjoy an adequate standard of living*'[115] (emphasis added).

Neither the UDHR nor the ICESCR mandates any particular methods to ensure the material interests of authors. The intellectual property system can be used to protect the author's material interests, but it is not the only modality for such protection.[116] Other methods, such as 'lead time advantages, government or private contracts and research grants, contests, bonuses, prizes, tenure, and professorial chairs'[117] can be employed to

---

109 Peter K. Yu 'Reconceptualizing Intellectual Property Interests in a Human Rights Framework' (2007) 40 *UC Davis Law Review* 1039–49, 1082.

110 CESCR, GC No. 17 (n 3) para. 16.

111 Article 43 of the 'Cassin Draft': Suggestions Submitted by the Representative of France for Articles of the International Declaration of Human Rights, in Glendon (n 7) 275–80: 'The authors of all artistic, literary and scientific works and inventors shall retain, in addition to the just remuneration of their labour, a moral right to their work or discovery which shall not disappear even after such work or discovery has become the common property of mankind.'

112 Morsink (n 4) 220–21.

113 Yu (n 109) 1087.

114 CESCR, GC No. 17 (n 3) para. 2.

115 Ibid., para. 39.

116 Yu (n 109) 1089.

117 Dreyfuss (n 106) 81.

ensure adequate remuneration for intellectual labour. In fact, the strong protection of intellectual property may be less desirable, in a human rights context, given that the current intellectual property system grants the exclusive right to the first applicant to file a claim over an invention, potentially restricting other independent inventors' liberty with their own invention. The CESCR clarifies that the protection under Article 15.1(c) 'need not necessarily reflect the level and means of protection found in present copyright, patent and other intellectual property regimes'.[118] It further states that the protection of the material interests of authors can 'be achieved through one-time payments or by vesting an author, for a limited period of time, with the exclusive right to exploit his scientific, literary or artistic production'.[119]

Traditional knowledge

From a human rights perspective, special attention should be given to traditional knowledge holders since their knowledge might be subject to appropriation, adaptation and patenting of their knowledge without their prior and informed consent.[120] The protection of the rights of traditional knowledge holders entails preventing misappropriation of traditional knowledge (moral interests) and ensuring traditional knowledge holders a fair share of the benefits of any further innovations resulting from the traditional knowledge (material interests).[121] Documentation of traditional knowledge could provide a starting point for such protection.[122] States are required to recognise traditional knowledge holders' contributions to preserving biological diversity and enriching knowledge, and take measures to protect their moral and material interests resulting from their contribution.[123]

Conclusion

This chapter has examined the right to enjoy the benefits of scientific progress and its applications and the right to benefit from the protection of the moral and material interests of the author. Importantly, these two rights must be read together. Moreover, to be consistent with the objectives of the Covenant, the protection of these two rights must be considered in view of other internationally recognised human rights, e.g. the rights to life, privacy, health, food, education, and not to be subject to inhumane treatment. This reading is in line with Article 5.1 of the ICESCR, '[n]othing in the present Covenant may be interpreted as implying for any State, group or person any right to engage in any activity or to perform any act aimed at the destruction of any of the rights or freedoms

---

118 CESCR GC No. 17 (n 3) para. 10.

119 Ibid., para. 16.

120 Report of the High Commissioner for Human Rights: The Impact of the Agreement on Trade-Related Aspects of Intellectual Property Rights on Human Rights (27 June 2001), UN Doc. E/CN.4/Sub.2/2001/13, para. 41; Philippe Cullet, 'Human Rights and Intellectual Property Protection in the TRIPS Era' (2007) 29(2) *Human Rights Quarterly* 403–30, 426.

121 Cullet (n 120) 426–9; Correa (n 100).

122 Correa (n 100).

123 CESCR GC No 17 (n 3) para. 32; Cullet (n 120) 426–7.

recognized herein, or at their limitation to a greater extent than is provided for in the present Covenant'.

The CESCR stresses, in its general comment on Article 15.1(c), that:

> States parties are therefore obliged to strike an adequate balance between their obligations under Article 15, paragraph 1 (c), on one hand, and under the other provisions of the Covenant, on the other hand, with a view to promoting and protecting the full range of rights guaranteed in the Covenant. In striking this balance, the private interests of authors should not be unduly favoured and the public interest in enjoying broad access to their productions should be given due consideration.[124]

Universal access to the benefits of scientific progress, which is essential for a life with dignity, is a core element of the right to enjoy the benefits of scientific progress. In order to fulfil this right, the States, individually and through international cooperation, must take appropriate measures to invest in research and development for priority needs of people and to ensure affordable access to the outcomes of those scientific developments by all, including disadvantaged and marginalised people. These measures should include effective mechanisms for ensuring equitable access to the scientific development, as well as protecting the moral and material interests of the inventors. This integrated understanding of these two rights can constitute an important basis of a human rights framework within which the rights of contributors to knowledge creation and the rights of users of such knowledge are protected in a balanced manner.

---

124 CESCR GC No 17 (n 3) para. 35.

Chapter 6

Relationship between TRIPS and International Human Rights Law in the Context of Access to Medicines

Introduction

The relationship between TRIPS and human rights has often been conceived as conflicting. This chapter begins with a brief overview of the debate about TRIPS and human rights. In order to enhance conceptual clarity, a clarification is provided as to distinctive features of the entitlements under the existing intellectual property system, in comparison to the right to the protection of the moral and material interests of the author under Article 15.1(c) of the ICESCR. Also, the relationship between intellectual property rights on one hand, and the right to property recognised in international human rights instruments on the other is briefly discussed. This chapter then redirects its attention to TRIPS and human rights concerning the issue of access to medicines. It considers the definition of normative conflicts in international law, drawing upon recent relevant studies, and examines how norms in TRIPS and norms in international human rights law relate to each other in the context of access to medicines. Stress is placed on the importance of interpreting TRIPS in light of international human rights law. Inquiry is made as to whether the understanding of TRIPS has evolved or is able to evolve so as to be responsive to values and concerns intrinsic to international human rights law. While a harmonised interpretation of TRIPS and international human rights enables the State to utilise appropriate policy measures that promote access to medicines, this chapter also notes, it may be of limited benefit to the issue of health innovation and access to its outcome in developing countries, which requires the development of an alternative or complementary R&D system.

The Early Interface between TRIPS and Human Rights

UN Sub-Commission on Human Rights

The adoption of TRIPS in 1994 and the following bilateral and regional 'TRIPS-plus' treaties has revealed that the way intellectual products are regulated through the grant of exclusive rights may have significant human rights implications. The first response to the issue, directly devoted to the relationship between human rights and intellectual property, came from the UN Sub-Commission on the Protection and Promotion of Human Rights ('Sub-Commission') in 2000. In its resolution 2000/7 'Intellectual property rights and human rights'[1] with its focus on TRIPS, the Sub-Commission warned that 'actual or potential conflicts exist between the implementation of TRIPS and the realization of economic, social and cultural rights'.[2] The Sub-Commission listed as areas of human rights concern: (a) impediments to the transfer of technology to developing countries; (b) the consequences for the enjoyment of the right to food of plant variety rights and the patenting of genetically modified organisms; (c) 'bio-piracy' and the protection of traditional knowledge; and (d) the implications for the right to health of restrictions on access to patented pharmaceuticals.[3]

To resolve potential conflicts between intellectual property and human rights, the Sub-Commission urged all States to recognise 'the primacy of human rights over economic policies' when designing national law and policy concerning intellectual property.[4] Furthermore, the Sub-Commission requested the WTO to 'take fully into account the existing State obligations under international human rights'.[5] The various UN bodies, including the Secretary-General, the High Commissioner for Human Rights, the Committee on Economic, Social and Cultural Rights (CESCR), and the World Intellectual Property Organization were recommended to analyse the human rights implications of TRIPS.[6] A significant number of reactions from other UN human rights bodies, various intergovernmental organisations, governments and NGOs followed.[7]

WTO and WIPO

The WTO drew an analogy between the intellectual property system and human rights in its reply to the Sub-Commission's critique of TRIPS. It took special note of authors' rights to the protection of moral and material interests resulting from their work under Article 27(2) of the UDHR and Article 15(1)(c) of the ICESCR.[8] The

---

1 See, for the detailed account of the background, content and impact of Sub-Commission Resolution 2000/7, David Weissbrodt and Kell Schoff, 'Human Rights Approach to Intellectual Property Protection: The Genesis and Application of Sub-Commission Resolution 2000/7' (2003) 5 *Minnesota Intellectual Property Review* 1–46.

2 Sub-Commission on Human Rights Resolution 2000/7, Intellectual Property Rights and Human Rights, UN Doc. E/CN.4/Sub.2/Res/2000/7 (17 August 2000) Preamble.

3 Ibid.

4 Ibid., para. 3.

5 Ibid., para. 8.

6 Ibid., paras 8–15.

7 Report of the High Commissioner for Human Rights, The Impact of the Agreement on Trade-Related Aspects of Intellectual Property Rights on Human Rights (27 June 2001) UN Doc. E/CN.4/Sub.2/2001/13; Report of the Secretary-General, Intellectual Property Rights and Human Rights (14 June 2001) UN Doc. E/CN.4/Sub.2/2001/12; The addendum to the Report of the Secretary-General (3 July 2001) UN Doc. E/CN.4/Sub.2/2001/12/Add.1. The Secretary-General's report and its addendum comprise reactions to Resolution 2000/7 from diverse governments and international organisations, including the WTO and WIPO, and NGOs.

8 Reply from the WTO is found in Section II, B in the Report of the Secretary-General (n 7) 7–9; Reply from the WIPO is in Section II, in Addendum to the Report of the Secretary-General (n 7).

WTO stated that 'it can be argued that TRIPS also seeks to give effect ... to article 15(1)(c) [of the ICESCR]'.[9] It also considered that Article 7 setting out the objectives of TRIPS 'corresponds with the objectives of article 15(1)(a) and (b) of the ICESCR' recognising the right of everyone to take part in cultural life and to enjoy the benefits of scientific progress and its applications.[10] Article 7 of TRIPS (Objectives) states that 'the protection and enforcement of intellectual property rights should contribute to the promotion of technological innovation and to the transfer and dissemination of technology, to the mutual advantage of producers and users of technological knowledge and in a manner conducive to social and economic welfare, and to a balance of rights and obligations'.[11] The WIPO, similarly, stated that intellectual property and human rights both require 'resolving tensions and striking balances' between 'the rights of creators and those of users',[12] referring to Article 15 of the ICESCR and Article 27.2 of the UDHR.[13]

UN High Commissioner for Human Rights

The UN High Commissioner for Human Rights also recognised that there exist links between TRIPS and human rights. However, the High Commissioner posed a question as to 'whether TRIPS strikes a balance that is consistent with a human rights approach'.[14] On this question, the High Commissioner for Human Rights made several preliminary remarks, which can be summarised as follows: (1) 'The promotion of public health, nutrition, environment and development', which has close links with human rights, 'are generally expressed in terms of exceptions to the rule' in TRIPS, whereas 'a human rights approach ... would explicitly place the promotion and protection of human rights ... at the heart of objectives of intellectual property protection'.[15] (2) TRIPS does not provide the content of the responsibilities of intellectual property holders, as opposed to the detailed rules of their rights, and thus the balance under TRIPS may not be consistent with a human rights approach.[16] (3) TRIPS might restrict States' capacities to protect and promote human rights.[17] (4) The protection of traditional knowledge is not provided for in TRIPS.[18] Further, the report of the High Commissioner for Human Rights provided an analysis of the impact of TRIPS in the context of the right to health, substantiating the need to review TRIPS in light of human rights.

---

9 Reply from the WTO (n 8), para. 4.

10 Ibid.

11 Agreement on Trade-Related Aspects of Intellectual Property Rights (TRIPS), 15 April 1994, Marrakesh Agreement Establishing the World Trade Organization, Annex 1C.

12 Reply from the WIPO (n 8), para. 6.

13 Ibid.

14 Report of UN High Commissioner for Human Rights (n 7), paras 11, 20, 21.

15 Ibid., para. 22.

16 Ibid., para. 23.

17 Ibid., para. 24.

18 Ibid., para. 26.

Other UN Human Rights Bodies

Besides the responses from the WTO, WIPO and the UN High Commissioner for Human Rights, a series of reports and resolutions of UN human rights bodies have addressed the issue of human rights and intellectual property since the adoption of the Sub-Commission's resolution 2000/7. The CESCR released a 'statement on Human Rights and Intellectual Property'[19] in 2001 and provided a preliminary analysis of the relationship between human rights and intellectual property. From 2001 to 2003, the UN Commission on Human Rights adopted three annual resolutions on 'Access to medication in the context of pandemics such as HIV/AIDS, tuberculosis and malaria', and requested States and the relevant intergovernmental organisations to ensure access to essential medicines.[20] The UN Special Rapporteur on the Right to Food mentioned 'concerns that patents on seeds limit the access of peasant farmers to seeds for replanting' in his 2002 and 2003 reports.[21] The UN Special Rapporteur on the Right to Health recommended States make use of provisions in TRIPS, such as compulsory licensing, with a view to promote access to affordable drugs, and further cautioned the potential negative impact of 'TRIPS-plus' legislation on the right to health.[22]

These early debates concerning the relationship between intellectual property and human rights, described so far, have given rise to the need for clarification as to how intellectual property relates to human rights, whether there is conflict between TRIPS and human rights, and if so, how it can be resolved. These questions are central to characterising and reshaping the relationship between intellectual property and human rights. The following sections of this chapter ask these questions, specifically in the context of access to medicines.

Distinction between Intellectual Property Rights and Human Rights

Intellectual Property Rights and the Right to Benefit from the Protection of the Moral and Material Interests of the Author (Art. 15.1(c) of the ICESCR)

Different types of intellectual property
It is necessary to clarify the distinctive features of intellectual property rights in comparison to human rights, before exploring the issue of normative conflicts. The mention of

---

19 Ibid.

20 Commission on Human Rights Resolution 2001/33 (23 April 2001) UN Doc. E/CN.4/RES/2001/33; Commission on Human Rights Resolution 2002/32 (22 April 2002) UN Doc. E/CN.4/RES/2002/32; Commission on Human Rights Resolution 2003/29 (22 April 2003) UN Doc. E/CN.4/RES/2003/29.

21 Report of the first Special Rapporteur on the Right to Food, Jean Ziegler (10 January 2002) UN Doc. E/CN.4/2002/58, para. 119; (28 August 2003) UN Doc. A/58/330, para. 29; Report of the second Special Rapporteur on the Right to Food, Olivier De Schutter (23 July 2009) UN Doc. A/64/170.

22 Report of the first Special Rapporteur on the Right to Health, Paul Hunt, 'Mission to the World Trade Organization' (1 March 2004) UN Doc. E/CN.4/2004/49/Add.1, paras 81–82; (13 September 2006) UN Doc. A/61/338; Report of the second Special Rapporteur on the Right to Health, Anand Grover (31 March 2009) UN Doc. A/HRC/11/12.

Article 15.1(c) of the ICESCR and Article 27 of the UDHR, in the responses from the WTO and WIPO to the Sub-Commission's resolution 2000/7, indicates a tendency to equate intellectual property rights with the right to benefit from the protection of the moral and material interests of the author, recognised in international human rights instruments.[23] There are various types of intellectual property rights and each of them may have a different relationship with human rights. For instance, the moral rights of authors in Article 6*bis* of the Berne Convention may share the characteristics of human rights,[24] although the provisions on copyrights in TRIPS have excluded the protection of the moral interests of authors from its scope.[25] On the other hand, corporate trademarks, one type of intellectual property right, may share few commonalities with the human right under Article 15.1(c) of the ICESCR, since they are not to protect intellectual creations of individuals but to facilitate competition by distinguishing different goods and services.[26] The scope of analysis here is restricted to patent rights among other types of intellectual property since patent rights are of particular relevance in the context of access to medicines.

Differing foundational principles

> The fact that the human person is the central subject and primary beneficiary of human rights distinguishes human rights, including the right of authors to the moral and material interests in their works, from legal rights recognized in intellectual property systems. Human rights are fundamental, inalienable and universal entitlements belonging to individuals, and in some situations groups of individuals and communities. Human rights are fundamental as they derive from the human person as such, whereas intellectual property rights derived from intellectual property systems are instrumental, in that they are a means by which States seek to provide incentives for inventiveness and creativity from which society benefits. In contrast with human rights, intellectual property rights are generally of a temporary nature, and can be revoked, licensed or assigned to someone else. While intellectual property rights may be allocated, limited in time and scope, traded, amended and even forfeited, human rights are timeless expressions of fundamental entitlements of the human person. Whereas human rights are dedicated to assuring satisfactory standards of human welfare and well-being,

---

23 Reply from the WTO (n 8); Reply from the WIPO (n 8).

24 Article 6*bis* of the Berne Convention for the Protection of Literary and Artistic Works (Berne Convention), para. 1: 'Independently of the author's economic rights, and even after the transfer of the said rights, the author shall have the right to claim authorship of the work and to object to any distortion, mutilation or other modification of, or other derogatory action in relation to, the said work, which would be prejudicial to his honor or reputation.'

25 Article 9 (Relation to the Berne Convention) of TRIPS (n 11): '1. Members shall comply with Articles 1 through 21 of the Berne Convention (1971) and the Appendix thereto. *However, Members shall not have rights or obligations under this Agreement in respect of the rights conferred under Article 6*bis *of that Convention or of the rights derived therefrom*' (emphasis added).

26 Peter Yu, 'Ten Common Questions about Intellectual Property and Human Rights (2007) 23(4) *Georgia State University Law Review* 709–53, 727; Jan Brinkhof, '8. On Patents and Human Rights', in Willem Grosheide (ed.), *Intellectual Property and Human Rights: A Paradox*, Edward Elgar (2010) 140–54, 140.

intellectual property regimes, although they traditionally provide protection to individual authors and creators, are increasingly focused on protecting business and corporate interests and investments. Moreover, the scope of protection of the moral and material interests of the author provided for under article 15 of the Covenant does not necessarily coincide with what is termed intellectual property rights under national legislation or international agreements.[27]

This statement by the UN CESCR succinctly describes differences between intellectual property and the right under Article 15.1(c) of the ICESCR.[28] What follows further elaborates these distinctive features of patent rights and the right under Article 15.1(c) of the ICESCR.

Most significantly, patent rights and the right to the protection of moral and material interests are different from each other in terms of foundational principles. As the CESCR identified, a human right 'derives from the inherent dignity and worth of all persons', 'whereas intellectual property rights are first and foremost means by which States seek to provide incentives for inventiveness and creativity, encourage the dissemination of creative and innovative productions, ... for the benefit of society as a whole'.[29] The historical overview of intellectual property in Chapter 1 has shown that patent rights are created to serve a social function, and are not an end in themselves. This is illustrated by section 6 of the Statute of Monopolies of 1623 (England),[30] the foundation of the modern patent system, and section 8 of the US Constitution.[31] The analysis of different perspectives on patents in Chapter 2 has also indicated that the main ground for a patent is that it is a policy tool to stimulate knowledge creation, balancing with access to knowledge. Objectives set out in Article 7 of TRIPS reflect this perspective.[32]

---

27 CESCR, Statement: Human Rights and Intellectual Property (14 December 2001) UN Doc. E/C/12/2001/15, para. 6.

28 Article 15, para. 1(c) of ICESCR recognises the right of everyone 'to benefit from the protection of the moral and material interests resulting from any scientific, literary or artistic production of which he is the author'.

29 CESCR, General Comment No. 17: The Right of Everyone to Benefit from the Protection of the Moral and Material Interests Resulting from Any Scientific, Literary or Artistic Production of which He is the Author (Art. 15(1)(c) of ICESCR) (12 January 2006) UN Doc. E/C.12/2005, para. 1.

30 'IV. Provided also and be it declared and enacted that any declaration before mentioned shall not extend to any letters of patent and grants of privilege for the term of fourteen years or under, hereafter to be made, of the sole working or making of any manner of new manufactures within this realm, to the true and first inventor and inventors of such manufactures which others at the time of making such letters patent and grants shall not use, so also they be not contrary to the law or mischievous to the state, by raising prices of commodities at home, or hurt of trade, or generally inconvenient.'

31 Section 8 'The Congress shall have power ... To promote the progress of science and useful arts, by securing for limited times to authors and inventors the exclusive right to their respective writings and discoveries'.

32 Article 7 of TRIPS (n 11) reads 'The protection and enforcement of intellectual property rights should contribute to the promotion of technological innovation and to the transfer and dissemination of technology, to the mutual advantage of producers and users of technological knowledge and in a manner conducive to social and economic welfare, and to a balance of rights and obligations.'

Patents as a policy instrument

Distinctive features of patent rights follow from their instrumental nature. States, through legislative acts, grant the exclusive rights, adjust the scope and duration of those rights, permit exceptions to the exclusive rights, and may even make provisions for the revocation or forfeiture of the rights.[33] Not all inventions are patentable.[34] One important criterion for patentability is industrial applicability, which reflects the main purpose of patents, i.e. encouraging inventions useful to society. The life of a patent is limited, and after a certain period of time, the subject matter of the patent belongs to the public domain.[35] Determining the duration of the patent protection is a balancing exercise between private interests and public interests. An applicant for a patent is also required to disclose the details of the invention he or she is seeking a patent for, which is to facilitate further innovation.[36] A patent system provides exceptions and limitations to the exclusive rights, such as compulsory licensing.[37] Chapter 3 of this book has elaborated various exceptions and limitations to the exclusive rights, provided in Articles 27(2) and (3), 30 and 31 of the TRIPS Agreement. All these features illustrate that patent rights are granted, protected and limited, with a view to achieving social ends. While the human right under Article 15.1(c) is not without limitations, human rights require stringent rules regarding limitations.[38] Even among human rights, the scope of permissible limitations differs according to the

---

33 Rochelle Cooper Dreyfuss, 'Patents and Human Rights: Where is the Paradox?', in Grosheide (n 26) 75–80. Grounds for revocation may include (1) the subject matter of the patent in question is not patentable; (2) the patent does not sufficiently disclose the information about the invention for it to be carried out by a skilled person in the art; (3) the content of the patent extends beyond the content of the application as filed. See, for instance, Arts 100–102 of the European Patent Convention or section 25(2) of the Patent Act of India. As to forfeiture of a patent, Article 5A(3) of the Paris Convention allows it as a secondary measure available only 'where the grant of compulsory licenses would not have been sufficient to prevent' 'failure to work' the patent in question.

34 The standard criteria for patentability can be found in Art. 27 of TRIPS, which reads '... provided that they are new, involve an inventive step and are capable of industrial application'.

35 The duration of patent rights has been subject to changes over time. Article 33 of TRIPS prescribes the protection of a patent for a period of 20 years after the filing date.

36 Article 29.1 of TRIPS provides that '1. Members shall require that an applicant for a patent shall disclose the invention in a manner sufficiently clear and complete for the invention to be carried out by a person skilled in the art and may require the applicant to indicate the best mode for carrying out the invention known to the inventor at the filing date or, where priority is claimed, at the priority date of the application.'

37 Exceptions to the exclusive rights include the so-called Bolar exception, which is the use of a pharmaceutical invention to conduct tests and obtain the approval from the health authority during the patent term for commercialisation of a generic version just after such expiry; experimental use, preparation of medicines for individual cases according to prescription; and private non-commercial use by individuals. Daniel Gervais, *The TRIPS Agreement: Drafting History and Analysis*, 3rd edn, Sweet & Maxwell (2008) 382; Holger Hestermeyer, *Human Rights and the WTO: The Case of Patents and Access to Medicines*, Oxford University Press (2007) 238–9; Carlos Correa, *Trade Related Aspects of Intellectual Property Rights: A Commentary on the TRIPS Agreement*, Oxford University Press (2007) 303.

38 See Arts 2.1, 4 and 5 of the ICESCR, concerning the scope of justifiable limitations upon Art. 15.1(c).

moral importance of the right in question. The scope of limitations upon human rights is discussed in detail in Chapter 7.

Rights holder

Who is entitled to a right is another major issue distinguishing patent rights from the right under Article 15.1(c). Under the patent system, a patent right is granted to the first to file an application, with the exception of the US where the first to invent is granted a patent. Neither the first-to-file nor the first-to-invent system provides a patent right to other independent inventors of the same or similar piece of invention. Such systems are justified by several reasons, e.g. promoting prompt disclosure of inventions, providing sufficient incentives to innovation, and easing the burden of administration.[39] However, in case several persons or groups independently come up with a same invention, all independent inventors, not only the first applicant of a patent, are within the scope of Article 15.1(c) of the ICESCR.[40]

Whether assignees and corporations can be the right holder highlights a further difference between the patent rights and the human right under Article 15.1(c). According to the CESCR, the protection of Article 15.1(c) requires a personal link between the creators and the creations, and thus can be enjoyed only by 'individuals and, under certain circumstances, groups of individuals and communities',[41] as discussed under 'Authors' in Chapter 5. On the other hand, patent rights are mostly held by corporations.[42] The corporations may hold the patent rights 'by assignment from the actual, human creators'.[43] While patent rights can be assigned to someone else and traded,[44] the human right owed to the inventor is inalienable.[45] The CESCR has noted that '[u]nder the existing international treaty protection regimes, legal entities are included among the holders of intellectual property rights. However, ... their entitlements, because of their different nature, are not protected at the level of human rights'.[46]

Issue of traditional knowledge

The issue of traditional knowledge also exposes a divergence between the human right under Article 15.1(c) and patent rights. While traditional knowledge is within the scope of Article 15.1(c),[47] it does not easily fit with the existing intellectual property system. Most

---

39 Wendy J. Gordon, 'Current Patent Laws Cannot Claim the Backing of Human Rights', in Grosheide (n 26) 164, 166, 167.

40 The issue of other independent inventors is discussed in Chapter 2 of this book, particularly under 'Boundaries of the Natural Property Right' and 'Sufficiency condition'. See also Gordon (n 39) 162, 166, 167.

41 CESCR GC No. 17 (n 29) paras 1, 7, 8.

42 Ibid., paras 2 and 7.

43 Gordon (n 39) 167.

44 CESCR, GC No. 17 (n 29) para. 2.

45 Peter K. Yu 'Reconceptualizing Intellectual Property Interests in a Human Rights Framework' (2007) 40 *UC Davis Law Review* 1131; CESCR, GC No. 17 (n 29) paras 1, 2.

46 CESCR, GC No. 17 (n 29) para. 7.

47 Ibid., paras 8, 9 and 32.

traditional knowledge would be considered to belong to prior art, thus failing to meet the novelty criteria for the protection of intellectual property.[48] A *sui generis* intellectual property system, that is, 'a legal regime "of its own kind" which is specifically adapted to the nature and characteristics of traditional knowledge',[49] can be established in order to protect traditional knowledge holders.[50] However, for the most part, traditional and indigenous communities may not pursue private ownership over their knowledge. Instead, they may seek other measures to preserve and safeguard traditional knowledge, e.g. the identification, documentation, transmission, revitalization and promotion of traditional knowledge.[51] Therefore, the grant of exclusive rights, a typical form of the existing intellectual property system, may not be one of the essential features of the protection of the moral and material interests of traditional knowledge holders under Article 15.1(c).

So far, it has been discussed that a patent right under the existing intellectual property system is different from the human right under Article 15.1(c) of ICESCR, in terms of the foundation and purpose of each right, and the manner in which each right is implemented.[52] To the extent that these differing features are recognised, a patent system can be used as a means to protect the human right of the inventor. Nonetheless, it is worth revisiting some of the points explained in Chapter 5 on material interests within the meaning of Article 15.1(c) of the ICESCR.[53] What is protected as a human right under Article 15.1(c) is adequate and just remuneration for intellectual labour so as to enable the author/inventor to enjoy an adequate standard of living.[54] These basic material interests of the author/inventor under Article 15.1(c) can be satisfied by other measures, such as one-time payments, as well as the grant of exclusive rights for a limited period of time.[55] When a patent system is used to protect the material interests of the inventor, States must make sure that it does not negatively affect other independent inventors.

---

48 Laurence R. Helfer, 'Toward a Human Rights Framework for Intellectual Property' (2007) 40 *UC Davis Law Review* 982–3.

49 Carlos Correa, *Traditional Knowledge and Intellectual Property – Issues and Options Surrounding the Protection of Traditional Knowledge*, Quaker United Nations Office Discussion Paper (2001) 14.

50 The protection of traditional knowledge has been discussed in diverse international forums such as the Conference of the Parties (COP) to the Convention on Biological Diversity (CBD), WIPO and the WTO. For the CBD, see http://www.cbd.int/tk/, last accessed 15 March 2015; for the discussion in WIPO, see http://www.wipo.int/tk/en/, last accessed 15 March 2015; for the discussion in the WTO, see http://www.wto.org/english/tratop_e/trips_e/art27_3b_e.htm, last accessed 15 March 2015.

51 WIPO, The Report of the Intergovernmental Committee on Intellectual Property and Genetic Resources, Traditional Knowledge and Folklore (Consolidated Analysis of the Legal Protection of Traditional Knowledge), Fifth Session (7–13 July 2003) paras 10 and 11, available at http://www.wipo.int/edocs/mdocs/tk/en/wipo_grtkf_ic_5/wipo_grtkf_ic_5_3.pdf, last accessed 15 March 2015.

52 CESCR, GC No. 17 (n 29) para. 1.

53 Article 15.1(c) protects *the moral and material interests* of the author/inventor. Here, the focus of the discussion is on the material interests.

54 Yu (n 45) 1129–31. CESCR, GC No. 17 (n 29) para. 15.

55 CESCR, GC No. 17 (n 29) para. 10; Dreyfuss (n 33) 75–80.

Patent Rights and the Human Right to Property

There is a separate question of whether a patent falls within the right to property under international human rights law. If the answer to this question is positive, a discussion has to follow as to the scope of permissible limitations of a patent right. A similar question was raised when 39 global pharmaceutical companies brought a legal action against the South African government, claiming that the Medicines Act 1997, limiting a patent right with a view to increasing access to medicines, contravenes, *inter alia*, the right-to-property provision of South Africa's Constitution (section 25).[56] The lawsuit was, however, dropped by the companies as a consequence of mounting pressure from civil society worldwide. What follows briefly discusses the relationship between a patent and the right to property in the context of international human rights law.

The right to property in international human rights law

Article 17 of the UDHR recognises everyone's right to own property alone as well as in association with others, and prohibits arbitrary deprivation of property.[57] There is no provision on right to property, however, in either the ICESCR or the ICCPR. The drafting history indicates that although there was a consensus on the recognition of the right to property, disagreement over the formulation of the right and the scope of limitations upon the right was insurmountable.[58] The Annotations on the text of the draft International Covenants on Human Rights[59] are instructive in understanding differing views about the right to property that can be characterised as a human right.

The Annotations report three different views about the formulation of the universal human right to property. One view proposes the formulation of the right in broad and general terms, modelling Article 17 of the UDHR, considering 'the differences of views regarding property rights embodied in the social and political systems of various States'.[60] Another view was in favour of the formulation 'drafted in precise legal terms and spel[t] out the necessary qualifications and limitations to which the right of property would be subject', and proposed texts which 'would not only provide that States parties should undertake to respect the right of property, but would indicate that the right was not

---

56 Case No. 4183/98, South African High Court. Section 25(1) of the South African Constitution: 'No one may be deprived of property except in terms of law of general application, and no law may permit arbitrary deprivation of property ...'.

57 Article 17 of the UDHR: '(1) [e]veryone has the right to own property alone as well as in association with others. (2) No one shall be arbitrarily deprived of his property.' For the drafting history of this provision, see Mary Ann Glendon, *A World Made New: Eleanor Roosevelt and the Universal Declaration of Human Rights*, Random House (2001) 182–3.

58 Catarina Krause, '11. The Right to Property' in Asbjørn Eide et al. (eds), *Economic, Social and Cultural Rights*, 2nd edn, Kluwer Law International (2001) 191–209, 194; Christophe Golay and Ioana Cismas, *Legal Opinion: The Right to Property from a Human Rights Perspective* (2010) 3–5, available at http://papers.ssrn.com/sol3/papers.cfm?abstract_id=1635359, last accessed 15 March 2015.

59 Annotations on the text of the draft International Covenants on Human Rights (1 July 1955) UN Doc. A/2929, paras 195–212.

60 Ibid., para. 199.

absolute and would specify the conditions under which a person might be deprived of his property'.[61] A third view was that the article should delineate the scope of the right to property that is qualified as a human right. From this point of view, only to the extent that is 'necessary for decent living and for maintaining the dignity of the individual and the home ... could the right of property be regarded as fundamental and inviolable'.[62]

What was generally agreed was that 'the right to own property was not absolute'[63] and 'the right to own property was subject to some degree of control by the State'.[64] However, it was not possible to reach an agreement on the extent of not only the limitations of the right, but also the restrictions on State action.[65] In the absence of the right to property provision in the two Covenants, Eibe Riedel suggests that the right to property in the UDHR can 'still serve, for instance, to legitimize the concept of "smaller ownership", i.e. property rights limited to subsistence guarantees of individuals, but it could not be utilized as a justification for large-scale capital accumulation'.[66]

While 'it was not possible to reach a consensus on the permissible restrictions in the context of a universal convention', the similar 'legal and social traditions' within geographical areas made it possible to include the right to property and relevant limitation clauses in regional human rights treaties.[67] Thus, the right to property is provided in Article 23 of the American Declaration[68] and Article 21 of the ACHR.[69] The right to property was included in Article 1 of Protocol 1 to the ECHR[70] and in Article 17 of the Charter of Fundamental Rights of the European Union.[71] Article 14 of the African Charter on Human

---

61 Ibid., para. 200.

62 Ibid., para. 201.

63 Ibid., para. 202.

64 Ibid., para. 206.

65 Ibid., paras 202–212; Golay and Cismas (n 58) 3–5.

66 Eibe Riedel, 'Standards and Sources. Farewell to the Exclusivity of the Sources Triad in International Law?' (1991) 2 *European Journal of International Law* 58–84, 69.

67 Krause (n 58) 194.

68 Article 23 of the American Declaration on the Rights and Duties of Man (ADRD) OAS Res. XXX, adopted by the Ninth International Conference of American States (1948): 'Every person has a right to own such private property as meets the essential needs of decent living and helps to maintain the dignity of the individual and of the home,'

69 Article 21 of the American Convention on Human Rights (ACHR) 'Pact of San Jose, Costa Rica', adopted on 22 November 1969. '1. Everyone has the right to the use and enjoyment of his property. The law may subordinate such use and enjoyment to the interest of society. 2. No one shall be deprived of his property except upon payment of just compensation, for reasons of public utility or social interest, and in the cases and according to the forms established by law ...'.

70 Article 1 of the First Protocol to the ECHR (1952): 'Every natural or legal person is entitled to the peaceful enjoyment of his possessions. No one shall be deprived of his possessions except in the public interest and subject to the conditions provided for by law and by the general principles of international law. The preceding provisions shall not, however, in any way impair the right of a State to enforce such laws as it deems necessary to control the use of property in accordance with the general interest or to secure the payment of taxes or other contributions or penalties.'

71 It has come into effect through the entry into force of the Lisbon Treaty in 2009. The Charter sets out civil, political, economic and social rights of European citizens and all persons

and Peoples' Rights[72] and Article 31 of the Arab Charter on Human Rights[73] also recognise the right to property. All the above provisions in regional human rights instruments include limitation clauses. This indicates that while the right to property is widely recognised since the security of individual possession is necessary for one's autonomy and personal development, a property system is constantly adjusted according to the economic and social policies of States on e.g. land, tax, welfare and the environment.[74] For this reason, Catarina Krause observed that, in the context of international human rights law, 'there will always be a certain amount of reluctance towards international supervision of these rights [property rights]'.[75]

An expectation of obtaining a patent

When examining a question of whether a patent right is within the scope of the human right to property, a distinction should be made between those who have an *expectation* of obtaining a patent on one hand, and those who *have acquired a patent* on the other. The human right to property does not apply to those who seek a patent over an invention, since there is no *existing* property.[76] The formulations of the right to property provisions in international human rights instruments are commonly understood to protect only 'acquired property rights' from arbitrary interference by the State.[77] This implies that the right to property in international human rights law does not give rise to a positive obligation upon States to provide a specific form of property to a person.

The scope of the right to property may be extended so as to imply that everyone is entitled to a certain minimum of property necessary for a decent standard of living

---

resident in the EU. Article 17: '1. Everyone has the right to own, use, dispose of and bequeath his or her lawfully acquired possessions. No one may be deprived of his or her possessions, except in the public interest and in the cases and under the conditions provided for by law, subject to fair compensation being paid in good time for their loss. The use of property may be regulated by law in so far as is necessary for the general interest. 2. Intellectual property shall be protected.'

72 Article 14 of the African Charter on Human and Peoples' Rights (ACHPR) (1981): 'The right to property shall be guaranteed. It may only be encroached upon in the interest of public need or in the general interest of the community and in accordance with the provisions of appropriate laws.'

73 Article 31 of the (revised) Arab Charter on Human Rights (2004): 'Everyone has a guaranteed right to own private property, and shall not under any circumstances be arbitrarily or unlawfully divested of all or any part of his property.'

74 Peter Drahos, 'Intellectual Property and Human Rights' (1999) 3 *Intellectual Property Quarterly* 349–71, 360; Philippe Cullet, 'Human Rights and Intellectual Property Protection in the TRIPS Era' (2007) 29 *Human Rights Quarterly* 405.

75 Krause (n 58) 193.

76 *British-American Tobacco Company Ltd v. the Netherlands* (19 May 1994), Opinion of the Commission, §§ 71–72; *Anheuser-Busch Inc v. Portugal*, Application no. 73049/01, Judgment of Grand Chamber, 11 January 2007, paras 49 and 69.

77 See Art. 21 of the ACHR, Art. 1 of the First Protocol to ECHR, and Art. 17 of the Charter of Fundamental Rights of the European Union. Krause (n 58) 191 and 197; Council of Europe, *The Right to Property under the European Convention on Human Rights: A Guide to the Implementation of the European Convention on Human Rights and its Protocols* (2007) 7.

and a life with dignity.[78] Such a reading can be supported by how the right to property is phrased in Article 23 of the American Declaration.[79] With this universal right to have a minimum of personal property as a potential exception, the right to property provisions in international human rights conventions 'emphasize the negative aspects of the right by spelling out the conditions for permissible interference with one's property'.[80] It is doubtful that an expectation of acquiring a patent falls within the scope of a potentially justifiable positive right to property.

Moreover, Article 17 of the UDHR suggests that the right to property is not predicated on a specific form of property, by containing the phrase 'alone as well as in association with others'. The drafting history confirms this reading.[81] Peter K. Yu noted that this article can provide 'an equally compelling basis for the creation of a rich public domain and for unrestricted access to protected materials [intellectual products]'.[82] The natural right to property argument, based on Locke's theory, also does not favour private property in intellectual products over the common ownership, as discussed in Chapter 2. Therefore, determining what kind of property rights in intellectual products should be prescribed by the relevant law is a matter of social agreement.

In fact, a modern patent system does not grant all inventors the exclusive right in their invention. It combines time-limited exclusive rights and public domain, as explained earlier in chapters 1, 2 and 3. A set of criteria for patentability is set out by the relevant domestic law, subject to the TRIPS Agreement.[83] These criteria for patentability may change, reflecting relevant policy changes. Any patent claim over an invention is subject to an examination by the granting office as to whether it satisfies the criteria for patentability. Therefore, some inventions become part of the public domain from their inception, and other inventions, those that have met the conditions for patentability, are subject to the exclusive rights for a certain period of time and then belong to the public domain.

This question of an expectation of holding a patent was examined by the European human rights system. In *British-American Tobacco Company Ltd v. the Netherlands*, the Commission was of the opinion that an application for a patent was not covered by the right to property provision in Article 1 of Protocol No. 1 to the ECHR.[84] This view was

---

78 Henry G. Schermers, 'The International Protection of the Right of Property' in Franz Matscher et al. (eds), *Protecting Human Rights: The European Dimension*, Carl Heymanns Verlag KG (1988) 565–80, 569; Krause (n 58) 191, 209; Jeremy Waldron, '12 Property for All', in *The Right to Private Property*, Clarendon Press (1990) 423–45.

79 'Every person has a right to own such private property *as meets the essential needs of decent living and helps to maintain the dignity of the individual and of the home*' (emphasis added).

80 Krause (n 58) 197.

81 Johannes Morsink, *The Universal Declaration of Human Rights: Origins, Drafting, and Intent*, University of Pennsylvania Press (1999) 151.

82 Yu (n 45) 1087.

83 Articles 27 (Patentable Subject Matter) and 29 (Conditions on Patent Applicants) of TRIPS.

84 *British-American Tobacco Company Ltd v. the Netherlands* (n 76) §§ 71–2. 'The applicant company did not succeed in obtaining an effective protection for their invention by means of a patent. Consequently, the company were denied a protected intellectual property right but were not deprived of their existing property.'

reiterated by the European Court of Human Rights in a case concerning a trade mark, stating that 'the applicant company could not be sure of being the owner of the trade mark in question until after final registration and then only on condition that no third party raised an objection, as the applicable legislation permitted. ... Prior to such registration, the applicant did, of course, have a hope of acquiring such a "possession", but not a legally-protected legitimate expectation.'[85]

An acquired patent

Does the human right to property apply to the person having acquired the patent after having met the conditions set out by relevant law? First of all, this question has to surmount a conceptual difficulty raised by the fact that patents are mostly held by corporations. As seen above in relation to the right to the protection of moral and material interests, the CESCR is of the view that human rights are 'fundamental entitlements of the human person'[86] and intellectual property rights, held by legal entities, 'are not protected at the level of human rights'.[87] Article 1.2 of the ACHR clarifies that '2. For the purposes of this Convention, "person" means every human being'. However, Article 1 of the First Protocol to the ECHR is extended to claims by corporations. This is the only provision of the ECHR that expressly recognises the rights not only of natural persons, but also of legal persons.[88]

Specifically regarding intellectual property, the European Commission and Court of Human Rights have been requested, very occasionally, to examine the applicability of Article 1 of the First Protocol to intellectual property. The resultant case law has ruled that patents, copyrights and trademarks are 'possessions' in the sense of Article 1 of Protocol 1 to the Convention,[89] often referring to *Smith Kline and French Laboratories Ltd v. the Netherlands*:[90] 'The Commission notes that under Dutch law the holder of a patent is referred to as the proprietor of a patent and that patents are deemed, subject to the provisions of the Patent Act, to be personal property which is transferable and assignable. The Commission finds that a patent accordingly falls within the scope of the term "possessions" in Article 1 of Protocol No. 1.' The Charter of Fundamental Rights of the European Union, adopted in 2000, specifically included intellectual property in the right to property provision.[91]

---

85 *Anheuser-Busch Inc v. Portugal* (n 76) paras 49 and 69.

86 CESCR, GC No. 17 (n 29) para. 2.

87 Ibid., para. 7.

88 'Every natural or *legal person* is entitled to the peaceful enjoyment of his possessions ...' (emphasis added).

89 *Smith Kline & French Laboratories Ltd v. the Netherlands*, Application No. 12633/87, 66 European Commission of Human Rights (4 October 1990) (patents); *Dima v. Romania*, Application No. 58472/00, ECtHR, para. 87 (2005) (admissibility decision) (copyrighted works); *Melnychuk v. Ukraine*, Application No. 28743/03, ECtHR, para. 8 (2005) (admissibility decision) (IP); *Anheuser-Busch Inc v. Portugal* (n 76) paras 66–72.

90 *Smith Kline & French Laboratories Ltd. v. the Netherlands* (n 89), cited in *Anheuser-Busch Inc v. Portugal* (n 76) para. 69.

91 Article 17 (Right to Property) '... 2. Intellectual property shall be protected'.

In short, in Europe, intellectual property, including a patent, is within the scope of the human right. The caveat should be entered that this analysis of patents and the right to property should not lead to a presumption that a patent is universally recognised as a human right to property. Also, the right to property provision under the ECHR makes it clear that the recognition of the right to property 'shall not ... impair the right of a State to enforce such laws as it deems necessary to control the use of property in accordance with the general interest or to secure the payment of taxes or other contributions or penalties'. On the status of the right to property, Henry Schermers, a former member of the European Commission of Human Rights (1981–1996), observed that 'either the right to property is only a minor kind of human right, subject to so many limitations', or 'the fundamental human right of property only concerns the property' necessary to sustain personal life.[92] Restrictions prescribed in Article 1 of the First Protocol to the ECHR are discussed under 'Cross-cutting Topics' in Chapter 7.

Re-examination of Conflicts between TRIPS and Access to Medicines

The Question of Inter-regime Conflict

Most documents of the UN human rights bodies on this subject discussed in the first section of this chapter expressed general human rights concerns in relation to the existing intellectual property system. In the following years, there were studies that made a close inquiry into the impacts of intellectual property rights on societal interests, including human rights.[93] This section revisits the findings of those recent studies, in particular on the existence of conflicts between intellectual property and the right to access to medicines. The purpose of re-examination of the alleged conflict between the two regimes is to deepen discussion on how to create and enhance a mutually beneficial relationship between the two regimes taking into account human rights concerns.

---

92 Schermers (n 78) 575.

93 For more thorough analysis of social impacts of intellectual property rights, see Report of the Commission on Intellectual Property Rights (UK), *Integrating Intellectual Property Rights and Development Policy* (2002); for the impact on the right to food, see Report of the second Special Rapporteur on the Right to Food, Olivier De Schutter (23 July 2009) UN Doc. A/64/170; particularly for the impact on health of intellectual property, see Reports of the first UN Special Rapporteur on the Right to Health, Paul Hunt (1 March 2004) UN Doc. E/CN.4/2004/49/ Add.1; (13 September 2006) UN Doc. A/61/338; Reports of the second Special Rapporteur on the Right to Health, Anand Grover (31 March 2009) UN Doc. A/HRC/11/12; (1 May 2013) UN Doc. A/HRC/23/42; Report of the High Commissioner for Human Rights (n 7) paras 29–58; WHO, Report of the Commission on Intellectual Property Rights, Innovation and Public Health (CIPIH), *Public Health, Innovation and Intellectual Property Rights* (2006); WHO, WIPO and WTO, *Promoting Access to Medical Technologies and Innovation: Intersections between Public Health, Intellectual Property and Trade* (2013); Philippe Cullet, 'Patents and Medicines: The Relationship between TRIPS and the Human Right to Health' (2003) 79(1) *International Affairs* 139–60; Hestermeyer (n 37).

The issue of how to regulate knowledge over pharmaceuticals invites the application of two different rules in international law: norms contained in TRIPS, which is part of WTO law on one hand, and norms concerning the right to health and the right to life guaranteed in international human rights law on the other.[94] The existence of conflicts between two sets of norms can be ascertained by the analysis of whether the two rules point to different directions.[95]

Imagine a situation where the protection of pharmaceutical patents leads to increased prices of medicines so as to render them unaffordable to a significant number of people in a country. This State conduct may comply with TRIPS, but may constitute a breach of the rights to life and health under international human rights treaties. It is a widely held view that TRIPS, requiring all the States to provide patent protection for both pharmaceutical processes and products, is likely to lead to substantial increases in the price of medicines, particularly in developing countries, where there used to be no patent protection for pharmaceutical products. Such price increases of medicines negatively affect capabilities of governments to ensure access to affordable essential medicines and thus the right of individuals to access to essential medicines.

Narrow Definition of Conflict

This situation may not necessarily lead one to conclude that there is a conflict between rules in international law. In a narrow definition of a conflict of laws formulated by Wilfred Jenks, 'a conflict in the strict sense of direct incompatibility arises only where a party to the two treaties cannot simultaneously comply with its obligations under both treaties'.[96] In other words, 'conflict exists if it is possible for a party to two treaties to comply with one rule only by thereby failing to comply with another rule'.[97] In the case of TRIPS and access to medicines, an examination has to be undertaken as to whether compliance with TRIPS necessitates a violation of the right to access to medicines.[98] TRIPS allows for substantial

---

94 'That two norms are valid in regard to a situation means that they each cover the facts of which the situation consists. That two norms are applicable in a situation means that they have binding force in respect to the legal subjects finding themselves in the relevant situation.' ILC, *Difficulties Arising from the Diversification and Expansion of International Law* (2006) footnote 1.

95 Report of the Study Group of the ILC, 'Fragmentation of International Law: Difficulties Arising from the Diversification and Expansion of International Law', finalised by Martti Koskenniemi (13 April 2006) UN Doc. A/CN.4/L.682, para. 23; Joost Pauwelyn, 'The Role of Public International Law in the WTO' (2001) 95 *American Journal of International Law* 535–78; Gabrielle Marceau, 'The WTO Dispute Settlement and Human Rights', in Frederick Abbott et al. (eds), *International Trade and Human Rights: Foundations and Conceptual Issues*, University of Michigan Press (2006) 181–260; Hans Morten Haugen, 'The Nature of Social Human Rights Treaties and Standard-Setting WTO Treaties: A Question of Hierarchy?' (2007) 76 *Nordic Journal of International Law* 435–64.

96 Wilfred Jenks, 'The Conflict of Law-Making Treaties' (1953) 30 *British Yearbook of International Law* 401–53.

97 Report of the Study Group of the ILC (n 95) para. 24.

98 Marceau (n 95) 791.

flexibility in the application of intellectual property standards with a view to protecting public health, as analysed in detail in Chapter 3. Furthermore, the adoption of the Doha Declaration confirmed the right of WTO Members to adopt measures necessary to protect public health.[99] Therefore, it can be argued that the existence of TRIPS flexibilities may allow States to simultaneously comply with obligations both under TRIPS and the right to access to medicines, suggesting that there is no conflict, in a strict sense, between norms under TRIPS and international human rights law.

Broad Definition of Conflict

While a conflict of norms may be understood strictly as a notion of incompatibility between obligations upon a single party as above, it may be useful for discussions about a conflict of norms to include 'a situation where two rules or principles suggest different ways of dealing with a problem',[100] albeit not necessarily causing strict incompatibility. As the Study Group of the International Law Commission noted, 'a treaty may sometimes frustrate the goals of another treaty without there being any strict incompatibility between their provisions'.[101] Joost Pauwelyn considers that the strict notion of conflict of norms that 'limits the situation of conflict between norms to two norms imposing mutually exclusive obligations ignores other situations, such as where permissive norms and obligations are incompatible'.[102]

If we take this broad definition of conflict between rules in international law, the existence of flexibility in TRIPS may not preclude conflict between TRIPS and the right to access to medicines. As noted earlier, the High Commissioner for Human Rights raised a question of 'whether the TRIPS Agreement strikes a balance that is consistent with human rights'.[103] This question is apt in understanding the relationship between TRIPS and international human rights law beyond the strict notion of conflict.

Suppose that TRIPS strikes a balance between the protection of commercial interests of the patent holder and the promotion of public health in a way that places the protection of commercial interests of the patent holder at the centre of their concerns and the promotion of public health as an exception. In such cases, States have to justify that there is no alternative that is less restrictive to the protection of commercial interests of the patent holder when adopting measures for the purpose of ensuring access to essential medicines. This particular balancing exercise creates a 'collateral' relationship of human rights to private interests of the patent holder and thus limits policy space for complying with international human rights standards.[104] A strict notion of conflict between norms

---

99 WT/MIN(01)/DEC/2, adopted on 14 November 2001.

100 Report of the Study Group of the ILC (n 95) para. 24.

101 Ibid.

102 Pauwelyn (n 95); Joost Pauwelyn, *Conflict of Norms in Public International Law: How WTO Law Relates to other Rules of International Law*, Cambridge University Press (2003) 170–71.

103 Report of the High Commissioner for Human Rights (n 7) para. 21.

104 For a critique of the collateral role of human rights in shaping and adjusting economic activities, see Sheldon Leader, 'The Collateral Protection of Rights in the Global Economy' (2008–2009) 53 *New York Law School Law Review* 805–14. Also, see GATT, *Thailand – Restrictions*

may not capture this kind of divergence between TRIPS and human rights. As discussed in Chapter 3, it is possible to factor the promotion of public health into the objectives of TRIPS and thus readjust a balance between the commercial interests and public health. However, to resolve divergence through interpretation, one has to first realise that there is a potential conflict.[105]

This discussion on how to define conflicts could help to better understand a relationship of different legal regimes and to enhance consistency in light of the functions of the international legal system as a whole. The first section of this chapter has discussed a series of reports and statements issued by various UN human rights bodies that highlighted potential inconsistencies between TRIPS and human rights.[106] These reports and statements are mainly directed at the divergence of the normative objectives of the different norms, rather than a strict notion of incompatibilities between obligations upon a single State party. Such discussions contributed to forming a pressure on the WTO regime to assess the potential and actual impact of TRIPS on human rights and to give adequate normative weight to human rights norms in interpreting its objective and purpose.[107]

Interpreting TRIPS in Light of Human Rights

Interpretation comes into play when ascertaining the existence of a conflict, as well as resolving a conflict that has been established.[108] The Study Group of the International Law Commission notes that '[i]n international law, there is a strong presumption against normative conflict'.[109] In its view, although two sets of norms may appear to conflict, in most situations 'it is still possible to apply or understand them in such way that no overlap or conflict will remain'.[110] Resolving certain conflicts between different rules may necessitate interventions at the legislative level.[111] On other occasions, potential conflicts between two sets of norms can be avoided by judicious interpretation.

From this perspective, the key question in the present context is whether TRIPS can be interpreted so as to serve general interests, in particular the right to access to medicines.

---

on Importation of and Internal Taxes on Cigarettes, adopted 20 February 1990, BISD 37S/200, para. 75. In this case, the Panel observed that '[t]he import restrictions [on Tobacco] imposed by Thailand could be considered to be "necessary" in terms of Article XX(b) [of GATT] only if there were no alternative measure consistent with the General Agreement, or less inconsistent with it, which Thailand could reasonably be expected to employ to achieve its health policy objectives'.

105 Hestermeyer (n 37) 169–76. Pauwelyn (n 102) 178.

106 Sub-Commission on Human Rights Resolution 2000/7 (n 2); Report of the High Commissioner for Human Rights (n 7).

107 Andrew T.F. Lang, '7. Inter-regime Encounters', in Sarah Joseph et al. (eds), *The World Trade Organization and Human Rights*, Edward Elgar (2009) 163–89.

108 Report of the Study Group of the ILC (n 95) para. 412.

109 Ibid., para. 37; Pauwelyn (n 102) 240–44.

110 Report of the Study Group of the ILC (n 95) para. 43.

111 Ibid., para. 412.

The focus of inquiry should move from whether there is a conflict between norms under TRIPS and the ICESCR, to whether potential conflicts between these two sets of norms can be resolved through interpretation. As the Sub-Commission on Human Rights and the High Commissioner for Human Rights suggested,[112] there is a potential conflict between TRIPS and the right to access to medicines, among other human rights. Is such *prima facie* conflict irreconcilable?

To begin with, the notion of *jus cogens*. which is referenced customarily in the search of hierarchy of norms, may not be of much relevance in the context of the right to access to medicines. The VCLT recognises this concept as 'a norm accepted and recognized by the international community of States as a whole as a norm from which no derogation is permitted and which can be modified only by a subsequent norm of general international law having the same character'.[113] What qualifies as *jus cogens* is subject to debate, with there being no agreed criteria for the norms.[114] The most often cited candidates for *jus cogens* include the prohibition of aggressive use of force other than in self-defence; and the prohibitions of slavery and the slave trade, genocide, racial discrimination, apartheid and torture.[115] Although the content of *jus cogens* may be expanding in response to the development of international law and moral values of the international community,[116] it is doubtful that the right to access to affordable medicines has been widely accepted as *jus cogens*. In addition, while the legal consequence of *jus cogens* is, according to the VCLT, to void other norms conflicting with *jus cogens*, what matters in the present context is whether TRIPS can be interpreted so as to serve the right to access to medicines.

Interpretive role of international human rights law in weighing and balancing

While no definite hierarchical order is established with regard to norms in international treaties, with the exception of *jus cogens*, balancing different rights and obligations always involves evaluating the normative weight of concerns at stake and prioritising more important concerns over less important ones. Norms in international human rights law that give legal expressions to fundamental human values or interests accepted by States can help the process of weighing and balancing different interests.

Weighing the importance of interests or values is not alien to the interpretation of WTO law. In the *EC – Asbestos* case,[117] where the 'necessity' of a measure regarding asbestos fibres adopted by France was considered in accordance with Article XX(b) of the GATT (General Agreement on Tariff and Trade),[118] the Appellate Body reiterated a view held in

---

112 Sub-Commission on Human Rights Resolution 2000/7 (n 2); Report of the High Commissioner for Human Rights (n 7).

113 Article 53 of the VCLT (1969).

114 Dinah Shelton, 'Normative Hierarchy in International Law' (2006) 100, April, *American Journal of International Law* 291–323, 302–3.

115 Report of the Study Group of the ILC (n 95) para. 374.

116 Shelton (n 114) 303.

117 *European Communities – Measures Affecting Asbestos and Asbestos-Containing Products* (12 March 2001) WT/DS135/AB/R.

118 Article XX of the GATT (1947) sets out general exceptions. Article XX(b) concerns domestic regulatory action 'necessary to protect human, animal or plant life or health'.

the *Korea – Beef* case[119] that "'[t]he more vital or important [the] common interests or values" pursued, the easier it would be to accept as "necessary" measures designed to achieve those ends'.[120] The Appellate Body considered that '[i]n this case, the objective pursued by the measure is the preservation of human life and health through the elimination, or reduction, of the well-known, and life-threatening, health risks posed by asbestos fibres. The value pursued is both vital and important in the highest degree'.[121] '[A] process of weighing and balancing'[122] is a necessary feature of the interpretation of WTO law.

The role of international human rights law in the interpretation of WTO Agreements is supported by Article 31.3(c) of the VCLT.[123] This article recognises the interpretive role of other international instruments, as 'relevant rules of international law'.[124] The WTO Appellate Body affirmed that the WTO Agreement is not to be interpreted in 'clinical isolation from public international law'.[125] In *US – Shrimp*, the Appellate Body interpreted the terms 'exhaustible natural resources' in GATT Article XX(g) with reference to a number of environmental treaties.[126] In this case, the Appellate Body justifies its reasoning, citing the view of the International Court of Justice that 'where concepts embodied in a treaty are "by definition, evolutionary", their interpretation cannot remain unaffected by the subsequent development of the law ... Moreover, an international instrument has to be interpreted and applied within the framework of the entire legal system prevailing at the time of interpretation'.[127] It is also suggested that a good-faith interpretation of WTO provisions, which is required by general principles of international law,[128] must lead to a reading of WTO law, as far as it is possible to do so, as consistent with other relevant international law, including international human rights law.[129]

---

119 WTO Appellate Body Report, *Korea – Measures Affecting Imports of Fresh, Chilled and Frozen Beef* (11 December 2000) WT/DS161/AB/R, WT/DS169/AB/R, para. 162: 'a treaty interpreter ... may take into account the relative importance of the common interests or values that the law or regulation to be enforced is intended to protect. The more vital or important those common interests or values are, the easier it would be to accept as "necessary" a measure designed as an enforcement instrument'.

120 *European Communities – Measures Affecting Asbestos and Asbestos-Containing Products* (n 117) para. 172.

121 Ibid.

122 *Korea – Measures Affecting Imports of Fresh, Chilled and Frozen Beef* (n 119) para. 164.

123 See Marceau (n 95); Joost Pauwelyn, 'Human Rights in WTO Dispute Settlement', in Thomas Cottier, Joost Pauwelyn and Elisabeth Bürgi (eds), *Human Rights and International Trade*, Oxford University Press (2005) 205–31, 208–9.

124 Article 31.3 of the VCLT: 'There shall be taken into account, together with the context: ... (c) any relevant rules of international law applicable in the relations between the parties'.

125 WTO Appellate Body Report, *United States – Standard for Reformulation and Conventional Gasoline* (20 May 1996), WT/DS2/AB/R, 17.

126 WTO Appellate Body Report, United States – Import Prohibition of Certain Shrimp and Shrimp Products (12 October 1998), WT/DS/58/AB/R, paras 128–132.

127 Ibid., para. 130. International Court of Justice Report, Namibia (Legal Consequences) Advisory Opinion (1971), 31.

128 Article 31.1 of the VCLT.

129 Marceau (n 95).

International human rights law should be taken into account when evaluating the normative importance of competing values, and, further, seeking a right balance between different values and interests involved in TRIPS. For instance, when commercial interests of the patent holder and access to medicines are at stake in the implementation of TRIPS, States must identify whether either of them is recognised as a human right and, if so, what normative weight the human right(s) should be accorded in international human rights law. In this regard, it is useful to consider how international human rights law deals with a situation when a legitimate interest and a human right compete or two human rights compete through limitation clauses. This is an important discussion when constituting a human rights framework for intellectual property and access to medicines, as considered in Chapter 7.

Crucially, TRIPS is not propelled exclusively towards strengthening and harmonising the protection of intellectual property rights throughout the world, as discussed in Chapter 3.[130] The objectives of TRIPS require a balance between the promotion of technological innovation and the transfer and dissemination of technology, and between the users and producers of technology.[131] The principles of TRIPS acknowledge the right of WTO Members to adopt measures necessary to protect public health.[132] Flexibilities in TRIPS relating to the standards for patentability, compulsory licensing, parallel importing and other exceptions to exclusive rights provide tools for striking a balance between the promotion of innovation and access to the outcome of such innovation. International human rights law can provide guidance in this process of weighing and balancing different interests or values, prescribed by TRIPS, with a view to achieving a fair balance,[133] ensuring that the measures adopted to achieve economic goals do not frustrate other objectives that TRIPS serves.

Evolving norms under TRIPS in response to 'normative environment'[134]

State practice in the use of TRIPS flexibilities, and other developments around the issue of access to medicines in the last decade, indicates that it is possible to interpret TRIPS in a manner consistent with the values embodied in international human rights

---

130 Henning Grosse Ruse-Khan, 'Proportionality and Balancing within the Objectives', in Paul Torremans (ed.), *Intellectual Property and Human Rights: Enhanced Edition of Copyright and Human Rights*, Kluwer Law International (2008) 161–94, 174–5; UNCTAD-ICTSD, *Resource Book on TRIPS and Development*, Cambridge University Press (2004) 125.

131 Article 7 of TRIPS: 'The protection and enforcement of IPR should contribute to the promotion of technological innovation and to the transfer and dissemination of technology, to the mutual advantage of producers and users of technological knowledge and in a manner conducive to social and economic welfare, and to a balance of rights and obligations.'

132 Article 8.1 of TRIPS: 'Members may, in formulating or amending their laws and regulations, *adopt measures necessary to protect public health and nutrition*, and to promote the public interest in sectors of vital importance to their socio-economic and technological development, provided that such measures are consistent with the provisions of this Agreement' (emphasis added).

133 Robert Howse, 'The WTO and Human Rights', in Sarah Joseph et al. (eds), *The World Trade Organization and Human Rights: Interdisciplinary Perspectives*, Edward Elgar (2009) 39–68, 59.

134 Report of the Study Group of the ILC (n 95) paras 413–23.

law so that potential conflicts between TRIPS and the right to access to medicines may be avoided or resolved. The function of TRIPS flexibilities in the context of access to medicines has been crystallised by several events, such as the HIV/AIDS crisis, pharmaceutical companies' lawsuit against the government of South Africa over legislation incorporating the flexibilities in TRIPS,[135] and the WTO dispute initiated by the US against Brazil over the issue of compulsory licensing.[136] These cases prompted intense debate on TRIPS and access to medicines. The UN human rights mechanisms stressed that access to medicines is a crucial element of the right to health and expressed their concerns over the implication of TRIPS for the right to access to medicines in various forms.[137]

The Doha Declaration was adopted amid heightening demand for reassurance that TRIPS does not prevent States from adopting measures to protect public health.[138] The Declaration critically reaffirmed the right of Members to take measures necessary to protect public health by clarifying the flexibilities in TRIPS. Although the language of human rights is not explicit in the Declaration, Frederick Abbott observed that 'the Doha Declaration is implicitly a human rights instrument, as well as a trade instrument'.[139] Gabrielle Marceau also considered the Doha Declaration to be exemplary for 'coherent reading of WTO provisions taking into account potentially relevant human rights law'.[140]

Furthermore, jurisprudence from national courts has solidified access to medicines as a justiciable human right.[141] An outstanding case was *Minister of Health v. Treatment Action Campaign*, where the Constitutional Court of South Africa found that the failure of the government to take appropriate measures to ensure access to Nevirapine, to prevent mother-to-child transmission of HIV, within its jurisdiction constituted a violation of

---

135 In 1998, a group of 39 global pharmaceutical companies sued the government of South Africa, alleging that the Amended Medicines Act violated the TRIPS Agreement and the South African Constitution. In 2001, the pharmaceutical companies dropped the lawsuit under a high level of international pressure. For more details, see 'The Doha Declaration on the TRIPS Agreement and Public Health' in Chapter 1.

136 In 2001, the US filed a WTO case against Brazil, disputing the compatibility of the Brazilian compulsory licensing legislation with the TRIPS Agreement. The US later withdrew its case against Brazil in the face of intense international criticism. For more details, see 'The Doha Declaration on the TRIPS Agreement and Public Health' in Chapter 1.

137 Commission on Human Rights Resolution 2001/33 (n 20), particularly paras 1, 4; Report of the High Commissioner for Human Rights (n 7) paras 11, 20, 21.

138 For the circumstances that led to the adoption of the Doha Declaration, see 'The Doha Declaration on the TRIPS Agreement and Public Health' in Chapter 1. For detailed analysis of the flexibilities, see Chapter 3.

139 Frederick M. Abbott, 'The "Rule of Reason" and the Right to Health: Integrating Human Rights and Competition Principles in the Context of TRIPS' in Cottier et al. (n 123) 283.

140 Marceau (n 95) 755–6.

141 See 'Access to Medicine: An Element of the Right to Health' in Chapter 4. Hans V. Hogerzeil, Melanie Samson, Jaume Vidal Casanovas and Ladan Rahmani-Ocora, 'Is Access to Essential Medicines as Part of the Fulfilment of the Right to Health Enforceable through the Courts?' (2006) 368 *The Lancet* 305–11.

constitutional rights.[142] In a raised awareness of access to medicine as a human right, the TRIPS flexibilities, reaffirmed by the Doha Declaration, have been used by several countries, such as Brazil, Egypt, Malaysia, Zimbabwe, Zambia, Ghana, Indonesia, Thailand and Ecuador,[143] in order to lower prices of patented medicines and thus ensure access to affordable medicines.

Access to affordable medicines in developing countries lacking pharmaceutical manufacturing capacity is one of the remaining challenges in making TRIPS compatible with international human rights law. This issue was recognised in paragraph 6 of the Doha Declaration,[144] culminating in the 2003 WTO Decision[145] and the following modification of the provision on compulsory licensing in TRIPS.[146] The 2003 WTO Decision provides a waiver from Article 31(f) obligations for countries manufacturing patented products under compulsory licence to export the products to eligible importing countries. The functioning of this new system (the so-called 'Paragraph 6' system) is subject to annual review, in accordance with paragraph 8 of the Decision on the Implementation of Paragraph 6 of the Doha Declaration.[147] This review process may provide an opportunity for the right to access to medicines to be considered, in the context of poor countries in terms of

---

142 *Minister of Health and Others v. Treatment Action Campaign and Others*, CCT 8/02, SA 721 (5 July 2002).

143 See Reed Beall and Randall Kuhn, 'Trends in Compulsory Licensing of Pharmaceuticals Since the Doha Declaration: A Database Analysis' (2012) 9(1) *PloS Medicine*; WHO, Briefing Note Access to Medicines – Country Experiences in Using TRIPS Safeguards (February 2008); UNDP, Good Practice Guide: Improving Access to Treatment by Utilizing Public Health Flexibilities in the WTO TRIPS Agreement (2010); Sisule Musungu and Cecilia Oh, 'The Use of Flexibilities in TRIPS by Developing Countries: Can They Promote Access to Medicines?' in WHO, Report of the Commission on Intellectual Property Rights, Innovation and Public Health (CIPIH) (n 93); Frederick M. Abbott and Jerome H. Reichman, 'The Doha Round's Public Health Legacy: Strategies for the Production and Diffusion of Patented Medicines under the Amended TRIPS Provisions' [2007] *Journal of International Economic Law* 921–87, 949–57.

144 Paragraph 6 of the Doha Declaration on the TRIPS Agreement and Public Health, WT/MIN(01)/DEC/W/2: 'We recognize that WTO Members with insufficient or no manufacturing capacities in the pharmaceutical sector could face difficulties in making effective use of compulsory licensing under the TRIPS Agreement. We instruct the Council for TRIPS to find an expeditious solution to this problem and to report to the General Council before the end of 2002.'

145 Decision of the General Council, 'Implementation of paragraph 6 of the Doha Declaration on the TRIPS Agreement and Public Health', WT/L/540 and Corr.1, 1 September 2003.

146 Decision of General Council, Amendment of the TRIPS Agreement, 6 December 2005, WT/L/641. This amendment to the TRIPS Agreement has formally incorporated the 2003 WTO waiver decision and will replace it once two-thirds of Members accepts the amendment. For more details, see 'Compulsory Licensing: Countries with Few Manufacturing Capacities in the Pharmaceutical Sector' in Chapter 3.

147 Decision of the General Council of 30 August 2003 (Implementation of Paragraph 6 of the Doha Declaration on the TRIPS Agreement and Public Health), paragraph 8 states: 'The Council for TRIPS shall review annually the functioning of the system set out in this Decision with a view to ensuring its effective operation and shall annually report on its operation to the General Council. This review shall be deemed to fulfil the review requirements of Article IX:4 of the WTO Agreement.'

pharmaceutical manufacturing capacity. This process may further prompt a discussion as to whether a better implementation of the 2003 WTO Decision will suffice or whether further modification of TRIPS will be required to enable these countries to ensure access to affordable medicines for their population.[148]

What has been discussed so far indicates that, in the context of access to medicines, the norms in TRIPS evolve seeking a better balance between different interests, and international human rights law has become recognised as a crucial part of 'a normative environment',[149] in light of which TRIPS should be understood and reviewed.

Exploring a New Model for Health Innovation beyond TRIPS

The right to health and the right to enjoy the benefits of scientific progress and its application entail the promotion of essential health innovation and affordable access to new medicines as well as existing ones. How to implement TRIPS plays an important role in helping or obstructing access to existing medicines, yet the unavailability of medicines for 'neglected diseases' requires new models for health innovation.[150] In this regard, it is necessary to note efforts that have been made over the last 10 years to address this huge research gap for health needs of people in developing countries since an effective coordination is required among policy makers in this field with a view to enhancing access to medicines and thus fulfilling obligations under international human rights law.

A conventional market-based intellectual property system fails to correspond with health needs of people living in developing countries where the purchasing power of both patients and the government is limited. In order to overcome this market failure, the World Health Assembly endorsed a Global Strategy and Plan of Action on Public Health, Innovation and Intellectual Property, the overall objective of which is 'to secure, inter alia, an enhanced and sustainable basis for needs-driven, essential health research and development relevant to diseases that disproportionately affect developing countries'.[151]

---

148 There are concerns about the onerous conditions set out in the 2003 WTO Decision which may still place an obstacle for countries lacking their own manufacturing capacity to take advantage of the waiver so as to improve access to affordable medicines. For instance, see also the statement of Brazil to the WTO TRIPS Council, 1 March 2011. 'As we have mentioned last meeting, the TRIPS Council and other fora should analyze whether the economic and political incentives provided by the system are adequate to secure investment in the production of generic medicines at affordable prices. The fact that in seven years there has been only one case of use of the system is strong evidence that they are not', available at http://keionline.org/node/1086, last accessed 12 April 2014. Carlos Correa, 'Access to Drugs under TRIPS: A Not So Expeditious Solution' (2004) 8(1) *Bridges* 21–2; Graham Dutfield, 'Delivering Drugs to the Poor: Will the TRIPS Amendment Help?' (2008) 34 *American Journal of Law & Medicine* 107–24.

149 Report of the Study Group of the ILC (n 95) paras 413–23.

150 For the discussion of market failure in innovation, see 'Other Incentive Mechanisms: Public Sponsorship' in Chapter 2 and 'Implications for Scientific Knowledge Production' in Chapter 5.

151 WHA Resolution 61.21, 'Global Strategy and Plan of Action on Public Health, Innovation and Intellectual Property' (24 May 2008).

A key concept in search of alternative ways for needs-based health R&D is the de-linkage of the final product price from the costs of R&D, that is, 'costs and risks associated with R&D should be rewarded, and incentives for R&D provided, other than through the price of the product'.[152]

In order to find such alternative financing mechanisms for health innovation, the World Health Assembly set up two expert working groups, i.e. the Expert Working Group on Research and Development: Coordination and Financing (EWG), and subsequently the Consultative Expert Working Group on Research and Development: Financing and Coordination (CEWG). The CEWG analysed the proposals for new health R&D that EWG assembled in its report,[153] and made a number of recommendations on global policy efforts to promote R&D for health needs of developing countries in 2012.[154] A key recommendation is that of open-knowledge approaches to innovation, i.e. R&D outcomes should be in the public domain or made available through the use of equitable open licensing and patent pools.[155] Given the market failures in relation to health needs of developing countries, financing for R&D needs to be based on increased contributions from governments and relevant to health needs of developing countries. The CEWG recommended spending by all countries of at least 0.01 per cent of GDP on government-funded R&D for this purpose.[156] A far-reaching recommendation is to negotiate and adopt an international convention on global health R&D that will ensure sustainable and effective financing and coordination of health R&D.[157] Carlos Correa commented that a new model of R&D recommended by the CEWG would 'lead to a reduction of R&D costs and increase innovation through a more focused, health-driven research agenda and through improved monitoring, cooperation and sharing of research results' as well as 'much more affordable, accessible treatments'.[158]

Conclusion

This chapter has re-examined the relationship between TRIPS and international human rights law in the context of access to medicines. It began by clarifying the different

---

152 WHO, WIPO and WTO (n 93) 116.

153 WHO, Report of the Expert Working Group on Research and Development Financing, Geneva (2010).

154 WHO, *Research and Development to Meet Health Needs in Developing Countries: Strengthening Global Financing and Coordination*, Report of the Consultative Expert Working Group on Research and Development: Financing and Coordination (CEWG), Geneva (2012).

155 John-Arne Røttingen, Claudia Chamas, L.C. Goyal, Hilda Harb, Leizel Lagrada and Bongani Mawethu Mayosi, 'Securing the Public Good of Health Research and Development for Developing Countries' [2012] *Bulletin of the World Health Organization* 398–400.

156 WHO, *Research and Development to Meet Health Needs in Developing Countries: Strengthening Global Financing and Coordination* (n 154) 110.

157 Ibid., 120–22.

158 Carlos Correa, 'Towards a New Model for Pharmaceutical Research' [2012] *Bulletin of the World Health Organization* 90.

features of a patent under the existing intellectual property regime and the right to benefit from the protection of authors' moral and material interests under Article 15.1(c) of the ICESCR. Then, as a separate question, the relationship between a patent and the right to property was examined. In the European context, a human or legal person who has acquired a patent is within the scope of the right to property, although susceptible to restrictions provided by relevant laws.

The discussion of normative conflicts in international law sheds light on the interplay between norms under TRIPS and international human rights law. A potential conflict exists between TRIPS, mandating all WTO Members to provide intellectual property protection in all fields of technology including pharmaceuticals on one hand, and international human rights treaties obliging States parties to ensure access to affordable medicines for all on the other. The resolution of such potential conflicts can begin with the recognition that TRIPS, as part of the international legal system, has to be viewed along with other international treaties. The balancing activities necessary to realise the objectives and principles of TRIPS invite the role of international human rights law in the interpretation and implementation of TRIPS. The normative evolution in relation to TRIPS has widened the possibility that TRIPS is implemented and reviewed in light of international human rights norms.

Challenges remain as to the lack of appropriate treatment for many of the diseases in developing countries, another significant part of access to medicines. States have obligations under the right to health and the right to enjoy the benefits of scientific progress to promote innovation of new medicines addressing health needs of people and to ensure access to its outcome. Fulfilling these obligations may go beyond the scope of how to implement TRIPS and require a new model for health R&D. Considering this wider context, the following chapter discusses a human rights framework for considering health innovation, intellectual property and access to medicines.

Chapter 7

Human Rights, Intellectual Property, Innovation and Access to Medicines

Introduction

Along with domestic bills of rights, international human rights law requires States to make their domestic law and policies compatible with human rights standards.[1] The area of intellectual property law and policy is no exception. A series of reports or statements from the UN human rights mechanisms directly or indirectly addressed the role of human rights in relation to intellectual property. The CESCR stated that intellectual property protection should serve 'the objective of human well-being' and 'international human rights instruments give legal expression' to it.[2] The CESCR has attached 'fundamental importance' to 'the integration of international human rights norms into the enactment and interpretation of intellectual property law'.[3] The High Commissioner for Human Rights recommended ways that human rights can be factored into the objectives of the implementation of TRIPS.[4] The first Special Rapporteur on the Right to Health (Paul Hunt) has set out the right-to-health responsibilities of States[5] and has also developed human rights guidelines for pharmaceutical companies,[6] each of which bear upon intellectual property law and policy. The second Special Rapporteur on the Right to Health (Anand Grover) has highlighted intellectual property policies that States can use to guarantee the right to health.[7] Building upon the existing human rights recommendations for intellectual property and access to medicines, this chapter aims to develop a human rights framework for intellectual property, innovation and access to medicines that can guide States in enacting and implementing intellectual property law and policy.

---

1 Dinah Shelton, 'Protecting Human Rights in a Globalized World' (2002) 25 *Boston College International and Comparative Law Review* 273–322, 304.

2 CESCR, Statement: Human Rights and Intellectual Property, Follow-up to the Day of General Discussion on Article 15.1(c) (14 December 2001), E/C.12/2001/15, para. 4.

3 Ibid., para. 18.

4 Report of the High Commissioner for Human Rights, 'The Impact of the Agreement on Trade-Related Aspects of Intellectual Property Rights on Human Rights' (27 June 2001) UN Doc. E/CN.4/Sub.2/2001/13, paras 59–69.

5 Report of the first Special Rapporteur on the Right to Health, Paul Hunt (13 September 2006) UN Doc. A/61/338.

6 Report of the first Special Rapporteur on the Right to Health, Paul Hunt (11 August 2008) UN Doc. A/63/263.

7 Report of the second Special Rapporteur on the Right to Health, Anand Grover (31 March 2009) UN Doc. A/HRC/11/12.

Importantly, a human rights framework for intellectual property, innovation and access to medicines should be firmly embedded within the right to health. Therefore, the right-to-health framework in relation to access to medicines, developed by the UN human rights mechanisms, is a cornerstone for any further discussion on a human rights framework for intellectual property and access to medicines. On the other hand, it also has to be noted that there are other human rights relevant to this human rights framework for intellectual property, innovation and access to medicines, for instance the right to enjoy the benefits of scientific progress and its applications (Art. 15.1(b) ICESCR), the right to benefit from the protection of the moral and material interests of authors (Art. 15.1(c) ICESCR), and the right to property in the European context.

This chapter highlights essential features of primarily the right to health, but also other human rights listed above.[8] All these human rights have been analysed in earlier chapters. While clarifying human rights responsibilities of pharmaceutical companies is equally important to ensure access to affordable medicines, this chapter focuses on States' human rights obligations in relation to the issue of intellectual property and access to medicines. Delineating the boundary of justifiable limitations upon relevant human rights is crucial for preserving the nature of the human rights at stake and for shaping the appropriate relationship between intellectual property and access to medicines. Clauses on limitations in the ICESCR are analysed for this purpose, as these can provide guidance in balancing different human rights and interests in the context of access to medicines. This chapter concludes with a series of human rights recommendations for States concerning the issue of intellectual property and access to medicines.

Relevant Human Rights

The human rights listed here as relevant to the issue of intellectual property and access to medicines have already been analysed in chapters 4, 5 and 6. This section highlights the relevant aspects of each of them in developing a human rights framework for intellectual property, innovation and access to medicines.

Right to Access to Medicines

The right to access to medicines is an essential element of the right to health and the right to life. The right to health and the right to life are enshrined in numerous international and regional human rights instruments.[9] The right to access to medicines in the context of pandemics is emerging as part of customary international law.[10] Intellectual property law and policy has a particular bearing upon the promotion of

---

8 This does not suggest that the human rights listed here as relevant to the present subject are exhaustive.

9 See 'Access to Medicine: An Element of the Right to Health' and 'Access to Essential Medicines: An Element of the Right to Life' in Chapter 4.

10 See 'The Right to Access to Medicines as Customary International Law' in Chapter 4.

research and development for primary health needs, and access to affordable essential medicines.[11] The right to access to medicines should be embedded in a human rights framework for this issue.

Where primary health needs are not effectively addressed by existing medicines, the right to access to medicines places an obligation upon States parties to the ICESCR to take reasonable measures to ensure research and development for new medicines addressing primary health needs.[12] Diseases predominantly affecting people in developing countries, known as 'neglected diseases', have attracted little medical research and development because effective market demand does not exist due to the insufficient purchasing power of people in those countries.[13] The UN General Assembly recognised that insufficient market incentive to the development of new medicines addressing diseases primarily affecting people in developing countries directly impacts upon the right to health in those countries and thus requires international cooperation, in its Resolution 58/173 which highlights:

> the need for further international cooperation and research to promote the development of new drugs, vaccines and diagnostic tools for diseases causing a heavy burden in developing countries, and stresses the need to support developing countries in their efforts in this regard, taking into account that the failure of market forces to address such diseases has a direct negative impact on the progressive realization in these countries of the right of everyone to the highest attainable standard of physical and mental health.[14]

Accordingly, States, individually and through international assistance and cooperation, have to take effective measures to promote the development and the availability of new essential medicines addressing the primary health needs of people.

Also, the right to access to medicines obliges States parties to ensure that existing medicines are available, accessible, culturally acceptable and of good quality.[15] At least, in the context of pandemics, all States, not only States parties, are bound to ensure access to medicines treating pandemics. While the right to access to medicines in general is subject to progressive realisation in accordance with Article 2.1 of the ICESCR, the provision of essential medicines is a minimum core obligation of States under the right to health. States must, as a minimum core obligation, make sure that essential medicines on the

---

11 Report of the High Commissioner for Human Rights (n 4) para. 30.

12 Ibid., para. 31; Report of the Special Rapporteur on the Right to Health, Paul Hunt (2006, n 5) paras 47–48; Report of the Special Rapporteur on the Right to Health, Paul Hunt: Mission to Uganda (19 January 2006), UN doc. E/CN.4/2006/48/Add.2, paras 62–6.

13 See 'Other Incentive Mechanisms: Public Sponsorship' in Chapter 2 and 'Availability, accessibility, acceptability and good quality' and 'The duties to respect, protect and fulfil' in Chapter 4.

14 GA Resolution 58/173. The Right of Everyone to the Enjoyment of the Highest Attainable Standard of Physical and Mental Health, 58th session (22 December 2003) UN Doc. A/RES/58/173, para. 13.

15 CESCR, GC No. 14 The Right to Health (Art. 12 of the ICESCR), adopted in 22nd session (2000) UN Doc. E/C.12/2000/4, para. 12.

national list[16] are available in sufficient quantity and economically accessible throughout their jurisdiction.[17]

Right of Everyone to Enjoy the Benefits of Scientific Progress and its Applications

One important factor in progressively realising the right to access to medicines is 'our ability to enjoy the benefits of scientific progress and its applications'.[18] Intellectual property systems can have a significant impact upon the realisation of the right to enjoy the benefits of scientific progress and its applications (REBSP). Thus, this right is another necessary feature of a human rights framework for intellectual property, innovation and access to medicines.

Considering the provisions in Article 15 of the ICESCR[19] and the Venice Statement on the Right to Enjoy the Benefits of Scientific Progress and its Applications,[20] two elements of REBSP are pertinent to intellectual property law and policy: freedom of scientific research, and equitable access to scientific information and applications.[21] There are scientific applications and technologies that have particularly significant impacts on people's lives. Innovations essential for a life with dignity must be made accessible to all as a matter of the right to enjoy the benefits of scientific progress. In the context of access to medicines, duties of States parties to fulfil REBSP include taking measures to promote medical research and development, and making products resulting from this development available and accessible. Where medical research and development is necessary for addressing primary health needs, States parties have duties to facilitate an environment where such development is undertaken, and also to ensure its outcome is accessible for those who need it.

---

16 The right to access to essential medicines requires States to put into place a national list of essential medicines, based on their primary health needs, consulting the WHO Model Lists. WHO, 'WHO Model Lists of Essential Medicines' (latest version is available at http://www.who.int/medicines/publications/essentialmedicines/en/, last accessed 15 March 2015).

17 CESCR, GC No. 14 (n 15) para. 43; Report of the first Special Rapporteur on the Right to Health, Paul Hunt (13 September 2006, n 5) para. 57.

18 William A. Shabas, '7 Study of the Right to Enjoy the Benefits of Scientific and Technological Progress and Its Applications', in Yvonne Donders and Vladimir Volodin (eds), *Human Rights in Education, Science and Culture: Legal Development and Challenges*, UNESCO and Ashgate (2007) 273–307, 296.

19 Article 15.2: 'The steps to be taken by the States Parties to the present Covenant to achieve the full realization of this right shall include those necessary for the conservation, the development and the diffusion of science and culture.' 15.3: 'The States Parties to the present Covenant undertake to respect the freedom indispensable for scientific research and creative activity.' 15.4: 'The States Parties to the present Covenant recognize the benefits to be derived from the encouragement and development of international contacts and co-operation in the scientific and cultural fields.'

20 UNESCO, The Right to Enjoy the Benefits of Scientific Progress and its Applications: The Outcome of the Experts' Meeting held 16–17 July 2009 in Venice, Italy. This initiative was undertaken in cooperation with the European Inter-University Centre for Human Rights and Democratisation (EIUC), the Amsterdam Center for International Law and the Irish Centre for Human Rights.

21 See 'The Right of Everyone to Enjoy the Benefits of Scientific Progress and its Applications (Art. 15.1(b) of ICESCR)' in Chapter 5.

Right to Benefit from the Protection of the Moral and Material Interests of the Author

The right of everyone to benefit from the protection of the moral and material interests of the author can provide guidance on how the society should treat creators, including authors and inventors. A caveat should be entered that entitlements provided by the existing intellectual property system are different, both conceptually and functionally, from the right to benefit from the protection of the moral and material interests of the author.[22] In the context of medicines, researchers[23] developing new medicines in academic institutions, the biotechnology industry and the pharmaceutical industry, as well as individuals and communities who preserve and develop traditional medicines, are entitled to the right to benefit from the protection of the moral and material interests of the author. As the CESCR clarified, companies cannot claim this human right.[24] The protection of moral interests of authors refers to 'safeguard[ing] the personal link between authors and their creations and between peoples, communities, or other groups and their collective cultural heritage'.[25] The protection of material interests of authors within the human rights context is essentially to enable authors to enjoy the right to an adequate standard of living under Article 11.1 of the ICESCR, as enunciated by the CESCR.[26] The obligation of States is, therefore, 'to respect and protect the basic material interests of authors resulting from their scientific, literary or artistic productions, which are necessary to enable those authors to enjoy an adequate standard of living'.[27]

---

22 See 'Distinction between Intellectual Property Rights and Human Rights' in Chapter 6.

23 According to the interpretation of the CESCR, inventors as well as artists and writers are within the scope of protection, although there is no explicit mention of inventors in the wording of the text. See CESCR, GC No. 17, The Right of Everyone to Benefit from the Protection of the Moral and Material Interests Resulting from Any Scientific, Literary or Artistic Production of Which He or She is the Author (Art. 15, para. 1 (c), of the ICESCR) (12 January 2006) para. 9.

24 For this, see 'The Right to Benefit from the Protection of the Moral and Material Interests Resulting from any Scientific, Literary or Artistic Production of which He is the Author (Art. 15.1(c) of ICESCR)' in Chapter 5 and 'Distinction between Intellectual Property Rights and Human Rights' in Chapter 6. Ibid., para. 7.

25 For this purpose, States must provide measures to protect 'the right of authors to be recognised as the creators of their scientific, literary and artistic productions and to object to any distortion, mutilation or other modification of, or other derogatory action in relation to, such productions, which would be prejudicial to their honour and reputation'. Ibid., paras 2 and 13.

26 Ibid., paras 2, 16, 23. The rationale for the protection of the material interests of authors including inventors is to ensure intellectual workers, e.g. inventors, artists and authors, the enjoyment of an adequate standard of living, through just remuneration for work protected under Art. 7.1 of the ICESCR, which states: '[t]he States Parties to the present Covenant recognize the right of everyone to the enjoyment of just and favourable conditions of work which ensure, in particular; (a) Remuneration which provides all workers, as a minimum, with: (i) fair wages and equal remuneration for work of equal value without distinction of any kind, ... ; (ii) a decent living for themselves and their families in accordance with the provisions of the present Covenant; ...'.

27 Ibid., para. 39.

Right to Property

The right to property provisions in international human rights conventions protect those who have acquired property, according to the relevant laws that apply, from arbitrary interference with their property, and spell out the conditions for permissible limitations to the right.[28] A proposition that rights borne by companies are human rights deviates from the idea that human rights derive from the recognition of the dignity of human persons.[29] The CESCR implied that companies are outside the protection of human rights by stating that entitlements owed to corporations under intellectual property regimes 'are not protected at the level of human rights'.[30] However, under Article 1 of the First Protocol to the ECHR, even a patent held by companies falls within the scope of protection.[31] Therefore, the right to property should also be considered in developing a human rights framework for intellectual property, innovation and access to medicines, although its application is confined to the States parties to the ECHR.

Cross-cutting Topics

Non-discrimination and Equality

Non-discrimination and equality are among the most fundamental principles in international human rights law. They are enshrined in various international human rights instruments, such as the UDHR, ICESCR and ICCPR.[32] General Comment No. 3 of the CESCR affirms that

---

28 See 'Patent Rights and the Human Right to Property' in Chapter 6. Article 21 of the ACHR, Art. 1 of the First Protocol to the ECHR, and Art. 14 of the ACHPR. Catarina Krause, '11. The Right to Property', in Asbjørn Eide et al. (eds), *Economic, Social and Cultural Rights*, 2nd edn, Kluwer Law International (2001) 191–209, 191 and 197.

29 See 'Scope of the Right to Benefit from the Protection of the Moral and Material Interests Resulting from any Scientific, Literary or Artistic Production of which He is the Author' in Chapter 5.

30 CESCR, GC No. 17 (n 23) para. 7. See also Art. 1.2 of the ACHR: '2. For the purposes of this Convention, "person" means every human being.'

31 See 'An acquired patent' in Chapter 6. Article 1 of the First Protocol to the ECHR: 'Every natural or legal person is entitled to peaceful enjoyment of his possessions. No one shall be deprived of his possessions except in the public interest and subject to the conditions provided for by law and by the general principles of international law. The preceding provisions shall not, however, in any way impair the right of a State to enforce such laws as it deems necessary to control the use of property in accordance with the general interest or to secure the payment of taxes or other contributions or penalties.' *Smith Kline & French Laboratories Ltd v. the Netherlands*, Application No. 12633/87, 66 European Commission of Human Rights (1990) (patents); *Dima v. Romania*, Application No. 58472/00, ECtHR, para. 87 (2005) (admissibility decision) (copyrighted works); *Melnychuk v. Ukraine*, Application No. 28743/03, ECtHR, para. 8 (2005) (admissibility decision) (IP); *Anheuser-Busch Inc. v. Portugal*, Application No. 73049/01, Judgment of Grand Chamber (ECtHR) (11 January 2007) paras 66–72 (registered trademarks).

32 Article 2 of the UDHR states that 'Everyone is entitled to all the rights and freedoms set forth in this Declaration, without distinction of any kind, such as race, colour, sex, language, religion,

'even in times of severe resources constraints … the vulnerable members of society[33] can and indeed must be protected by the adoption of relatively low-cost targeted programmes'.[34] The principle of non-discrimination and equality calls for special attention to be paid to the needs of vulnerable people, including women, children and people living in poverty.[35]

In the context of access to medicines, States must prohibit any discrimination in access to medicines on internationally prohibited grounds.[36] This constitutes a minimum core obligation under the right to health. This obligation also relates to REBSP in that medicines are an outcome of scientific application.[37] In addition, States parties have a core obligation 'to ensure equitable distribution of all health facilities, goods and services' according to General Comment No. 14 of the Committee.[38] Addressing inequitable access to medicines involves a positive duty to take measures in favour of disadvantaged individuals and communities:[39] i.e. a State has to collect disaggregated data on access to medicines in relation to each of the vulnerable groups and a national medicines policy should include programmes specifically designed to enhance access to medicines of vulnerable people, considering economic, social and cultural factors that inhibit vulnerable people's access to medicines.[40]

---

political or other opinion, national or social origin, property, birth or other status. Furthermore, no distinction shall be made on the basis of the political, jurisdictional or international status of the country or territory to which a person belongs, whether it be independent, trust, non-self-governing or under any other limitation of sovereignty'. Article 7 of the UDHR enshrines 'equality before the law' and 'equal protection of the law'. Article 2.2 of the ICESCR: '[t]he States Parties to the present Covenant undertake to guarantee that the rights enunciated in the present Covenant will be exercised without discrimination of any kind as to race, colour, sex, language, religion, political or other opinion, national or social origin, property, birth or other status'. Article 3 of the ICESCR: '[t]he States Parties to the present Covenant undertake to ensure the equal right of men and women to the enjoyment of all economic, social and cultural rights set forth in the present Covenant'. See also Arts 2 and 26 of the ICCPR.

33 The vulnerable members of society include children, women, people living in poverty, rural communities, indigenous populations, national (ethnic, religious, linguistic) minorities, internally displaced persons, the elderly, people with disabilities, and prisoners. See Hans V. Hogerzeil, 'Essential Medicines and Human Rights: What Can They Learn from Each Other?' (2006) *Bulletin of the World Health Organization* 373.

34 CESCR, GC No. 3: The Nature of States Parties Obligations (Art. 2, para. 1 of the Covenant), adopted in fifth session (1990) UN Doc. E/1991/23, para. 12.

35 CESCR, GC No. 14 (n 15) para. 19; Report of the first Special Rapporteur on the Right to Health, Paul Hunt (13 September 2006, n 5) para. 53.

36 CESCR, GC No. 14 (n 15) paras 18, 43.

37 Paragraph 16(b) of the Venice Statement on the REBSP provides that the duty to fulfil should include 'to promote access to the benefits of science and its applications on a non-discriminatory basis including measures necessary to address the needs of disadvantaged and marginalized groups'.

38 CESCR, GC No. 14 (n 15) para. 43.

39 Ibid., para. 19; Report of the first Special Rapporteur on the Right to Health, Paul Hunt (13 September 2006, n 5) para. 53.

40 Hogerzeil (n 33) 373; Report of the first Special Rapporteur on the Right to Health, Paul Hunt (13 September 2006, n 5) para. 54.

Extraterritorial Obligations

The concept of international assistance and cooperation is embodied in Article 2(1) of the ICESCR, a covering article for the implementation of the provisions, which states: '[e]ach State Party to the present Covenant undertakes to take steps individually and *through international assistance and cooperation, especially economic and technical,* to the maximum of its available resources' (emphasis added). International assistance and cooperation implies the existence of certain extraterritorial obligations of States parties to realise the rights in the ICESCR.[41] Notably, the ICESCR does not place a territorial or jurisdictional restriction to its application, in contrast to the ICCPR, ECHR and ACHR.[42] The principle of international cooperation among States is initially established in Articles 55 and 56 of the Charter of the United Nations, which is legally binding on all UN Members.[43] It is also reflected in Articles 22 and 28 of the UDHR.[44]

Based on Articles 55 and 56 of the UN Charter and Article 2(1) of the ICESCR, the CESCR notes that 'international co-operation for development and thus for the realization of economic, social and cultural rights is an obligation of all States'.[45] The CESCR

---

41 Michal Gondek, *The Reach of Human Rights in a Globalising World: Extraterritorial Application of Human Rights Treaties,* Intersentia (2009) 295, 334.

42 Article 2 of ICCPR: 'Each State Party to the present Covenant undertakes to respect and to ensure to all individuals *within its territory and subject to its jurisdiction* the rights recognized in the present Covenant …'. Article 1 of the ECHR reads: 'The High Contracting Parties shall secure to everyone within their jurisdiction the rights and freedoms defined in Section I of this Convention'. Article 1.1 of the ACHR: 'The States Parties to this Convention undertake to respect the rights and freedoms recognized herein and to ensure to all persons subject to their jurisdiction the free and full exercise of those rights and freedoms …'.

43 Adopted 26 June 1945. Article 1 sets 'to achieve international co-operation in solving international problems of an economic, social, cultural, or humanitarian character, and in promoting and encouraging respect for human rights and for fundamental freedoms for all without distinction as to race, sex, language, or religion' as one of the purposes of the UN. Article 56 affirms that '[a]ll Members pledge themselves to take joint and separate action in co-operation with the Organization for the achievement of the purposes set forth in Article 55'. Article 55 of the Charter states 'universal respect for, and observance of, human rights and fundamental freedoms for all without distinction as to race, sex, language, or religion' as one of the purpose of the United Nations.

44 Article 22 of the UDHR reads: 'Everyone, as a member of society, has the right to social security and is entitled to realization, *through national effort and international co-operation* and in accordance with the organization and resources of each State, of the economic, social and cultural rights indispensable for his dignity and the free development of his personality' (emphasis added). Article 28 states '[e]veryone is entitled to a social and international order in which the rights and freedoms set forth in this Declaration can be fully realized'.

45 CESCR, GC No. 3 (n 34) para. 14. 'The Committee wishes to emphasize that in accordance with Articles 55 and 56 of the Charter of the United Nations, with well-established principles of international law, and with the provisions of the Covenant itself, international cooperation for development and thus for the realization of economic, social and cultural rights is an obligation of all States. It is particularly incumbent upon those States which are in a position to assist others in this regard.'

explained that '"to the maximum of its available resources" was intended by the drafters of the Covenant to refer to both the resources existing within a State and those available from the international community through international cooperation and assistance'.[46] The embodiment of the concept of international assistance and cooperation in the ICESCR indicates that international assistance and cooperation for the realisation of economic, social and cultural rights is not only a moral obligation but also a legal obligation of States parties to the ICESCR, although its scope and content as a legal obligation is in a formative stage.[47] International cooperation has also been given particular importance in the CRC.[48] Article 4 of the CRC provides that 'States Parties shall undertake all appropriate legislative, administrative, and other measures for the implementation of the rights recognized in the present Convention. With regard to economic, social and cultural rights, States Parties shall undertake such measures to the maximum extent of their available resources and, where needed, *within the framework of international co-operation*' (emphasis added). Explicit reference to international cooperation is found in many substantive articles of the CRC including Article 24 on the right of the child to health, which states that '4. States Parties undertake to promote and encourage *international co-operation* with a view to achieving progressively the full realization of the right recognized in the present article. In this regard, particular account shall be taken of *the needs of developing countries*' (emphasis added).

The principle of international assistance and cooperation also appears in numerous soft-law documents. The normative importance of international cooperation lies at the heart of the right to development, recognised in the Declaration on the Right to Development (DRD)[49] While the DRD recognises that individual States have the primary duty to realise all human rights, including the right to development of individuals and peoples within their territory or jurisdiction,[50] it importantly creates the duty of States 'to co-operate with each other in ensuring development and eliminating obstacles to development'.[51] Such emphasis on the duty to cooperate came from the recognition that the realisation of human rights can be constrained by global institutional arrangements in this increasingly

---

46 Ibid., para. 13.

47 Gondek (n 41) 325.

48 Convention on the Rights of the Child, adopted on 20 November 1989 and entered into force on 2 September 1990; 194 States are parties to the Convention as of 1 November 2014.

49 Adopted by GA Resolution 41/128 (4 December 1986).

50 Article 2(3) of the DRD reads '[s]tates have the right and the duty to formulate appropriate national development policies that aim at the constant improvement of the well-being of the entire population and of all individuals, on the basis of their active, free and meaningful participation in development and in the fair distribution of the benefits resulting therefrom'.

51 Article 3(3) of the DRD provides that '[s]tates have the duty to co-operate with each other in ensuring development and eliminating obstacles to development. States should realize their rights and fulfil their duties in such a manner as to promote a new international economic order based on sovereign equality, interdependence, mutual interest and co-operation among all States, as well as to encourage the observance and realization of human rights.' In a similar spirit, Art. 6 states that '[a]ll States should co-operate with a view to promoting, encouraging and strengthening universal respect for and observance of all human rights and fundamental freedoms for all without any distinction as to race, sex, language or religion'.

interconnected world, and an equitable and just national and international order is a condition for the enjoyment of all human rights.[52] The UN Millennium Declaration[53] also reaffirmed that 'in addition to our separate responsibilities to our individual societies, we have a collective responsibility to uphold the principles of human dignity, equality and equity at the global level'.[54]

While the legal character of the obligation of international assistance and cooperation is not yet certain, the Maastricht Principles on Extraterritorial Obligations of States in the Area of Economic, Social and Cultural Rights (hereinafter Maastricht Principles), adopted in September 2011 by leading experts in international law and human rights, help to clarify the scope of extraterritorial obligations of States on the basis of existing international law.[55] As to obligations to respect, States must refrain from not only direct interferences (Principle 20) but also indirect interferences such that impair 'the ability of another State or international organisation to comply with that State's or that international organisation's obligations as regards economic, social and cultural rights' (Principle 21). To prevent causing harm to the enjoyment of human rights in other countries, the Maastricht Principle 14 provides that States must carry out 'impact assessments, with public participation, of the risks and potential extraterritorial impacts of their laws, policies and practices on the enjoyment of economic, social and cultural rights'. Concerning obligations to protect, the Maastricht Principle 24 affirms that 'all States must take necessary measures to ensure that non-State actors which they are in a position to regulate ... such as private individuals and organisations, and transnational corporations and other business enterprises, do not nullify or impair the enjoyment of economic, social and cultural rights'.

Regarding the fulfil aspect, the Maastricht Principles highlight the obligation of international cooperation for the creation of an international enabling environment (Principle 29), as well as a procedural obligation to establish an international system of responsibility allocation (Principle 30) and mobilisation of resources for the universal fulfilment of economic, social and cultural rights (Principle 31). While the CESCR has affirmed that international assistance and cooperation is 'particularly incumbent upon

---

52 Margot Salomon, 'International Human Rights Obligations in Context: Structural Obstacles and the Demands of Global Justice', in Bard Andressen and Stephen Marks (eds), *Development as a Human Right: Legal, Political, and Economic Dimensions*, Harvard School of Public Health (2006) 96–118, 99–101; Benjamin Mason Meier, 'Development as Health: Employing the Collective Right to Development to Achieve the Goals of the Individual Right to Health' (2008) 30(2) *Human Rights Quarterly* 259–355, 331; Alicia Ely Yamin, 'Our Place in the World: Conceptualizing Obligations beyond Borders in Human Rights-based Approaches to Health' (2010) 12(1) *Health and Human Rights* 3–14, 11.

53 Adopted at the Millennium Summit of the UN on 8 September 2000. UN GA Resolution A/RES/55/2.

54 Ibid., para. 2.

55 The Maastricht Principles on Extraterritorial Obligations of States in the Area of Economic, Social and Cultural Rights, adopted on 28 September 2011 at a gathering convened by Maastricht University and the International Commission of Jurists. Available at http://www.maastrichtuniversity. nl/web/Institutes/MaastrichtCentreForHumanRights/MaastrichtETOPrinciples.htm, last accessed 15 March 2015.

States parties and other actors in a position to assist',[56] international human rights law does not provide precise criteria for States in a position to assist in determining how to allocate responsibilities and mobilise necessary resources. The Maastricht Principles 30 and 31 highlight procedural requirements to establish a system of international coordination, which are complementary to the substantive obligation of international cooperation.[57] Principles for priorities in cooperation such as the obligation to prioritise the realisation of the rights of disadvantaged, marginalised and vulnerable groups and the core obligations to realise minimum essential levels of economic, social and cultural rights are also enunciated, based on the views of the CESCR (Principle 32).

In the context of intellectual property and access to medicines, the CESCR's interpretive comment on the right to health sheds light on the relevant extraterritorial obligations of States parties:

> To comply with their international obligations in relation to article 12, States parties have to respect the enjoyment of the right to health in other countries, and to prevent third parties from violating the right in other countries, if they are able to influence these third parties by way of legal or political means, in accordance with the Charter of the United Nations and applicable international law. Depending on the availability of resources, States should facilitate access to essential health facilities, goods and services in other countries, wherever possible and provide the necessary aid when required. States parties should ensure that the right to health is given due attention in international agreements and, to that end, should consider the development of further legal instruments. In relation to the conclusion of other international agreements, States parties should take steps to ensure that these instruments do not adversely impact upon the right to health. Similarly, States parties have an obligation to ensure that their actions as members of international organizations take due account of the right to health.[58]

International assistance and cooperation is also crucial to enabling States to build their capacities in the field of science and technology, which are necessary to ensure the availability of new medicines for addressing the primary health needs of people in their own territory. In this regard, Article 15.4 also states that '[t]he States Parties to the present Covenant recognize the benefits to be derived from the encouragement and development of international contacts and co-operation in the scientific and cultural fields'. Accordingly, States must ensure that domestic and international law and policy, including intellectual property rules, are conducive, rather than restrictive, to the transfer of technology and cooperation in scientific fields,[59] with a view to assisting capacity building in countries

---

56 CESCR, GC No. 14 (n 15) para. 45.

57 Olivier de Schutter, Asbjørn Eide, Ashfaq Khalfan, Marcos Orellana, Margot Salomon and Ian Seiderman, 'Commentary to the Maastricht Principles on Extraterritorial Obligations of States in the Area of Economic, Social and Cultural Rights' (2012) 34 *Human Rights Quarterly* 1084–169, 1149–53.

58 CESCR, GC No. 14 (n 15) para. 39; Gondek (n 41) 352–63.

59 For instance, an intellectual property system that provides a strong protection for the patent holder may have a restrictive effect on the transfer of technology and cooperation in the scientific

where the scientific inquiry and the diffusion of scientific knowledge is not active.[60] States should also internationally cooperate in the mobilisation of resources for innovation addressing unmet health needs of people living in poverty as well as ensuring access to essential medicines for all with a view to fulfilling a core obligation under the rights to life and health.[61]

Limitations upon Human Rights

Given that these several human rights and potentially other interests are relevant to the issue of intellectual property and access to medicines, a human rights framework for intellectual property, innovation and access to medicines has to clarify the relationship among these human rights, as well as between human rights and other interests relating to intellectual property, and should provide guidance upon how to achieve a fair balance of human rights and other interests. For this purpose, this section examines the boundary of justifiable limitations to the right to access to medicines, the right to enjoy the benefits from scientific progress and its applications, and the right to benefit from the protection of the moral and material interests of the author. Human rights, with certain exceptions mentioned earlier under 'Interpreting TRIPS in Light of Human Rights' in Chapter 6,[62] are also subject to derogations and limitations. The ICESCR does not contain any derogation clause, but does have clauses regulating limitations. These clauses should be considered with respect to the human rights in question. In delineating the scope of justifiable limitations upon human rights, it is necessary to reflect upon the concept of core obligations that the CESCR has developed through its General Comments. In the European context, permissible limitations in relation to the right to property should also be taken into account. This analysis may shed light on how to strike a right balance among human rights, and between human rights and other interests, which is crucial to a human rights framework for intellectual property, innovation and access to medicines.

Limitations clauses in the International Covenant on Economic, Social and Cultural Rights

A general limitation clause is found in Article 4 of the ICESCR. While Article 2.1 does not explicitly regulate limitations, the notion of 'progressive realisation' and 'maximum available resources' in the provision requires the clarification as to the permissible scope of 'retrogressive measures' in relation to resource constraints. General Comment No. 3

---

fields, and thus undermine the capacity building for the realisation of the REBSP in many low-income countries or even middle-income countries. The Report of the High-Level Task Force on the Right to Development, Technical mission: MDG 8 target F on technology transfer: WIPO Development Agenda, para. 13 (19 November 2009) UN Doc. A/HRC/15/WG.2/TF/CRP.1; Audrey Chapman, 'Towards an Understanding of the Right to Enjoy the Benefits of Scientific Progress and Its Applications' (2009) 8(1) *Journal of Human Rights* 1–36, 26, 28, 29.

60 Paragraphs 9 and 16(d) of the Venice Statement.

61 See the Maastricht Principles (n 55) 28–35 regarding obligations to fulfil through international cooperation and principles and priorities in cooperation.

62 See Art. 4 of ICCPR, Art. 27 of ACHR, and Art. 15 of the ECHR.

of the CESCR addresses the issue of 'retrogressive measures' as it elaborates Article 2.1.[63] Article 5.1 is also relevant to the present discussion as it concerns the relationship among the rights in the ICESCR. In order to understand the boundary of justifiable limitations to the right to access to medicines, the right to enjoy the benefits from scientific progress and its application, and the right to benefit from the protection of the moral and material interests of the author, this section begins with an analysis of Article 4, Article 2.1 and Article 5.1 of the ICESCR in turn.

> Article 4: The States Parties to the present Covenant recognize that, in the enjoyment of those rights provided by the State in conformity with the present Covenant, the State may subject such rights only to such limitations as are determined by law only in so far as this may be compatible with the nature of these rights and solely for the purpose of promoting the general welfare in a democratic society.

Article 4 permits States parties to limit the rights contained in the Covenant, but there are conditions upon such limitations.

'General welfare' and 'determined by law' The solely legitimate purpose of limitations to the rights in the Covenant is the promotion of the general welfare in a democratic society. Alston and Quinn suggest that the term 'general welfare' should be interpreted restrictively, and reasons such as 'national security' or 'economic development' can be invoked only to the extent that 'they are genuinely synonymous with "the general welfare"'.[64] In accordance with Article 4, any limitations on the rights must be determined by national law and 'solely for the purpose of promoting the general welfare in a democratic society'.

'Compatible with the nature of rights' Critically, any limitations must be 'compatible with the nature of these rights' in the Covenant. According to the negotiating history of the Covenant, this condition was included to make sure that 'the problem of restrictions, and limits to their scope, should be closely studied in connexion with each of the rights contained in the Covenant'.[65] 'Minimum core obligations' with respect to each of the rights are understood to elaborate 'the nature of these rights'. In General Comment No. 3, the CESCR notes that 'a minimum core obligation to ensure the satisfaction of, at the very least, minimum essential levels of each of the rights is incumbent upon every State party'.[66] The CESCR stresses that without the minimum core contents and obligations, the Covenant 'is largely deprived of its raison d'être'.[67] Commentators also suggest that the

---

63 CESCR, GC No. 3 (n 34) para. 9.

64 Philip Alston and Gerard Quinn, 'The Nature and Scope of States Parties' Obligations under the International Covenant on Economic, Social and Cultural Rights' (1987) 9 *Human Rights Quarterly* 156–249, 202.

65 Summary Record of the 235th meeting of the UN Commission on Human Rights (2 July 1951) E/CN.4/SR/235, 13, cited in Alston and Quinn (n 64) 201.

66 CESCR, GC No. 3 (n 34) para. 10.

67 Ibid.

concept of human rights presumes the existence of a minimum core within each right that is not subject to limitations.[68] The African Commission on Human and Peoples' Rights has also used 'the minimum core obligations' in the context of the African Charter on Human and Peoples' Rights,[69] and the Inter-American Commission on Human Rights has taken a similar concept, 'a minimum threshold of rights'.[70] Thus, no limitations to minimum core obligations are permitted because such limitations are not compatible with 'the nature of these rights'.[71]

Implicit condition: Proportionality   This phrase also leads to another implicit requirement for limitations to the rights: the principle of proportionality. Limitations are restricted to such that are necessary to promote 'general welfare', and the least restrictive limitations on a particular right in question, where several types of limitations are available, must be adopted. The proportionality of limitations is stressed by the CESCR in its General Comment on the right to health.[72]

> Article 2.1: Each State Party to the present Covenant undertakes to take steps, individually and through international assistance and co-operation, especially economic and technical, to the maximum of its available resources, with a view to achieving progressively the full realization of the rights recognized in the present Covenant by all appropriate means, including particularly the adoption of legislative measures.

The notion of 'progressive realisation' and 'to the maximum of its available resources' in Article 2.1 indicates that retrogressive measures with respect to the rights in the Covenant due to resource constraints may not automatically constitute a violation of the rights. If Article 2.1 is read in isolation from Article 4, a State may readily rely on the ground of resource constraints to justify its failure to fulfil its obligation rather than making efforts to meet conditions upon limitations, required by Article 4.[73] Therefore, as Alston and Quinn

---

68 Philip Alston, 'Out of the Abyss: The Challenges Confronting the New UN Committee on Economic, Social and Cultural Rights' (1987) 9 *Human Rights Quarterly* 332–81, 352–2; Joel Feinberg, *Social Philosophy*, Prentice-Hall, Inc. (1973) 79–83; Manisuli Ssenyonjo, *Economic, Social and Cultural Rights in International Law*, Hart Publishing (2009) 65–9.

69 *The Social and Economic Rights Action Center and the Center for Economic and Social Rights v. Nigeria*, Communication 155/96 (27 May 2002) paras 65–6.

70 On 'the realization of economic, social and cultural rights in the region', the Inter-American Commission on Human Rights states that 'the obligation of member states to observe and defend the human rights of individuals within their jurisdictions, as set forth in both the American Declaration and the American Convention, obligates them, regardless of the level of economic development, to guarantee a minimum threshold of these rights', Inter-American Commission on Human Rights, Annual Report of the Inter-American Commission on Human Rights (1994) 524.

71 Amrei Müller, 'Limitations to and Derogations from Economic, Social and Cultural Rights' (2009) 9(4) *Human Rights Law Review* 557–601, 581.

72 CESCR, GC No. 14 (n 15) para. 29.

73 Alston and Quinn (n 64) 205.

suggested and Müller recently further elaborated, it seems reasonable to read Article 2.1 as requiring any retrogressive measures under Article 2.1 to meet the conditions under Article 4.[74] The CESCR stated that 'any deliberately retrogressive measures in that regard would require the most careful consideration and would need to be fully justified by reference to the totality of the rights provided for in the Covenant and in the context of the full use of the maximum available resources'.[75] States parties must justify not only that retrogressive measures are unavoidable due to resource constraints, but also that the retrogressive measures are adopted in a manner that takes into account 'general welfare' under Article 4.[76] The Committee illustrates criteria for assessing whether any retrogressive steps can be attributable to resources constraints:

a. the country's level of development;
b. the severity of the alleged breach, in particular whether the situation concerned the enjoyment of the minimum core content of the Covenant;
c. the country's current economic situation, in particular whether the country was undergoing a period of economic recession;
d. the existence of other serious claims on the State party's limited resources; for example, resulting from a recent natural disaster or from recent internal or international armed conflict;
e. whether the State party had sought to identify low-cost options;
f. whether the State party had sought cooperation and assistance or rejected offers of resources from the international community for the purposes of implementing the provisions of the Covenant without sufficient reason.[77]

In principle, 'minimum core obligations' must not be subject to retrogressive measures. This line of interpretation is consistent with the view of the CESCR in General Comment No. 14 on the right to health that non-compliance with the core obligations constitutes violations.[78] On the other hand, in General Comment No. 3, the CESCR appears not to exclude an exceptional situation where non-implementation of even a core obligation may be justified, provided that a State party 'demonstrate[s] that every effort has been made to use all resources that are at its disposition in an effort to satisfy, as a matter of priority, those minimum obligations'.[79] Such circumstances may be comparable to *force majeure*, 'the occurrence of an irresistible force or of an unforeseen event, beyond the control of the State, making it materially impossible in the circumstances to perform the obligation', recognised as circumstances precluding wrongfulness in the International Law Commission's final draft Articles on Responsibility of States for International Wrongful

---

74 Ibid., 205–6; Müller (n 71) 584–91.
75 CESCR, GC No. 3 (n 34) para. 9.
76 Müller (n 71) 587–8.
77 CESCR, Statement: An Evaluation of the Obligation to Take Steps to the 'Maximum Available Resources' under an Optional Protocol to the Covenant' (10 May 2007) UN Doc. E/C.12/2007/1, para. 10.
78 CESCR, GC No. 14 (n 15) paras 47–8.
79 CESCR, GC No. 3 (n 34) para. 10.

Acts.[80] However, even in such situations, States have 'an obligation to do the utmost to remedy the situation, be it in asking and receiving foreign assistance'.[81] All in all, it can be concluded that retrogressive measures due to resource constraints have to meet the general conditions set out in the general limitation clause, Article 4. Logically, retrogressive measures inconsistent with minimum core obligations, as other limitations under Article 4, *prima facie* constitute a violation of the respective right.

> Article 5.1: Nothing in the present Covenant may be interpreted as implying for any State, group or person any right to engage in any activity or to perform any act aimed at the destruction of any of the rights or freedoms recognized herein, or at their limitation to a greater extent than is provided for in the present Covenant.

Article 5, paragraph 1 aims at preventing a State from interpreting any provision of the Covenant in a way to neglect or violate one right on the grounds that protecting another right in the Covenant makes it unavoidable.[82] Considering that there exist circumstances where rights in the Covenant compete, the question is what amounts to 'the destruction of any of the rights or freedoms' within the meaning of Article 5.1. In accordance with Article 4, parameters should be whether a measure to promote one right is compatible with the nature of other rights in the Covenant. Given that minimum core obligations are to ensure the very nature of the rights in the Covenant, a State party cannot justify an act inconsistent with the minimum core obligations of any of the rights in the Covenant on the ground of promoting the realisation of some other rights in the Covenant.

Limitation to the right to property under the European Convention on Human Rights

Varying forms of property, including patents, fall within the meaning of 'possessions' under Article 1 of the First Protocol to the ECHR. A legal person is also entitled to the protection of the right to property under this provision, unlike under other international human rights instruments such as the UDHR and ACHR.[83] However, do all types of property receive the same level of protection under the ECHR? Henry Schermers made distinctions between different kinds of property, and concluded that only the right to property without which any normal way of life is impossible may qualify as a fundamental human right.[84] Schermers adds that what kinds of property are necessary for a life with dignity may vary depending on economic and social circumstances,[85] and that drawing the

---

80 Article 23, ILC, Responsibility of States for International Wrongful Acts, adopted at the 53rd Session (2001), available at http://legal.un.org/ilc/texts/instruments/english/commentaries/9_6_2001.pdf, last accessed 15 March 2015.

81 Allan Rosas and Monika Sandvik-Nylund, '22. Armed Conflicts', in Eide (n 28) 407–21, 414.

82 Alston and Quinn (n 64) 207.

83 Section 'Patent Rights and the Human Right to Property' in Chapter 6.

84 Henry G. Schermers, 'The International Protection of the Right of Property', in Franz Matscher et al. (eds), *Protecting Human Rights: The European Dimension*, Carl Heymanns Verlag KG (1988) 565–80, 572–5.

85 Ibid., 572–3.

line between the fundamental rights to property from the other property rights is 'gradual rather than absolute'.[86] The scope of permissible limitations upon the right to property has been determined taking into account the degree of importance of the property in question to leading a normal way of life in a particular society, along with other social and economic considerations.[87]

In *Sporrong and Lönnroth v. Sweden*, the European Court of Human Rights (ECtHR) clarified three rules contained in this provision:

> Article (P1–1) [Article 1 of Protocol No.1] comprises three distinct rules. The first rule, which is of a general nature, enounces the principle of peaceful enjoyment of property; it is set out in the first sentence of the first paragraph. The second rule covers deprivation of possessions and subjects it to certain conditions; it appears in the second sentence of the same paragraph. The third rule recognizes that the States are entitled, amongst other things, to control the use of property in accordance with the general interest, by enforcing such laws as they deem necessary for the purpose; it is contained in the second paragraph.[88]

In applying Article 1 of Protocol No. 1, the ECtHR allows States a wide margin of appreciation with regard to the public interest in regulating or expropriating property. In *James v. United Kingdom*,[89] the ECtHR made a seminal statement and this jurisprudence has been followed by subsequent cases[90] concerning the establishment of measures in the public interest under Article 1 of Protocol No. 1:

> Because of their direct knowledge of their society and its needs, the national authorities are in principle better placed than the international judge to appreciate what is "in the public interest". Under the system of protection established by the Convention, it is thus for the national authorities to make the initial assessment both of the existence of a problem of public concern warranting measures of deprivation of property and of the remedial action to be taken … Furthermore, the notion of "public interest" is necessarily extensive. In particular, as the Commission noted, the decision to enact laws expropriating property will commonly involve consideration of political, economic and social issues on which opinions within a democratic society may reasonably differ widely. The Court, finding it natural that the margin of appreciation available to the legislature in implementing social and economic policies should be a wide one, will respect the legislature's judgment as to what is "in the public interest" unless that judgment be manifestly without reasonable foundation.[91]

---

86 Ibid., 566, 579.

87 Ibid., 359, 360.

88 *Sporrong and Lönnroth v. Sweden*, Application no. 7151/75; 7152/75 (Judgment of 23 September 1982) para. 61.

89 *James and others v. United Kingdom*, Application no. 8793/79 (Judgment of 21 February 1986) para. 46.

90 For instance, see *Draon v. France*, Application no. 1513/03 (6 October 2005) paras 75–6.

91 *James and others v. United Kingdom* (n 89) para. 46.

Regarding the reasonableness of government measures under Article 1 of Protocol 1, the ECtHR often applies three tests: (1) the government measure must be prescribed by law and the law must be accessible; (2) it must pursue a legitimate aim, i.e. the general interest or public interest; and (3) it must be necessary in a democratic society, which requires proportionality to the public interest, i.e. striking a fair balance between the demands of the general interest of the community and the private interests of the property owner.[92] The ECtHR distinguishes 'the control of property', i.e. regulation,[93] and 'deprivation of property'.[94] In comparison to cases of deprivation or expropriation, in cases of the control of property the Court tends to apply a low level of standard of proportionality, therefore giving more weight to social considerations and being more deferential to the national authorities.[95] The ECtHR's jurisprudence on proportionality in relation to expropriation or regulation was adopted by the *Tecmed* arbitration tribunal in examining whether a regulatory measure amounts to indirect expropriation.[96]

The case of compulsory licence   Compulsory licensing is one of the limitations permitted by the TRIPS Agreement[97] upon the exclusive rights of a patent holder.[98] In *Smith Kline & French Laboratories Ltd v. the Netherlands*,[99] the European Commission of Human Rights examined the grant of a compulsory licence, under Dutch law, over a patented medicine in relation to Article 1 of the First Protocol, and found no violation. The Commission held that the compulsory licence granted under Dutch law, thereby limiting the sole right of exploitation by the patent holder, constituted 'a control of the use of property',[100] not 'deprivation of property'. Note that compulsory licences do not prevent the patent holder from continuing to use and sell the patented product.

---

92 Ibid., paras 47, 50; *Sporrong and Lönnroth v. Sweden* (n 88) para. 69; *Mellacher and others v. Austria*, Application nos 10522/83; 11011/84; 11070/84, Strasbourg (19 December 1989) para. 48; Christophe Golay and Ioana Cismas, 'Legal Opinion: The Right to Property from a Human Rights Perspective' (2010) 15, available at http://papers.ssrn.com/sol3/papers.cfm?abstract_id=1635359, last accessed 11 April 2014; Council of Europe, *The Right to Property under the European Convention on Human Rights: A Guide to the Implementation of the European Convention on Human Rights and its Protocols* (2007) 12–14.

93 The third paragraph of Art. 1 of the First Protocol to the ECHR: 'The preceding provisions shall not, however, in any way impair the right of a State to enforce such laws as it deems necessary to control the use of property in accordance with the general interest or to secure the payment of taxes or other contributions or penalties' (emphasis added).

94 The second paragraph of Art. 1 of the First Protocol to the ECHR: 'No one shall be deprived of his possessions except in the public interest and subject to the conditions provided for by law and by the general principles of international law.'

95 Golay and Cismas (n 92); Krause (n 28) 203.

96 *Técnicas Medioambientales Tecmed S.A v. Mexico*, ICSID Case No. ARB(AF)/00/2 (29 May 2003) para. 119.

97 Article 31 of TRIPS.

98 See relevant discussions under 'Access to Essential Medicines: An Element of the Right to Life' in Chapter 4.

99 Application No. 12633/87 (n 31).

100 Ibid.

The Commission paid attention to the fact that a law prescribing compulsory licences is found in many countries, stating that 'the exclusive rights of a patentee are limited in many of the Contracting States and that provision for other persons to make use of a particular patented product or process is commonly made for the purpose of preventing the long term hampering of technological progress and economic activity'.[101]

In this case, a compulsory licence for a patent was granted for the working of a dependent patent, which could not work without the earlier/dominant patent. Such compulsory licensing is prescribed by Dutch law. The Commission viewed that 'the grant of the compulsory licence was lawful and pursued a legitimate aim of encouraging technological and economic development'. The grant of compulsory licence, in this circumstance, was 'intended to prevent abuse of monopoly situations and encourage development'. The Commission held that 'this method of pursuing that aim falls within the margin of appreciation according to the Contracting State'. Considering this aim and the way in which the compulsory licence was granted, including royalties for each compulsory licence payable to the owner of the dominant patent, the Commission found that 'the control of use in the circumstances of this case did not fail to strike a fair balance between the interests of the applicant company and the general interest ...'.[102]

In short, the ECtHR and the former European Commission allow the States a wide 'margin of appreciation' to limit the right to property in the public interest, provided that the relevant laws are in place and applied in a foreseeable manner, the limitation pursues a legitimate aim and is deemed proportionate to the stated aim and the rights of individuals affected.[103] The case law regarding a compulsory licence indicates that the right to property provision does not impair the right of States to limit the exclusive rights of the patent holder when in pursuit of a legitimate aim.[104] In so far as the human right to property applies to a patent under the ECHR, the government measures regulating a patent with a view to striking a fair balance between public interests and private interests of the patent holder are presumed to be compatible with the right to property. This discussion indicates a strong presumption that when a compulsory licence is granted for the purpose of enhancing access to medicines, in accordance with national law and the TRIPS Agreement, it constitutes measures proportionate to the aim and a legitimate policy choice available to a democratic society in operating a patent system to serve advancing the realisation of the rights to life and health.

Intellectual property as a limitation upon the right to access to medicines
Articles 2.1, 4 and 5.1 of the ICESCR provide guidance on how to strike a right balance between rights and other public interests in the context of intellectual property and access to medicines. The analysis of the relevant human rights indicates that intellectual property may

---

101 Ibid.

102 Ibid.

103 Golay and Cismas (n 92); Krause (n 28) 202–3.

104 Laurence R. Helfer, 'The New Innovation Frontier? Intellectual Property and the European Court of Human Rights'. (2008) 49 *Harvard International Law Journal* 1–52, 36–9; Peter Drahos, 'Intellectual Property and Human Rights' (1999) (3) *Intellectual Property Quarterly* 360.

relate to human rights in the context of access to medicines in several ways, which include the following. First, the protection of pharmaceutical patents may be provided as a means to protect the moral and material interests of the author in accordance with Article 15.1(c), although few patents fall within this scope.[105] Among other reasons, most pharmaceutical patents are held by legal entities, lacking the personal link between authors and their creations which, as the CESCR considers, is an essential feature of the right recognised in Article 15.1(c). Secondly, an appropriate level of the protection of intellectual property in pharmaceuticals may indirectly contribute to the realisation of the right to access to medicines and the right to enjoy the benefits from scientific progress and its applications, by stimulating innovation necessary to address health needs. However, the strengthened protection of pharmaceutical patents required by the adoption of TRIPS may have a negative impact on the very same rights by raising the price of medicines and making them unaffordable to many who need them.[106] Also, patents alone cannot induce health innovation addressing health needs of people living in poverty. This is due to a lack of market incentive crucial for the function of patents.[107] Thirdly, an acquired pharmaceutical patent, in the European context, is protected from unjustified interference by the State. The use of TRIPS flexibilities, such as compulsory licences for the purpose of enhancing access to medicines, *prima facie* fall within the margin of appreciation of States parties to the ECHR.[108]

The above analysis of Articles 2.1 and 4 of the ICESCR indicates that the right to access to medicines, the right to enjoy the benefits from scientific progress and its applications, and the right to benefit from the protection of the moral and material interests of the author may be subject to limitations. However, any limitations to these rights must meet conditions set forth in Article 4 so that a State party must justify that any of the limitations is strictly necessary for the promotion of general welfare, proportionate, and determined by law in a manner compatible with the nature of the rights.

So far as it can be demonstrated that a limitation imposed by the protection of intellectual property is necessary for the inducement of technological development, its purpose can be considered to meet one of the conditions, namely the promotion of the general welfare. Nevertheless, in accordance with the principle of proportionality, it also has to be asked whether there are any other measures that are less restrictive to the right to access to medicines. In other words, even if fostering technological development is necessary for the promotion of general welfare, in order to achieve the stated aim, a State party must adopt the least restrictive measure, among several choices, to the right to access to medicines, either through using public health flexibilities within intellectual property

---

105 See 'The Right to Benefit from the Protection of the Moral and Material Interests Resulting from any Scientific, Literary or Artistic Production of which He is the Author (Art. 15.1(c) of ICESCR)' in Chapter 5 and 'Intellectual Property Rights and the Right to Benefit from the Protection of the Moral and Material Interests of the Author (Art. 15.1(c) of the ICESCR)' in Chapter 6.

106 See 'Re-examination of Conflicts between TRIPS and Access to Medicines' in Chapter 6.

107 See 'Economic Incentive Perspective' in Chapter 2 and 'The Right of Everyone to Enjoy the Benefits of Scientific Progress and its Applications (Art. 15.1(b) of ICESCR)' in Chapter 5.

108 See 'Limitation to the right to property under the European Convention on Human Rights' above.

or through adopting other policy measures. As examined earlier, Article 1 of the First Protocol to the ECHR also places conditions upon limitations of the right to property: limitations of the right to property are permissible when they are prescribed by law, in the public interest, and necessary in a democratic society.[109] Nevertheless, the ECtHR and the former European Commission generally show deference to the judgment of national authorities as to what is in the public interest, and apply a low level of proportionality test, particularly in relation to 'the control of use' under the right to property provision.[110]

Limitations upon human rights are circumscribed, as the analysis of Articles 4, 2.1 and 5 in above suggested. The States parties cannot impose limitations or retrogressive measures that are inconsistent with minimum core obligations of the respective right because those limitations or retrogressive measures destroy the nature of the right, which is not compatible with Article 4 of the Covenant. In the present context, the most obvious core obligation is ensuring access to essential medicines under the right to health (Art. 12). The CESCR confirms that the minimum core obligations of States under the right to the highest attainable standard of health include the provision of essential medicines, as defined by the WHO.[111] According to the WHO:

> Essential medicines are those that satisfy the priority health care needs of the population. They are selected with due regard to public health relevance, evidence on efficacy and safety, and comparative cost effectiveness. Essential medicines are intended to be available within the context of functioning health systems at all times in adequate amounts, in the appropriate dosage forms, with assured quality and adequate information, and at a price the individual and the community can afford.[112]

The WHO has prepared and updated its Model Lists of Essential Medicines since 1977.[113] States have a responsibility to prepare a national essential medicines list, guided by the WHO Model Lists of Essential Medicines,[114] and must make those medicines on the national essential medicines list available and accessible for all as a core obligation under the right to health. Therefore, although the right to access to non-essential medicines may be subject to progressive realisation[115] and to limitations, so far as such

---

109 *James and others v. United Kingdom* (n 89) para. 47, 50; *Sporrong and Lönnroth v. Sweden* (n 88) para. 69; *Mellacher and others v. Austria* (n 92) para. 48; Golay and Cismas (n 92) 15; Council of Europe (n 92) 12–14.

110 *James and others v. United Kingdom* (n 89) paras 47, 50; Golay and Cismas (n 92) 15; Council of Europe (n 92) 12–15.

111 See 'Core obligations' in Chapter 4. CESCR, GC No. 14 (n 15) para. 43(d): 'to provide essential drugs, as from time to time defined under the WHO Action Programme on Essential Drugs'.

112 WHO, The Selection and Use of Essential Medicines, Technical Report Series 920 (2003) 54.

113 See the latest edition of the WHO Model Lists of Essential Medicines (n 16).

114 WHO, The Selection and Use of Essential Medicines (n 112) 54.

115 Report of the first Special Rapporteur on the Right to Health, Paul Hunt (13 September 2006, n 5) para. 58.

conditions as defined by Article 4 of the ICESCR are met, no limitations upon the right to access to essential medicines are justifiable in the absence of *force majeure*.[116] While the right to benefit from the protection of the moral and material interests of the author gives rise to a minimum core obligation to protect 'the means which are necessary to enable authors to enjoy an adequate standard of living',[117] it should be emphasised that intellectual property is not the only means to fulfil this core obligation. The concept of core obligation does not appear to be used in the European human rights system, but not all types of property receive the same level of protection. It may be useful to recall Henry Schermers' observation that only the kind of right to property without which human persons cannot lead a normal way of life falls within a fundamental human right. Other types of the right to property constitute an ordinary legal right, subject to limitations.[118]

Therefore, the States must make sure that their intellectual property system is designed and implemented so as not to reduce their ability to fulfil their core obligations in relation to access to essential medicines. Furthermore, promoting the totality of all human rights in accordance with Article 5 of the ICESCR, the CESCR calls for 'strik[ing] an adequate balance between the effective protection of the moral and material interests of authors and States parties' obligations in relation to the rights to food, health, and education, as well as the rights to take part in cultural life and to enjoy the benefits of scientific progress and its applications, or any other right recognised in the Covenant' as a core obligation under Article 15.1(c) of the ICESCR.[119] As to adequate balancing, the CESCR noted that 'the private interests of authors [under Article 15.1(c)] should not be unduly favoured and the public interest in enjoying broad access to their productions should be given due consideration'.[120]

A Human Rights Framework for Intellectual Property, Innovation and Access to Medicines

Building upon the foregoing discussions, a human rights framework is suggested with regard to the issue of intellectual property, innovation and access to medicines.[121] One of

---

116 Article 23, ILC (n 80).

117 CESCR, GC No. 17 (n 23), paras 22 and 39(c).

118 Schermers (n 84) 572–5.

119 CESCR, GC No. 17 (n 23) para. 39(e).

120 Ibid., para. 35.

121 The ideas of formulating the following principles were initially informed by Peter Drahos, 'An Alternative Framework for the Global Regulation of Intellectual Property Rights' [2005] *Australian Journal of Development Studies* 44 and have been developed drawing upon the Report of the High Commissioner for Human Rights (n 4); Margaret Chon, 'Intellectual Property and the Development Divide' (2005–2006) 27 *Cardozo Law Review* 2821–912; Report of the first Special Rapporteur on the Right to Health, Paul Hunt, Annex: Mission to GlaxoSmithKline (5 May 2009) UN Doc. A/HRC/11/12/Add.2; Report of the second Special Rapporteur on the Right to Health, Anand Grover (31 March 2009) UN Doc. A/HRC/11/12; Criteria for Periodic Evaluation of Global Development Partnerships from a Right to Development Perspective, Report of the

the important outcomes expected from the application of this human rights framework is to reorient intellectual property law and policy as a tool to serve human rights. A patent system is not a mechanism that protects purely the private interests of patent holders, but is an instrument to achieve certain social objectives.[122] By conforming to the human rights framework, intellectual property can serve as a tool for the realisation of the right to access to medicines and other related human rights. The following human rights framework for intellectual property, innovation and access to medicines aims at enhancing access to the *existing* essential medicines for all, placing a particular importance on access for people living in poverty. In the long term, this human rights framework is expected to contribute to enlarging the capabilities of countries, individually and collectively, to ensure the availability of *new* medicines to address neglected diseases. In short, this human rights framework for intellectual property, innovation and access to medicines, when reflected in an intellectual property system, functions as an internal limit upon the interpretation of the existing intellectual property norms and the setting of new related norms. This human rights framework also provides a normative base for international cooperation of States in creating a new innovation system that can ensure the availability and accessibility of medicines addressing unmet health needs of people living in poverty.

A Balanced Approach to Intellectual Property in Accordance with Human Rights

Intellectual property law must be enacted and construed in accordance with norms in international human rights law, such as the right to life, the right to health, the right to benefit from scientific progress and its applications, and the right to benefit from the protection of the moral and material interests of the author. The patent system may be justified as a policy tool to achieve social objectives, e.g. the promotion of technological innovation and the transfer and dissemination of technology.[123] Even so, States must strike an appropriate balance between different objectives and values inherent to intellectual property, taking into account the norms in international human rights law. When the protection of the exclusive rights of the patent holder is likely to restrict the enjoyment of a particular human right contained in the ICESCR, such as the right to access to medicines, international human rights law imposes on States an obligation to adopt a measure that can minimise such impact on human rights, among other available measures, to achieve the promotion of technological innovation, in accordance with Article 4 of the ICESCR. Policies relating to the standards for patentability, compulsory licensing, parallel importing, and other exceptions to exclusive rights constitute an integral part of TRIPS for this important balancing exercise. Even in the light of Article 1 of Protocol No. 1 to the ECHR, which extends its protection to companies, those alternatives adopted to comply with States' obligations in relation to human rights, such

---

High-Level Task Force on the Implementation of the Right to Development on its fourth session (January 2008) UN Doc. A/HRC/8/WG.2/TF/2, Annex II.

122 See discussions in Chapter 2.

123 For instance, see Art. 7 of TRIPS.

as the rights to life and health, are, *prima facie*, covered by the margin of appreciation that States parties to the ECHR enjoy to regulate 'the use of property in accordance with the general interest'.

Access to essential medicines as a human right constitutes a minimum core obligation of States under the ICESCR.[124] In accordance with Articles 4 and 5.1 of the ICESCR, no limitations to a minimum core obligation to ensure access to essential medicines are permitted in the absence of 'the occurrence of an irresistible force or of an unforeseen event, beyond the control of the State, making it materially impossible in the circumstances to perform the obligation'.[125] Therefore, States must ensure that their national intellectual property law and policy do not impede their ability to comply with their obligations to ensure access to essential medicines, but are enacted and implemented in a manner assisting States to fulfil such obligations.

Ensuring Access to Affordable Existing Medicines

In accordance with the rights to life and health enshrined in international human rights instruments, States must assess the impact on affordability of medicines before adopting any new intellectual property rules.[126] States must ensure that their national intellectual property law and policy have all the necessary safeguards to protect access to existing medicines. Examples of such provisions include defining standards for patentability such as inventive step; considering the implications for access to medicines; issuing compulsory licensing and authorising government use; differential pricing; importing essential medicines by countries with little manufacturing capacity; parallel importing; Bolar exception, which is the use of a pharmaceutical invention to conduct tests and obtain the approval from the health authority during the patent term for commercialisation of a generic version just after the patent's expiry; and experimental use.[127]

Ensuring Availability of New Medicines Addressing Primary Health Needs: Neglected Diseases

In accordance with the rights to life and health, and the right to enjoy the benefits from scientific progress and its applications, States must establish transparent priority-setting mechanisms for medical research, and provide incentives to research and development for unmet primary health needs of people. States can use diverse forms of incentive schemes, including public procurements, prizes, grants and tax credits. The Special Rapporteur on the Right to Health noted, '[s]tates should resort to a variety of economic, financial and commercial incentives in order to influence research and development into specific health

---

124 CESCR, GC No. 14 (n 15) para. 43. See also 'Access to Medicine: An Element of the Right to Health' in Chapter 4.

125 Article 23, ILC (n 80).

126 Report of the first Special Rapporteur on the Right to Health, Paul Hunt: Mission to the WTO (1 March 2004) UN Doc. E/CN.4/2004/49/Add.1, para. 82.

127 These measures are examined in detail in Chapter 3.

needs'.[128] While intellectual property is an important tool to promote the development of new medicines and other health technology, '[t]his incentive alone does not meet the need for the development of new products to fight diseases where the potential paying market is small or uncertain', as the WHO has pointed out.[129]

Freedom of Scientific Research

Consistent with the obligation to respect the freedom of scientific research under Article 15.1(b) and 15.3 of the ICESCR, States parties must make sure that intellectual property law and policy do not impose undue restrictions on the freedom of scientific research, by impeding access to knowledge for further research. There are occasions where patents on research tools, such as genes and cell lines, delay or block the conduct of further medical research by increasing costs in terms of time and/or money, as the Commission on Intellectual Property, Innovation and Public Health noted.[130] In this regard, States should consider incorporating such measures into intellectual property law and policy as strict criteria for patentability, research exemptions to the exclusive rights, and compulsory licensing to allow access to technology.[131]

Protecting the Moral and Material Interests of the Author

In accordance with the right to benefit from the protection of the moral and material interests of the author under Article 15.1(c) of the ICESCR, in the context of pharmaceutical innovation, States parties have to protect the rights of the researchers, to be recognised as the creators of their scientific productions, and to object to any distortion, mutilation or other modification of, or other derogatory action in relation to, their productions that would be prejudicial to their honour or reputation.[132] States parties also have to respect and protect the basic material interests of the researchers resulting from their scientific research, which are necessary to enable those authors to enjoy an adequate standard of living.[133] While States may consider the grant of exclusive rights as a measure to provide the protection of, particularly, the material interests of the researchers, in such circumstance, States must make sure that such exclusive rights do not unduly restrict other, independent, inventors' enjoyment of moral and material interests resulting from

---

128 Report of the Special Rapporteur (Paul Hunt) on the Right to Health (13 September 2006, n 5).

129 WHA Resolution 61.21 'Global Strategy and Plan of Action on Public Health, Innovation and Intellectual Property' (24 May 2008), Annex, para. 7, available at http://apps.who.int/gb/ebwha/pdf_files/A61/A61_R21-en.pdf, last accessed 15 March 2015; Doha Declaration on the TRIPS Agreement and Public Health, WT/MIN(01)/DEC/2 (14 November 2001) para. 3.

130 WHO, Report of the Commission on Intellectual Property Rights, Innovation and Public Health, *Public Health, Innovation and Intellectual Property Rights* (2006) 49.

131 For further discussion on each measure, see Chapter 3 of this book; WHO, *Report of the Commission on Intellectual Property Rights, Innovation and Public Health* (n 130) 51–5.

132 CESCR, GC No. 17 (n 23) para. 39(b).

133 Ibid., para. 39(c).

the same invention.[134] States can adopt other measures to ensure adequate remuneration for the intellectual labours, such as 'lead time advantages, government or private contracts and research grants, contests, bonuses, prizes, tenure, and professorial chairs'.[135] States also have to ensure that traditional medical knowledge and subsequent health innovation of indigenous and local communities are protected from any appropriation, adaptation and patenting with little or no compensation to, and without the free, prior and informed consent of, the original knowledge holders.[136]

International Assistance and Cooperation for the Issue of Intellectual Property, Innovation and Access to Medicines

Given that a majority of patents are owned by companies domiciled in a small number of high-income countries,[137] the effect of intellectual property on access to affordable essential medicines, when they are patented, is profound, particularly in developing countries.[138] There is another concern that current medical R&D scarcely addresses the health needs of people in developing countries.[139] In accordance with the Charter of the United Nations and other applicable international instruments,[140] States have to internationally cooperate to ensure access to affordable essential medicines and availability of medicines addressing unmet primary health needs of people.

---

134 Note that, under the current international patent system, a patent is granted only to the first applicant for an invention.

135 Rochelle Dreyfuss, 'Patents and Human Rights: Where Is the Paradox?', in Willem Grosheide (ed.), *Intellectual Property and Human Rights: A Paradox*, Edward Elgar (2010) 72–96; CESCR, GC No. 17 (n 23) para. 16.

136 Report of the High Commissioner for Human Rights (n 4) para. 41; Philippe Cullet, 'Human Rights and Intellectual Property Protection on the TRIPS Era' (2007) 29 *Human Rights Quarterly* 403–30, 426; CESCR, GC No. 17 (n 23) para. 32.

137 Jeffrey Sachs, 'The Global Innovation Divide' (2003) 3, January, *Innovation Policy and the Economy* 131–41.

138 Chon (n 121) 2866–7, 2898–9.

139 Patrice Trouiller, Piero Olliaro, Els Torreele, James Orbinsk, Richard Laing and Nathan Ford, 'Drug Development for Neglected Diseases' (2002) 359(9324) *The Lancet* 2188–94, 2189; Pierre Chirac and Els Torreele, 'Global Framework on Essential R & D' (2006) 367(9522) *The Lancet* 1560–61.

140 Articles 55 and 56 of the UN Charter, Arts 22 and 28 of the UDHR, Arts 2(1), 12, 15.4, 22 and 23 of the ICESCR, Arts 4, 23, 24, 28 of the CRC, the Alma-Ata Declaration on Primary Health Care (adopted in the International Conference on Primary Health Care, convened by the WHO and UNICEF in September 1978), the DRD (1986), and the Millennium Development Goal 8. In 2000, all the heads of States and Governments adopted the UN Millennium Declaration committing their nations to reducing extreme poverty and setting out a series of targets, which are called the Millennium Development Goals (MDGs). Target 5 of Goal 8: Develop a Global Partnership for Development is to '[i]n cooperation with pharmaceutical companies, provide access to affordable essential drugs in developing countries'. See, for the full list of the MDGs, http://www.un.org/millenniumgoals/global.shtml, last accessed 15 March 2015.

Duty to respect

States must refrain from unreasonable measures that undermine the right to health in other countries. Particularly, States have to ensure that their trade and other international policies do not restrict the ability of another State to use 'TRIPS flexibilities' to ensure access to affordable medicines. When negotiating and implementing bilateral or multilateral trade agreements, States, individually and collectively, have to make sure that 'these instruments do not adversely impact upon the right to health'.[141] Also, States must ensure that 'they [trade agreements] include safeguards recognising the right and duty of countries to adopt measures to protect human life and health and the right to health'.[142] Any country acceding to those trade agreements, with technical assistance where appropriate, should make use of the right to health impact assessments before identifying the most appropriate intellectual property rules. If States adopt policies shifting the balance in favour of the patent-holding pharmaceutical companies without a proper consideration of the impact on access to medicines and a justifiable basis of those changes, they are *prima facie* in breach of their obligation under the right to health.

Duty to protect

States have to take steps to ensure that patent-holding pharmaceutical companies domiciled in their territory or jurisdiction respect the obligation of hosting States in relation to access to medicines and thus do not undermine the right to health of people in those States.[143] For this purpose, States have to take reasonable measures to encourage and, where appropriate, require those companies to carry out human rights due diligence regarding their policy on patenting, licensing and pricing so as to avoid negatively impacting on the right to access to medicines of people abroad.[144] States should encourage patent-

---

141 Paragraph 39 of GC No. 14 (n 15). See also the Maastricht Principles (n 55) 13–15, 21.

142 Paul Hunt, Neglected Diseases: A Human Rights Analysis, WHO: Special Topics No. 6 (2007) 37.

143 Paragraph 39 of GC No. 14 (n 15). See also the Maastricht Principles (n 55) 23–27.

144 See 'Human Rights Responsibilities of Pharmaceutical Companies' in Chapter 4. For the concept of human rights due diligence applicable to business enterprises, see Report of the Special Representative of the Secretary-General on Business and Human Rights, John Ruggie, 'Protect, Respect and Remedy: A Framework for Business and Human Rights' (7 April 2008) UN Doc. A/HRC/8/5, paras 54–57; For States' duty to protect in relation to business activities in general, see Report of the Special Representative of the Secretary-General on Business and Human Rights, John Ruggie, Guiding Principles on Business and Human Rights: Implementing the United Nations 'Protect, Respect and Remedy' Framework (21 March 2011) UN Doc. A/HRC/17/31, paras 1–3; Particularly on the right to access to medicines, see Report of the first Special Rapporteur on the Right to Health, Paul Hunt, Annex: Human Rights Guidelines for Pharmaceutical Companies in Relation to Access to Medicines (11 August 2008) UN Doc. A/63/263 (2008); Report of the Special Rapporteur on the Right to Health, Paul Hunt: Mission to GlaxoSmithKline (5 May 2009) UN Doc. A/HRC/11/12/Add.2; Joo-Young Lee and Paul Hunt, 'Human Rights Responsibilities of Pharmaceutical Companies in Relation to Access to Medicines' (2012) 40(2) *The Journal of Law, Medicine & Ethics: Special Issue: Symposium: Pharmaceutical Firms and the Right to Health* 220–23.

holding pharmaceutical companies to manage their intellectual property in a manner that facilitates access to patented medicines, e.g. differential pricing and open (non-exclusive) voluntary licensing.[145]

Duty to fulfil

The right to health requires States to take reasonable measures, individually and collectively, to assist the fulfilment of the right of access to medicines of all individuals. Particularly, States in a position to do so should assist other countries, in light of available resources, where assistance is required for those countries to meet their minimum core obligation to ensure access to essential medicines.[146] For instance, countries with pharmaceutical manufacturing capacities should cooperate in facilitating the transfer of technology to countries lacking such capacities, and, if necessary, use the 2003 WTO waiver Decision in relation to compulsory licensing for export so as to supply essential medicines to those countries.[147]

States' obligations of international assistance and cooperation under the right to health also require the establishment of global partnerships to enhance access to medicines. In other words, States should establish a system of coordination for the allocation of responsibilities, in order to advance the universal realisation of access to essential medicines.[148] Some pioneering examples, although not explicitly human rights based, include UNITAID and the Global Fund to Fight AIDS, Tuberculosis and Malaria (Global Fund). UNITAID is an international drug purchase facility which was founded in 2006 by Brazil, France, Chile, Norway and the United Kingdom.[149] Its mission is to reduce the prices of medicines using its purchasing power based on a tax on air fares, accelerate the distribution of medicines and provide incentives for the development of new medicines with a particular focus on HIV/AIDS, tuberculosis and malaria.[150] The Global Fund is a global public–private partnership established in 2002 and it is the largest source of funding for programmes to prevent and treat the diseases and helps countries to strengthen their health systems. It aims to increase access to treatment for AIDS, tuberculosis and malaria for people in low-income countries.[151]

International cooperation accompanying the appropriate allocation of responsibilities and mobilisation of resources is also needed to ensure the availability of new medicines

---

145 Report of the first Special Rapporteur on the Right to Health, Paul Hunt (11 August 2008, n 144) para. 30.

146 Paragraph 39 of GC No. 14 (n 15); See the Maastricht Principles (n 55) 32–3. Gorik Ooms, The Right to Health and the Sustainability of Health Care: Why a New Global Health Aid Paradigm is Needed, unpublished doctoral thesis (2008) 193, 202, available at https://biblio.ugent. be/publication/4098368, last accessed 15 March 2015.

147 Decision of the General Council, Implementation of Paragraph 6 of the Doha Declaration on the TRIPS Agreement and Public Health (30 August 2003) WT/L/540 and Corr.1; for more detailed discussion of this decision, see Chapter 3.

148 See the Maastricht Principles (n 55) 29–32.

149 UNITAID's members include 28 States and 1 foundation as of April 2014.

150 See www.unitaid.org/en/, last accessed 15 March 2015.

151 See http://www.theglobalfund.org/en/, last accessed 15 March 2015.

addressing health needs of people in developing countries.[152] States should explore and implement new R&D systems that can address unmet health needs of people, as well as facilitate the transfer of health technology that is most needed for capacity building in developing countries in order to ensure sustainable access to medicines. A far-reaching, compelling proposal has emerged from the World Health Organization Global Strategy and Plan of Action on Public Health, Innovation and Intellectual property,[153] and its subsequent two expert working groups (EWG and CEWG).[154] A key concept in the proposal is the need for a new model for health innovation, based on de-linking of R&D costs from final product prices, and more coordinated financing for health innovation.[155] A number of creative policy suggestions, such as prizes, government grants, public procurements, the use of patent pools and open-source drug development, have been put forward as alternative approaches to medical innovation.

Within intellectual property systems, States should encourage the management of intellectual property in a manner that facilitates access to technologies necessary for medical R&D.[156] The new Medicines Patent Pool Foundation (MPPF), which was initially established by UNITAID, is a promising example. The MPPF is established as a voluntary medicines patent pool with a view to fostering research and development for the primary health needs of people in developing countries and also enhancing access to affordable medicines.[157] The patent pool enables two or more patent holders to agree to license their patents to third parties with a one-stop licensing mechanism. The open licensing of inventions, encouraged by the MPPF, would help to accelerate the availability of low-priced, newer medicines through facilitating generic competition. For instance, in October 2010, the National Institute of Health (NIH), an agency of the US Department of Health and Human Services, became the first research institution to join the MPPF.[158] The NIH

---

152 Criterion 1(g)(iv) for Implementation of the Right to Development: Attributes, Criteria, Sub-criteria and Indicators, Report of the High-Level Task Force on the Implementation of the Right to Development on its sixth session (8 March 2010) UN Doc. A/HRC/15/WG.2/TF/2/Add.2, 11. See also the Maastricht Principles (n 55) 29–32.

153 WHA Resolution 61.21 (n 129).

154 WHO, Report of the Expert Working Group on Research and Development Financing, Geneva (2010); WHO, *Research and Development to Meet Health Needs in Developing Countries: Strengthening Global Financing and Coordination*, Report of the Consultative Expert Working Group on Research and Development: Financing and Coordination (CEWG), Geneva (2012).

155 See 'Exploring a New Model for Health Innovation beyond TRIPS' in Chapter 6.

156 Criteria (a), (e), (n) for Periodic Evaluation of Global Development Partnerships from a Right to Development Perspective (n 121).

157 Patent holders voluntarily put their patents into this proposed 'pool' and researchers or other pharmaceutical companies can obtain open licences to use multiple patents necessary for their research in return for the payment of royalties. See http://www.medicinespatentpool.org/, last accessed 13 April 2014; See also UK All-Party Parliamentary Group on AIDS, The Treatment Timebomb, July 2009, available at http://www.appg-aids.org.uk/publications.htm, last accessed 15 March 2015.

158 Reuters, 'NIH joins patent pool for AIDS drugs' (30 September 2010); *The Guardian*, 'Time for the drug companies to hand over their patents' (30 September 2010).

holds a number of patents on the inventions of its scientists, and the royalty-free licence agreement between the NIH and the MPPF covers the patent on *darunavir*, a class of AIDS drugs for treating drug-resistant HIV infection.

Conclusion

In order to assess intellectual property law and policy in light of human rights, we should have a good understanding of human rights relevant to this issue. While the right to access to medicines is a cornerstone for a human rights framework for intellectual property, innovation and access to medicines, this book considers the right to enjoy the benefits of scientific progress and its applications and the right to the protection of the moral and material interests of authors, among other human rights, to be also necessary features of a human rights framework for this issue. Discussion of justifiable limitations in the ICESCR provides guidance on how to strike an appropriate balance between human rights and other interests in this context, and also clarifies that the core elements necessary for preserving the nature of the rights cannot be subject to limitations.

A cardinal rule in a human rights framework for intellectual property, innovation and access to medicines is that ensuring the right to access to essential medicines for all is a core obligation of States parties to the ICESCR, and thus States must make sure that their intellectual property law and policies do not undermine this core element. Furthermore, States must regulate patent-holding pharmaceutical companies in order that their management of patents do not impede States' compliance with their human rights obligations in relation to access to medicines. Under international human rights law, States are also obliged, alone and through international cooperation, to promote innovation of new medicines to address the unmet primary health needs of people.

Conclusion

At the time of writing this, the world is struggling to contain the worst outbreak of Ebola since its discovery nearly 40 years ago. With no approved cure yet available for this disease, 23,969 people had contracted the virus and 9,807 had died from it, according to the WHO.[1] Since the outbreak, people mostly in West African countries such as Sierra Leone, Liberia and Guinea have been devastated by the rapid spread of the virus and the related social breakdown. This state of affairs presses an urgent question of why there are no vaccines or treatments even after 40 years. As to the main reason for the lack of treatments, '[i]t's a market failure because this is typically a disease of poor people in poor countries where there is no market,' the WHO Assistant Director-General Marie-Paul Kieny says.[2] Indeed, Ebola is another devastating example of 'neglected diseases', which figure prominently in the intersections between intellectual property and access to medicines.

This book highlighted two primary areas of concern regarding intellectual property in the context of access to medicines. One is where intellectual property, by enabling proprietary pricing becomes a key barrier to access to affordable medicines. The other is where intellectual property fails to function as an incentive mechanism for innovation for diseases mostly relevant to people living in poverty due to little prospect of profits. This book proposed a human rights framework for intellectual property, innovation and access to medicines.

The proposed human rights framework intended to overcome two distinctive tendencies in the discussion of intellectual property and human rights in the context of access to medicines. One prevalent view is to conceive intellectual property as the antithesis of human rights in the context of access to medicines. Another tendency, increasingly observed over the last two decades, is to elevate intellectual property to the level of a human right. As Laurence Helfer and Graeme Austin analysed, these opposing views share a methodology within which they selectively invoke human rights in order to argue for either maximalist or minimalist intellectual property protection.[3] A view that focuses on external conflicts between intellectual property and human rights might carry a rhetorical force against the expansion of intellectual property protections. However, taking no account of the creators' rights falls short of a rigorous analysis of human rights. On the other hand, an expansionist claim on the ground of human rights is misleading in that it does not appreciate the significant differences between human rights and intellectual property rights.

---

1 WHO: Ebola Situation Report, 4 March 2015.

2 WHO Virtual Press Conference following a panel of medical ethicists to explore experimental treatment in the ongoing Ebola outbreak in West Africa, 12 August 2014.

3 Laurence R. Helfer and Graeme W. Austin, *Human Rights and Intellectual Property: Mapping the Global Interface*, Cambridge University Press (2011) 511.

This book's approach is guided by the basic understanding that intellectual property is not an end in itself, but has been developed as a means by which States promote innovation and encourage the dissemination of valuable products for the benefit of society, as addressed by the UN Committee on Economic, Social and Cultural Rights.[4] Interpreting and implementing intellectual property law with a view to serving broader social objectives is not alien to an intellectual property system in that intellectual property is a social institution created to achieve certain social objectives. The intellectual property system has been regulated by norms that evolve in response to various factors, such as economic changes and societal needs. While balancing between different interests in the intellectual property system has been informed by economic perspectives traditionally, the globalisation of patent protection, by increasing its impact on the life of people, makes it imperative to have intellectual property law and policy integrate a normative framework based on such human values as embodied in international human rights law.

Increasingly, human rights have been used as a language that can add moral authority to the access to medicines campaigns. Also, human rights have been invoked as legal norms to reinvigorate policy tools built in intellectual property rules that can help the States to strike a balance between providing incentives to innovation and improving access to such innovation.[5] This book also joined the calls for the use of a range of policies such as compulsory licensing, the standards for patentability, parallel importing, differential pricing between and within countries, and other exceptions to exclusive rights, with the aim of a better balance between commercial interests and public health objectives. From the right-to-health perspective, these policies can significantly contribute to reducing costs and improving access to essential medicines by facilitating local production or the importation of generic medicines.

A major concern raised by some observers against compulsory licensing is a reduction of incentives to innovate. However, in the case of investment in cures for diseases occurring in both rich and poor countries, developed country markets are a primary factor since potential returns from developing countries are low in present-day conditions. Therefore, compulsory licensing for such medicines in developing countries would engender little impact on incentives to innovate in developed countries.[6]

At the same time, we should also acknowledge the gaps in fulfilling the right to health that cannot adequately be closed by the flexibility measures alone, however valuable they are. Most of all, neglected research into health needs of developing countries highlights the limitations of seeking the solutions within the existing intellectual property system. This book agrees with the analysis of Helfer and Graeme that 'intellectual property flexibility mechanisms expand the regulatory space available to government. Yet they offer at best only limited guidance for restructuring creativity and innovation policies to promote human rights.'

---

4 CESCR, General Comment No. 17: The Right of Everyone to Benefit from the Protection of the Moral and Material Interests Resulting from Any Scientific, Literary or Artistic Production of which He is the Author (Art. 15(1)(c) of the ICESCR) (12 January 2006) UN Doc. E/C.12/2005.

5 Duncan Matthews, *Intellectual Property, Human Rights and Development: The Role of NGOs and Social Movements*, Edward Elgar (2011) 202–3.

6 Jerome H. Reichman, 'Comment: Compulsory Licensing of Patented Pharmaceutical Inventions: Evaluating the Options' (2009) 37 *Journal of Law, Medicine and Ethics* 247–63.

Greater attention should be paid to the ways in which research and development on the vaccines and medicines for neglected diseases can be encouraged locally and internationally.

Even with the existing medicines, the lack of capacities presents a great challenge to many developing countries in utilising the flexibility measures. While several developing countries, such as Brazil, India and Thailand, have successfully used flexibilities in order to lower prices of patented medicines and thus ensure access to affordable medicines, it is far from a common practice.[7] The emerging studies on the national situation regarding the implementation of the flexibility measures reveal the disparities in State capacities within developing countries.[8] Only a small number of developing countries have capacities in resisting strong pressures from intellectual property exporting countries. Manufacturing capacities in the fields of pharmaceuticals are lacking in many developing countries. The drug markets are not particularly competitive even without intellectual property. The assumption, if not for intellectual property, the market would produce generic medicines of good quality at a competitive price, does not fit all developing countries. As Angelina Snodgrass Godoy alerted, we should be careful not to place blind faith in 'market mechanisms as adjudicators of access'.[9] The flexibility mechanisms can be of limited success in removing barriers to access to medicines unless there are efforts to strengthen the capacity of developing countries in regulating the drug markets and purchasing the drugs that address the priority health needs of people.

The human rights framework proposed in this book can help to overcome some of the weaknesses found in the existing views and strategies to reconcile intellectual property and access to medicines. First of all, this book has brought together human rights relevant to the issue of intellectual property, innovation and access to medicines. While the right to access to medicines lies at the centre of this human rights framework, the right to enjoy the benefits of scientific progress and its applications, the right to benefit from the protection of the moral and material interests of the author, and the right to property, among other human rights, provide important elements for a human rights framework for intellectual property, innovation and access to medicines. In this way, the human rights framework obtains a comprehensive perspective and enables us to avoid viewing intellectual property and human rights as the relationship of a stark conflict. This approach is indebted to the respective work of Peter K. Yu and Laurence Helfer[10] and has become more solid in a concrete context of access to medicines.

---

7 UN, *MDG Gap Taskforce Report: Millennium Development Goal 8 The Global Partnership for Development: Making Rhetoric a Reality* (2012) 67.

8 UN Conference on Trade and Development (UNCTAD), *The Least Developed Countries Report 2007: Knowledge, Technological Learning and Innovation for Development*, UN Doc. UNCTAD/LDC/2007 (2007); Kenneth C. Shadlen, Samira Guennif, Alenka Guzman and N. Lalitha, *Intellectual Property, Pharmaceuticals and Public Health: Access to Drugs in Developing Countries*, Edward Elgar (2011); Angelina Snodgrass Godoy, *Intellectual Property and Human Rights in the Free Trade Era of Medicines and Markets*, Stanford University Press (2013); Jennifer Sellin, *Access to Medicines: The Interface Between Patents and Human Rights. Does One Size Fit All?* Intersentia (2014).

9 Godoy (n 8) 131.

10 Peter K. Yu 'Reconceptualizing Intellectual Property Interests in a Human Rights Framework' (2007) 40 *UC Davis Law Review* 1039–149; Peter K. Yu, 'Intellectual Property and Human Rights

Secondly, this human rights framework for intellectual property, innovation and access to medicines is guided by the analysis of the boundary of justifiable limitations upon human rights. It helps to find human rights-consistent ways of reconciling internal conflicts between the access dimension of human rights and the protection of authors' dimension of human rights, as well as external conflicts between intellectual property and human rights. This book sees that conflicts between intellectual property and the right to access to medicines can be avoided in most cases. At the same time, it is not a natural process that intellectual property functions as a tool to serve human rights. Conscious efforts are required to reorient law and policy regulating intellectual property towards being responsive to human rights.

A cardinal rule is that States must make sure that their intellectual property laws and policies do not impede their compliance with their core obligations to ensure access to affordable essential medicines. When it comes to access to non-essential medicines, subject to progressive realisation, States must strike an appropriate balance between different rights or between intellectual property rights and human rights. While the moral and material interests of inventors are recognised as a human right, States have wide latitude to tailor methods in which the inventor's rights are protected. When a restriction upon the inventor's rights is necessary for securing other human rights, the baseline for the inventor's rights is a safeguard against arbitrary exercise of State power and a right to remuneration, not exclusive rights. Where intellectual property is assessed as an impediment to access to medicines, among other factors, in particular contexts, States are required to adjust intellectual property rules to ensure access to medicines. The safeguard provisions include, but are not limited to, compulsory licensing, government use, parallel importation, exemptions from patent protection for early working, and research and development of diagnostics.

Thirdly, this human rights framework embraces the efforts to seek new incentive schemes, complementary to intellectual property, which promote socially valuable innovation and access to the products resulting from it. Such incentive schemes are expected to provide a sustainable remedy for the lack of innovation addressing health needs of developing countries. There are increasing initiatives exploring alternatives that both ensure access and encourage needed health innovation. The World Health Organization's Global Strategy and Plan of Action on Public Health, Innovation and Intellectual Property (2008)[11] was a result of increased attention from States, NGOs and health sectors on this issue and prompted further actions. A scholarly analysis has been provided as to a number of creative policy suggestions, including prizes for medical innovation, a Health Impact Fund, the use of patent pools, and open-source drug development, such as in Thomas Pogge, Matthew Rimmer and Kim Rubenstein's book, *Incentives for Global Public Health: Patent Law and Access to Essential Medicines*.[12] From a human rights perspective, there is strong merit in

---

in the Nonmultilateral Era' (2012) 64 *Florida Law Review* 1045–100; Laurence R. Helfer, 'Toward a Human Rights Framework for Intellectual Property' (2007) 40 *UC Davis Law Review* 971.

11 WHA Resolution 61.21 'Global Strategy and Plan of Action on Public Health, Innovation and Intellectual Property' (24 May 2008).

12 Thomas Pogge, Matthew Rimmer and Kim Rubenstein (eds), *Incentives for Global Public Health: Patent Law and Access to Essential Medicines*, Cambridge University Press (2010); See also Amy

promoting incentive schemes that ensure both access and worthwhile health innovation in that there are better chances for securing the right to health, the right to enjoy the benefits of scientific application, and the right of inventors without compromising one over another.

Fourthly, this human rights framework acknowledges the significance of international cooperation in securing the right to health and advocates the recognition of extraterritorial obligations of States under international human rights law. Most of the literature on intellectual property and access to medicines addresses the policy tools available to individual countries. However, any policy framework for intellectual property is fundamentally limited without addressing international dimensions of this issue. Although the flexibility mechanisms within intellectual property can help enhance access to medicines, as discussed above, least-developed countries generally lack the relevant expertise and resources to make use of them. Frederick Abbott and Jerome Reichman thus highlighted the advantage of a pooled procurement strategy by developing countries,[13] for which international cooperation should be promoted. Furthermore, innovation of 'missing' medicines to address the unmet primary health needs of people cannot be sufficiently achieved by any one developing country. It is true that the responsibility of securing human rights primarily lies with individual States, and the legal status of the extraterritorial obligations of States under international human rights law is not clear. Nevertheless, the universality of human rights cannot just pass by the fact that diseases and human suffering do not stop before the national boundary. The evolving human rights norms regarding extraterritorial obligations, as clarified by the Maastricht Principles,[14] can be an important tool in addressing the issue of access to medicines among other contemporary transnational human rights challenges.

This human rights framework calls for the international cooperation of States in ensuring access to existing and new medicines, as well as worthwhile health innovation. Pioneering examples of international cooperation in this regard include a global observatory of health R&D, UNITAID, the Global Fund to Fight AIDS, Tuberculosis, and Malaria (Global Fund) and the Medicines Patent Pool Foundation.

Fifthly, this human rights framework acknowledges the ability of companies to impact on human rights both positively and negatively, and emphasises the State's responsibility to regulate pharmaceutical companies in order that their management of intellectual property does not undermine but assists the fulfilment of the right to access to medicines. This book also advocates the recognition of the human rights responsibilities of companies as emerging norms, given that many developing countries lack the relevant regulatory capacities

---

Kapczynski, 'Commentary: Innovation Policy for a New Era' (2009) 37 *Journal of Law, Medicine and Ethics* 264–8.

13 Frederic M. Abbott and Jerome H Reichman, 'The Doha Round's Public Health Legacy: Strategies for the Production and Diffusion of Patented Medicines Under the Amended TRIPS Provisions' (2007) 10(4) *Journal of International Economic Law* 921–87, 969–81; Reichman (n 6) 258.

14 The Maastricht Principles on Extraterritorial Obligations of States in the area of Economic, Social and Cultural Rights, adopted on 28 September 2011 at a gathering convened by Maastricht University and the International Commission of Jurists. Available at http://www.maastrichtuniversity. nl/web/Institutes/MaastrichtCentreForHumanRights/MaastrichtETOPrinciples.htm, last accessed 28 October 2014.

and the cooperation of companies is essential for health innovation.[15] These emerging norms help to overcome some of the structural obstacles that the existing intellectual property system places to the efforts to govern intellectual property and innovation in a more balanced manner. In the existing intellectual property system, intellectual property owners are the only 'rights' holders, and the responsibilities of the intellectual property rights holders are mentioned but not elaborated.

Differently, various UN human rights treaty bodies have dealt with responsibilities of non-State actors, including companies, in addition to the obligations of States.[16] The Guiding Principles on Business and Human Rights, adopted by the UN Human Rights Council, represents a significant step forward in setting out human rights responsibilities of companies, and places responsibilities upon companies to carry out due diligence in order to avoid and mitigate any human rights impacts they cause or contribute to.[17] The Human Rights Guidelines for Pharmaceutical Companies in Relation to Access to Medicines, prepared by the first Special Rapporteur on the Right to Health, made a number of specific recommendations to pharmaceutical companies: the companies respect the right of countries to use TRIPS flexibilities for promoting access to medicines, including compulsory licensing and parallel importing;[18] and 'take all reasonable steps to make the medicine as accessible as possible, as soon as possible, to all those in need, within a viable business model',[19] which includes differential pricing between and within countries, non-exclusive commercial voluntary licences, non-commercial voluntary licences, and public-private partnerships.[20] They also include a recommendation regarding neglected diseases that companies should 'engage constructively with key international and other initiatives that are searching for new, sustainable and effective approaches to accelerate and enhance research and development for neglected diseases'.[21] These emerging norms on human rights and business can help to fill the governance gaps in this context of access to medicines.

Finally, this human rights framework stresses the importance of empirical evidence in decision making in this area. It recommended that States should conduct human rights impact assessments before adopting any new intellectual property rules or polices. While it may not be easy to measure human rights impacts, human rights indicators developed by

---

15 See Chapter 4 of this book.

16 See e.g. CRC, GC No. 5, 'General Measures of Implementation of the Convention on the Rights of the Child' (27 November 2003) paras. 43–44, in relation to the context of privatisation; CESCR, GC No. 12, 'The Right to Adequate Food (Art.11)' (12 May 1999) paras 19–20; CESCR, GC No. 14, The Right to Health (Art. 12 of the ICESCR), adopted at the 22nd session (2000) UN Doc. E/C.12/2000/4 para 42.

17 Human Rights Council Resolution 17/4, Human Rights and Transnational Corporations and Other Business Enterprises, adopted without a vote (6 July 2011) UN Doc. A/HRC/RES/17/4.

18 Report of the Special Rapporteur on the Right to Health, Paul Hunt (11 August 2008) UN Doc. A/63/263, paras 26–29.

19 Ibid., para. 41.

20 Ibid., paras 30–38; Report of the first Special Rapporteur on the Right to Health, Paul Hunt, Mission to GlaxoSmithKline, A/HRC/11/12/Add.2, 5 May 2009, para. 38.

21 Ibid., para. 25.

the UN Office of the High Commissioner for Human Rights can assist States in assessing impacts on human rights of the new rules or policies.[22] It should also be kept in mind that the human rights impact assessments can be only meaningful if States act upon the gathered evidence so as to resolve any impediments to the compliance of international human rights obligations.[23]

In short, this human rights framework can help to solidify a normative basis for creative innovation models for promoting needs-driven research, protecting the moral and material interests of inventors as well as the right to health of people. The debates and practice in relation to intellectual property and access to medicines reveal a vast disparity among States in their capacity to address these issues. While the primary responsibility to ensure human rights lies with each State, international cooperation and appropriate regulation of the pharmaceutical industry should be part of any realistic strategy for reconciling intellectual property and access to medicines in a sustainable way. Drawing upon the developments at the UN human rights forums, this human rights framework provides for the normative grounds of international cooperation for access to medicines, as well as assessing the impacts of any new intellectual property rules and behaviours of the pharmaceutical industry. This human rights framework envisions national and international systems for intellectual property, innovation and health, in which vaccines and treatments for diseases are developed in a timely fashion and made accessible so that no human beings need to die from preventable diseases.

---

22 UN Office of the High Commissioner for Human Rights, *Human Rights Indicators: A Guide to Measurement and Implementation* (2012).

23 Yu, 'Intellectual Property and Human Rights in the Nonmultilateral Era' (n 10) 1098.

Bibliography

Books and Articles

Abbott, Frederick M., 'The Doha Declaration on the TRIPS Agreement and Public Health: Lighting a Dark Corner at the WTO' (2002) 5 *Journal of International Economic Law* 469–505.

Abbott, Frederick M., '11. The TRIPS-legality of Measures Taken to Address Public Health Crises: Responding to USTR-State-industry Positions that Undermine the WTO', in Daniel L.M. Kennedy (ed.), *Political Economy of International Trade law: Essays in Honor of Robert E. Hudec*, Cambridge University Press (2002) 311–48.

Abbott, Frederick M., *WTO TRIPS Agreement and Its Implications for Access to Medicines in Developing Countries*, The Commission on Intellectual Property Rights (UK) (2002).

Abbott, Frederick M., *The Doha Declaration on the TRIPS Agreement and Public Health and the Contradictory Trend in Bilateral and Regional Free Trade Agreements*, Occasional Paper No. 14, Geneva: QUNO (2004).

Abbott, Frederick M., 'The "Rule of Reason" and the Right to Health: Integrating Human Rights and Competition Principles in the Context of TRIPS', in Thomas Cottier, Joost Pauwelyn and Elisabeth Burgi (eds), *Human Rights and International Trade*, Oxford University Press (2005) 279–300.

Abbott, Frederick M., 'The WTO Medicines Decision: World Pharmaceutical Trade and the Protection of Public Health' (2005) 99(2) *The American Journal of International Law* 317–58.

Abbott, Frederick M., 'Toward a New Era of Objective Assessment in the Field of TRIPS and Variable Geometry for the Preservation of Multilateralism' (2005) 8(1) *Journal of International Economic Law* 77–100.

Abbott, Frederick M., Introductory Note to World Trade Organization Canada First Notice to Manufacture Generic Drug for Export (2007) 46 *International Legal Materials* 1127–31.

Abbott, Frederick M., 'The Judgment in *Novartis v. India*: What the Supreme Court of India Said', *Intellectual Property Watch* (Inside Views) 3 April 2013.

Abbott, Frederick M. and Jerome H. Reichman, 'The Doha Round's Public Health Legacy: Strategies for the Production and Diffusion of Patented Medicines under the Amended TRIPS Provisions' (2007) 10 *Journal of International Economic Law* 921–87.

Abegunde, Dele O., Colin Mathers, Taghreed Adam, et al., 'The Burden and Costs of Chronic Diseases in Low-Income and Middle-Income Countries (2007) 370 *The Lancet* 1029–38.

Akehurst, Michael, 'Custom as a Source of International Law' (1974–1975) 47 *The British Year Book of International Law* 1–53.

Alston, Philip, 'Out of the Abyss: The Challenges Confronting the New UN Committee on Economic, Social and Cultural Rights' (1987) 9 *Human Rights Quarterly* 332–81.

Alston, Philip and Gerard Quinn, 'The Nature and Scope of States Parties' Obligations under the International Covenant on Economic, Social and Cultural Rights' (1987) 9 *Human Rights Quarterly* 156–249.

Arno, Peter S. and Michael H. Davis, 'Why Don't We Enforce Existing Drug Price Controls? The Unrecognized and Unenforced Reasonable Pricing Requirements Imposed upon Patents Deriving in Whole or in Part from Federally Funded Research' (2001) 75 *Tulane Law Review* 631–91.

Ariyanuntaka, Vichai, 'Intellectual Property and International Trade Court: A New Dimension for Intellectual Property Rights Enforcement in Thailand' (2010) available at http://www.wipo.int/wipolex/en/details.jsp?id=6822, last accessed 15 March 2015.

Arrow, Kenneth J., 'Economic Welfare and the Allocation of Resources for Invention', in *The Rate and Direction of Inventive Activity: Economic and Social Factors: A Report of the National Bureau of Economic Research*, Universities-National Bureau (1962) 609–26.

Bale, Harvey E. Jr., 'The Conflicts Between Parallel Trade and Product Access and Innovation: The Case of Pharmaceuticals' (1998) 1 *Journal of International Economic Law* 637–53.

Basheer, Shamnad and T. Prashant Reddy, 'The "Efficacy" of Indian Patent Law: Ironing out the Creases in Section 3(d)' (2008) 5(2) *SCRIPTed* 232–66.

Beall, Reed and Randall Kuhn, 'Trends in Compulsory Licensing of Pharmaceuticals Since the Doha Declaration: A Database Analysis' (2012) 9(1) *PloS Medicine*.

Bhattacharya, Radhika, 'Are Developing Countries Going Too Far on TRIPS? A Closer Look at the New Laws in India' (2008) 34 *American Journal of Law & Medicine* 395–421.

Bilchitz, David, 'Towards a Reasonable Approach to the Minimum Core: Laying the Foundations for Future Socio-economic Rights Jurisprudence' (2003) 19 *South African Journal on Human Rights* 1–26.

Brinkhof, Jan, 'On Patents and Human Rights', in Willem Grosheide (ed.), *Intellectual Property and Human Rights: A Paradox*, Edward Elgar (2010) 140–54.

Burgers, J.M., 'Rights and Duties Concerning Creative Expression in Particular in Science', in UNESCO (ed.), *Human Rights: Comments and Interpretations* 215–20.

Champ, Paul and Amir Attaran, 'Patent Rights and Local Working Under the WTO TRIPS Agreement: An Analysis of the U.S.-Brazil Patent Dispute' (2002) 27 *Yale Journal of International Law* 365–93.

Chapman, Audrey R., 'A Human Rights Perspective on Intellectual Property, Scientific Progress, and Access to the Benefits of Science', in *Intellectual Property and Human Rights*, WIPO (1998) 10. Available at http://www.oapi.wipo.net/edocs/mdocs/tk/en/wipo_unhchr_ip_pnl_98/wipo_unhchr_ip_pnl_98_5.pdf, last accessed 15 March 2015.

Chapman, Audrey R., 'Core Obligations Related to ICESCR Article 15(1)(c)', in Audrey Chapman and Sage Russell (eds) *Core Obligations: Building a Framework for Economic, Social and Cultural Rights*, Intersentia (2002).

Chapman, Audrey R., 'Development of Indicators for Economic, Social and Cultural Rights', in Yvonne Donders and Vladimir Volodin (eds), *Human Rights in Education, Science and Culture: Legal Developments and Challenges*, UNESCO (2007) 111–52.

Chapman, Audrey R., 'Towards an Understanding of the Right to Enjoy the Benefits of Scientific Progress and Its Applications (2009) 8(1) *Journal of Human Rights* 1–36.

Charney, Jonathan, 'The Persistent Objector Rule and the Development of Customary International Law' (1985) 56 *British Yearbook of International Law* 1.

Chasombat, Sanchai, Cheewanan Lertpiriyasuwat, Sombat Thanprasertsuk, et al., 'The National Access to Antiretroviral Program for PHA (NAPHA) in Thailand' (2006) 37(4) *The Southeast Asian Journal of Tropical Medicine and Public Health* 704–15.

Chatterjee, Patralekha, 'India's New Patent Laws Still Hurt Generic Drug Supplies' (2005) 365(9468) *The Lancet* 1378.

Chirac, Pierre and Els Torreele, 'Global Framework on Essential Health R&D' (2006) 367(9522) *The Lancet* 1560–61.

Chirwa, Danwood Mzikenge, 'The Right to Health in International Law: Its Implications for the Obligations of State and Non-State Actors in Ensuring Access to Essential Medicine' (2003) 19 *South African Journal on Human Rights* 541–66.

Chon, Margaret, 'Intellectual Property and the Development Divide' (2005–2006) 27 *Cardozo Law Review* 2821–912.

Clapham, Andrew, *Human Rights Obligations of Non-State Actors*, Oxford University Press (2006).

Claude, Richard Pierre, 'Scientists' Rights and the Human Rights to the Benefits of Science' in Audrey Chapman and Sage Russell (eds), *Core Obligations: Building a Framework for Economic, Social and Cultural Rights*, Intersentia (2002) 247–78.

Cohen, Morris R., 'Property and Sovereignty' (1927–1928) 13 *Cornell Law Quarterly* 8–30.

Cohen, Wesley, Richard Nelson and John Walsh, 'Appropriability Conditions and Why Firms Patents and Why They Do Not'. Manuscript (1997).

Commission on Intellectual Property Rights (UK), *Integrating Intellectual Property Rights and Development Policy* (2002).

Cook, Rebecca J. and Bernard M. Dickens, 'Human Rights Dynamics of Abortion Law Reform' (2003) 25 *Human Rights Quarterly* 1–59.

Cornish, William and David Llewelyn, *Intellectual Property: Patents, Copyright, Trade Marks and Allied Rights*, 5th edn, Sweet & Maxwell (2003).

Correa, Carlos M., 'Public Health and Patent Legislation in Developing Countries' (2001) 3, Spring, *Tulane Journal of Technology and Intellectual Property* 1–53.

Correa, Carlos M., *Traditional Knowledge and Intellectual Property – Issues and Options Surrounding the Protection of Traditional Knowledge*, Quaker United Nations Office Discussion Paper (2001).

Correa, Carlos M., 'Implications of the Doha Declaration on the TRIPS Agreement and Public Health', World Health Organization (2002).

Correa, Carlos M., 'Access to Drugs under TRIPS: A Not So Expeditious Solution' (2004) 8(1) *Bridges* 21–2.

Correa, Carlos M., 'Investment Protection in Bilateral and Free Trade Agreements: Implications for the Granting of Compulsory Licenses' (2004–2005) 26 *Michigan Journal of International Law* 331–53.

Correa, Carlos M., 'Implications of Bilateral Free Trade Agreements on Access to Medicines' (2006) 84(5) *Bulletin of the World Health Organization* 399–404.

Correa, Carlos M., *Guidelines for the Examination of Pharmaceutical Patents: Developing a Public Health Perspective*, WHO-ICTSD-UNCTAD (2007).

Correa, Carlos M., *Trade Related Aspects of Intellectual Property Rights: A Commentary on the TRIPS Agreement*, Oxford University Press (2007).

Correa, Carlos M., 'Towards a New Model for Pharmaceutical Research', *Bulletin of the World Health Organization* (2012).

Cottier, Thomas, 'TRIPS, the Doha Declaration and Public Health' (2003) 6(2) *Journal of World Intellectual Property* 373–8, 386.

Courtis, Christian, 'Socio-economic Rights before the Courts in Argentina', in Fons Coomans (ed.), *Justiciability of Economic and Social Rights: Experiences from Domestic Systems*, Intersentia (2006).

Cullet, Philippe, 'Patents and Medicines: The Relationship between TRIPS and the Human Right to Health' (2003) 79(1) *International Affairs* 139–60.

Cullet, Philippe, 'Human Rights and Intellectual Property Protection in the TRIPS Era' (2007) 29(2) *Human Rights Quarterly* 403–30.

D'Amato, Anthony, *The Concept of Custom in International Law*, Cornell University Press (1971).

Daniels, Norman, *Just Health: Meeting Health Needs Fairly*, Cambridge University Press (2008).

David, Paul, 'New Technology, Diffusion, Public Policy, and Industrial Competitiveness' in Ralph Landau and Nathan Rosenberg (eds), *The Positive Sum Strategy: Harnessing Technology for Economic Growth*, Washington, D.C.: National Academy Press (1986) 373–92.

Dickson, Michael, Jeremy Hurst and Stéphane Jacobzone, *Survey of Pharmacoeconomic Assessment Activity in Eleven Countries*, OECD Health Working Papers No. 4, DELSA/ELSA/WD/HEA (2003).

Drahos, Peter, *A Philosophy of Intellectual Property*, Ashgate Publishing (1996).

Drahos, Peter, 'Intellectual Property and Human Rights' (1999) 3 *Intellectual Property Quarterly* 349–71.

Drahos, Peter, *Bilateralism in Intellectual Property*, Oxfam Policy Paper, December (2001).

Drahos, Peter, '10 Negotiating Intellectual Property Rights: Between Coercion and Dialogue', in Peter Drahos and Ruth Mayne (eds), *Global Intellectual Property Rights Knowledge, Access and Development*, Palgrave Macmillan (2002) 161–82.

Drahos, Peter, 'An Alternative Framework for the Global Regulation of Intellectual Property Rights (2005) 1 *Austrian Journal of Development Studies* 16, available at http://papers.ssrn.com/sol3/papers.cfm?abstract_id=850751, last accessed 15 March 2015.

Drahos, Peter and John Braithwaite, *Information Feudalism: Who Owns the Knowledge Economy?*, The New Press (2002).

Dreyfuss, Rochelle Cooper, 'Varying the Course in Patenting Genetic Material: A Counter Proposal to Richard Epstein's Steady Course', Public Law and Legal Theory Research Paper Series, Research Paper No. 59 (April 2003).

Dreyfuss, Rochelle Cooper, 'Patents and Human Rights: Where is the Paradox?', in Willem Grosheide (ed.), *Intellectual Property and Human Rights: A Paradox*, Edward Elgar (2010) 72–96.

Dutfield, Graham, *Intellectual Property Rights and the Life Science Industries: A Twentieth Century History*, Ashgate Publishing (2003).

Dutfield, Graham, 'Delivering Drugs to the Poor: Will the TRIPS Amendment Help?' (2008) 34 *American Journal of Law & Medicine* 107–24.

Dutton, Harold Irvin, *The Patent System and Inventive Activity during the Industrial Revolution 1750–1852*, Manchester University Press (1984).

Eide, Asbjørn, 'Realisation of Social and Economic Rights and the Minimum Threshold Approach' (1989) 10 *Human Rights Law Journal* 35.

Eisenberg, Rebecca S., 'Public Research and Private Development: Patents and Technology Transfer in Government-Sponsored Research' (1996) 82 *Virginia Law Review* 1663–727.

Eisenberg, Rebecca S., '9 Bargaining over the Transfer of Proprietary Research Tools: Is This Market Failing or Emerging?', in Rochelle Dreyfuss, Diane L. Zimmerman and Harry First (eds), *Expanding the Boundaries of Intellectual Property: Innovation Policy for the Knowledge Society*, Oxford University Press (2001) 223–49.

Elliott, Richard, 'Delivery Past Due: Global Precedent Set under Canada's Access to Medicines Regime' (2008) 13(1) *HIV/AIDS Policy & Law Review*.

El Said, Mohammed K., *Public Health-related TRIPS-Plus Provisions in Bilateral Trade Agreements: A Policy Guide for Negotiators and Implementers in the WHO Eastern Mediterranean Region*, ICTSD and WHO (2010).

Farmer, Paul, *Pathologies of Power: Health, Human Rights and the New World on the Poor*, University of California Press (2005).

Feinberg, Joel, *Social Philosophy*, Prentice-Hall, Inc. (1973).

Ferraz, Octavio Luiz Motta, 'The Right to Health in the Courts of Brazil: Worsening Health Inequities?' (2009) 11(2) *Health and Human Rights* 33–45.

Fisher, William, 'Theories of Intellectual Property', in Stephen R. Munzer (ed.), *New Essays in the Legal and Political Theory of Property*, Cambridge University Press (2001) 194–9.

Flynn, Sean, *Analysis of Thai Law on Government Use Licenses*, available at http://www.wcl. american.edu/pijip/thai_comp_licenses.cfm, last accessed 15 March 2015.

Flynn, Sean, Aidan Hollis and Mike Palmedo, 'An Economic Justification for Open Access to Essential Medicine Patents in Developing Countries' (2009) 37(2) *Journal of Law, Medicine & Ethics* 2–25.

Gallini, Nancy, 'Patent Length and Breadth with Costly Imitation' (1992) 44 *RAND Journal of Economics* 52–63.

Gallini, Nancy and Suzanne Scotchmer, 'Intellectual Property: When is it the Best Incentive System?' (2002) 2 *Innovation Policy and the Economy* 51–77.

Gathii, James Thuo, 'Construing Intellectual Property Rights and Competition Policy Consistently with Facilitating Access to Affordable AIDS Drugs to Low-end Consumers' (2001) 53 *Florida Law Review* 727–78.

Gathii, James Thuo, 'The Legal Status of the Doha Declaration on TRIPS and Public Health under the Vienna Convention on the Law of Treaties' (2002) 15 *Harvard Journal of Law and Technology* 291–317.

Gervais, Daniel, *The TRIPS Agreement: Drafting History and Analysis*, 3rd edn, Sweet & Maxwell (2008).

Gilbert, Richard and Carl Shapiro, 'Optimal Patent Length and Breadth' (1990) 21 *RAND Journal of Economics* 106–12.

Glendon, Mary Ann (ed.), *A World Made New: Eleanor Roosevelt and the Universal Declaration of Human Rights*, Random House (2001).

Godoy, Angelina Snodgrass, *Intellectual Property and Human Rights in the Free Trade Era of Medicines and Markets*, Stanford University Press (2013).

Golay, Christophe and Ioana Cismas, *Legal Opinion: The Right to Property from a Human Rights Perspective* (2010), available at http://papers.ssrn.com/sol3/papers.cfm?abstract_id=1635359, last accessed 15 March 2015.

Gormley, W. Paul, 'The Right to Life and the Rule of Non-derogability: Peremptory Norms of Jus Cogens', in Bertrand G. Ramcharan (ed.), *The Right to Life in International Law*, Martinus Nijhoff (1985).

Gondek, Michal, *The Reach of Human Rights in a Globalising World: Extraterritorial Application of Human Rights Treaties*, Intersentia (2009).

Gordon, Wendy J., 'Current Patent Laws Cannot Claim the Backing of Human Rights', in Willem Grosheide (ed.), *Intellectual Property and Human Rights: A Paradox*, Edward Elgar (2010) 155–71.

Grossman, Gene M. and Edwin L.C. Lai, 'International Protection of Intellectual Property' (2004) 94(5) *The American Economic Review* 1635–13.

Grubb, Philip, *Patents for Chemicals, Pharmaceuticals and Biotechnology: Fundamentals of Global Law, Practice and Strategy*, Clarendon Press (1999).

Gruskin, Sofia and Michael A. Grodin (eds), *Perspectives on Health and Human Rights*, Routledge (2005).

Gumbel, Mike, 'Is Article 31*bis* Enough? The Need to Promote Economies of Scale in the International Compulsory Licensing System' (2008) 22 *Temple International and Comparative Law Journal* 161–85.

Haugen, Hans Morten, 'The Nature of Social Human Rights Treaties and Standard-Setting WTO Treaties: A Question of Hierarchy?' (2007) 76 *Nordic Journal of International Law* 435–64.

Haugen, Hans Morten, '6 The Right to Benefit from the Moral and Material Interests of Scientific Production and the Right to Enjoy Benefits from Scientific Progress and Its Applications', in *The Right to Food and the TRIPS Agreement*, Martinus Nijhoff (2007) 169–212.

Helfer, Laurence R., 'Toward a Human Rights Framework for Intellectual Property' (2007) 40 *UC Davis Law Review* 971.

Helfer, Laurence R., 'The New Innovation Frontier? Intellectual Property and the European Court of Human Rights' (2008) 49 *Harvard International Law Journal* 1–52.

Helfer, Laurence R. and Graeme W. Austin, *Human Rights and Intellectual Property: Mapping the Global Interface*, Cambridge (2011).

Heller, Michael A. and Rebecca S. Eisenberg, 'Can Patents Deter Innovation? The Anticommons in Biomedical Research' (1998) 280 *Science* 698–701.

Henkin, Louis, 'The Universal Declaration at 50 and the Challenge of Global Markets' (1999) 25(1) *Brooklyn Journal of International Law* 17–25.

Hess, Charlotte and Elinor Ostrom, 'Ideas, Artifacts, and Facilities: Information as a Common-Pool Resource' (2003) 66 *Law & Contemporary Problems* 121–2.

Hesse, Carla, 'Enlightenment Epistemology and the Law of Authorship in Revolutionary France, 1777–1793', in Robert Post (ed.), *Law and the Order of Culture*, University of California Press (1991) 109–37.

Hestermeyer, Holger, 'Canadian-made Drugs for Rwanda: The First Application of the WTO Waiver on Patents and Medicines' (2007) 11(28) *The American Society of International Law Insights*, available at http://www.asil.org/insights/volume/11/issue/28/canadian-made-drugs-rwanda-first-application-wto-waiver-patents-and, last accessed 4 March 2015.

Hestermeyer, Holger, *Human Rights and the WTO: The Case of Patents and Access to Medicines*, Oxford University Press (2007).

Hettinger, Edwin C., 'Justifying Intellectual Property' (1989) 18(1) *Philosophy and Public Affairs* 31–52.

Heywood, Mark, 'Debunking "Conglomo-talk": A Case Study of the Amicus Curiae as an Instrument for Advocacy, Investigation and Mobilisation', *Law, Democracy and Development* (2001).

Ho, Cynthia M., 'Patent Breaking or Balancing?: Separating Strands of Fact from Fiction under TRIPS' (2009) 34 *North Carolina Journal of International Law & Commercial Regulation* 371–469.

Ho, Cynthia M., *Access to Medicine in the Global Economy: International Agreements on Patents and Related Rights*, Oxford University Press (2011).

Hogerzeil, Hans V., 'Essential Medicines and Human Rights: What Can They Learn from Each Other?' (2006) 84(5) *Bulletin of the World Health Organization* 371–5.

Hogerzeil, Hans V., Melanie Samson, Jaume Vidal Casanovas and Ladan Rahmani-Ocora, 'Is Access to Essential Medicines as Part of the Fulfilment of the Right to Health Enforceable through the Courts?' (2006) 368, 22 July, *The Lancet* 305–11.

Hohfeld, Wesley Newcomb, *Fundamental Legal Conceptions* [1919] David Campbell and Philip Thomas (eds), Ashgate Publishing (2001).

Howse, Robert, 'The Canadian Generic Medicines Panel: A Dangerous Precedent in Dangerous Times' (2000) 3(4) *Journal of World Intellectual Property* 493–507.

Howse, Robert, 'The WTO and Human Rights', in Sarah Joseph et al. (eds), *The World Trade Organization and Human Rights: Interdisciplinary Perspectives* (2009) 39–68.

Hughes, David and Songkramchai Leethongdee, 'Universal Coverage in the Land of Smiles: Lessons from Thailand's 30 Baht Health Reforms' (2007) 36(4) *Health Affairs* 999–1008.

Hughes, Justin, 'The Philosophy of Intellectual Property' (1988) 77 *Georgetown Law Journal* 287–366.

Hunt, Paul, *Neglected Diseases: A Human Rights Analysis*, World Health Organization: Special Topics No. 6 (2007).

International Committee of the Red Cross, *Customary International Humanitarian Law, Volume I Rules*, Cambridge University Press (2004).

International Council on Human Rights Policy, *Beyond Voluntarism: Human Rights and the Developing International Legal Obligations of Companies* (2002) available at http://www.ichrp.org/en/projects/107?theme=10, last accessed 15 March 2015.

International Law Association, *Final Report of the Committee on the Formation of Customary (General) International Law, Statement of Principles Applicable to the Formation of General Customary International Law*, International Law Association Conference, London, 2000.

Jenks, Wilfred, 'The Conflict of Law-Making Treaties' (1953) 30 *British Yearbook of International Law* 401–53.

Jones, Peter, 'Human Rights, Group Rights, and Peoples' Rights' (1999) 21 *Human Rights Quarterly* 80–107.

Jongudomsuk, P. (ed.), *NHSO Annual Report 2004: Implementation of Universal Health Care Coverage*, SPS Printing Co Ltd (2004).

Joseph, Sarah, 'Pharmaceutical Corporations and Access to Drugs: The "Fourth Wave" of Corporate Human Rights Scrutiny', *Human Rights Quarterly* 25.2 (2003) 425–52.

Joseph, Sarah, *Corporations and Transnational Human Rights Litigation*, Hart Publishing (2004).

Kapczynski, Amy, 'Commentary: Innovation Policy for a New Era' (2009) 37 *Journal of Law, Medicine and Ethics* 264–8.

Kastriner, Lawrence G., 'The Revival of Confidence in the Patent System' (1991) 73(1) *Journal of the Patent and Trademark Office Society* 5–23.

Kennedy, Daniel L.M. (ed.), *Political Economy of International Trade Law: Essays in Honor of Robert E. Hudec*, Cambridge University Press (2002).

Kinley, David and Rachel Chambers, 'The UN Human Rights Norms for Corporations: The Private Implications of Public International Law' (2006) 6(3) *Human Rights Law Review* 447–97.

Kinney, Eleanor D. and Brian Alexander Clark, 'Provisions for Health and Health Care in the Constitutions of the Countries of the World' (2004) 37 *Cornell International Law Journal* 285–355.

Kitch, Edmund W., 'The Nature and Function of the Patent System' (1977) 20(2) *Journal of Law and Economics* 265–90.

Kobak, James Jr., 'The Misuse Defense and Intellectual Property litigation' (1915) 1(2) *Boston University Journal of Science and Technology Law* 1–43.

Krause, Catarina, '11. The Right to Property', in Asbjørn Eide et al. (eds), *Economic, Social and Cultural Rights*, 2nd edn, Kluwer Law International (2001) 191–209.

Kremer, Michael, 'Patent Buyouts: A Mechanism for Encouraging Innovation' (1998) 113(4) *Quarterly Journal of Economics* 1137–68.

Kuanpoth, Jakkrit, 'TRIPS-Plus Intellectual Property Rules: Impact on Thailand's Public Health' (2006) 9(5)*The Journal of World Intellectual Property* 573–91.

Laing, Richard, Brenda Waning, Andy Gray, et al., '25 Years of the WHO Essential Medicines Lists: Progress and Challenges' (2003) 361*The Lancet* 1723–9.

Landes, William M. and Richard A. Posner, *The Economic Structure of Intellectual Property Law*, The Belknap Press of Harvard University Press (2003) 294–333.

Lang, Andrew T.F., '7. Inter-regime Encounters', in Sarah Joseph, David Kinley and Jeff Waincymer (eds), *The World Trade Organization and Human Rights*, Edward Elgar (2009) 163–89.

Leader, Sheldon, 'The Collateral Protection of Rights in the Global Economy' (2008–2009) 53 *New York Law School Law Review* 805–14.

Joo-Young Lee and Paul Hunt, 'Human Rights Responsibilities of Pharmaceutical Companies in Relation to Access to Medicines' (2012) 40(2) *The Journal of Law, Medicine & Ethics: Special Issue: Symposium: Pharmaceutical Firms and the Right to Health* 220–33.

Lee, Linda L., 'Trials and TRIPS-ulations: Indian Patent Law and *Novartis AG v. Union of India*' (2008) 23 *Berkeley Technology Law Journal* 281–313.

Leisinger, Klaus M., 'Corporate Responsibilities for Access to Medicines', *Journal of Business Ethics* (2009) 85(1) 3–23.

Levin, R.C., A.K. Klevorick, R.R. Nelson and S.G. Winter, 'Appropriating the Returns from Industrial Research and Development' *Brookings Papers on Economic Activity* 3 (1987) 783–820.

Llewelyn, Margaret, 'Schrodinger's Cat: An Observation on Modern Patent Law', in Peter Drahos (ed.), *Death of Patents*, Lawtext Publishing Limited and Queen Mary Intellectual Property Research Institute (2005) 67–109.

Locke, John, *Two Treatises of Government* [1698], Peter Laslett (ed.) 2nd edn, Cambridge University Press (1994).

Lopez, Alan and Colin Mathers, 'Inequities in Health Status: Findings from the 2001 Global Burden of Disease Study', *Global Forum Update on Research for Health 4: Equitable Access: Research Challenges for Health in Developing Countries*, 163–75, available at http://announcementsfiles.cohred.org/gfhr_pub/assoc/s14812e/s14812e.pdf, last accessed 15 March 2015.

Machlup, Fritz and Edith Penrose, 'The Patent Controversy in the Nineteenth Century' (1950) 10(1) *Journal of Economic History* 1–29.

MacLeod, Christine, 'Would There Have Been No Industrial Revolution Without Patents?' Paper presented at ESRC Research Seminar Series, Intellectual Property Rights, Economic Development and Social Welfare: What Does History Tell Us? Ironbridge Gorge Museum, Coalbrookdale, UK, 26 April 2004.

Mann, Jonathan, Sofia Gruskin, Michael Grodin, et al. (eds), *Health and Human Rights: A Reader*, Routledge (1999).

Mansfield, Edwin, 'Patents and Innovation: An Empirical Study' (1986) 32 *Management Science* 173–81.

Marceau, Gabrielle, 'WTO Dispute Settlement and Human Rights' (2002) 13(4) *European Journal of International Law* 753–814.

Marceau, Gabrielle, 'The WTO Dispute Settlement and Human Rights', in Frederick Abbott, Christine Kaufmann and Thomas Cottier (eds), *International Trade and Human Rights: Foundations and Conceptual Issues* (2006) 181–260.

Maskus, Keith E., *Intellectual Property Rights in the Global Economy*, Institute for International Economics (2000).

Maskus, Keith M. and M Ganslandt, 'Parallel Trade in Pharmaceutical Products: Implications for Procuring Medicines for Poor Countries', in B. Granville (ed.), *The Economics of Essential Medicines*, RIIA (2002) 57–80.

Matlin, Stephen, 'Introduction: Poverty, Equity and Health Research' in *Global Forum Update on Research for Health 2: Poverty, Equity and Health Research*, 10–3, available at http://announcementsfiles.cohred.org/gfhr_pub/assoc/s14810e/s14810e.pdf, last accessed 15 March 2015.

Matthews, Duncan, 'WTO Decision on Implementation of Paragraph 6 of the Doha Declaration on the TRIPS Agreement and Public Health: A Solution to the Access to Essential Medicines Problem?' (2004) 7(1) *Journal of International Economic Law* 73–107.

Matthews, Duncan, 'TRIPS Flexibilities and Access to Medicines in Developing Countries: The Problem with Technical Assistance and Free Trade Agreements' (2005) 27(11) *European Intellectual Property Review* 420–27.

Matthews, Duncan, *Intellectual Property, Human Rights and Development: The Role of NGOs and Social Movements*, Edward Elgar (2011).

Maurer, Stephen M. and Suzanne Scotchmer, 'The Independent Invention Defense in Intellectual Property' John M. Olin Working Paper No. 98-11. Boalt Hall School of Law, University of California, Berkeley (1998).

Maurer, Stephen M. and Suzanne Scotchmer, 'Procuring Knowledge, National Bureau of Economic Research Working Paper 9903' (2003) available at http://www.nber.org/papers/w9903.pdf, last accessed 15 March 2015.

May, Christopher and Susan Sell, *Intellectual Property Rights: A Critical History*, Lynne Rienner (2006).

Mayer, Carl J., 'Personalizing the Impersonal: Corporations and the Bill of Rights' (1989–1990) 41 *Hastings Law Journal* 577–667.

Mazzoleni, Robert and Richard R. Nelson, 'The Benefits and Costs of Strong Patent Protection: A Contribution to the Current Debate' (1998) 27 *Research Policy* 273–84.

McCalman, Phillip, 'Reaping What You Sow: An Empirical Analysis of International Patent Harmonization', (2001) 55(1) *Journal of International Economics* 161–86.

McCalman, Phillip, 'National Patents, Innovation and International Agreements' (2002) 11(1) *The Journal of International Trade & Economic Development* 1–14.

Meier, Benjamin Mason, 'Development as Health: Employing the Collective Right to Development to Achieve the Goals of the Individual Right to Health' (2008) 30(2) *Human Rights Quarterly* 259–355.

Menghistu, F., 'III. The Satisfaction of Survival Requirements', in B.G. Ramcharan (ed.), *The Right to Life in International Law*, Martinus Nijhoff (1985) 63–83.

Merges, Robert P., Peter S. Menell and Mark A. Lemley, *Intellectual Property in the New Technological Age*, Aspen Publishers, 2nd edn (2000).

Merges, Robert P. and Richard R. Nelson, 'On the Complex Economics of Patent Scope', (1990) 90(4) *Columbia Law Review* 839–916.

Moore, Adam, 'Toward a Lockean Theory of Intellectual Property', in Adam Moore (ed.), *Intellectual Property*, Rowman and Littlefield (1997) 81–103.

Morsink, Johannes, *The Universal Declaration of Human Rights: Origins, Drafting, and Intent*, University of Pennsylvania Press (1999).

Müller, Amrei, 'Limitations to and Derogations from Economic, Social and Cultural Rights' (2009) 9(4) *Human Rights Law Review* 557–601.

Muller, Janice M., 'The Tiger Awakens: The Tumultuous Transformation of India's Patent System and the Rise of Indian Pharmaceutical Innovation' (2007) 68 Spring, *University of Pittsburgh Law Review* 491–641.

Muller, Janice M., 'Taking TRIPS to India – Novartis, Patent Law, and Access to Medicines', (8 February 2007) *The New England Journal of Medicine* 541–3.

Murdur, Ganapati, 'Indian Patients Go to Court Over Cancer Drug' (2004) 329 *British Medical Journal* 419.

Musungu, Sisule F. and Cecilia Oh, 'The Use of Flexibilities in TRIPS by Developing Countries: Can They Promote Access to Medicines?' Study 4C of the Commission on Intellectual Property Rights, Innovation and Public Health (CIPIH) (2005).

Nelson, Richard and Steven Winter, *An Evolutionary Theory of Economic Change*, Belknap Press of Harvard University Press (1982).

Nolan, Justin, 'With Power Comes Responsibility: Human Rights and Corporate Accountability' (2005) 28 *The University of New South Wales Law Journal* 581–613.

Nordhaus, William, *Invention, Growth and Welfare: A Theoretical Treatment of Technological Change*, MIT Press (1969).

Nozick, Robert, *Anarchy, State, and Utopia*, Basil Blackwell (1974).

Ooms, Gorik, 'The Right to Health and the Sustainability of Health Care: Why a New Global Health Aid Paradigm is Needed', unpublished doctoral thesis (2008) available at https://biblio.ugent.be/publication/4098368, last accessed 15 March 2015.

Outterson, Kevin, 'Should Access to Medicines and TRIPS Flexibilities be Limited to Specific Diseases?' (2008) 34 *American Journal of Law & Medicine* 279–301.

Parker, Scott and Kevin Mooney, 'Is "Evergreening" a Cause for Concern? A Legal Perspective' (2007) 13(4) *Journal of Commercial Biotechnology* 235–44.

Pauwelyn, Joost, 'The Role of Public International Law in the WTO' (2001) 95 *American Journal of International Law* 535–78.

Pauwelyn, Joost, *Conflict of Norms in Public International Law: How WTO Law Relates to Other Rules of International Law*, Cambridge University Press (2003).

Pauwelyn, Joost, 'Human Rights in WTO Dispute Settlement', in Thomas Cottier, Joost Pauwelyn and Elisabeth Burgi (eds), *Human Rights and International Trade*, Oxford University Press (2005) 205–31.

Penrose, Edith Tilton, 'International Patenting and the Less-developed Countries' (1973) 83(331) *The Economic Journal* 768–86.

Penrose, Edith Tilton, *The Economics of the International Patent System*, originally published by the Johns Hopkins Press, 1951; Greenwood Reprinting (1973).

Perehudoff, Katrina, Richard Laing and Hans Hogerzeil, 'Access to Essential Medicines in National Constitutions' (2010) 88(11) *Bulletin of the World Health Organization*.

Pingali, Prabhu L. and Greg Traxler, 'Changing Locus of Agricultural Research: Will the Poor Benefit from Biotechnology and Privatization Trends?' (2002) 27 *Food Policy* 223–38.

Pogge, Thomas, Matthew Rimmer and Kim Rubenstein (eds), *Incentives for Global Public Health: Patent Law and Access to Essential Medicines*, Cambridge University Press (2010).

Priest, George, 'What Economists Can Tell Lawyers About Intellectual Property' (1986) 8 *Research in Law and Economics* 19–21.

Ramanna, Anitha, 'Chapter 5. Shifts in India's Policy on Intellectual Property: The Role of Ideas, Coercion and Changing Interests', in *Death of Patents*, Queen Mary Intellectual Property Institute and Lawtext Publishing Limited (2005) 150–74.

Ramcharan, Bertrand G., 'I. The Concept and Dimensions of the Right to Life', in Betrand Ramcharan (ed.), *The Right to Life in International Law*, Martinus Nijhoff (1985) 1–32.

Ratner, Steven, 'Corporations and Human Rights: A Theory of Legal Responsibility' (2001–2002) 111 *Yale Law Journal* 443–545.

Rawls, John, *A Theory of Justice*, Harvard University Press (1971), reprinted in 2005.

Reichman, Jerome H., 'Comment: Compulsory Licensing of Patented Pharmaceutical Inventions: Evaluating the Options (2009) 37 *Journal of Law, Medicine and Ethics* 247–63.

Revenga, Ana, Mead Over, Emiko Masaki, Wiwat Peerapatanapokin, Julian Gold, Viroj Tangcharoensathien and Sombat Thanprasertsuk, *The Economics of Effective AIDS Treatment: Evaluating Policy Options for Thailand*, The World Bank (2006).

Riedel, Eibe, 'Standards and Sources. Farewell to the Exclusivity of the Sources Triad in International Law?' (1991) 2 *European Journal of International Law* 58–84.

Roberts, Anthea Elizabeth, 'Traditional and Modern Approaches to Customary International Law: A Reconciliation' (2001) 95 *American Journal of International Law* 757–91.

Rosas, Allan and Monika Sandvik-Nylund, '22. Armed Conflicts', in Asbjørn Eide, Catarina Krause and Allen Rosas (eds), *Economic, Social, and Cultural Rights: A Textbook*, 2nd edn (2001) 407–21.

Røttingen, John-Arne, Claudia Chamas, L.C. Goyal, Hilda Harb, Leizel Lagrada and Bongani Mawethu Mayosi, 'Securing the Public Good of Health Research and Development for Developing Countries' [2012] *Bulletin of the World Health Organization* 398–400.

Rozek, Richard P. and Renee L. Rainey, 'Broad-Based Compulsory Licensing of Pharmaceutical Technologies: Unsound Public Policy' (2001) 4(4) *Journal of World Intellectual Property* 463–80.

Ruse-Khan, Henning Grosse, 'Proportionality and Balancing within the Objectives', in Paul Torremans (ed.), *Intellectual Property and Human Rights: Enhanced Edition of Copyright and Human Rights*, Kluwer Law International (2008) 161–94.

Sachs, Jeffrey, 'The Global Innovation Divide' (2003) 3 *Innovation Policy and the Economy* 131–41.

Salomon, Margot, 'International Human Rights Obligations in Context: Structural Obstacles and the Demands of Global Justice', in Bard Andressen and Stephen Marks (eds), *Development as a Human Right: Legal, Political, and Economic Dimensions*, Harvard School of Public Health (2006) 96–118.

Savoie, Brent, 'Thailand's Test: Compulsory Licensing in an Era of Epidemiologic Transition' (2007–2008) 48 *Virginia Journal of International Law* 211–48.

Schabas, William A., '7 Study of the Right to Enjoy the Benefits of Scientific and Technological Progress and its Applications', in Yvonne Donders and Vladimir Volodin (eds), *Human Rights in Education, Science and Culture: Legal Developments and Challenges*, UNESCO, Ashgate Publishing (2007) 273–307.

Schachter, Oschar, 'New Custom: Power, Opinio Juris and Contrary Practice', in J. Makarczyk (ed.), *Theory of International Law at the Threshold of the 21st Century*, Kluwer Law International (1996) 531–2.

Scherer, F.M. and Jayashree Watal, 'The Economics of TRIPS Options for Access to Medicines', in B Granville (ed.), *The Economics of Essential Medicines* (2002) 32–56.

Schermers, Henry G., 'The International Protection of the Right of Property', in Franz Matscher and Herbert Petzold (eds), *Protecting Human Rights: The European Dimension*, Carl Heymanns Verlag KG (1988) 565–80.

Schiff, Eric, *Industrialisation Without National Patents: The Netherlands, 1869–1912; Switzerland, 1850–1907*, Princeton University Press (1971).

Olivier de Schutter, Asbjørn Eide, Ashfaq Khalfan, et al., 'Commentary to the Maastricht Principles on Extraterritorial Obligations of States in the Area of Economic, Social and Cultural Rights' (2012) 34 *Human Rights Quarterly* 1084–169.

Scotchmer, Suzanne, 'Standing on the Shoulders of Giants: Cumulative Research and the Patent Law' (1991) 5(1) *The Journal of Economic Perspectives* 29–41.

Scotchmer, Suzanne, 'The Political Economy of Intellectual Property Treaties' (2004) 20(2) *The Journal of Law, Economics, & Organization* 415–37.

Scott, Craig and Philip Alston, 'Adjudicating Constitutional Priorities in a Transnational Context: A Comment on Soobramoney's Legacy and Grootboom's Promise' (2000) 16 *South African Journal on Human Rights* 206–68.

Sell, Susan K., 'Intellectual Property as a Trade Issue: From the Paris Convention to GATT', (1989) XIII(4) *Legal Studies Forum* 407–22.

Sell, Susan K., *Private Power, Public Law: The Globalization of Intellectual Property*, Cambridge University Press (2003).

Sellin, Jennifer, *Access to Medicines: The Interface Between Patents and Human Rights. Does One Size Fit All?* Intersentia (2014).

Sen, Amartya, 'Why Health Equity?' (2002) 11(8) *Health Economics* 659–66.

Shadlen, Kenneth C., Samira Guennif, Alenka Guzman and N. Lalitha, *Intellectual Property, Pharmaceuticals and Public Health: Access to Drugs in Developing Countries*, Edward Elgar (2011).

Shavell, Steven and Tanguy Van Ypersele, 'Rewards versus Intellectual Property Rights' (2001) 44 *Journal of Law and Economics* 525–47.

Shaver, Lea, 'The Right to Science and Culture' [2010] *Wisconsin Law Review* 121–84.

Shelton, Dinah, 'Protecting Human Rights in a Globalized World' (2002) 25 *Boston College International and Comparative Law Review* 273–322.

Shelton, Dinah, 'Normative Hierarchy in International Law' (2006) 100, April, *American Journal of International Law* 291–323.

Sherman, Brad and Lionel Bently, *The Making of Modern Intellectual Property Law: The British Experience, 1760–1911*, Cambridge University Press (1999).

Shiffrin, Seana Valentine, 'Lockean Arguments for Private Intellectual Property', in Stephen R. Munzer (ed.), *New Essays in the Legal and Political Theory of Property*, Cambridge University Press (2001) 138–67.

Shue, Henry, *Basic Rights: Subsistence, Affluence, and U.S. Foreign Policy*, Princeton University Press (1980).

Simma, Bruno and Philip Alston, 'The Sources of Human Rights Law: Custom, Jus Cogens, and General Principles' (1988–1989) 12 *Australia Year Book of International Law* 82–108.

Singer, Joseph, *Entitlement: The Paradoxes of Property*, Yale University Press (2000).

Ssenyonjo, Manisuli, *Economic, Social and Cultural Rights in International Law*, Hart Publishing (2009).

Sterckx, Sigrid, 'The Ethics of Patenting – Uneasy Justifications', in Peter Drahos (ed.), *Death of Patents*, Queen Mary Intellectual Property Research Institute (2005).

Sterckx, Sigrid and Julian Cockbain, 'Purpose-limited Pharmaceutical Product Claims under the Revised European Patent Convention: A Camouflaged Attack on Generic Substitution?' (2010) 1 *Intellectual Property Quarterly* 88–107.

Stiglitz, Joseph E., 'Knowledge as a Global Public Good', in Inge Kaul, Isabelle Grunberg and Mare A. Stern (eds), *Global Public Goods: International Cooperation in the 21st Century*, UNDP/Oxford University Press (1999) 308–25.

Stoll, Peter-Tobias, Jan Busche and Katrin Arend (eds), *WTO-Trade-Related Aspects of Intellectual Property Rights: Max Planck Commentaries on World Trade Law*, Martinus Nijhoff Publishers (2009).

Taubman, Antony, 'Rethinking TRIPS: "Adequate Remuneration" for Non-voluntary Patent Licensing' (2008) 11(4) *Journal of International Economic Law* 927–70.

Taylor, Christopher T. and Aubrey Silberston, *The Economic Impact of the Patent System. A Study of the British Experience*, Cambridge University Press (1973).

The National Institute for Health Care Management Research and Educational Foundation, *Changing Patterns of Pharmaceutical Innovation*, May 2002, available at http://www.nihcm.org/pdf/innovations.pdf, last accessed 15 March 2015.

The US National Research Council of the National Academies (ed.), *Reaping the Benefits of Genomic and Proteomic Research: Intellectual Property Rights, Innovation, and Public Health*, National Academies Press (2006).

Tobin, John, *The Right to Health in International Law*, Oxford University Press (2012).

Torres, Mary Ann, 'The Human Right to Health, National Courts, and Access to HIV/AIDS Treatment: A Case Study from Venezuela', in Sofia Gruskin, Michael Grodin, George Annas, et al. (eds), *Perspectives on Health and Human Rights*, Routledge (2005) 507–18.

Touiller, Patrice, Piero Olliaro, Els Torreele, James Orbinski, Richard Laing and Nathan Ford, 'Drug Development for Neglected Diseases: A Deficient Market and a Public-Health Policy Failure' (2002) 359(9324) *The Lancet* 2188–94.

Towse, Adrian, Anne Mills and Viroj Tangcharoensathien, 'Learning from Thailand's Health Reforms' (2004) 328 *British Medical Journal* 103–5.

Tully, James, *A Discourse on Property: John Locke and His Adversaries*, Cambridge University Press (1980).

Vaitos, Constantine, 'Patents Revisited: Their Function in Developing Countries' (1972) 9(I) *Journal of Development Studies* 71–97.

Waldron, Jeremy, *The Right to Private Property*, Clarendon Press (1990).

Waldron, Jeremy, 'Chapter 13 Homelessness and the Issue of Freedom', in *Liberal Rights*, Cambridge University Press (1993) 309–38.

Weissbrodt, David and Muria Kruger, 'Norms on the Responsibilities of Transnational Corporations and Other Business Enterprises with Regard to Human Rights' (2003) 97(4) *The American Journal of International Law* 901–22.

Weissbrodt, David and Kell Schoff, 'Human Rights Approach to Intellectual Property Protection: The Genesis and Application of Sub-Commission Resolution 2000/7' (2003) 5 *Minnesota Intellectual Property Review* 1–46.

Weissman, Robert, 'A Long Strange TRIPS: The Pharmaceutical Industry Drive to Harmonize Global Intellectual Property Rules, and the Remaining WTO Legal Alternatives Available to Third World Countries' (1996) 17 *University of Pennsylvania Journal of International Economic Law* 1069–125.

Wolff, Jonathan, *The Human Right to Health*, W.W. Norton & Company (2012).

Yamane, Hiroko, 'Impacts of Scientific and Technological Progress on Human Rights: Normative Response of the International Community', in Christopher Gregory Weeramantry (ed.), *Human Rights and Scientific and Technological Development*, United Nations University Press (1990).

Yamin, Alicia Ely, 'Not Just a Tragedy: Access to Medications as a Right under International Law' (2003) 21 *Boston University International Law Journal* 325–71.

Yamin, Alicia Ely, 'Our Place in the World: Conceptualizing Obligations beyond Borders in Human Rights-based Approaches to Health' (2010) 12(1) *Health and Human Rights* 3–14.

Yamin, Alicia Ely and Oscar Parra-Vera, 'How Do Courts Set Health Policy? The Case of the Colombian Constitutional Court' (2009) 6(2) *PLoS Medicine* 1–4.

Yu, Peter K., 'Reconceptualizing Intellectual Property Interests in a Human Rights Framework' (2007) 40 *UC Davis Law Review* 1039–149.

Yu, Peter K., 'Ten Common Questions about Intellectual Property and Human Rights' (2007) 23(4) *Georgia State University Law Review* 709–53.

Yu, Peter K., 'Intellectual Property and Human Rights in the Nonmultilateral Era' (2012) 64 *Florida Law Review* 1045–100.

Zinner, Darren E., 'Medical R&D at the Turn of the Millennium', *Health Affairs*, September–October 2001.

Zuniga, Jose M., Stephen P. Marks and Lawrence O. Gostin, *Advancing the Human Right to Health*, Oxford University Press (2013).

International Instruments

Additional Protocol to the American Convention on Human Rights in the Area of Economic, Social and Cultural Rights (adopted by Organization of American States on 27 June 1988 and entered into force 21 October 1999) (Protocol of San Salvador).

African Charter on Human and Peoples' Rights (adopted by Organization of African Unity on 27 June 1981 and entered into force 21 October 1986) (ACHPR).

Agreement on Trade-Related Aspects of Intellectual Property Rights (adopted on 15 April 1994, Marrakesh Agreement Establishing the World Trade Organization, Annex 1C).

Alma-Ata Declaration on Primary Health Care (adopted in the International Conference on Primary Health Care, convened by the WHO and UNICEF in September 1978).

American Convention on Human Rights (signed at the Inter-American Specialized Conference on Human Rights, 22 November 1969) (ACHR).

American Declaration of the Rights and Duties of Man (adopted by the Ninth International Conference of America States in 1948) (ADRD).

Arab Charter on Human Rights (adopted by the League of Arab States on 22 Mary 2004 and entered into force on 15 March 2008).

Berne Convention for the Protection of Literary and Artistic Works (Berne Convention).

Charter of Fundamental Rights of the European Union (proclaimed by the Presidents of the European Parliament, the Council and the Commission at the European Council meeting on 7 December 2000 and came into effect through the entry into force of the Lisbon Treaty in 2009).

Charter of the United Nations (adopted on 26 June 1945 and entered into force on 24 October 1945).

Constitution of the World Health Organization (adopted by the World Health Assembly on 22 July 1946 and entered into force on 7 April 1948).

Convention on Biological Diversity (signed at the Earth Summit in Rio de Janeiro, Brazil, in 1992 and entered into force on 29 December 1993).

Convention on the Elimination of All Forms of Discrimination against Women (adopted by the UN General Assembly on 18 December 1979 and entered into force on 3 September 1981).

Convention on the Rights of the Child (adopted by the UN General Assembly on 20 November 1989 and entered into force on 2 September 1990).

Convention on the Rights of Persons with Disabilities (adopted by the UN General Assembly on 13 December 2006 and entered into force on 3 May 2008).

Decision 486 of Andean Community of Nations 'Common Intellectual Property Regime'

Decision of the Council for TRIPS, 'Extension of the Transition Period under Article 66.1 of the TRIPS Agreement for Least-Developed Country Members for Certain Obligations with Respect to Pharmaceutical Products', IP/C/25 (1 July 2002).

Decision of the Council for TRIPS, 'Extension of the Transition Period under Article 66.1 for Least Developed Country Members', IP/C/64 (12 June 2013).

Decision of the WTO General Council, 'Implementation of paragraph 6 of the Doha Declaration on the TRIPS Agreement and Public Health', WT/L/540 and Corr.1, 1 September 2003.

Decision of the WTO General Council, 'Amendment of the TRIPS Agreement', WT/L/641, 6 December 2005.

Declaration on the Right to Development, UN General Assembly Resolution 41/128, (4 December 1986).

Doha Declaration on the TRIPS Agreement and Public Health (adopted on 14 November 2001 by the Fourth WTO Ministerial Conference, Doha, Qatar, WT/MIN(01)/DEC/2).

European Convention on Human Rights (Convention for the Protection of Human Rights and Fundamental Freedoms: adopted by the Council of Europe on 4 November 1950 and entered into force on 3 September 1953) (ECHR).

European Patent Convention (adopted on 5 October 1973, Amended version of 2000 entered into force on 13 December 2007).

European Social Charter (adopted by the Council of Europe in 1961 and revised in 1996. The Revised European Social Charter entered into force in 1999). General Agreement on Tariffs and Trade (adopted on 15 April 1994 and entered into force 1 January 1995) Marrakesh Agreement Establishing the World Trade Organization, Annex 1A (GATT).

ILO Tripartite Declaration of Principles Concerning Multinational Enterprises and Social Policy (adopted in November 1977 by the International Labour Organisation).

International Convention on the Elimination of All Forms of Racial Discrimination (adopted by the UN General Assembly on 21 December 1965 and entered into force on 4 January 1969).

International Convention on the Protection of the Rights of All Migrant Workers and Members of their Families (adopted by the UN General Assembly on 18 December 1990 and entered into force on 1 July 2003).

International Covenant on Civil and Political Rights (adopted by the UN General Assembly on 16 December 1966 and entered into force on 23 March 1976) (ICCPR).

International Covenant on Economic, Social, and Cultural Rights (adopted by the UN General Assembly on 16 December 1966 and entered into force on 3 January 1976) (ICESCR).

Protocol No. 1 to the European Convention on Human Rights (adopted on 20 March 1952 and entered into force on 18 May 1954).

Statute of International Court of Justice (adopted on 26 June 1945 and entered into force on 24 October 1945).

Understanding on Rules and Procedures Governing the Settlement of Disputes, Annex 2 of the WTO Agreement (1994).

United Nations Millennium Declaration (adopted by the Millennium Summit of the United Nations, 6–8 September 2000, General Assembly Resolution 55/2).

United States-Australia Free Trade Agreement (entered into force on 1 January 2005) (US-Australia FTA).

United States-Bahrain Free Trade Agreement (entered into force on 11 January 2006) (US-Bahrain FTA).

United States-Chile Free Trade Agreement (entered into force on 1 January 2004) (US-Chile FTA).

United States-Dominican Republic-Central America Free Trade Agreement (signed on 5 August 2004) (US-CAFTA).

United States-Jordan Free Trade Agreement (entered into force on 17 December 2001) (US-Jordan FTA).

United States-Morocco Free Trade Agreement (entered into force on 1 January 1 2006) (US-Morocco FTA).

Universal Declaration of Human Rights (adopted by the UN General Assembly on 10 December 1948).

US-Singapore Free Trade Agreement (entered into force on 1 January 2004) (US-Singapore FTA).

Vienna Convention on the Law of Treaties (adopted on 23 May 1969 and entered into force on 27 January 1980) (VCLT).

Domestic Legislation

Bayh-Dole Act (US) P.L. 96–517, Patent and Trademark Act Amendments of 1980.

Bill C-9 (Canada), an Act to Amend the Patent Act and the Food and Drug Act (known as the 'Jean Chrétien Pledge to Africa) available at http://www2.parl.gc.ca/Sites/LOP/LegislativeSummaries/Bills_ls.asp?Parl=37&Ses=3&ls=C9, last accessed 15 March 2015.

Bill C-393 (Canada) An Act to amend the Patent Act (drugs for international humanitarian purposes) and to make a consequential amendment to another Act, available at http://openparliament.ca/bills/40–3/C-393/, last accessed 15 March 2015.

Brazilian Industrial Property Law No. 9,279 of 14 May 1996.

Canadian Patent Act (R.S.C., 1985, c. P-4, last amended in 2006), available at http://laws.justice.gc.ca/eng/P-4/index.html, last accessed 15 March 2015.

Constitution of the Kingdom of Thailand 2007, available at http://www.asianlii.org/th/legis/const/2007/1.html#C03P09, last accessed 15 March 2015.

Constitution of the Republic of South Africa No. 108 of 1996.

Constitution of the United States.

Indian Patents Act of 1970, available at http://ipindia.nic.in/ipr/patent/patAct1970-3-99.html, last accessed 15 March 2015.

Indian Patents Act (Amendment) of 2005, available at http://www.wipo.int/wipolex/en/details.jsp?id=2407 last accessed 15 March 2015.

Medicines and Related Substances Control Amendment Act, No. 90 of 1997 (South Africa).

National Health Security Act of 2002 (Thailand), available at http://www.nhso.go.th/eng/content/uploads/files/Thailand_NHS_Act.pdf.

Section 1(a) Executive Order No 13155 (United States), Access to HIV/AIDS Pharmaceuticals and Medical Technologies, 10 May 2000.

Statute of Monopolies 1623 (England).

Thailand's Patent Act B.E. 2522 (A.D. 1979) as amended by the Patent Act (No. 3) B.E. 2542 (A.D. 1999).

Trade Act of the US (Bipartisan Trade Promotion Authority Act of 2002).

Use of Patented Products for International Humanitarian Purposes Regulations (SOR/2005–143).

US Patent Act (United States Code Title 35 -Patents) available at http://www.uspto.gov/web/offices/pac/mpep/consolidated_laws.pdf, last accessed 15 March 2015.

International Cases and Decisions

Abbot Respiratory – Dosage regime, European Patent Office, Enlarged Board of Appeal, Decision No. G 02/08, 19 February 2010.

Anheuser-Busch Inc v. Portugal, Application 73049/01, ECtHR, Judgment of Grand Chamber, 11 January 2007.

Association X v. United Kingdom, Application 7154/75, European Commission of Human Rights, 14 Decision and Reports 31 (1978).

British-American Tobacco Company Ltd v. the Netherlands, Application 19589/92, ECtHR: Judgment of 20 November 1995.

Dima v. Romania, Application 58472/00, ECtHR (2005) (admissibility decision).

Draon v. France, Application 1513/03, ECtHR, 6 October 2005.

Fisheries Jurisdiction case (*Federal Republic of Germany v. Iceland*) 25 July 1974.

Fisheries Jurisdiction case (*United Kingdom v. Iceland*) 25 July 1974.

Gabčíkovo-Nagymaros Project case (*Hungary v. Slovakia*) 25 September 1997.

GATT, *Thailand – Restrictions on Importation of and Internal Taxes on Cigarettes*, 20 February 1990, BISD 37S/200.

James and others v. United Kingdom, Application 8793/79, ECtHR, 21 February 1986.

Legal Consequences of the Construction of a Wall in the Occupied Palestinian Territory, Advisory Opinion, 9 July 2004.

Mellacher and others v. Austria (Application nos 10522/83; 11011/84; 11070/84) ECtHR, 19 December 1989.

Melnychuk v. Ukraine, Application No. 28743/03, ECtHR, 5 July 2005 (admissibility decision).

Military and Paramilitary Activities in and against Nicaragua case (*Nicaragua v. United States*), Merits, ICJ, 27 June 1986.

North Sea Continental Shelf cases (*Federal Republic of Germany v. Denmark*; *FRG v. the Netherlands*) International Court of Justice, 20 February 1969.

Smith Kline & French Laboratories Ltd v. the Netherlands, Application No. 12633/87, European Commission of Human Rights, 4 October 1990.

Social and Economic Rights Action Centre and the Centre for Economic and Social Rights v. Nigeria, Communication No. 155/1996, ACHRP/COMM/A044/1, 27 May 2002.

South West Africa case (*Ethiopia v. South Africa*), ICJ, 18 July 1966.

Sporrong and Lönnroth v. Sweden, Application nos 7151/75; 7152/75, ECtHR, 23 September 1982.

Tavares v. France, Application No. 16593/90, 12 September 1991, European Commission of Human Rights.

Técnicas Medioambientales Tecmed S.A. v. Mexico, ICSID Case No. ARB(AF)/00/2, 29 May 2003.

Villagran-Morales et al. v. Guatemala (Street Children Case), Judgment Inter-American Court of Human Rights, 19 November 1999 (Merits).

WTO, *Brazil – Measures Affecting Patent Protection*, WT/DS199/3, 9 January 2001.

WTO, *Canada – Patent Protection of Pharmaceutical Products*, WT/DS114/R, 17 March 2000.

WTO, *European Communities – Measures Affecting Asbestos and Asbestos-Containing Products*, WT/DS135/AB/R, 12 March 2001.

WTO, *Japan – Taxes on Alcoholic Beverages*, WT/DS8/AB/R, 4 October 1996.

WTO, *Korea – Measures Affecting Imports of Fresh, Chilled and Frozen Beef*, WT/DS161/AB/R, WT/DS169/AB/R, 11 December 2000.

WTO, *United States – Import Prohibition of Certain Shrimp and Shrimp Products (US – Shrimp)*, WT/DS58/AB/R, 12 October 1998.

WTO, *United States – Sections 301–310 of the Trade Act of 1974*, WT/DS152/R, 22 December 1999.

WTO, *United States – Standard for Reformulation and Conventional Gasoline*, WT/DS2/AB/R, 20 May 1996.

Domestic Cases

Corte Constitucional de Colombia, Sala Segunda de Revision, Sentencia T-760. 31 July 2008.

Cruz Bermudez et al. v. Ministerio de Sanidad y Asistencia Social, Sala Polico Administrativa. Corte Suprema de Justica, Republica de Venezuela, Expediente Numero: 15.789 (1999).

Darcy v. Allein 77 Eng Rep 1260 (KB *1602*).

Minister of Health and Others v. Treatment Action Campaign and Others CCT 8/02, South Africa 721, 5 July 2002.

Novartis AG v. The Controller General of Patents, Designs and Trade Marks, M.P. Nos 1 to 5/2007 in TA/1 to 5/2007/PT/CH, M.P. No. 33/2008 in TA/1/2007/PT/CH, TA/1 TO 5/2007/ PT/CH, IP Appellate Board (India).

Novartis AG v. Union of India W.P. Nos 24759 and 24760 of 2006, High Court of Madras (India) 6 August 2007.

Novartis v. India, Supreme Court of India, Civil Appeal Nos 2706–2716 of 2013 (Arising out of SLP(C) Nos 20539–20549 of 2009) 1 April 2013.

Paschim Banga Khet Samity v. State of West Bengal, Case No. 169, Judgment of 6 May 1996, Indian Supreme Court.

Pharmaceutical Manufacturers' Association of South Africa v. Government of South Africa and others, Case No. 4183/98, South African High Court; Affidavits of the Treatment Action Campaign submitted regarding this case, www.tac.org.za/Documents/Medicine ActCourtCase/MedicineActCourtCase.htm, last accessed 2 April 2011.

Thiagraj Soobramoney v. Minister of Health (Kwazulu-Natal), Constitutional Court of South Africa, Case CCT 32/97, 27 November 1997.

Viceconte v. Ministry of Health and Social Welfare, National Court of Appeals for the Federal Contentious-Administrative Jurisdiction of Argentina Poder Judicial de la Nación Causa no. 31.777/96, 2 June 1998.

Documents of the United Nations and Other International Organisations

Annotations on the text of the draft International Covenants on Human Rights, UN Doc. A/2929, 1 July 1955.

Background Paper submitted to UN Economic and Social Council, Committee on Economic, Social and Cultural Rights, Twenty-fourth Session, Green, Maria, 'Drafting History of the Article 15 (1) (c) of the International Covenant on Economic, Social and Cultural Rights', UN Doc. E/C.12/2000/15, 9 October 2000.

Commission on Human Rights Resolution 2001/33, Access to Medication in the Context of Pandemics such as HIV/AIDS, 23 April 2001.

Commission on Human Rights Resolution 2002/32, Access to Medication in the Context of Pandemics such as HIV/AIDS, 22 April 2002.

Commission on Human Rights Resolution 2003/29, Access to Medication in the Context of Pandemics such as HIV/AIDS, Tuberculosis and Malaria, 22 April 2003.

Commission on Human Rights Resolution 2004/26, Access to Medication in the Context of Pandemics such as HIV/AIDS, Tuberculosis and Malaria, 16 April 2004.

Commission on Human Rights, Resolution 2005/23, Access to Medication in the Context of Pandemics such as HIV/AIDS, Tuberculosis and Malaria, 15 April 2005, UN Doc. E/CN.4/RES/2005/23.

CESCR, General Comment No. 3: The Nature of States Parties Obligations (Art. 2(1) of the Covenant) (1990) UN Doc. E/1991/23.

CESCR, General Comment No. 12: The Right to Adequate Food (Art. 11 of ICESCR) (1999) UN Doc. E/C.12/1999/5.

CESCR, General Comment No. 14: The Right to Health (Art. 12 of ICESCR) (2000) UN Doc. E/C.12/2000/4.

CESCR, General Comment No. 17: The Right of Everyone to Benefit from the Protection of the Moral and Material Interests Resulting from Any Scientific, Literary or Artistic Production of which He is the Author (Art. 15(1)(c) of ICESCR) (12 January 2006) UN Doc. E/C.12/2005.

CESCR, General Comment No. 21: The Right of Everyone to Take Part in Cultural Life (Art. 15.1(a) of ICESCR) (2009) UN Doc. E/C.12/GC/21.

CESCR, Statement: Human Rights and Intellectual Property, Follow-up to the Day of General Discussion on Article 15.1(c) (14 December 2001), UN Doc. E/C/12/2001/15.

CESCR, Statement: An Evaluation of the Obligation to Take Steps to the 'Maximum Available Resources' under an Optional Protocol to the Covenant' (10 May 2007), UN Doc. E/C.12/2007/1.

Communication from the European Communities and their Member States to the Council for Trade-Related Aspects of Intellectual Property Rights, IP/C/W/280, 12 June 2001.

Council of Europe, *The Right to Property under the European Convention on Human Rights: A Guide to the Implementation of the European Convention on Human Rights and its Protocols* (2007).

CRC, General Comment No. 5: General Measures of Implementation of the Convention on the Rights of the Child, 27 November 2003 UN Doc. CRC/GC/2003/5.

General Assembly, Declaration of Commitment on HIV/AIDS, Twenty-sixth special session (2 August 2001) UN Doc. A/RES/S-26/2.

General Assembly Resolution 3384 (XXX), Declaration on the Use of Scientific and Technological Progress in the Interests of Peace and for the Benefit of Mankind (10 November 1975).

General Assembly Resolution 58/173, The Right of Everyone to the Enjoyment of the Highest Attainable Standard of Physical and Mental Health (22 December 2003).

General Assembly Resolution 58/179, Access to Medication in the Context of Pandemics such as HIV/AIDS, Tuberculosis and Malaria (22 December 2003).

General Assembly Resolution 60/262, Political Declaration on HIV/AIDS (2 June 2006) UN Doc. A/RES/60/262.

General Assembly Resolution 65/277, Political Declaration on HIV and AIDS: Intensifying Our Efforts to Eliminate HIV and AIDS (8 July 2011) UN Doc. A/RES/65/277.

General Assembly Resolution S-26/2, Declaration of Commitment on HIV/AIDS (27 June 2001).

Global Compact, launched by the Secretary-General (26 July 2000).

Guidelines on Treaty-Specific Documents to be Submitted by States parties under Articles 16 and 17 of the ICESCR (24 May 2009) E/C.12/2008/2.

Human Rights Commission, Resolution 2004/116, Responsibilities of Transnational Corporations and Related Business Enterprises with regard to Human rights, contained in E/CN.4/2004/L.11/Add.7.

Human Rights Committee, General Comment No. 6: The Right to Life (Art. 6 of ICCPR) (1982) UN Doc. 30/04/1982.

Human Rights Council Decision 2/107, Access to Medication in the Context of Pandemics such as HIV/AIDS, Tuberculosis and Malaria (27 November 2006).

Human Rights Council Resolution 8/7, Mandate of the Special Representative of the Secretary-General on the Issue of Human Rights and Transnational Corporations and other Business Enterprises (18 June 2008).

Human Rights Council Resolution 12/24, Access to Medicine in the Context of the Right of Everyone to the Enjoyment of the Highest Attainable Standard of Physical and Mental Health, adopted without a vote (12 October 2009) UN Doc. A/HRC/RES/12/24.

Human Rights Council Resolution 17/4, Human Rights and Transnational Corporations and Other Business Enterprises, adopted without a vote (6 July 2011) UN Doc. A/HRC/RES/17/4.

Human Rights Council Resolution 23/14, Access to Medicines in the Context of the Right of Everyone to the Enjoyment of the Highest Attainable Standard of Physical and Mental Health, adopted with a vote of 31 to 0, with 16 abstentions (24 June 2013) UN Doc. A/HRC/RES/23/14.

ILC, Responsibility of States for International Wrongful Acts (adopted by the International Law Commission at its 53rd session, in November 2001, reported to the General Assembly at 56th session 85th meeting on 12 December 2001, included in the annex to General Assembly Resolution 56/83 of 12 December 2001).

ILC, *Difficulties Arising from the Diversification and Expansion of International Law* (2006).

Inter-American Commission on Human Rights, *Annual Report of the Inter-American Commission on Human Rights* (1994).

Johannesburg Declaration on Sustainable Development (adopted at the Johannesburg World Summit on Sustainable Development (26 August–4 September 2002) UN Doc. A/CONF.199/20/Corr.1.

Keeping the Promise: United to Achieve the Millennium Development Goals, adopted by the High-Level Plenary Meeting of the General Assembly at its 64th session on 22 September 2010, UN Doc. A/RES/65/1.

Monterrey Consensus (adopted at the International Conference on Financing for Development, at Monterrey, Mexico, 18–22 March 2002, endorsed by the UN General Assembly in its Resolution 56/210 B of 9 July 2002).

Norms on the Responsibilities of Transnational Corporations and Other Business Enterprises with regard to Human Rights (adopted by the UN Sub-Commission on the Promotion and Protection of Human Rights on 26 August 2003 UN Doc. E/CN.4/Sub.2/2003/12/Rev.2).

OECD, Guidelines for Multinational Enterprises, the latest revision (2011) available at http://www.oecd.org/daf/inv/mne/48004323.pdf, last accessed 1 March 2014.

OECD, Main Science and Technology Indicators (2012) available at http://stats.oecd.org/Index.aspx?DataSetCode=MSTI_PUB, last accessed 19 March 2015.

OHCHR, Human Rights Indicators: A Guide to Measurement and Implementation (2012).

Proclamation of Teheran, Final Act of the International Conference on Human Rights, 22 April to 13 May 1968, UN Doc. A/CONF. 32/41 at 3 (1968).

Report of the High Commissioner for Human Rights: The Impact of the Agreement on Trade-Related Aspects of Intellectual Property Rights on Human Rights (27 June 2001) UN Doc. E/CN.4/Sub.2/2001/13.

Report of the High-level Task Force on the Implementation of the Right to Development – Annex II, Criteria for Periodic Evaluation of Global Development Partnerships from a Right to Development Perspective, January 2008, UN Doc. A/HRC/8/WG.2/TF/2.

Report of the High-Level Task Force on the Right to Development, Technical Mission: MDG 8 Target F on Technology Transfer: WIPO Development Agenda, 19 November 2009, UN Doc. A/HRC/15/WG.2/TF/CRP.1.

Report of the Independent Expert in the field of Cultural Rights, Farida Shaheed, 22 March 2010, UN Doc. A/HRC/14/36.

Report of the Secretary-General, Intellectual Property Rights and Human Rights (14 June 2001) UN Doc. E/CN.4/Sub.2/2001/12.

Report of the Secretary-General (Addendum), Intellectual Property Rights and Human Rights (3 July 2001) UN Doc. E/CN.4/Sub.2/2001/12/Add.1.

Report of the Secretary-General, Declaration of Commitment on HIV/AIDS and Political Declaration on HIV/AIDS: Midway to the Millennium Development Goals, 1 April 2008, UN Doc. A/62/780.

Report of the Secretary-General, Accelerating the AIDS Response: Achieving the Targets of the 2011 Political Declaration, 3 April 2013, UN Doc. A/67/8.

Report of the Special Rapporteur in the field of Cultural Rights, Farida Shaheed, 14 May 2012, UN Doc. A/HRC/20/26.

Report of the Special Rapporteur on the Right to Food, Jean Ziegler 10 January 2002, UN Doc. E/CN.4/2002/58.

Report of the Special Rapporteur on the Right to Food, Jean Ziegler, 28 August 2003, UN Doc. A/58/330.

Report of the Special Rapporteur on the Right to Food, Jean Ziegler, 9 February 2004, UN Doc. E/CN.4/2004/10.

Report of the Special Rapporteur on the Right to Health, Anand Grover, 31 March 2009, UN Doc. A/HRC/11/12.

Report of the Special Rapporteur on the Right to Health, Anand Grover, 1 May 2013, UN Doc. A/HRC/23/42.

Report of the Special Rapporteur on the Right to Health, Paul Hunt, 17 April 2003, UN Doc. E/CN.4/2003/58.

Report of the Special Rapporteur on the Right to Health, Paul Hunt, 'Mission to the World Trade Organization', 1 March 2004, UN Doc. E/CN.4/2004/49/Add.1.

Report of the Special Rapporteur on the Right to Health, Paul Hunt, 19 January 2006, UN Doc. E/CN.4/2006/48/Add.2.

Report of the Special Rapporteur on the Right to Health, Paul Hunt, Addendum: Mission to Uganda, 19 January 2006, UN doc. E/CN.4/2006/48/Add.2.

Report of the Special Rapporteur on the Right to Health, Paul Hunt, 13 September 2006, UN Doc. A/61/338.

Report of the Special Rapporteur on the Right to Health, Paul Hunt, 17 January 2007 UN Doc. A/HRC/4/28.

Report of the Special Rapporteur on the Right to Health, Paul Hunt, 8 August 2007, UN Doc. A/62/214.

Report of the Special Rapporteur on the Right to Health, Paul Hunt, Annex: The Human Rights Guidelines for Pharmaceutical Companies in relation to Access to Medicines, 11 August 2008, UN Doc. A/63/263.

Report of the Special Rapporteur on the Right to Health, Paul Hunt, Annex: Mission to GlaxoSmithKline, 5 May 2009, UN Doc. A/HRC/11/12/Add.2.

Report of the Special Representative of the Secretary-General on the Issue of Human Rights and Transnational Corporations and other Business Enterprises (Business and

Human Rights), John Ruggie, 'Protect, Respect and Remedy: A Framework for Business and Human Rights', 7 April 2008, UN Doc. A/HRC/8/5.

Report of the Special Representative of the Secretary-General on the Issue of Human Rights and Transnational Corporations and Other Business Enterprises, John Ruggie, Business and Human Rights: Towards operationalizing the 'Protect, Respect and Remedy' Framework, 22 April 2009, A/HRC/11/13.

Report of the Special Representative of the Secretary-General, Business and Human Rights, John Ruggie, Further Steps Toward the Operationalization of the 'Protect, Respect and Remedy' Framework, 9 April 2010, UN Doc. A/HRC/14/27.

Report of the Special Representative of the Secretary-General, Business and Human Rights, John Ruggie, Guiding Principles on Business and Human Rights: Implementing the United Nations 'Protect, Respect and Remedy' Framework, 21 March 2011, UN Doc, A/HRC/17/31.

Report of the Study Group of the ILC, 'Fragmentation of International Law: Difficulties arising from the Diversification and Expansion of International Law' finalised by Martti Koskenniemi, 13 April 2006, UN Doc. A/CN.4/L.682.

Statement of Brazil at the WTO TRIPS Council regarding the Doha Paragraph 6 system, 1 March 2011.

Sub-Commission on Human Rights Resolution 2000/7, Intellectual Property Rights and Human Rights (17 August 2000) UN Doc. E/CN.4/Sub.2/Res/2000/7.

Sub-Commission on the Promotion and Protection of Human Rights, Commentary on the Norms on the Responsibilities of Transnational Corporations and other Business Enterprises with regard to Human rights (26 August 2003) UN Doc. E/CN.4/Sub.2/2003/38/Rev.2.

UNAIDS, The Road Towards Universal Access (1 August 2008).

UNAIDS, Global Report: UNAIDS Report on the Global AIDS Epidemic (2013).

UNAIDS and WHO, AIDS Epidemic Update (2007).

UNCTAD, The Least Developed Countries Report 2007: Knowledge, Technological Learning and Innovation for Development, UN Doc. UNCTAD/LDC/2007 (2007).

UNCTAD-ICTSD (F.M. Abbott and C. Correa as principal consultant), *Resource Book on TRIPS and Development*, Cambridge University Press (2005) available at http://www.iprsonline.org/unctadictsd/ResourceBookIndex.htm.

UNDP, *Human Development Report 2001: Making New Technologies Work for Human Development* (2001) available at http://hdr.undp.org/en/media/completenew1.pdf, last accessed 3 April 2010.

UNDP, Good Practice Guide: Improving Access to Treatment by Utilizing Public Health Flexibilities in the WTO TRIPS Agreement (2010).

UNESCO, The Right to Enjoy the Benefits of Scientific Progress and its Applications: The Outcome of the Experts' Meeting held on 16–17 July 2009 in Venice, Italy, available at http://unesdoc.unesco.org/images/0018/001855/185558e.pdf, last accessed 15 March 2015.

United Nations, MDG Gap Taskforce Report: The Global Partnership for Development at a Critical Juncture (2010).

United Nations, MDG Gap Taskforce Report: Millennium Development Goal 8 The Global Partnership for Development: Making Rhetoric a Reality (2012).

United Nations Millennium Declaration, adopted on 8 September 2000, General Assembly Resolution A/55/L.2, UN Doc. A/RES/55/2.

Universal Declaration on Bioethics and Human Rights, adopted by UNESCO's General Conference on 19 October 2005.

Vienna Declaration and Programme of Action, Adopted by the World Conference on Human Rights on 25 June 1993, UN Doc. A/CONF.157/24.

Venice Statement on the Right to Enjoy the Benefits of Scientific Progress and its Applications (2009), adopted at the Experts' Meeting on the Right to Enjoy the Benefits of Scientific Progress and its Applications, convened by UNESCO, available at http://unesdoc.unesco.org/images/0018/001855/185558e.pdf, last accessed 15 March 2015.

WHA Resolution 53.14 'HIV/AIDS: Confronting the Epidemic', May 2000.

WHA Resolution 54.10 'Scaling up the Response to HIV/AIDS', 21 May 2001.

WHA Resolution 55.14, 'Ensuring Accessibility to Essential Medicines', 18 May 2002.

WHA Assembly Resolution 56.27 'Intellectual Property Rights, Innovation and Public Health', 28 May 2003.

WHA Resolution 56.30 'Global Health-sector Strategy for HIV/AIDS', 28 May 2003.

WHA Resolution 57.14 'Scaling up Treatment and Care Within a Coordinated and Comprehensive Response to HIV/AIDS', 22 May 2004.

WHA Resolution 59.24 'Public Health, Innovation, Essential Health Research and Intellectual Property Rights: Towards a Global Strategy and Plan of Action', 27 May 2006.

WHA Resolution 60.20 'Better Medicines for Children', 23 May 2007.

WHA Resolution 60.30 'Public Health, Innovation and Intellectual Property', 23 May 2007.

WHA Resolution 61.21 'Global Strategy and Plan of Action on Public Health, Innovation and Intellectual Property', 24 May 2008.

WHA Resolution 65.22 'Follow-up of the report of the Consultative Expert Working Group on Research and Development: Financing and Coordination', 26 May 2012.

WHA Resolution 66.22 'Follow-up of the report of the Consultative Expert Working Group on Research and Development: Financing and Coordination', 27 May 2013.

WHO, Remuneration guidelines for non-voluntary use of a patent on medical technologies, WHO/TCM/2005.1, available at http://www.who.int/medicines/areas/technical_cooperation/WHOTCM2005.1_OMS.pdf, last accessed 15 March 2015.

WHO, 'WHO Model Lists of Essential Medicines' http://www.who.int/medicines/publications/essentialmedicines/en/, last accessed 15 March 2015.

WHO, The Selection and Use of Essential Medicines, Technical Report Series 920 (2003).

WHO, *The World Health Report* (2004).

WHO, *The World Medicines Situation* (2004).

WHO, Preventing Chronic Diseases: A Vital Investment (2005), available at http://www.who.int/chp/chronic_disease_report/contents/en/index.html, last accessed 15 March 2015.

WHO, Regional Office for South-East Asia and the Ministry of Public Health, *External Review of the Health Sector Response to HIV/AIDS in Thailand* (2005).

WHO, Report of the Commission on Intellectual Property Rights, Innovation and Public Health (CIPIH), 'Public Health, Innovation and Intellectual Property Rights' (2006).

WHO, MDG Gap Taskforce Report 2008 'Delivering on the Global Partnerships for Achieving the Millennium Development Goals' (2008).

WHO, Briefing Note: Access to Medicines – Country Experiences in Using TRIPS Safeguards (February 2008), available at http://searo.who.int/entity/intellectual_ property/IPT_Briefing_note_country_experiences.pdf last accessed 15 March 2015.

WHO, Improving Access to Medicines in Thailand: The Use of TRIPS Flexibilities (31 January to 6 February 2008).

WHO, MDG Gap Taskforce Report 2008 'Delivering on the Global Partnerships for Achieving the Millennium Development Goals' (2008).

WHO, Continuity and Change: Implementing the Third WHO Medicines Strategy 2008–2013 (2009).

WHO, Report of the Expert Working Group on Research and Development Financing (2010).

WHO, *The World Medicines Situation 2011: Access to Essential Medicines as Part of the Right to Health* (2011).

WHO, *Research and Development to Meet Health Needs in Developing Countries: Strengthening Global Financing and Coordination*, Report of the Consultative Expert Working Group on Research and Development: Financing and Coordination (CEWG) (2012).

WHO, Virtual Press Conference following a panel of medical ethicists to explore experimental treatment in the ongoing Ebola outbreak in West Africa, 12 August 2014.

WHO, Ebola Situation Report, 4 March 2015.

WHO, WIPO and WTO, *Promoting Access to Medical Technologies and Innovation: Intersections between Public Health, Intellectual Property and Trade* (2013).

WIPO, Committee of Experts on the Harmonization of Certain Provisions in Laws for the Protection of Inventions, Eighth Session, Geneva, 11–22 June 1990, Draft Treaty on the Harmonization of patent Laws; Draft Regulations Under the Draft Treaty (Articles 9 to 24; Rule 7).

WIPO, The Report of the Intergovernmental Committee on Intellectual Property and Genetic Resources, Traditional Knowledge and Folklore (Consolidated Analysis of the Legal Protection of Traditional Knowledge) 7–13 July 2003, available at http://www. wipo.int/edocs/mdocs/tk/en/wipo_grtkf_ic_5/wipo_grtkf_ic_5_3.pdf, last accessed 15 March 2015.

WTO, General Council Chairperson's Statement, WT/GC/M/82, 13 November 2003.

Documents of Governments

Letter from European Commissioner for External Trade, Peter Mandelson to Thai Minister of Commerce Krirk-krai Jirapaet (10 July 2007) http://www.wcl.american. edu/pijip/thai_comp_licenses.cfm, last accessed 15 March 2015.

Letter from European Commissioner for External Trade, Peter Mandelson to Thai Minister of Commerce, Mingkwan Saengsuwan (21 February 2008) http://www.ip-watch.org/

files/Peter_Mandelson_letter_Febr_21_2008_to_Thai_Minister_of_Commerce.pdf, last accessed 15 March 2015.

Office of the United States Trade Representative, 2007 Special 301 Report, available at http://www.ustr.gov/sites/default/files/asset_upload_file230_11122.pdf, last accessed 15 March 2015.

Thai Ministry of Public Health and the National Health Security Office, Facts and Evidences on the 10 Burning Issues related to the Government Use of Patents on Three Patented Essential Drugs in Thailand (February 2007) available at http://www.moph.go.th/hot/White%20Paper%20CL-EN.pdf, last accessed 15 March 2015.

Thai Ministry of Public Health and the National Health Security Office, The 10 Burning Questions on the Government Use of Patents on the four anti-cancer drugs in Thailand, February 2008, available at http://www.moph.go.th/hot/White%20paper%20CL%20 II%20FEB%2008-ENG.pdf, last accessed 15 March 2015.

UK Department for International Development, Increasing People's Access to Essential Medicines in Developing Countries: A Framework for Good Practice in the Pharmaceutical Industry: A UK Government Policy Paper, March 2005 available at http://apps.who.int/medicinedocs/en/d/Js18384en/, last accessed 15 March 2015.

UK All-Party Parliamentary Group on AIDS, The Treatment Timebomb, July 2009, available at http://www.appg-aids.org.uk/publications.htm, last accessed 15 March 2015.

Statements of NGOs and Companies

American Association for the Advancement of Science (AAAS), Statement on the Human Right to the Benefits of Scientific Progress, adopted by the AAAS Board of Directors, 16 April 2010, available at http://www.aaas.org/sites/default/files/migrate/uploads/Article15_AAASBoardStatement.pdf, last accessed 15 March 2015.

GlaxoSmithKline, Statement in Response to Paul Hunt's Report on GSK (A/HRC/11/12/Add.2), June 2009, available at http://198.170.85.29/GSK-response-to-Paul-Hunt-report-June-2009.pdf, last accessed 15 March 2015.

Institute for Human Rights and Business, *Setting Boundaries: Clarifying the Scope and Content of the Corporate Responsibility to Respect Human Rights*, Submission to the UN Special Representative on Business and Human Rights, December 2009. Available at http://www.ihrb.org/pdf/Setting_Boundaries-Clarifying_Scope_and_Content_of _Corporate_Responsibility_to_Respect_Human_Rights.pdf, last accessed 15 March 2015.

Maastricht Principles on Extraterritorial Obligations of States in the area of Economic, Social and Cultural Rights, adopted on 28 September 2011, available at http://www.maastrichtuniversity.nl/web/Institutes/MaastrichtCentreForHumanRights/Maastricht ETOPrinciples.htm, last accessed on 15 March 2015.

Médecins Sans Frontières (MSF), *Neither Expeditious, Nor a Solution: The WTO August 30th Decision is Unworkable* (2006), available at http://www.msfaccess.org/content/neither-expeditious-nor-solution-wto-august-30th-decision-unworkable, last accessed 15 March 2015.

Merck & Co., Inc., to the Human Rights Guidelines for Pharmaceutical Companies in relation to Access to Medicines prepared by United Nations Special Rapporteur, Paul Hunt, 29 February 2008, available at http://www.merck.com/corporate-responsibility/docs/access_developing_response_feb08.pdf, last accessed 15 March 2015.

NGO Statement of Support for the UN Human Rights Norms for Business, delivered at the 60th Session of the Commission on Human Rights (15 March–23 April 2004).

Novartis Challenges Gleevec Patent Rejection in the Supreme Court, 28 August 2009, available at http://www.lawyerscollective.org/node/1042, last accessed 3 June 2010.

Novartis, History of Glivec in India, available at http://www.novartis.com/downloads/about-novartis/glivec-history-india.pdf, last accessed 10 July 2010.

Oxfam, All Costs, No Benefits: How TRIPS-plus Intellectual Property Rules in the US-Jordan FTA Affect Access to Medicines, Oxfam Briefing Paper, May 2007, available at http://donttradeourlivesaway.files.wordpress.com/2011/01/all-costs-no-benefits.pdf, last accessed 15 March 2015.

Press Release of Apotex, Life Saving AIDS Drug for Africa Gets Final Clearance, 20 September 2007, available at https://www.apotex.com/ca/en/about/press/20070920.asp, last accessed 15 March 2015.

Press Release of PhRMA, *Protecting Patent Rights in Thailand*, 1 December 2006.

Press Release of PhRMA, *PhRMA Response to 2007 Special 301 Report*, 30 April 2007.

Statement of Civil Society Organizations Working for Health and Human Rights (Canada), 'Parliament Fails to Fix Law to Save Lives - BILL C-393 Stalled to Death in Senate' (25 March 2011), available at http://www.aidslaw.ca/site/parliament-fails-to-fix-law-to-save-lives-bill-c-393-stalled-to-death-in-senate/, last accessed 15 March 2015.

Media Reports

Basheer, Shamnad, 'First Mailbox Opposition (Gleevec) Decided in India' *Spicy IP*, 11 March 2007, available at http://spicyipindia.blogspot.com/2006/03/first-mailbox-opposition-gleevec.html, last accessed 15 March 2015.

The Guardian, 'Time for the drug companies to hand over their patents' (30 September 2010).

The Nation, 'NHSO wants licence extended for two AIDS drugs' (15 June 2010).

Kaiser Daily HIV/AIDS Report, 'Politics and Policy, President Bush Signs PEPFAR [President's Emergency Plan for AIDS Relief] Reauthorization Bill', 31 July 2008, available at http://kaiserhealthnews.org/morning-breakout/dr00053609/, last accessed 15 March 2015.

Schoen-Angerer, Tido von, 'India: Will Pharma, Trade Agreements Shut Down the Pharmacy of the Developing World?', *The Huffington Post*, 19 April 2010, available at http://www.huffingtonpost.com/tido-von-schoenangerer/india-will-pharma-trade-a_b_543572.html, last accessed 15 March 2015.

Silverman, Ed, 'Novartis Strikes Deal With Thailand over Gleevec', *Pharmalot* (31 January 2008), available at www.pharmalot.com/2008/01/novartis-strikes-deal-with-thailand-over-gleevec/, last accessed 10 April 2011.

Sukumar, C.R., 'Novartis Loses Patent Claim on Cancer Drug – Patents Controller Upholds Natco Contention', The Hindu Business Line, 25 January 2005, available at http://www.thehindubusinessline.in/bline/2006/01/26/stories/2006012601150500. htm, last accessed 15 March 2015.

Websites

Medicines Patent Pool Foundation (MPPF) http://www.medicinespatentpool.org/, last accessed 15 March 2015.

The Global Fund to Fight AIDS, Tuberculosis and Malaria, http://www.theglobalfund. org/en/, last accessed 15 March 2015.

UNITAID, available at http://www.unitaid.org/en, last accessed 15 March 2015.

WTO Secretariat, TRIPS and Health: Frequently Asked Questions, Compulsory Licences of Pharmaceuticals and TRIPS, available at http://www.wto.org/english/tratop_e/ trips_e/public_health_faq_e.htm, last accessed 15 March 2015.

WTO Secretariat, 'What does "generic" mean', in fact sheet on TRIPS and pharmaceutical patents, available at http://www.wto.org/english/tratop_e/trips_e/factsheet_pharm 03_e.htm, last accessed 15 March 2015.

Index

Introductory Note

References such as '178–9' indicate (not necessarily continuous) discussion of a topic across a range of pages. Wherever possible in the case of topics with many references, these have either been divided into sub-topics or only the most significant discussions of the topic are listed. Because the entire work is about 'intellectual property' and 'human rights', the use of these terms (and certain others which occur constantly throughout the book) as entry points has been restricted. Information will be found under the corresponding detailed topics.

Lightning Source UK Ltd.
Milton Keynes UK
UKHW051203080721
386836UK00007B/1120

9 781138 094444